P9-CEA-108

MAYOR
HAROLD
WASHINGTON

MAYOR
HAROLD
WASHINGTON

Champion of
Race and Reform
in Chicago

ROGER BILES

**UNIVERSITY OF
ILLINOIS PRESS**
Urbana, Chicago, and Springfield

© 2018 by the Board of Trustees
of the University of Illinois
All rights reserved
Manufactured in the United States of America
C 5 4 3 2 1
♾ This book is printed on acid-free paper.

Library of Congress Cataloging-in-Publication Data
Names: Biles, Roger, 1950– author.
Title: Mayor Harold Washington : champion of race
    and reform in Chicago / Roger Biles.
Description: Urbana : University of Illinois Press, 2018.
    | Includes bibliographical references and index.
Identifiers: LCCN 2017048407 | ISBN 9780252041853
    (hardcover : alk. paper)
Subjects: LCSH: Washington, Harold, 1922–1987. |
    Chicago (Ill.)—Politics and government—1951–
    | Mayors—Illinois—Chicago—Biography. |
    Legislators—United States—Biography. | Chicago
    (Ill.)—Biography. | Chicago (Ill.)—Race relations—
    History—20th century. | United States. Congress.
    House—Biography.
Classification: LCC F548.52.W36 B55 2018 | DDC
    977.3/043092 [B]—dc23
LC record available at https://lccn.loc.gov/2017048407

RO451870224

For Tony, who left us much too soon

Contents

Acknowledgments

I relied heavily on materials in the Harold Washington Papers, so first and foremost I must praise the superb staff members of the Harold Washington Archives and Collections. Thanks to the efforts of those dedicated professionals, I thoroughly enjoyed my time working in the beautiful reading room on the ninth floor of the Harold Washington Library Center. My sincere thanks, therefore, go to Glenn Humphreys, Evelyn Johnson, Roslyn Mabry, Johanna Russ, Jeff Thivel, Morag Walsh, Teresa Yoder, and Sarah Zimmerman. Archivists at the Chicago History Museum, the Richard J. Daley Library at the University of Illinois at Chicago (UIC), and the Illinois State Historical Library were also very helpful.

My completion of this book owed in no small measure to the financial and moral support I received from the History Department at Illinois State University. My department chair, Tony Crubaugh, shared with me what little travel funds were available to faculty during perilous economic times for higher education in Illinois; after I retired, he allowed me to retain an office in the department so that I could finish the manuscript. My understanding of black politics deepened because of long conversations with my former colleague Touré Reed, a talented scholar of race and class in the United States. Working with the University of Illinois Press has been a rewarding experience, largely because of Daniel Nasset's avid support of the project.

As always, I am indebted to the members of my family. Although my three children have scattered throughout the country, residing in suburban San Diego, Chicago, and New York City, I think about them constantly. My wife, Mary Claire, tolerates my excessive work habits and serves during our long walks as my sounding board for ideas. Her support has been unwavering.

MAYOR HAROLD WASHINGTON

INTRODUCTION
Race, Reform, and Redistribution

On November 24, 2015, the city of Chicago released a chilling dash-cam video that showed a police officer repeatedly shooting a seventeen-year-old African American male, Laquan McDonald, without cause. The administration of Mayor Rahm Emanuel had refused to make the video public for more than a year after the October 20, 2014, incident, defying the state's open-records law, and relented only at the order of a Cook County judge. Chicagoans and Internet viewers around the world recoiled at the graphic, gratuitous violence. After briefly waving a folding knife, McDonald had skirted a contingent of police officers who were monitoring his movements. According to numerous witnesses, the teenager made no menacing motions toward the authorities as he walked away from them. Arriving late at the scene, Officer Jason Van Dyke opened fire six seconds after exiting his squad car and continued to shoot after McDonald fell to the ground. In all the policeman shot the victim sixteen times in fourteen seconds before stopping to reload. In his report, an account corroborated by seven other police officers present, Van Dyke claimed to have fired in self-defense when McDonald threatened him with the knife—an assertion contradicted by the video and bystander accounts. The Cook County state's attorney charged Van Dyke with first-degree murder, the first time a Chicago police officer had been accused of an on-duty fatality in nearly thirty-five years. Even before filing a civil suit, the McDonald family received a five-million-dollar wrongful-death payment from the city. It was business as usual in the Windy City, complained members of the black community, for city hall had spent more than fifty million dollars in 2014 to settle wrongful-death complaints against the Chicago Police Department (CPD), in most cases involving the killing of young African American males by white police officers.[1]

Laquan McDonald's death sparked massive protests in Chicago's central business district during December 2015, where demonstrators chanting "Sixteen times!" halted traffic and disrupted the Christmas shopping season in the Loop and on Michigan Avenue's Magnificent Mile. Public attention shifted in the following months to a series of candlelight vigils denoting a concern over the city's soaring gun-related homicide rates, which far exceeded the death tolls in more populous New York City and Los Angeles. In August 2016 alone, reported police officials, 92 Chicagoans became homicide victims. At the conclusion of a lethal Labor Day weekend, in which shooters wounded 65 people and killed 13, the city's homicide total of 488 fatalities for 2016 already surpassed the previous year's 481 for all of 2015. The homicide rate, the highest in the city since the 1990s, increased most dramatically in African American neighborhoods on the South and West Sides, where entrenched segregation, grinding poverty, illegal drug trafficking, and a dearth of economic opportunity plagued the population. The surge in violence led to a U.S. Justice Department investigation and promises by Chicago's embattled mayor to find a solution to the worsening problem. Emanuel fired Garry McCarthy, the police superintendent, replacing him with twenty-seven-year CPD veteran Eddie Johnson, and collaborated with the city council to hire one thousand more police officers.[2]

De-emphasizing the animus between white police officers and African American residents, Johnson attributed the escalating violence to the deplorable situation in the heavily black South and West Sides. "It's not a police issue, it's a society issue," said the new superintendent. "Impoverished neighborhoods, people without hope do these kinds of things." What Johnson left unsaid, but what many Chicagoans of color asserted, was that the "society issue" to which he referred stemmed largely from local government's chronic neglect of the city's disadvantaged. The wretched conditions prevailing in the city's declining neighborhoods owed to the priorities of a white ruling class committed to an unbending policy of downtown enrichment at the expense of Chicago's downtrodden residents. Emanuel and Richard M. Daley, the two occupants of the mayor's office since 1989, boasted about the Windy City's successful transition under their leadership from declining regional hub to thriving postindustrial service center, from gritty manufacturing metropolis to cosmopolitan global city. In the thrumming downtown of Rahm Emanuel's Chicago, corporate headquarters, business service firms, and financial institutions shared space with internationally renowned cultural attractions, swank hotels, glittering fashion outlets, and gourmet restaurants. Affluent yuppies and empty nesters lived comfortably in tony neighborhoods on the gentrifying North Side. Meanwhile, the benefits of the city's remarkable metamorphosis failed to trickle down to the forlorn residents trapped in the blighted areas of postindustrial Chicago. The undeniable disparity, glaringly evident in the city for decades, continued to generate frustration and anger among the unfortunates left behind in poor districts where high levels of unemployment and violence prevailed.[3]

Thirty years earlier, the election of Chicago's first black mayor had provided hope that a progressive regime might address some of the fundamental inequities eroding amity in the city. Harold Washington narrowly prevailed in the 1983 mayoral contest when an unprecedented grassroots effort to mobilize the city's large but politically inert black population succeeded and created an unstoppable popular movement; latent black political power became real as thousands of West and South Side residents registered and voted for the first time. Exultant African Americans joyously celebrated the unexpected triumph, rightfully crediting the black political awakening as the key to victory. But Washington worked to assemble a broader alliance, and he pointed out that the electoral support of Latinos and liberal whites had been crucial to his election as well. Indeed, in 1983 Washington spoke repeatedly of fashioning a rainbow coalition and campaigned on behalf of progressive ideals aimed at the sweet spot where race and class interests intersected. He insisted that a municipal government based on fairness and genuine economic opportunity would benefit all of Chicago's disparate races and ethnicities. His sudden death in office barely four years later abruptly terminated the reform effort, paved the way for a political restoration by conservative interests, and left the black community in despair.

The death of Harold Washington triggered a widespread outpouring of grief in Chicago's African American neighborhoods, where he was a beloved figure with an unshakable following. Gauging the sentiment in the city's overwhelmingly white precincts, the press reported decidedly less anguish over the mayor's demise. Reporters from the Windy City and elsewhere identified race as the key variable that explained the very different reactions. Sensational accounts of the virulent racism pervading his election in 1983 and the antipathy that split the city council into two warring factions in subsequent years painted a distressing picture of a metropolis riven by racial animosity. Shocked and bereaved by the fifty-six-year-old Washington's unexpected death, which the local coroner immediately attributed to natural causes, deeply suspicious African Americans in Chicago promptly concocted conspiracy theories to explain how his white enemies had assassinated him. The unseemly scramble to succeed the fallen mayor played out not just as a free-for-all between power-hungry Democratic Party factions but also as a tense confrontation between the races. For many journalists, the election and the ongoing tribulations of the city's first black mayor served as a microcosm of the mistrust and fear between African Americans and whites rampant in the nation at the time. Washington joked that a leading local television personality never failed in his interviews, regardless of the topic, to pose some variation or other of his favorite question: "Well, Governor—or Well, Senator—or, Well, Mayor—when you get right down to it, doesn't it all come down to a matter of race?"[4]

As a black man who had grown up in Chicago, Washington intimately understood the salience of race in the city. Born in Cook County Hospital, Harold Washington lived almost his entire life on the city's South Side. On a few occasions, circumstances took him elsewhere temporarily. As a member of the U.S. Army during the Second World War, he bunked in a series of training camps stateside and then served a tour of duty in the Pacific theater. After the war, he commuted from his home daily while attending nearby Roosevelt College and Northwestern University Law School. Serving in the Illinois General Assembly for sixteen years, he maintained his primary residence in Chicago and stayed in Springfield only on weeknights during legislative sessions. Throughout his brief tenure as a member of the U.S. Congress, he rented a room in Washington, D.C., but returned home to Chicago at every opportunity (usually two or three long weekends per month) to tend the political home fires. His deep understanding of the Windy City's folkways and mores owed to a lifetime spent traversing its thoroughfares, observing its interest groups, and interacting with its people.

As a lifelong occupant of the city, an African American who had grown up in the rigidly segregated metropolis, Washington intuitively knew the economic, political, and cultural ramifications of Chicago's racial divisions. He understood when his good friend Dempsey Travis sardonically wrote that "waking up a black in Chicago was always a continuation of the previous night's bad dream."[5] Tutored in politics from an early age by his father, a popular precinct captain and respected community leader on the South Side, he saw the operation of the infamous Cook County Democratic machine at close hand and in vivid detail. As he rose within the local political hierarchy and contemplated the possibility of perhaps someday running for mayor, Washington fully grasped the difficulties a black candidate for citywide office would encounter. A savvy politician, he knew that a successful mayoral race for any African American would be impossible without harnessing the untapped potential of the city's large black population through a massive voter registration drive and without a successful campaign to motivate members of the expanded electorate to turn out and vote. He knew that an African American candidate must enlarge the black base to have any chance of winning and then seek pockets of votes in other racial and ethnic communities where possible. That would be the only feasible formula for success. The black vote was undeniably crucial for any African American office seeker to prevail in a citywide election. Race remained central to the calculation of how to forge a winning coalition for mayor in Chicago.

Not surprisingly, when Washington won in 1983, the reporting in local and national media revolved around the election of an African American mayor in the nation's third-largest city. Given the clear-cut voting patterns in largely homogeneous wards and the centrality of race to the campaign just concluded, which was inarguably the most vituperative in the city's history, the continuing focus on racial discord can be readily understood. No one could reasonably dispute that Washington's race played a crucial role in the election. The bitter Council Wars that followed revealed lingering racial resentments that plagued city governance throughout the mayor's first term. As well, much of the academic literature on Washington's election and administration has adopted the trope of race as the most reliable means of understanding the events of 1983–87. Even members of the Washington administration who initially underestimated the singular importance of race relations in Chicago testified that they developed a keen appreciation for its significance. Commissioner of economic development Robert Mier, a university professor with no experience in electoral politics before moving into city hall in 1983, concluded that racial attitudes factored into every problem he confronted. He wrote:

I believe the fundamental lesson I learned from the Washington years is that race should be the *first* way a local economic development or planning problem should be framed. This inexorable presence of racism is my strongest realization from the Washington years. I now find it impossible to approach an economic development challenge without immediately seeing the race and gender dimensions of it, especially that of African-Americans.[6]

Another political neophyte in the Washington administration, Elizabeth Hollander, the commissioner of planning, likewise remembered encountering racial agendas whenever she addressed a new issue—even in the most innocuous settings. She concluded, "I can never again walk into a room without being instantly aware of who's there . . . and who's not there. It makes *all* the difference in the world."[7]

Race was clearly important in all aspects of Washington's political career, but the extraordinary story of his mayoralty cannot be understood solely as a black electoral triumph. To do so would be inaccurate and unfair to Washington, a significant number of the bureaucrats who served in his administration, and many of the Chicagoans who voted for him. The mayor's race figured prominently in the events of the mid-1980s, but so too did his ideas. "This political battle is not about race," he asserted in 1983 and repeatedly thereafter. "It is about money and power and morality." A dedicated progressive who carved out a record of reform over two decades in public life, he consistently outlined a program for Chicago that aided the minorities and the disadvantaged who had been poorly served by the city's autocratic political ruling class for generations. Organization Democrats in the city council vigorously opposed him at every juncture because of race but more important because of the fundamental changes he sought in Chicago's political economy. Washington's nemeses blanched at his frequent allusions to redistribution, both because such language conjured up images of a political upheaval and because of the potential for a reallocation of scarce resources in the city. In the first case, a changing of the guard in city hall menaced the longevity of an entrenched political machine fiercely protective of its exalted status. In the second case, challenges to the economic status quo jeopardized the concentration of funding in the central business district, scattered middle-class neighborhoods, and a few affluent enclaves to the exclusion of declining areas inhabited by people of color, the working class, and the indigent. Washington's recurrent calls for redistribution, invariably couched in his promise of fairness, inextricably bound race and class interests in a way that threatened privileged groups in Chicago. The leaders of the Democratic machine and the city's elites feared that he meant it.[8]

Just as Washington's political opponents took seriously his threat to the economic order, they and many later students of Chicago politics and government also impugned his idealistic declarations as just so much self-serving political rhetoric. Dismissing his break with the political organization he had served for many years as crass opportunism, they saw his apparent conversion to reform as a calculated tactic designed to advance his own career. In their view, Washington remained essentially a machine politician who disguised his reliance on old-fashioned power politics with high-minded oratory. Shortly after Washington's break with the regular Democrats, Illinois Republican governor James Thompson attributed the schism simply to a dispute over "power, politics, contracts and patronage." Chicago alderman Bernard Stone concurred, saying, "Washington is a pretend reformer. There's absolutely no question in my mind he's no different than any of the bosses that preceded him." In the words of historian Steven P. Erie, "Chicago's 'antimachine' Mayor Harold Washington ransacked city hall and special district governments for additional patronage to pay off his supporters and consolidate power." The editors of a highly regarded book on the 1983 campaign, historian Melvin G. Holli and political scientist Paul M. Green, described Washington's reforms as nothing more than "affirmative action patronage," a "new wrinkle" on the "spoils system" that had prevailed in the city for decades. Similarly dubious of Washington's opposition to machine politics, sociologist Gerald D. Suttles commented that the mayor "did shift patronage toward a new population, but also one that showed strong signs of forthcoming obedience."[9]

Skeptics found Washington guilty of playing the race card to seize control of city hall and then utilizing the perquisites of the mayor's office to reward his African American constituents. In their accounting of the Democratic machine's decline and fall, journalists Bill Granger and Lori Granger said, "Like the long-ago Oscar De Priest, Washington had always been a 'race man.' In 1983 he waved the bloody flag of racism for political edge and it worked." In their interpretation, Washington "was doing no more than becoming a boss and using racial confrontation to do it." Holli and Green decried "the mayor's monochromatic vision of the public good, which generously translated into the need to satisfy his black constituency," and rued the fact that "affirmative action had become the be-all and end-all of city policy, often to the exclusion of larger citywide and metropolitan-wide concerns."[10]

The same skeptics characterized Washington as a canny tactician and mesmerizing orator whose indisputable political talents far outdistanced his managerial ability, which they thought became evident during his mayoral tenure. Granger and Granger found that, once ensconced in city hall, the mayor "remained lazy in administrative matters and bored by details." Disregarding the implacable opposition Washington encountered in the city council, they mentioned another important reason for his administration's difficulties:

> There was no ready-made cadre of Machine-trained operatives to handle the ins and outs of Chicago's extremely complex and fragmented governmental system for him. Because blacks had been out of power for so long and Washington had no intention of heading an administration run by whites, he found himself relying on neophytes who were more schooled in race rhetoric than in administrative reality. They were frequently outmaneuvered by the remnants of the old Machine.[11]

In his biography of Chicago mayor Richard M. Daley, Keith Koeneman largely agreed with this unflattering assessment by sketching his subject's "focus on effective government" in contrast to Washington, "who as mayor had been full of good ideas but ineffective as manager of the city." His overall assessment of Mayor Washington concluded:

> Harold Washington was a great campaigner—charismatic, full of life—and a wonderful orator. Washington was also a pathbreaker for black Chicagoans, inspiring a belief that the local Democratic Party could be changed and made more open and diverse. Unfortunately, Washington turned out to be relatively ineffective as mayor of Chicago for two reasons: he was a weak administrator and he did not understand—or perhaps did not care—how power worked in white Chicago.[12]

Stories of Washington's lassitude, inattention to detail, and haphazard managerial practices, promulgated by his enemies in the city council and mimicked by the local press, fed a shorthand summary of his political career that gained widespread currency throughout Chicago and Illinois: charismatic public figure and effective vote getter, but undisciplined and ineffectual officeholder. Such a terse appraisal, convenient in its succinct explanation of Washington's pathbreaking electoral victory in 1983, his narrow reelection in 1987, and the reputed dearth of achievements during a contentious mayoralty, fitted comfortably with a racist analysis that grudgingly granted the mayor credit for effective politicking but leveled sharp criticism for his failure at the much more demanding and important task of governing the city effectively. This cynical view starkly contradicts the observations and firsthand experiences of many elected officials and presents an incomplete and inaccurate picture of the mayor's time in office. As well, this simplistic summary provides an insubstantial foundation for understanding the impact of Washington's truncated time in city hall during the 1980s.[13]

Making sense of the Washington mayoralty not only clarifies an important period in Chicago history but also sheds light on the temper of racial politics nationally. Analysis of events in Cook County during the 1980s contributes to the discussion among historians, political scientists, sociologists, and black studies scholars about the nature of racial politics and the role of African Americans in reform during the twentieth century. In an influential analysis of post–World War II black culture and politics, historian Manning Marable charged African American office seekers during the 1980s with moving further to the right ideologically to take advantage of the conservative shift in the nation's electorate. To capture the votes of the white upper and middle classes, Marable contended, successful politicians such as Atlanta mayor Andrew Young, Virginia governor Douglas Wilder, Pennsylvania congressman William Gray, and Democratic National Committee chairman Ronald Brown deserted politics long aligned with the black freedom struggle and distanced themselves from the militant activism practiced by earlier generations of African American leadership. This pursuit of personal gain by ambitious individuals diminished the chances of improving the lives of ghetto residents and predictably fed a growing alienation with politics among minority inner-city populations.[14]

Marable's depiction of African American politics and politicians in the 1980s, an effort to reconcile the triumph of Reagan conservatism nationally with the concurrent African American electoral successes in local and state politics, lacked explanatory power in Chicago, where Washington made no such accommodations to the prevailing political currents. An unrelenting critic of the Reagan administration during his tenure in the U.S. House of Representatives, the years immediately preceding his election to the office of mayor, Washington continued to condemn the Republican White House during his time in city hall. Having mobilized a grassroots coalition to win in 1983, singling out the malevolent presidential administration along with the incumbent mayor as his principal adversaries, he remained true to the ideals expressed in that year's campaign and became a leading national spokesman for endangered municipal governments fighting against hostile conservative forces in the nation's capital.

Rather than the parameters suggested by Marable, Washington's ascendance reflected more closely a picture sketched by other scholars in which black communities strove for progressive change over long periods of time and often achieved electoral success substantially after the period of principal civil rights breakthroughs. Proponents of the "long civil rights movement" have rejected the customary focus on the years 1954–65 and argued that the reform movement began as early as the 1930s and continued into the 1980s. In their view, dedicated reformers made noteworthy—and essential—progress in advance of the landmark legal and legislative achievements of the 1950s and 1960s; moreover, significant accomplishments after the mid-1960s completed the story of a far-ranging civil rights movement. Viewing the pursuit of reform through a wider lens and tracing the story over a greater length of time, these scholars criticized the tendency to celebrate only the perseverance of national organizations and the dramatic victories of heroic individuals rather than to recount lesser-known breakthroughs in a variety of locations across the nation. Additionally, historian Jacqueline Dowd Hall and others have denounced the traditional narrative for ignoring the durable connective tissue that bound race to class and civil rights to workers' rights. Hall concluded, "By confining the civil rights struggle to the South, to bowdlerized heroes, to a single halcyon decade, and to limited, noneconomic objectives, the master narrative simultaneously elevates and diminishes the movement." For Hall and like-minded revisionists, the drive for racial equality combined inextricably with opposition to economic exploitation in an elongated protest movement that spanned decades.[15]

A shift in geographical focus also accompanied the changing chronological approach, as revisionist scholars renounced the exclusive attention to the civil rights movement in the South. In delineating the impact of reform efforts beyond the states of the Old Confederacy, advocates of what became known as "Freedom North" studies in fact examined the struggle against racial discrimination in all other regions of the nation. In addition to their published work on the civil rights movement in northeastern and midwestern cities such as New York City, Chicago, Philadelphia, Detroit, St. Louis, and Milwaukee, scholars looked to the West Coast and completed illuminating books on Los Angeles, Oakland, and Seattle, among others. This literature rested primarily on a flurry of local case studies, with Thomas J. Sugrue's synthetic *Sweet Land of Liberty* being the principal exception. "Freedom North" studies affirmed that activists in communities throughout the nation contributed to the fight against racial inequality, both before and after passage of the seminal Civil Rights Act of 1964 and Voting Rights Act of 1965.[16]

Recent historiography has likewise taken aim at the notion of a monolithic reform movement based on a uniform set of participants, goals, and methods. An enhanced appreciation for diversity within the ranks of the civil rights movement has led, for instance, to an augmented appreciation for the role played by black nationalism in the fight against racism and economic exploitation. Whereas the old paradigm indicated that a number of restless African Americans embraced Black Power ideology in the mid-1960s and later because of widespread disenchantment with the dilatory pace of progress, a broader definition of the civil rights movement has incorporated black nationalism as an important variant in the multifaceted effort against racial inequality. Not just a rigid commitment to black separatism, black nationalism entailed a commonsensical alternative to liberalism's frustrating gradualism. (With a nod to Hall and her acolytes, historian Peniel E. Joseph has referred to the "long black power movement.") Challenging the image of Black Power as just a violent fringe movement and noting that a variety of constituencies worked alongside each other to improve ghetto conditions, black studies scholars have paid particular attention to the similar grassroots approaches effected by revolutionaries and political pragmatists alike—by Malcolm X and Stokely Carmichael, as presented in the traditional narrative, but also by such mayors as Richard Hatcher in Gary, Indiana; David Dinkins in New York City; and Harold Washington in Chicago.[17]

U.S. historians continue to debate the validity of the "long civil rights movement" as a conceptual tool. Academicians argue about whether the events of the 1930s and 1940s constituted merely an important precursor or an indispensable first phase of the campaign for racial equality and whether a more encompassing definition of the civil rights movement denies the events of the 1950s and 1960s their distinct character and significance. Critics contend that the interpretation of the civil rights movement as *longue durée* distorts the meaning of some crucial developments—by exaggerating the importance of Popular Front liberalism and wartime activism, for example, while underestimating the debilitating effect of domestic anticommunism during the early Cold War years. Whatever its shortcomings in explaining the precise nature of the African American freedom struggle nationally, the long civil rights paradigm is helpful in comprehending the remarkable 1983 regime change in Chicago as part of a larger quest for political empowerment and as a drive to address both economic exploitation and racial inequality. Washington's victory, the culmination of a political upheaval long in the making, came after decades of mounting disillusionment in the Windy City's black neighborhoods. As historian Jeffrey Helgeson put it, "Washington's progressive stance provided an opening for individuals and organizations that had been working to benefit local communities, workers, and businesses all along."[18]

A disparate cast of characters in Chicago, ranging across the political spectrum from cautious liberals to impatient black nationalists, joined forces in the hope of overthrowing the autocratic Democratic machine in the 1980s. Black nationalists cooperated with other dissidents from a wide array of backgrounds within the African American community—from churches, trade unions, block clubs, civil rights organizations, fraternal associations, and more—to work toward a common goal in 1983. The rainbow coalitions created by the Black Panthers in Chicago and other cities during the 1960s, though admittedly limited in scope and influence, served as models for the multiracial rainbow coalition that Washington and his followers cobbled together some twenty years later. Black nationalists had earlier participated in independent political movements against the political machine of Richard J. Daley—advancing affirmative action as a means of obliterating the color line in the construction industry, for example, and creating organizations such as the Kenwood Oakland Community Organization as an alternative to anemic interracial groups in declining African American neighborhoods—and later many of the same activists worked in Washington's political campaigns. Thus, Bobby Rush, the Black Panthers' defense minister for Illinois in the 1960s and later U.S. representative from the state's First Congressional District, drew a straight line connecting the 1960s' radical activism and the 1980s' electoral upheaval. Washington's election, he asserted, owed directly "to the 'assassination of Mr. [Fred] Hampton and the outcry and change that it prompted.'"[19]

A nuanced understanding of the Washington administration, one that makes the most sense of politics and policy making in mid-1980s Chicago, takes the mayor's spoken and written calls for change over a long career seriously and situates his reform ethos within the context of an African American community mounting meaningful challenges to the city's political economy. In the view suggested here, Washington's tenure in city hall represented a triumph of progressive politics no less than an unprecedented victory for African American voters—constituting an important story involving both reform and race working in tandem. Having long suffered from the degenerative effects of machine rule, the black community acted in the vanguard of reform politics. Rooted in an African American community that had chafed under the oppressive control of a white political machine for decades—and that viewed reform expansively as an engine for sweeping societal change—Washington's progressive sensibility took aim at inequality and unfairness in all manifestations. His vision of reform extended to the farthest reaches of Chicago and beyond. He saw the black community as a testing ground for the entire city and beyond, nostrums successfully used in South Side and West Side neighborhoods entirely suitable for implementation on a much grander scale. Unlike other politicians who promised sweeping changes during their campaigns and then sought less consequential breaks from existing practices once in office, Washington moved expeditiously after his election to alter city government in meaningful ways. Establishing fairness as the touchstone of his mayoralty, he pursued redistribution, balanced economic growth, industrial retention, and improved citizen access to government as workable solutions to Chicago's ills in a postindustrial world. Forged by a lifetime of observing how the existing political order abused many of its subjects, his vision entailed a reconfiguration of municipal government to benefit society's marginalized populations—people of color, women, and the economically disadvantaged, in particular.[20]

This reconsideration of Harold Washington, at odds with many of the traditional views of his mayoralty and informed by recent scholarship on African American politics, invites additional scrutiny of his administration's impact on Chicago in the late twentieth century. Ever mindful of the injustice and indignities suffered by the African American community in which he was raised, Washington labored to assemble a rainbow coalition that united blacks, Latinos, and forward-looking whites—an alliance that married minority interest in equal opportunity and redistribution with ideals popular among white liberals concerning good-government reform. A firm believer in the efficacy of democracy, he felt that repeated demonstrations of fairness in city hall would foster success at the polls. Shared class interests could overcome corrosive racial divisions that had been cynically utilized by a self-interested political machine to divide and conquer. No naive intellectual motivated by a romanticized view of civic engagement, hardened by decades of seeking change within and outside of the powerful Democratic machine, and confident in his ability to persuade the voters by implementing solutions that worked, Washington saw fairness and openness in city hall as the best ways to navigate Chicago through uncharted postindustrial waters. Equally important, he saw the fates of the city's African American population and other groups that had been systematically excluded from sharing in capitalism's bounty as seamlessly linked—and the key to Chicago's future.

The full impact of the 1983–87 interlude in the Windy City remains elusive in some instances, and students of urban history and urban politics in the twenty-first century will continue to seek answers to a number of important questions. This book, I hope, will at least start the process. To wit: Were Washington's years as mayor something more than a fleeting progressive interlude? If not, was political scientist Larry Bennett correct when he called the Washington mayoralty the "apotheosis of a particular form of political/civic culture that is unlikely ever to return"? Or could the mayor and his subordinates rightfully claim to have achieved meaningful, lasting breakthroughs in reforming the political economy? What significant changes, if any, survived the 1980s? How much of Richard M. Daley's administration—or, for that matter, Rahm Emanuel's—reflected Washington's influence? Would Chicago have developed any differently without the impetus for change provided during the Washington years? Could jobs really be assigned a higher priority than real estate without undermining a city's economy? And, as Washington fervently contended, could fairness be an effective organizing principle for city governance in a neoliberal age?[21]

1

FROM MACHINE REGULAR
TO PROGRESSIVE DEMOCRAT

For African Americans who traveled to Chicago during and immediately after World War I, fleeing the dangers and humiliations of Jim Crow in the South and lured by the promise of economic opportunity in the North, the community south of downtown variously called the South Side, the Black Belt, and Bronzeville served as the primary point of entry. A handful of much smaller residential settlements also developed immediately west and north of the Loop, but the vast majority of black newcomers headed straight for the South Side. Most of the wayfarers detrained at the Illinois Central Railroad terminal and promptly made their way to the city's predominant area of black settlement. During those years, the homogeneity of Chicago's neighborhoods remained largely undisturbed. Whites maintained a sturdy residential segregation through the use of residential covenants, the enforcement of which remained legal until the *Shelley v. Kraemer* U.S. Supreme Court decision in 1948. Thereafter, collusion among real estate agents and (if necessary) violence kept the burgeoning African American population bottled up south of the Loop between railroad yards on the west and Cottage Grove Avenue on the east, extending as far south as the Woodlawn and Englewood neighborhoods south of Thirty-Ninth Street. Bronzeville expanded incrementally as time passed to accommodate the growing number of African Americans arriving in a steady stream from Mississippi, Alabama, Louisiana, Tennessee, Arkansas, and other southern states. For the most part, however, the Black Belt remained a narrow, densely populated tract of land seldom more than a few blocks wide that bulged at the seams and spilled over into adjacent white neighborhoods only after fierce resistance. For decades, implacable white hostility kept the South Side's boundaries intact even as the black population increased inexorably.[1]

Despite overcrowding caused by the desperate housing shortage, African Americans residing in the Black Metropolis created a vibrant community in which a professional elite and the members of a commercial middle class lived alongside janitors, domestic workers, manual laborers, porters, and other blue-collar workers of modest means. Dozens of churches, running the gamut from ten-thousand-member Olivet Baptist Church to tiny storefront chapels, represented Pentecostal sects as well as mainstream denominations. The existence of small businesses (both licit and illicit), newspapers, schools, hospitals, jazz nightspots, professional baseball teams, and women's clubs testified to the richness of the cultural life available to the inhabitants of the confined area. South Side residents took great pride in Du Sable High School, Provident Hospital, the *Chicago Defender*, the Regal Theater, the Illinois National Guard Armory, and other venerable institutions. Social service organizations such as the Phyllis Wheatley Home, Frederick Douglass Center, the Young Men's Christian Association (YMCA), and the Young Women's Christian Association (YWCA) aided uprooted southerners who attempted to find lodging and employment. Organizations dedicated to racial uplift, including branch offices of the National Urban League and the National Association for the Advancement of Colored People, played prominent roles combating discrimination in the workplace and the exclusionary practices of trade unions. Severely constrained by segregation and regularly reminded of their second-class status, black Chicagoans launched enterprises that served South Side customers and founded variegated institutions to construct a wholesome environment. Battling racial inequality and pursuing economic opportunity, they endeavored to fashion a more just society.[2]

Following the lead of other oppressed minorities, African Americans sought to improve their condition by pursuing the benefits offered by politics. Blacks received a modicum of jobs, recognition, and social welfare disbursements in return for votes, but their fealty to the Republican Party ("the party of Lincoln") yielded few rewards in the years after emancipation. The local Republican organization nominated a handful of black candidates for minor offices and appointed a few token blacks to lesser city and county posts, all the while reserving important positions in city government for white politicians. In the first two decades of the twentieth century, as Chicago's African American population grew rapidly in the Second and Third Wards, an emerging cadre of professional politicians on the South Side worked tirelessly to expand black electoral influence. As Oscar De Priest, Ed Wright, Robert R. Jackson, and other black politicos foresaw, a unified African American vote could tip the balance of power between the two political parties or between the Republican Party's warring factions. De Priest became the city's first black alderman in 1915 and won election to the U.S. House of Representatives in 1929, but advancement came grudgingly overall for black office seekers. African Americans still exerted little influence within Chicago's Republican Party, and their compensation for unquestioning loyalty remained minimal.[3]

Like thousands of other African Americans who settled in the bustling African American community developing on the South Side, Harold Washington's parents traveled to Chicago during the First World War. Roy Washington came from a small town in Kentucky in 1918 and quickly found employment in the flourishing meatpacking industry. The son of a Methodist minister, he attended Garrett Theological Seminary and became an itinerant African Methodist Episcopal minister who preached at a number of churches in the city's Black Belt. While working long hours in the stockyards, he attended night classes at the Chicago Kent College of Law. Two years after graduating from law school, he quit his job in Packingtown's slaughterhouses and opened his own legal practice on the South Side. Bertha Jones journeyed to Chicago from the family farm near Centralia in southern Illinois, supported herself as a domestic worker, married Roy Washington, and quickly gave birth to four children. Harold, the third oldest, was born in Cook County Hospital on April 15, 1922. After the birth of the fourth child, when Harold was still a toddler, Bertha filed for divorce and remarried, leaving Roy with custody of their four children. Roy Washington also remarried but remained good friends with his first wife, who subsequently gave birth to six children with her second husband. Bertha lived nearby and never lost contact with her first family, but Roy Washington raised the four children substantially on his own and remained the dominant influence in their lives.[4] Harold Washington, who idolized his father, later said: "I was very fortunate. My father was my role model.

He was a real man, he was a good man. For many years he was not only my father, he was my mother. And so I knew who Santa Claus was. He came home every night, put his feet under the table and had dinner with me."[5]

In addition to preaching on Sundays, Roy Washington practiced law and invested extensively in South Side real estate. He became active in the Democratic Party during the 1920s, a time when the overwhelming majority of African Americans still voted for Republican candidates. "Even my mother wouldn't vote Democratic," remembered Harold Washington. As a successful precinct captain in the Democratic Party's Third Ward organization, Roy Washington parlayed his political connections into a job in the city's corporation counsel office as an assistant prosecutor. A conscientious precinct captain who attended promptly to the concerns of his constituents, he became known on the South Side as "Mr. Forty-Eighth Street."[6] Young Harold learned about politics at an early age, soaking up knowledge and observing legendary black politicos in operation. By the time he was sixteen years old, Harold was canvassing the precinct and working at the polls by his father's side. Commenting on the importance of politics to his early home life, he recalled, "My father discussed politics at the dinner table almost every night. . . . William L. Dawson, Oscar De Priest, Mike Sneed, Arthur W. Mitchell, and C. C. Wimbish were frequent visitors in our home. . . . The only subject that superseded politics in our home was religion."[7]

A group of African American businessmen and professionals, known as the "new breed" because of their desire to wrest power from the hands of unsavory Old Guard black politicians, condemned the bribery, graft, kickbacks, and favoritism they saw all around them on the South Side. They railed incessantly about the open tolerance of vice by corrupt politicians and crooked policemen on the take. In 1947 members of the indignant black elite approached Roy Washington, who was widely respected for his unflinching integrity, about running for Third Ward alderman. Democratic Third Ward committeeman Edward "Mike" Sneed, a crude, uneducated former janitor rumored to be involved with the South Side gambling cartel, ostensibly went along with Washington's candidacy but secretly worked on behalf of the Republican candidate, Archibald Carey Jr. Largely due to Sneed's treachery, Washington lost narrowly in a runoff election to Carey. Later that year, the *Chicago Defender*'s endorsement of Washington notwithstanding, the Democratic Party's leadership chose Illinois state senator Christopher Wimbish to replace the floundering Sneed as Third Ward committeeman.

Despite these setbacks, Roy Washington remained unswervingly loyal to the Democratic organization. Regardless of the cutthroat politics practiced in the upper echelons of the political machine, Third Ward residents continued to admire Washington as the benevolent face of the Democratic Party and a trusted ombudsman on Third Ward blocks.[8]

Roy Washington sent Harold and his younger brother, Edward, to St. Benedict the Moor Grammar School in Milwaukee, a Roman Catholic boarding school for black middle-class children, until their repeated acts of rebellion necessitated a change in plans. Revolting against the school's strict regimen and harsh discipline, the boys immediately ran away and hitchhiked home. When the audacious siblings had engineered the hundred-mile escape fourteen times, according to Harold's recollection, Roy capitulated and enrolled the brothers in Chicago's Forrestville Elementary School. Harold attended an overcrowded DuSable High School that had been designed for twenty-five hundred students but, bowing to the city's unyielding segregation policy, somehow made room for more than thirty-five hundred. A tough and determined high school athlete, he boxed as a middleweight and placed first in the 110-yard high hurdles and second in the 220-yard low hurdles at a citywide track meet. He read voraciously, sitting alone in the school cafeteria at lunchtime or secluded in the public library a few blocks from his home in the evenings. Friends recalled that he even read in the dugout in between at bats during baseball games. An intense and curious young man with far-ranging interests, he learned quickly but soon found little intellectual stimulation in his classes. Bored by a curriculum that he said offered no challenges, Harold left DuSable after his junior year and worked for six months at Civilian Conservation Corps camps in Illinois and Michigan before landing a full-time job at a Chicago meatpacking plant. He escaped the drudgery and dangers of the killing floors when Roy Washington used his political connections to land Harold a desk job in the local branch office of the U.S. Treasury. While working at the Treasury, the nineteen-year-old Washington married his childhood sweetheart, seventeen-year-old Dorothy "Nancy" Finch; they divorced, childless, in 1950, and Harold never remarried.[9]

Following the Japanese attack on Pearl Harbor, Harold Washington was drafted into the U.S. Army. Looking back at the Second World War, he spoke disparagingly about his three years in the armed forces. Beginning in boot camp, the site of several violent outbreaks between white and black soldiers, he balked at the regimentation and authoritarianism of military life. Jim Crow conditions in communities near several of the bases in the United States where he was stationed made the experience even more insufferable. Sent to the Pacific theater as a technician in the Army Air Force Engineers, he gathered and tested soil samples on a number of islands as the first step in the construction of landing strips for U.S. bombers. Eagerly taking the opportunity to enroll in the military's continuing education program, he completed thirty correspondence courses offered to overseas personnel. Although the army had promoted him to the rank of first sergeant by the time he received an honorable discharge on January 20, 1946, a disillusioned Washington named the high school equivalency diploma he earned as the only worthwhile outcome of his time in the armed forces.[10]

Near the end of the war, Nancy Washington began writing her husband about a new college forming downtown that everyone on the city's South Side was talking about. In 1945 sixty-eight professors from Chicago Central YMCA College walked out to protest the school's use of racial, religious, gender, and nationality quotas for admission and, with funding from trade unions and local philanthropists, founded an independent, coeducational college devoted to social justice and equal opportunity. Dedicated in 1945 and named after the recently deceased U.S. president, Roosevelt College opened as one of the few fully integrated institutions of higher learning in the nation. The college's commitment to diversity seemed all the more remarkable at a time when most of the hotels and restaurants in the surrounding downtown area refused to serve African American patrons. Providing extensive night school offerings and flexible class schedules, the institution catered to first-generation college students, racial minorities, and international students. In keeping with its reputation as a haven for nontraditional and avant-garde students, Roosevelt College became known as home to an extraordinary number of free thinkers, visionaries, and political radicals—"the little red schoolhouse" to its critics. Reclaiming his job at the U.S. Treasury office after returning to Chicago, Washington made use of his G.I. Bill benefits to enroll as a full-time student at Roosevelt College.[11]

Washington thrived in Roosevelt College's liberal environment, excelling in the classroom, involving himself extensively in student government organizations, and participating in protest activities led by a variety of student groups. The institution nurtured his independent, free-thinking inclinations. Prohibited from joining the college's social fraternities, which were bound by their national charters to exclude African Americans, he helped found a chapter of Phi Beta Sigma, a predominantly black collegiate and professional organization. As president of the college's student council, he extended its reach and broadened its portfolio to increase student influence on campus. In a predominantly white student body—with only about twenty blacks in a graduating class of four hundred—he won election as the college's first African American senior class president. His contemporaries remembered Washington as a calm voice of reason in frequently overheated campus politics, a moderate liberal who got along well with radicals but often stopped short of endorsing their nostrums and tactics. Opinionated but tolerant of other people's views, he defended his ideas firmly but accepted defeat graciously when the opposition prevailed. "He was regarded as an astute, honest, intelligent leader," recalled G. Nicholas Paster, the director of student activities. He chaired the college's first fund-raising drive by students and served on a campus committee that participated in a citywide effort to outlaw racially restrictive covenants in Chicago. In 1949, opposing a witch hunt to identify and punish alleged subversives, he led a delegation of students to the state capital to oppose measures outlawing the Communist Party in Illinois and mandating loyalty oaths for public school teachers. At the height of the Red Scare, the legislation passed.[12]

At Roosevelt College, Washington became acquainted with a number of young African Americans who later became influential figures in the South Side black community. His classmates at the school included, among others, novelist Frank London Brown; Bennett Johnson, a successful publisher and leading political independent; Gus Savage, owner of a weekly chain of community newspapers and later a member of the U.S. House of Representatives from the state's Second Congressional District; and Dempsey J. Travis, a mortgage banker, real estate mogul, civil rights activist, and historian. Travis recalled that, in one late-night bull session, Washington and Savage predicted that one day they would both represent Chicago in the U.S. Congress. In college and for many years thereafter, Travis unsuccessfully attempted to convince Washington to join him in a series of potentially lucrative real estate ventures. Washington repeatedly demurred, forsaking the affluence offered by a business career in favor of his first love, politics.[13]

Washington received a bachelor of arts degree with a major in political science from Roosevelt College in August 1949 and matriculated at Northwestern University Law School the following month. Leaving behind the heterogeneous student mix at Roosevelt College, he became the only African American in his first-year law school class of 185. The law school also accepted a handful of women that year, and only one—Dawn Clark Netsch, who later held several important positions in Illinois government—graduated three years later. In 1951 Washington won election as treasurer of the Junior Bar Association, a small and largely invisible student group that his energy and enthusiasm failed to transform into a more meaningful campus presence. Overall, he devoted much less time at Northwestern University to extracurricular pursuits than he had at Roosevelt College. For the most part, he studied, worked a series of part-time jobs in the evenings and on weekends to support himself, and kept a comparatively low profile on campus. He received his juris doctor degree in 1952 and joined his father's law practice on Chicago's South Side.[14]

Roy Washington died just a year after Harold joined the law practice, but not before the proud father pushed his son further into Democratic Party politics. Right across the hall from the Washingtons' law office, Ralph Metcalfe was settling in as the new Third Ward Democratic committeeman. A revered figure in black Chicago because of his athletic feats at the 1936 Olympics—he earned a silver medal in the 100-meter dash, finishing a fraction of a second behind Jesse Owens, and won a gold medal as a member of the U.S. team in the 400-meter relay—Metcalfe was working as a hotel manager when the Democratic machine installed him as alderman and committeeman to bring order to the fractious Third Ward. Roy Washington knew that a political neophyte like Metcalfe would need to rely on a seasoned veteran such as Harold, who had been accompanying his father on canvassing excursions and handing out leaflets on street corners since childhood. Despite his relative youth, the thirty-one-year-old Harold Washington knew the political terrain of the Third Ward much better than did the forty-three-year-old Metcalfe. In fact, according to Third Ward Democrats, the much younger Washington served as mentor to the older Metcalfe. Shortly after Roy Washington passed away in November 1953, Metcalfe persuaded Harold to take over his father's old precinct and also arranged to have him replace his father in the corporation counsel's office.[15]

On the evening of May 25, 1955, Roosevelt College celebrated its ten-year anniversary at a gala event attended by three thousand persons at the International Amphitheater. The college presented honorary doctoral degrees that night to Eleanor Roosevelt and Supreme Court chief justice Earl Warren. Chosen to speak on behalf of alumni, Washington shared the dais with the honored guests and sat next to Mayor Richard J. Daley. In his address, Washington spoke eloquently about the college's mission and its exemplary influence on the lives of many Chicagoans. Responding to the speaker's moving oratory and proud that a young South Sider, the college's first black senior class president, had acquitted himself well in such distinguished company, the hundreds of African Americans in the audience applauded enthusiastically. Duly impressed, Daley spoke at length with Washington after the festivities about local politics. The newly elected mayor, in office barely a month, was looking to shore up the Democratic Party's standing on the South Side by attracting capable young African Americans into the machine's orbit. The son of a respected Democratic loyalist, well educated, an impressive public speaker, and thoroughly conversant in the workings of ward politics, Harold Washington seemed to be precisely the kind of new talent the mayor was seeking. Shortly after the Roosevelt College dinner, the corporation counsel told Washington that his stock had suddenly risen dramatically in city hall and that he was being groomed for the coveted job of city prosecutor. Indeed, despite his status as a relative newcomer in the corporation counsel's office, he began receiving plum assignments in a variety of courtrooms throughout the city.[16]

Suddenly singled out as the rising star of the Chicago legal department, Washington encountered considerable hostility from many of the other attorneys working for the city, who saw his rapid ascent as a form of affirmative action. "The white folks were trying to get me out," he recalled, "because they thought I was Daley's favorite house nigger." Washington ignored the snide comments by coworkers at first, but finally exploded at an antagonist and threatened to throw him out a window. News of the contretemps reached Daley, who sent a black female attorney he trusted to urge Washington to be patient—to control his temper and try harder to ignore the harassment. "I couldn't get along with the racist mothers," Washington told the intermediary. Thereafter, he largely avoided the corporation counsel's office, staying away for weeks at a time, and left his city job altogether in 1958. Washington later admitted to being overly impetuous— "young and unsophisticated," in his own words—and acknowledged that he should have been content knowing that he had the most powerful patron of all in the mayor's office. "Instead of getting rough," he later confided to Dempsey Travis, "I should have jumped cool and bypassed them." No longer actively engaged in the business of the city's law office, he devoted his time exclusively to bolstering Metcalfe's Third Ward organization.[17]

In 1959 Metcalfe appointed Washington his aldermanic secretary and supervisor of all the ward's precinct captains. After these promotions, which made official his status as the second-highest-ranking Democrat in the Third Ward, Washington's elevated position afforded him an unimpeded overview of the ward's entire political scaffolding from top to bottom. Most important, Metcalfe put him in charge of the ward's moribund Young Democrats organization. Mayor Daley recognized the importance of the South Side black vote, which had proved crucial in his narrow victory in 1955, and sought to revive dormant youth groups in the Second, Third, Fourth, and Twentieth Wards. Washington worked tirelessly to recruit members to the Young Democrats, which quickly became the largest group of its kind in the city, with a membership of three thousand youngsters; soon blacks from around Chicago and the surrounding suburbs visited the Third Ward and began modeling their efforts after Washington's example. Scores of black politicians applied the lessons they had learned under Washington's tutelage in their own jurisdictions. The Young Democrats, who outnumbered all other participants at annual Third Ward affairs, boasted three times as many members as the regular organization by 1960. The Third Ward gave Daley his largest margin of victory in the 1963 mayoral election, and Washington could boast that he had trained fully half of the ward's Democratic precinct captains in his Young Democrat workshops. Thanks principally to Washington's hard work and political acumen, the Third Ward had become the electoral powerhouse in the Black Belt and the principal training ground for young African American Democrats citywide.[18]

Washington also served as an arbitrator for the Illinois Industrial Commission from 1960 to 1964, adjudicating disputes between labor and management regarding workplace injuries, but he continued to devote most of his energy to electoral politics. Along with Gus Savage, Bennett Johnson, and several other young African Americans, he founded the Chicago League of Negro Voters (CLNV) in 1959 to protest racial inequality and to foster increased political activism on the South Side. Exalting racial pride, the fledgling organization challenged the Democratic machine in Chicago to respond more fully to black grievances and urged African American voters to operate more independently. The CLNV tailored its appeals to both Democrats and Republicans and called for blacks to support whichever political party proved most responsive to their needs. Washington maintained good relations with the Democratic machine and continued to work hard for the Metcalfe organization, but his expressions of interest in an autonomous black political movement as early as the late 1950s could be seen as a harbinger of a later penchant for challenging the local establishment.[19]

Washington developed the reputation of a self-reliant free thinker and regularly asserted his independence in the Third Ward. Aware of his indispensability to the Metcalfe operation, he took liberties and bent the rules, relying on the political capital he had accrued. In addition to conducting mundane ward business and overseeing the work of the precinct captains, Washington successfully managed three of Metcalfe's aldermanic campaigns in the 1960s and two of his congressional campaigns in the 1970s. Whereas other precinct captains kept in regular contact with ward headquarters, Washington came and went as he pleased and often disappeared for days at a time. Charles Freeman, a young member of the Third Ward organization and later the first black Illinois Supreme Court justice, noted that Metcalfe sometimes became very impatient when he could not immediately confer with his lieutenant about an urgent matter and bellowed to others in the office, "Go find that goddamn Washington!" Metcalfe's frustration never led to a breach with Washington, however, doubtless because the alderman realized the value of the political wisdom and organizing ability supplied by his top aide. A wooden public speaker who depended on name recognition and the consistently outstanding performance of the ward's electoral machine, Metcalfe relied heavily on the talents of his canny and articulate second in command. If Washington's surpassing competence and increasing popularity made Metcalfe feel insecure, the perfect solution presented itself when the local state representative, Kenneth Wilson, resigned and won a seat on the Cook County Board of Commissioners. By slating Washington to replace Wilson in the Illinois House of Representatives, the Third Ward boss could dispatch his strongest potential rival to Springfield.[20]

In 1964 Washington ran for a seat in the state legislature, representing the Twenty-Sixth District, which encompassed the neighborhoods of Englewood, West Englewood, Grand Boulevard, and Woodlawn on Chicago's South Side. He won easily, accumulating the fortieth-highest vote total of the 177 representatives and senators elected to the Illinois General Assembly that year. Very quickly, he became known as a serious, hardworking legislator who did his homework, thoroughly understood the issues, and offered valuable insights during debates. Unlike many of his peers, Washington withstood the temptation to socialize in Springfield's many taverns and instead developed the reputation of a loner. He declined to join any Democratic study groups and spent most of his spare time in his hotel room reading, which he identified in a newspaper survey as his favorite pastime. Convivial to colleagues on the House floor and pleasant at all times to reporters, legislative staff, and other state employees around the capitol, he went his own way after hours and kept his own counsel.[21]

As a freshman in the House of Representatives who owed his election to the support of the Cook County Democratic machine, Washington arrived in Springfield burdened by a set of expectations about how he should behave and, most important, vote. Party leaders in Chicago expected unquestioned compliance from the legislators they chose to serve in the state capital, and indeed, with the exception of a very few independents, Democratic state senators and representatives from Cook County never thought about exercising individual initiative. Like clockwork, they read the "idiot sheets" the machine distributed that indicated without explanation how to vote—bill by bill—on the legislation to be considered each day. Unlike most of his peers, who gave the "idiot sheets" a cursory glance and quickly cast their votes as instructed, Washington gazed intensely at the instructions before voting. Adlai Stevenson III, Washington's seatmate on the House floor, described the recurring scenes: "I frequently saw the agony and tension in his face as he wrestled with the notions of what he wanted to do and what the Chicago machine wanted him to do." More often than not, even after prolonged deliberation, Washington followed the direction of the party bosses. Rote compliance with the machine took its toll on free-thinking black legislators such as Washington, however, leading to exasperation and restlessness. Political scientist William Grimshaw noted, "I think it's hard to appreciate the frustrations of some black politicians then. They had no power and they were being used, but it was the only game. It was a very hard thing for a bright black to submit to that. I've had old guys tell me about it with tears in their eyes. It was humiliating."[22]

Washington ignored his marching orders and supported progressive measures opposed by the Cook County delegation often enough to raise eyebrows in Chicago. He voted repeatedly for the Equal Rights Amendment, earning a 100 percent approval rating from the National Organization for Women, and against state aid for parents sending their children to parochial schools. His reputation as a nonconformist grew in 1969 when he joined several other African Americans to organize a black caucus in the House of Representatives. When Mayor Daley objected to the idea, demanding that there be no divisions within a unified Democratic Cook County delegation, most of the black legislators deserted the fledgling organization. Washington remained and assumed a leadership role in the black caucus. More friction ensued near the end of Washington's second term when he introduced a bill on behalf of Renault Robinson, head of the Chicago Police Department's Afro-American Patrolmen's League (AAPL), to create civilian review boards for monitoring the public's treatment by law enforcement authorities. Robinson's initiative reflected the outrage on the South Side about the long-standing mistreatment of blacks by Chicago's overwhelmingly white police force. Robinson knew that the bill had virtually no chance of passing but wanted to publicize the issue of police brutality, a concern of surpassing importance in the black community that continued to resonate into the twenty-first century. Mayor Daley strongly opposed the measure, disputing the need for reform and objecting to any tampering with his police department's independent operations. Having been rebuffed by several independent blacks and white liberals in the state legislature, who said that they agreed with the sentiment but feared angering Daley by introducing such a bill, Robinson approached Washington as a last resort. To the young policeman's surprise, the new legislator who had been elected with the Democratic machine's backing quickly agreed to sponsor the controversial legislation.[23]

Daley had told Metcalfe to dump the unpredictable Washington more than once before, but, recognizing the representative's large and loyal following in the Twenty-Sixth Legislative District and his value to black Democrats on the South Side, the Third Ward boss had resisted the pressure from city hall. The dispute over the police review board proved to be another matter, however, as Daley thought Washington guilty of insubordination on a sensitive matter that struck at the heart of the machine's unchecked power. Washington had to go, the mayor insisted. In a heated conversation at Third Ward headquarters, an exasperated Metcalfe told Washington, "You're on your own [with Daley]." Feeling betrayed by his boss, Washington responded, "You have your white man, and I've got mine." John Touhy, the powerful Speaker of the Illinois House of Representatives, came to the pugnacious representative's rescue and interceded on his behalf with the mayor. Washington kept his seat in Springfield but only after agreeing to serve on the commission Daley had formed to investigate the AAPL's charges of police brutality. Washington groused that his acquiescence in the commission's report, an obvious whitewash that absolved the police of any wrongdoing, made him feel like Daley's "showcase nigger." The entire episode left him humiliated and bitter. Deserted by his superior in an important organizational dispute, forced to rely on a powerful white politician to save his career, and compelled to participate in a bogus inquiry designed to protect the shameful status quo, he experienced firsthand the steep cost of challenging the potent Democratic machine over a matter of principle.[24]

Following the showdown with Daley in 1969, which nearly ended Washington's political career, he became more circumspect in his dealings with the Cook County Democratic organization. Ranked third among the state's 177 legislators by the liberal Independent Voters of Illinois (IVI) in 1967, Washington dropped to thirty-third by 1973 as he hewed more closely to the machine's party line. In effect, he traded some of his independence for security. When a detachment of fourteen policemen raided the home of several Black Panthers on the city's West Side in December 1969, initiating hostilities and killing Fred Hampton and Mark Clark in their beds, Washington rushed back to Chicago and toured the bullet-riddled apartment. Aghast and sickened by what he saw, he nevertheless refrained from commenting publicly on the incident. He subsequently kept a low profile when the AAPL, the Illinois Civil Liberties Union, and three independent aldermen demanded an investigation. Pushed forcefully in one direction by political necessity yet tugged in the other direction by temperament and conviction, he felt forced to choose expediency—and deeply regretted it. "I looked at myself as one of the [Uncle] Toms," he later told Dempsey Travis in discussing that period of his legislative career.[25]

Even though he felt hamstrung by the machine leadership in Chicago, Washington still exerted a striking measure of autonomy in the Cook County delegation that set him apart from his peers. He picked his battles more carefully after 1969, but Washington opposed the Chicago Democratic organization occasionally on matters he considered especially important. He sometimes ignored the instructions on the "idiot sheet" and voted according to the dictates of his conscience; at other times, when compliance seemed altogether unpalatable, he simply disappeared and could not be found when the time came for roll-call votes. (Metcalfe referred to that tactic as "one of Harold's famous walks out of the statehouse doors to get lost before the roll was called.") Even the occasional departure from the explicit directives communicated to state legislators upset party leaders in Chicago, an indication of the Cook County machine's powerful hold on its representatives in Springfield. Reflecting on Washington's career in the Illinois House, one of his colleagues noted admiringly: "He was the only black legislator ever to take such independent positions and survive." When he broke ranks with the Cook County Democrats and staked out more progressive positions than the Chicago leadership allowed its functionaries to take, his desertions usually involved issues of importance to racial minorities. In 1971, for example, Washington led a boycott of black legislators when Vice President Spiro Agnew addressed a joint session of the Illinois General Assembly. Having labeled Agnew "antiblack" and linked the vice president's policy positions to views held by the Ku Klux Klan, he persuaded nearly half of the African Americans in the state legislature not to attend the speech. By the early 1970s, Washington had emerged as one of the state legislature's most progressive voices and the most persistent spokesman in Springfield for African American rights.[26]

In alliance with other progressive legislators, Washington introduced a series of bills designed to protect racial minorities and other oppressed groups susceptible to exploitation by society's predatory interests. He quickly developed a reputation for the skillful exercise of the legislative chamber's rules and regulations, using an array of parliamentary tricks to forestall votes, marshal his forces, contest procedural customs, and confound his rivals. Conservative downstate and suburban interests often defeated reformist legislation he introduced or supported, but his efforts nonetheless resulted in some notable victories during his six terms in the Illinois House. He played an important role in the passage of the Consumer Credit Reform Act of 1965, for instance, which effectively curtailed the kind of fraud and deceptive business practices rampant in slums and ghettos. Working with law enforcement authorities concerned with the difficulty of securing convictions against criminals in gang-infested neighborhoods, he introduced and guided to passage the Witness Protection Act of 1972, which helped to ensure the safety of citizens willing to testify against defendants charged with violent crimes. His successful advocacy of the Medical Malpractice Insurance Revision of 1975 addressed the thorny problem of how to hold incompetent physicians accountable by preserving the right of patients to seek relief in the courts but also placing caps on the amounts awarded to litigants in malpractice suits.[27]

Washington worked for several years to improve the operation of the state's Fair Employment Practices Commission (FEPC), which after its creation in 1961 had attempted to root out discrimination in employment under state and local government contracts. Lack of adequate enforcement provisions had rendered the agency ineffective, however, and African Americans chafed at the continued lack of protection. In 1969, after a succession of failures in preceding legislative sessions, Washington steered through the House a series of contract compliance programs that ostensibly gave the FEPC more authority. Inadequate funding proved to be the next hurdle, and in 1971 Washington successfully championed an amendment to the FEPC law containing a new compliance apparatus along with an appropriation of one hundred thousand dollars to fund the new statewide program. In the same session, he received authorization to establish a special committee to investigate job discrimination under government contracts in Illinois. As chairman of the Illinois House Contracts Compliance Committee, he led an eight-month probe scrutinizing the hiring practices of businesses and the conduct of labor unions involved in government contracts. In 1972 the Illinois FEPC adopted many of the two dozen recommendations for combating racial discrimination listed in the committee's final report.[28]

To be sure, Washington's legislative forays did not always conclude so successfully. In 1973 he introduced a bill to repeal the state's controversial "stop and frisk" law, which allowed law enforcement authorities to search motorists and pedestrians who aroused suspicion for one reason or another. Statistics showed that the law had been used disproportionately against black and Latino populations. Washington contacted Renault Robinson to gather information about how the Chicago Police Department trained its officers to implement the law and to obtain a list of witnesses who could appear at congressional hearings to describe how the police abused "stop and frisk." Without citing his source, Washington noted in the House debate over the legislation that Chicago patrolmen boasted at police stations that they had violated the civil rights of innocent citizens during "stop and frisk" operations. Sometimes on Saturday nights, prayer meetings seemed to have broken out on the streets of his neighborhood, Washington sardonically claimed, because "every third man has his hands up in the air." Washington's measure received sixty-four of the eighty-nine votes needed for approval but lost to a coalition led by Henry J. Hyde of Chicago, which conceded that police had occasionally been "overzealous" in their implementation of the practice but called for preservation of "stop and frisk" as an invaluable law enforcement tool.[29]

Similarly, Washington made little headway for years in his efforts to dismantle the obstacles barring minority entrepreneurs from landing jobs in the construction industry. African American contractors faced insurmountable barriers securing contracts because of having to submit exorbitant bid deposits, the difficulty of securing loans from banks, and the problem of obtaining surety bonds guaranteed by the federal government's Small Business Administration without sufficient collateral. Thus, small minority businesses attempting to compete for bids with larger well-established firms failed repeatedly due to their lack of credit, collateral, and other necessary forms of capital. In 1974 Washington and Representative Bernard Epton sponsored a bill that obligated surety companies in Illinois to pool the risk of issuing bonds to small- and medium-size contractors with all of the other surety firms in the state; the bill died in the House's Industrial Affairs Committee.[30]

Nor did Washington's protracted battles against currency exchanges, which he condemned for preying mercilessly on ghetto residents, yield satisfactory results, despite years of effort. According to the findings of a four-month investigation by the *Chicago Sun-Times*, the Better Government Association (BGA), and the Legal Assistance Foundation of Chicago, currency exchanges in African American neighborhoods leveled usurious service charges on patrons who cashed checks, paid utility bills, purchased money orders, bought food stamps, and conducted other routine financial transactions. Bereft of alternatives nearby and lacking adequate transportation to conduct their business elsewhere, captive ghetto populations relied on the ubiquitous currency exchanges that lined the commercial streets of the city's South Side. (According to the *Sun-Times*, the five hundred currency exchanges in Chicago far outnumbered the ninety-nine banks that by state law could provide a limited number of financial services to the public.) The Community Currency Exchange Association, the powerful trade association that defended the interests of the currency exchanges, opposed any attempt by government agencies to oversee the kind of mundane business transactions conducted there. Washington introduced a bill that would have given the Illinois Department of Financial Institutions the authority to regulate rates charged by currency exchanges and comparable institutions. Members of the House approved the bill, but the measure perished in the Senate's Committee on Insurance and Licensed Activity. The fact that Washington's opposition to "stop and frisk," efforts to increase opportunity for minority contractors in the construction industry, and challenge of the currency exchanges all ended unsuccessfully mattered less to South Side voters than the intrepid legislator's repeated efforts on their behalf. Unlike the many timorous legislators who remained subservient to the Cook County Democratic machine, Washington was at least tackling issues of real consequence to vulnerable African American residents.[31]

Despite some discouraging setbacks, Washington's dogged pursuit of change on behalf of his African American constituency earned him plaudits back home in the Twenty-Sixth District. Two fights he successfully led—saving Provident Hospital from demolition and declaring Dr. Martin Luther King Jr.'s birthday a holiday in Illinois—especially resonated on the South Side. In the first instance, he introduced a bill that authorized the Illinois Department of Public Health to award a fifteen-million-dollar grant to the outmoded health care facility, one of Chicago's oldest African American institutions, as a supplement to federal grants and loans and the promise of additional funds from private foundations. The drive to refurbish facilities at Provident Hospital, a necessity for conforming to state licensure standards, allowed the continued delivery of critical medical services to a poor neighborhood desperate for good medical care.[32]

In the second instance, Washington's crusade began in 1969 when his bill to make Dr. King's birthday a state holiday passed both the House and the Senate before Republican governor Richard Ogilvie vetoed the measure. A year later, the governor signed a watered-down bill offered by Washington that made King's birthday a commemorative day on which the state's public schools would recognize the slain civil rights leader's accomplishments but not close; Washington accepted the halfway measure but only while continuing to work for more sweeping legislation. In 1971 another bill seeking a state holiday introduced by Washington passed both houses of the legislature, but the governor agreed to sign the measure only if King's birthday became a national holiday. After Ogilvie lost to Democrat Dan Walker in the 1972 gubernatorial election, Washington and his counterpart in the Senate Cecil A. Partee guided yet another version of the bill to passage and launched a massive public relations campaign among Chicago businessmen and clergymen to lobby the new governor in its favor. Walker signed the bill on September 17, 1973, making Illinois the first state to make Dr. King's birthday a legal holiday. Civil rights advocates in the state and beyond lauded Washington's perseverance in obtaining what they considered to be long-overdue recognition for the civil rights legend.[33]

Highly regarded for many years as a conscientious legislator with a keen interest in improving the lot of African Americans, Washington's profile reached new heights after his highly publicized success at making Dr. King's birthday a state holiday in 1973. Later that year, Representative Lewis A. H. Caldwell placed Washington's name in nomination for Speaker of the Illinois House—a singular honor signifying the nominee's rising status among the state's black political leaders. In 1974 the Chicago Committee for a Black Mayor, chaired by James Montgomery, president of the Cook County Bar Association, interviewed several potential candidates for the purpose of choosing an African American to contest Mayor Daley's reelection the following year. Impressed with Washington's record in Springfield, the committee invited him to a meeting to discuss his willingness to run. Washington attended the meeting, thanked the committee members for considering him, and endorsed their goal of supplanting Daley in city hall. He admitted having contemplated entering the race for mayor and claimed to have the requisite experience and name recognition to appeal to party regulars, independents, blacks, whites, Latinos, young, and old. But after discussing the matter with his political advisers, Washington told the committee, he had concluded that one person appeared even more qualified than he did at that time. "It is my considered opinion," Washington said, "that Congressman [Ralph] Metcalfe is your best candidate."[34] After lauding Metcalfe at length, he concluded, "Let me again repeat that I consider myself a servant of this Committee and I would be hard pressed to say no to a legitimate draft. But we are all interested in *promoting the empowerment* of blacks in this city and throughout the nation. Based on that premise I say let's go with *our best* . . . Ralph Metcalfe."[35]

A loyal member of the Democratic machine for many years, Metcalfe had always been a good soldier who followed orders without question. At least he had done so prior to clashing openly with Daley for the first time in the early 1970s. The murders of Black Panthers Fred Hampton and Mark Clark in 1969 had left Metcalfe uneasy but insufficiently so to venture any criticisms of the Democratic leadership at that time. In 1972 he refused to support the reelection of Edward Hanrahan, the Democratic state's attorney responsible for the killing of Hampton and Clark, in defiance of a mayoral directive. Repeated instances of police brutality against members of the black community, which Daley peremptorily dismissed when Metcalfe called for investigations, at last left the black leader prepared to sever relations with the Cook County organization. Metcalfe carefully considered challenging the mayor in 1975 but decided that he lacked the funds for a serious mayoral campaign that would give him a realistic chance of winning. Instead, in 1975 he endorsed a white reform alderman, William S. Singer, rather than the eventual black candidate, State Senator Richard Newhouse, against the incumbent mayor. His caution disappointed many blacks—none more so than Washington—who felt the time had come for a bold political challenge to the machine's plantation politics. Only Metcalfe had a reasonable chance of spearheading a black political movement and changing the political calculus in Chicago, reasoned Washington, who badgered the Third Ward leader unrelentingly about running against Daley. Metcalfe refused to reconsider, however, leading Washington to ridicule him as "a man who plotted every step of the way before he decided to cross a street." Washington never forgave Metcalfe for his timidity and refused to endorse him for reelection to his seat in the U.S. House of Representatives the following year.[36]

In 1976 Cecil Partee, president of the Illinois Senate, opted to seek the post of state attorney general, and Washington decided to run for Partee's seat in the state's Twenty-Sixth Senatorial District. Irritated by Washington's periodic flights from party orthodoxy in the House, Mayor Daley initially refused to slate him. Appreciative of Washington's prolabor voting record in the House, emissaries from the United Auto Workers lobbied the mayor to change his decision. So did Partee, who called Washington a "competent, articulate and concerned legislator." Daley finally relented, apparently without much enthusiasm, and Washington defeated Sixteenth Ward alderwoman Anna Langford, a vociferous critic of the mayor, by approximately two thousand votes in the March Democratic primary. Washington won the general election in November, unopposed by a Republican candidate. Calling himself an "organization liberal," Washington advanced to the state's upper chamber, prepared to walk the same tightrope he had traversed for the preceding years in the House. He owed his presence in Springfield to the backing of the Cook County Democratic organization but freelanced often enough to annoy party leadership. He had sustained this delicate balancing act in large measure because influential superiors in the general assembly—such powerful legislators as John Touhy and Cecil Partee—had recognized his ability and provided the necessary cover. He had also attended faithfully to constituents' concerns and fought the good fight over issues of concern to African Americans when the Daley machine appeared inattentive to their grievances. Still a member of the Cook County Democratic organization who voted along with his colleagues on most matters, his growing independence strained the tethers that bound him to the machine. It seemed unclear how long either member of such an uncomfortable alliance—the political machine that demanded unwavering loyalty or the contrary legislator with a progressive agenda—would be comfortable maintaining the uneasy accord.[37]

The irreparable breach came even before the eightieth session of the general assembly opened in January 1977, the product of Mayor Daley's unexpected death caused by a massive heart attack on December 20, 1976. Daley had appeared healthy at age seventy-four, so neither his supporters nor his adversaries seemed prepared for the urgent need to select a new mayor. At a time of great uncertainty, black alderman Wilson Frost of the Thirty-Fourth Ward argued that he should become acting mayor due to his position as city council president pro tempore. Faced with the prospect of swearing in Chicago's first African American mayor, white machine aldermen challenged Frost's reading of the pertinent city statutes. When none of the powerful white aldermen could muster enough support from competing factions to construct a winning coalition, they united behind Eleventh Ward alderman Michael A. Bilandic as an alternative to Frost. A bland apparatchik seemingly lacking in ambition, Bilandic emerged as the ideal caretaker to mind the store for a few months until a special citywide election could be held in April 1977; Bilandic assured everyone that he would not be a candidate in the special election. Convinced that he lacked the votes to win in a city council showdown, Frost agreed to a deal with the Democratic leadership: Frost became finance committee chairman, reputedly the second most powerful post in city government, in return for not contesting Bilandic's selection.[38]

Barely one week after his appointment as acting mayor, Bilandic reneged on his earlier pledge and announced his candidacy in the April election. The list of aspirants that spring also included two dissident white Democrats,

Forty-First Ward alderman Roman Pucinski, and former state's attorney Edward Hanrahan. Black community leaders, many of whom felt that Frost should have refused the deal offered by the machine aldermen and continued to fight as a representative of minority Chicagoans, quickly mobilized to choose a candidate as well. Infuriated with Frost, black political activists who had aggressively championed his claim to the mayoralty days earlier rapidly deserted his cause and began looking for another standard-bearer. At a December 28, 1976, meeting of African American community organizations, Washington introduced a resolution to field a black candidate in the election, organize a committee to raise funds for the campaign, and mobilize to increase voter turnout in the politically inert South Side wards. His recent hesitancy to challenge city hall notwithstanding, Metcalfe spoke enthusiastically for the resolution and issued a call for black unity. The Reverend Jesse Jackson also concurred with the plan of action and, echoing the sentiments of countless others present, argued that Frost had eliminated himself from consideration by accepting a tainted bargain that had embarrassed the African American community. The meeting concluded with the naming of a search committee, composed of state representative Jesse Madison, Renault Robinson, and a number of prominent local business leaders, charged with presenting the name(s) of one or more viable mayoral candidates at a meeting to be held in January 1977.[39]

The search committee, the composition of which underwent significant change in the ensuing weeks as some members withdrew and others came onboard, selected Washington as the best-qualified candidate. On January 21, just a few hours before a public announcement of the state senator's candidacy, Metcalfe told the *Chicago Sun-Times* that he had a "bill of particulars" against Washington and had decided not to support him in the election. Metcalfe's veiled remarks hinted that a scandal in Washington's past—he paid a fine and served a brief jail sentence for failing to file income tax returns in the 1960s—called his electability into question. Others suspected that poisoned personal relations and the burgeoning rivalry between the two dominant politicians of the Third Ward accounted for the rift. Ill will between the two Democrats, simmering for years, had boiled over when Metcalfe bowed out of the mayoral race in 1975 and Washington had withheld his support for Metcalfe's reelection to the U.S. Congress in 1976. Later that evening, after reading Metcalfe's remarks to a stunned audience gathered to endorse the search committee's choice, Washington removed his name from consideration. Following a prolonged and heated discussion, much of which criticized the unexpected Metcalfe statement and its chilling effect on the popular choice of a mayoral candidate, the meeting adjourned. The ad hoc Committee for a Black Mayor subsequently dissolved without accomplishing its principal task of selecting a candidate in the April election.[40]

Washington returned to Springfield, his mayoral campaign apparently stillborn and his willingness to seek the office having dissolved his last remaining ties to the Democratic machine. Washington and a biracial group of independent senators collectively known as the "Crazy Eight" immediately clashed with the Cook County Democratic organization over the selection of a senate president for the new legislative session. The Crazy Eight opposed the machine candidate, Thomas C. Hynes, a loyal machine Democrat and close associate of Richard M. Daley, son of the late boss. Anticipating his victory in the Senate vote, Hynes had announced his intention of appointing Senator Charles Chew of Chicago as leader of the Illinois Black Legislative Caucus. Citing Hynes's declaration as yet another example of the machine's arrogant exercise of power, Washington and his cohorts insisted on the right of black caucus members to pick their own president—in this case Kenneth Hall of East St. Louis. In an extremely close contest for the Senate presidency, with neither side able to muster a winning majority, the votes of the Crazy Eight held the balance through nearly two hundred inconclusive ballots. The prolonged stalemate, which delayed the obligatory selection of the legislative leadership, kept the Illinois General Assembly from commencing its work for nearly five weeks. Finally, after a seventeen-hour negotiating session in the state capital, the two sides reached a compromise whereby Hynes became president and several independent Democrats received influential leadership positions in the state senate (including Kenneth Hall, who became assistant majority leader).[41]

Washington's prominent leadership role in the Crazy Eight's success in wresting concessions from the machine convinced a cohort of black leaders in Chicago to resurrect his mayoral campaign. Regardless of Metcalfe's objections, they reasoned, Washington remained by far the most experienced and capable independent African American politician in the city. Without his knowledge, they collected the necessary number of signatures on a petition to activate his candidacy—and then conferred with him about running. Starting late, needing to fashion a campaign apparatus hastily, and knowing that his fund-raising would be grossly inadequate, Washington nevertheless agreed to enter the race. Given the imposing obstacles arrayed against him, the pragmatic legislator harbored no illusions about winning. Rather, he felt, his calculations reflected a realistic assessment of political exigencies in Chicago's post–Richard J. Daley era. The haughty dismissal of Wilson Frost's claim to the mayoralty by white power brokers rankled black Democrats, many of whom felt it essential to demonstrate their displeasure by fielding a candidate that year. No other viable black candidate existed, and Washington agreed with his suitors that someone needed to enter the race if African Americans seriously contemplated increasing their influence in local politics. His uneasy rapprochement with the machine having ruptured at last, he felt certain that the regular Democrats would attempt to unseat him in the next year's election regardless of what he did in 1977. The mayoral campaign would be an opportunity to mobilize voters for the 1978 state senate race. In the end, Washington shrugged, "I didn't have anything to lose."[42]

During the brief campaign leading to the Democratic primary on April 19, Washington employed many of the tactics and themes he used in his later mayoral contests. Repeatedly denying that he was seeking only black votes, he actively politicked in white neighborhoods and sought support from all racial and ethnic groups in the city. He linked race and class concerns in a broad definition of reform. His campaign created an Interethnic Citizens' Committee and won the endorsement of the Independent Voters of Illinois, the local affiliate of the liberal Americans for Democratic Action. Identifying himself as a good-government reformer, he called for an end to patronage and promised to replace the police superintendent, James Rochford, because of his blatant disregard for civil liberties. Frequently emphasizing the ties between Bilandic and the Daley administration that had guided the city's fortunes for more than two decades, he called for a sharp break with past practices and policies that had stifled the city's development. Ridiculing Chicago's reputation as "the city that works," he charged that the city worked only for Loop businesses and the influence-peddling politicians who engineered backroom deals that enriched a self-serving upper class. Chicago did not work, he asserted, for the overwhelming majority of its citizens.[43] He elaborated:

It does not work for our neighborhoods, which are unsafe and in various states of neglect and decay. It does not work for our children, who are not being educated by our schools. It does not work for blacks or Hispanic Americans or Polish-Americans, who have been written out of the social contract by the authoritarian rule of the Eleventh Ward. It does not work for the people of Chicago who are divided, afraid, paralyzed by the absence of great and inspiring leadership.[44]

Speaking to a large crowd at city hall, Washington indicted Bilandic as a "third-rate Boss Daley" who would blindly continue the Democratic machine's disastrous policies that had condemned Chicago to a prolonged period of decline. A police officer disconnected the microphone Washington was using, but he kept talking. Under Bilandic's uninspired leadership, Washington predicted, the city's tax base would continue to dwindle, businesses would continue fleeing to the suburbs, and both the educational and the welfare systems would continue to suffer chronic financial crises. Any hope for the city's future rested with a rejection of the entrenched political machine and a municipal government that worked only for moneyed interests. Instead, Washington offered an alternative vision of a Chicago that would work for all of the people and all of the neighborhoods.[45]

In the course of the mayoral campaign, the Chicago newspapers investigated Metcalfe's vague "bill of particulars" against Washington and published its findings without fanfare. Convicted of not filing income tax returns in 1964, 1965, 1967, and 1969, the press reported, Washington made restitution, paid a fine, and served a short jail sentence. In the 1970s, the Chicago Bar Association had suspended Washington's law license subject to complaints from clients that he had accepted retainer fees from them but not completed the work for which he had been paid. The abashed candidate admitted culpability in both instances, and the IVI acknowledged the reports matter-of-factly in announcing its endorsement of him. The story receded quickly from the local news scene, no doubt attracting very little attention because of Washington's marginal status in the mayoral race.[46]

Bilandic won the Democratic primary with slightly more than 50 percent of the ballots cast and went on to defeat Dennis Block (the lone Republican alderman in the city council) by nearly a four-to-one margin in the general election. Bowing to the pressure from city hall, the black Democratic committeemen unanimously endorsed the incumbent mayor. Metcalfe refused to support Washington, and Jesse Jackson of Operation PUSH (People United to Save Humanity) withheld his endorsement until the eleventh hour. Political factionalism continued to obstruct unity among black voters, and the machine's influence remained strong in a divided African American community. Washington won only 11 percent of the vote in the April primary but carried five wards (the Fifth, Sixth, Eighth, Ninth, and Twenty-First) and narrowly lost a sixth (the Seventeenth) on the South Side. While losing the predominantly black wards on the West Side, the independent Democrat polled surprisingly well in precincts still firmly controlled by the machine. With all of its handicaps, the hurriedly assembled, jerry-rigged, underfunded Washington campaign managed a surprisingly strong showing and hinted at the political potency a unified effort with adequate funding might produce. At the same time, many challenges remained for the black community leaders who aspired to mount a genuine threat to machine suzerainty. Black voter turnout remained strikingly low, as only 27 percent of voting-age blacks showed up at the polls in 1977—a shortcoming that had to be addressed for the goal of electing an African American mayor to be realized. Translating the city's substantial nonwhite population growth since the Second World War into a larger and more active electorate remained the greatest goal. "There is a sleeping giant in Chicago," noted an unbowed Washington. "And if this sleeping giant, the potential black vote, ever woke up, we'd control the city."[47]

Washington returned to Springfield, pledging to remain a staunch independent, impervious to the influence of the Cook County machine. "I'm going to do what maybe I should have done ten or twelve years ago," he said. "I'm going to stay outside that damn Democratic organization and give them hell." As Washington fully expected, the machine quickly took a number of actions to ensure that he would not be reelected to the state senate in 1978. When three of the five committeemen in the Twenty-Sixth District voted to reslate Washington, Bilandic ignored the long-standing principle of majority rule in such matters and allowed the two dissenting committeemen to run a candidate against the incumbent senator. Representative James Taylor, a bitter rival of Washington's from the Sixteenth Ward, chose one of his precinct captains, Clarence C. Barry, to run as the "regular" Democratic candidate. With Taylor supervising the allocation of funds, the machine funneled an unprecedented amount of cash into the Twenty-Sixth District to unseat the incumbent. Vandals destroyed Washington's billboards and campaign signs, while Barry's workers covered lampposts and bus stops with their own candidate's posters. The machine's dirty-tricks practitioners filed petitions for two other candidates, Denise Washington and Sabrina Washington, in an effort to confuse voters by listing three people on the ballot with the same surname. (The detection of defective petitions forced one of the two women to withdraw, but the other remained on the ballot to siphon votes away from the state senator.) Only an extraordinary effort by a dedicated band of independents offset the machine's chicanery that year; the incumbent won the Democratic primary by slightly more than two hundred votes. Washington narrowly survived against what he called "one of the worst combinations of low-brow politicians that I have ever dealt with in all my years in politics."[48]

Emboldened by the knowledge that he had withstood the machine's best efforts to unseat him, Washington returned to the state senate, determined to chart an independent course and aggressively represent the interests of African Americans and other disadvantaged groups. Persuaded by some of his colleagues to take a more active leadership role in the Illinois Black Legislative Caucus, he agreed to seek the chairmanship of the twenty-one-member group (fifteen representatives and six senators). Unanimously elected chairman in January 1979, he identified as the main goal of the caucus the strengthening of oversight functions to ensure that the achievements of recent years be enforced in various state agencies. Legislative advances in fair employment practices and affirmative action had not resulted in significant improvements, he charged, because chief executives, midlevel managers, and agency heads had scuttled the best efforts of reformers. Calling for the development of vigilant ad hoc committees to oversee state government operations, the ambitious senator likewise recommended the establishment of a clearinghouse in Chicago with regular business hours to encourage citizen participation, publicize problems, and coordinate the types of legislative responses necessary to ensure compliance with existing statutes.[49]

Several months later, Washington successfully concluded a six-year crusade he had commenced in the House to establish a minority set-aside program for employment by state agencies. Having failed to forge a majority for his bill every year since 1973, the senator finally recruited enough Republicans and downstate Democrats to offset machine opposition (underwritten by large contracting firms and some craft unions) to pass the Ten Per Cent Set-Aside Act of 1979. The pathbreaking law mandated that 10 percent of all contracts awarded by the Capital Development Board, the Department of Administrative Services, and the Department of Transportation (including all roads and bridges) be reserved for minority-owned businesses and that these firms be advanced payments as start-up funds to cover the initial cost of materials and labor. In all, estimated Washington, the set-asides would provide six hundred million dollars in contracts to minority entrepreneurs as well as a great number of jobs for minority workers.[50]

Concern for the harsh economic conditions confronting minorities and the poor also led Washington in 1979 to challenge budgetary decisions made in Washington, D.C., initiating a practice of loudly censuring national policy making that he repeated throughout the remainder of his political career. Reacting to the news that President Jimmy Carter's projected budget for fiscal year 1980 entailed significant cuts in social welfare programs, he audaciously announced that an Illinois state senate subcommittee would hold hearings to review federal spending priorities. Carter's proposed budget would cut housing assistance funds by 12.5 percent in Illinois, for example, while reduced allocations for the Comprehensive Employment and Training Act would translate into a loss of more than seventeen thousand jobs for the state in a summer youth program (mostly in poor inner-city neighborhoods). Curtailing funding for senior citizen programs would likewise lead to financial hardship for another especially vulnerable group in American society. "All of these cuts hit hardest on those least able to bear that burden," Washington protested, noting that the budget simultaneously provided for a 10 percent increase in military spending. Did not true national security reside in "a healthy, people-serving economy," he asked, "rather than an extravagant defense budget?"[51]

Just as he took advantage of his position in the Illinois General Assembly to assess federal policies, Washington commented freely in Springfield about political affairs in Chicago. In 1979 the reelection of Mayor Bilandic seemed inevitable, so much so that no African American politician thought it possible to unseat him. Bilandic's opposition instead came from Jane Byrne, a minor Democratic machine functionary who had been jettisoned from her city government post after Richard J. Daley's death and who had recast herself as a reformer. Byrne won in 1979 when the Bilandic administration's grievous mishandling of massive snowstorms a few months before the election showed that Chicago was no longer the city that worked. The hapless mayor's lame excuses mollified no one when the city stopped providing essential services. Streets and expressways remained clogged with snow, public transportation trains ceased running on time, mounds of noisome garbage rose in alleys, grocery store shelves stood empty as delivery trucks waited interminably for thoroughfares to become passable again, and O'Hare International Airport, the world's busiest, canceled so many flights that national air traffic remained disrupted for weeks. Bilandic's inept attempts to deal with the unfolding crisis exasperated and angered Chicagoans, especially the African Americans living in the South and West Side ghettos who stood freezing on public transit platforms while commuter train after commuter train bound for downtown sped by their stations without stopping. As a result of the mayor's overt hostility to the city's African American neighborhoods—the Chicago Transit Authority's (CTA) "skip-stop" policy that winter being just the most recent indignity suffered at the hands of the Bilandic administration—the victorious Byrne received her greatest electoral support from the black middle-class wards.[52]

The black electoral backing of Byrne in 1979, an extension of the protest vote for Washington two years earlier, constituted a clear rejection of the Democratic machine's long-standing racist policies. Byrne promptly renewed her ties to the Cook County organization after the election, however, leaving black voters feeling betrayed. The situation worsened as the new mayor sought to improve her standing with white ethnic voters by initiating the redrawing of ward boundaries to eliminate black voting majorities. At the same time, she reduced black representation on the public housing authority and the school board. "Mayor Byrne has contributed to the development of a slave/master mentality even more than [Richard J.] Daley," charged black community activist Lutrelle "Lu" Palmer. Black disaffection with Byrne surged during the first year of her "reform" administration, and in January 1980 Washington introduced a bill in the state senate to create a recall provision for the mayor of Chicago. "She has brought an injudicious, vindictive and just plain mean style of politics to Chicago," commented Washington in explaining why he had introduced the measure. The recall bill failed by seven votes in the senate. Washington's sponsorship of the legislation, which pundits in the capital gave little chance of passage, not only gave voice to black dissatisfaction with the Byrne administration but also offered more evidence of the Chicago senator's estrangement from the Cook County machine. So did his campaign for the seat in the U.S. House of Representatives long held by Metcalfe.[53]

When Metcalfe died shortly before the November 1978 election, Mayor Bilandic had selected an undistinguished machine hack, Twenty-First Ward alderman Bennett Stewart, to replace him on the ticket. Although incensed by the machine's imperious designation of an inferior (but malleable) candidate when so many qualified black politicians coveted the nomination, South Side voters remained loyal Democrats and gave Stewart a narrow victory over Republican A. A. "Sammy" Rayner, who competed that year with virtually no money or political organization. After Stewart served one lackluster term in Washington, D.C., three strong Democratic candidates emerged to contest his reelection. In addition to Stewart, who enjoyed the full support of Byrne and the Democratic organization, the list of candidates included John Stroger, Ralph Metcalfe Jr., and Harold Washington. One of the influential Democrats passed over two years earlier, Alderman Stroger of the Eighth Ward boasted close connections to wealthy South Side businessmen and enjoyed lavish financial support. A community college instructor with a dearth of political experience, Ralph Metcalfe Jr. nevertheless possessed a magical surname in black Chicago that provided instant name recognition. Despite having very little campaign funding and no semblance of an organization, Washington announced his candidacy on May 26, 1979.[54]

The First Congressional District of Illinois, blanketing much of Chicago's South Side from 31st Street to 101st Street, contained a variety of primarily black neighborhoods, including Grand Boulevard, Kenwood, Washington Park, Woodlawn, Grand Crossing, and Chatham, as well as Hyde Park, a racially integrated bastion of independent politics. The area housed much of the city's substantial black middle class, along with less affluent enclaves where an economically insecure working class and the poor struggled to make ends meet. Previous representatives of the First District, such estimable black politicians as Ralph Metcalfe, William Dawson, Clarence Mitchell, and Oscar De Priest, had in the past held the highest elective office to which an African American in Chicago could aspire. Washington's campaign for that office, a significant step up from the Illinois General Assembly, could be seen as the ultimate goal an ambitious black office seeker could pursue and the crowning achievement of a career in politics—the holy grail after which Harold Washington and Gus Savage had lusted decades earlier as idealistic young Roosevelt College students. Or alternatively, as some have suggested, the contest in 1980 for the U.S. House of Representatives may have been Washington's test run for the mayoral election in 1983—the job of U.S. congressman another impressive credential for a black antimachine politician who had already run for mayor once and harbored designs on doing so again. Washington's campaign rhetoric in 1980 opened the door to both interpretations, as he alternated comments on national affairs befitting a candidate for the U.S. Congress with the barbed criticisms of the Byrne administration a mayoral aspirant would naturally voice.[55]

In the course of the contest, Washington articulated a progressive philosophy of government and outlined a program that sought justice for blacks, other racial minorities, women, the elderly, and the poor. "The Washington Papers," a lengthy white paper distributed early in the campaign and updated periodically to reflect the candidate's positions on emerging national and international developments, discussed in detail a host of issues, ranging from foreign affairs and energy policy to drug abuse and crime. In the detailed document, the candidate underscored the limitations of action at the local and state levels and emphasized the importance of national policies to the residents of his district. In a conservative era of backlash and cutbacks, he asserted, ordinary citizens desperately needed an advocate for their interests in the nation's capital. Accordingly, his highest priorities included the creation of a full-employment economy; the public control of energy resources; the reduction of wasteful military spending; the guarantee of full rights for African Americans, other racial minorities, and women; and the preservation of civil liberties for all citizens. He promised to forge coalitions with progressive whites as well as to participate actively in the Congressional Black Caucus. Washington's views on critical issues and his broad approach to urban governance, which he articulated repeatedly throughout his mayoral years, could be found clearly laid out in his 1980 campaign literature.[56]

Although his official position papers devoted more attention to national affairs and dealt less fully with state and local issues, Washington's speeches and informal street-corner talks frequently referred to the Chicago political scene and especially to the shortcomings of the Byrne administration. While repeatedly excoriating the Democratic machine, he often discussed the feasibility of a black mayor in Chicago's immediate future. In a campaign speech that he gave at Chicago State University and repeated at countless other locations in 1980, he said, "They tell us no black person has the qualifications to be mayor. They tell us business wouldn't go along. They're saying everybody would move out. They're saying city officials wouldn't cooperate. Well, Sears Tower ain't going nowhere. And neither is LaSalle Street or City Hall. No black could run this town? He couldn't do any worse than Jane Byrne!"[57]

Whatever his principal motivation in 1980—laying the groundwork for a black mayoral candidacy in the future or simply advancing a progressive platform for the congressional election—Washington indefatigably scoured the South Side in search of votes. Widely praised as a trustworthy representative of his constituents who had built an impressive record in Springfield during the preceding sixteen years, he could justifiably claim to be the best-qualified candidate. Because of his well-known confrontations with the Democratic machine, he could boast credibly of being his own man. He loved politicking and obviously enjoyed himself on the stump. By all accounts the best orator among the four candidates that year, he spoke to groups of all sizes in a variety of locations—busy South Side intersections, parks, pool halls, public transit stations, Laundromats, Parent-Teacher Association meetings, and several churches every Sunday. Fully comfortable quoting Shakespeare, the Bible, or eighteenth-century philosophes to learned audiences, he could just as easily sprinkle his remarks with ungrammatical idioms when bantering with unlettered members of the working class and the indigent. In all, Washington clearly impressed voters by virtue of his communication skills, education, and experience as the best choice to represent them in Washington, D.C. Despite running his campaign on a shoestring budget, Washington won the Democratic primary in March 1980 with nearly 50 percent of the vote; the other three candidates split the remaining ballots, Metcalfe finishing a distant second, trailed by Stewart and Stroger. In the anticlimactic general election in November, Washington won more than 95 percent of the vote in defeating obscure Republican George Williams.[58]

Washington's election to the Ninety-Seventh U.S. Congress in 1980 coincided with the election of Ronald Reagan as the nation's fortieth president, a landmark event that many pundits felt completed a rightward tilt in American politics and initiated a period of conservative dominance in the federal government. Washington certainly shared that view and, from the beginning of his tenure in the U.S. House of Representatives, devoted the lion's share of his time to opposing the Reagan agenda in all of its dimensions. Whereas many Democratic legislators hesitated at first to challenge the immensely popular new president, the freshman representative from Chicago questioned the aims and actions of the so-called Reagan Revolution from the moment he arrived on Capitol Hill. In the capital less than a month, he boycotted a meeting between the Congressional Black Caucus and the president as a protest against the administration's retrograde budget. According to the *Congressional Quarterly*, Washington ranked fifth among the House's 435 members in antiadministration votes in 1982. He earned a perfect score (100) from the American Civil Liberties Union (ACLU) for opposing the administration on legislation involving abortion, school prayer, immigration restriction, and voting rights. He wasted no time opposing the deep cuts in domestic programs prescribed by the supply-side economics ("Reaganomics") advocates drafting the new administration's budgets and tax proposals. Reaganomics intended to "balance the budget on the backs of the poor and the near poor," warned Washington, and steer the greatest economic benefits to the wealthy. Instead of scrutinizing only the human services portions of the federal budget in search of places to reduce spending, he wrote to the chairman of the House Budget Committee, the Reagan administration should commission a thorough and objective analysis of the nation's spendthrift military expenditures. Such an investigation, Washington confidently predicted, would doubtless uncover wasteful and inefficient programs that could be cut or eliminated altogether without threatening national security.[59]

During his brief time on Capitol Hill, Washington not only challenged the high levels of military spending sustained by the Defense Department but also took aim at many of the fundamental tenets of the Reagan administration's foreign policy. The military buildup of the 1970s and 1980s, which Cold Warriors justified as a vital necessity in the nation's ongoing struggle to contain communism, seemed to the progressive congressman from Illinois part and parcel of an entrenched imperialism that wasted enormous amounts of money and threatened America's standing among emerging nations in Africa, Asia, and Latin America. He opposed the administration's support of the effort to preserve apartheid in South Africa, championed a nuclear freeze, called for the abrogation of the Pentagon's MX missile program, and condemned recurring U.S. imperialism in the Western Hemisphere. As one of the House's most vocal critics of the nation's adventurism in Latin America, he signed on as a coplaintiff in a lawsuit against the Reagan administration to compel the removal of U.S. troops from El Salvador. Explaining his defiance of presidential prerogative in an important aspect of the nation's diplomacy, Washington said, "The evidence is overwhelming that the President has certified more to what he wishes were the case in El Salvador than to what is actually taking place." He also participated actively in the congressional effort to preserve the Clark Amendment, which prohibited aid to private groups engaging in military and paramilitary activities in Angola.[60]

While opposing the Reagan administration over a host of foreign and domestic policies, Washington devoted most of his energy to issues revolving around racial inequality. Having become an active member of the Congressional Black Caucus as soon as he arrived in Washington, D.C., he was promptly elected the organization's secretary and rumored to be its next chairman. Much of the group's efforts dealt with the White House's pursuit of draconian budget cuts in social welfare programs, reductions that inevitably took the greatest toll in poor minority communities, while approving generous giveaways to wealthy individuals and giant corporations totaling an estimated $750 billion. Calling the drastic tax cuts prescribed by supply-side economics a "riverboat gamble," the membership of the Congressional Black Caucus closely monitored the rising unemployment rates resulting from Reaganomics. Just a year after the charting of the new economic course, reported the group in May 1982, unemployment stood at 18 percent among African American adults and 40–60 percent among black youth in various metropolitan areas. The fifty thousand small business bankruptcies during the administration's first year likewise occurred most frequently in inner-city minority neighborhoods. Although all Americans of modest means were suffering from the modern version of trickle-down economics, claimed the caucus, people of color were shouldering the greatest burden.[61]

Republican economic policies harmed the black community especially, Washington asserted, and the Reagan administration was seeking "to strip [African Americans] of every gain we've made over the last 30 years, particularly in the field of civil rights." In the Illinois congressman's view, the Reagan Justice Department had launched a systematic war on existing civil rights law in an effort to overturn many of the advances achieved in previous decades. On such issues as the tax status of private schools that practiced racial segregation, busing to achieve racial integration in public schools, affirmative action, and racial discrimination in public places, the administration introduced legislation and advocated constitutional amendments to restrict the jurisdiction of federal courts and to limit access to administrative agencies by racial minorities seeking redress of grievances. Washington charged that Reagan and his cronies in the White House had clearly set their sights on emasculating the two greatest achievements of the civil rights era, the Civil Rights Act of 1964 and the Voting Rights Act of 1965.[62]

Washington became intimately involved in the legislative struggle over the extension of the 1965 Voting Rights Act, which was scheduled to expire in August 1982. He cosponsored a bill (H.R. 3112) that extended the provisions of the original law, rejecting the claim by its opponents that the Voting Rights Act of 1965 needlessly and unfairly singled out for punishment certain jurisdictions in the South. Objecting to calls for home rule and states' rights, Washington recounted how minority voters in southern states had at long last been able to exercise the franchise only because of the federal supervision provided by the original legislation. He conducted staff briefings for members of the Black and Hispanic Caucuses and then represented the bill's cosponsors in the debates on the House floor, arguing that "H.R. 3112 . . . puts meat and gusto and verve to that long languishing 15th Amendment." The House and the Senate eventually agreed on a measure that extended voting-rights guarantees for twenty-five years. As a key figure in the fight to pass a bill preserving voting-rights safeguards, which Reagan signed into law on June 29, 1982, Washington received a ceremonial pen and a commemorative copy of the act from the president.[63]

Washington not only became a leader among black Democrats in Washington, D.C., but also in short order won the respect of legislators possessing considerably more seniority in Congress. Veteran Capitol Hill journalists wrote glowingly about the behind-the-scenes political skills exhibited by the new congressman from Chicago, who ignored the time-honored tradition of freshmen watching, learning, and biding their time before joining the political fray. Members of his staff spoke of him as a workaholic who refused to rely solely on their summaries of pending legislation and who read every bill carefully before casting a vote. As he had done for many years in Springfield, he generally avoided social gatherings in Washington, D.C., and spent much of his spare time pouring over proposed legislation in his spartan living quarters. Washington insisted on being available to his constituents, noted his staff, returning to Chicago at every opportunity and listening to all supplicants who came to his office or attended regular public meetings. He remained extremely popular in the First Congressional District, in large measure due to his accessibility and because of the efficiency of his political organization.[64]

Any doubts about his reelection in 1982 surfaced only because of an imminent reduction in the size of the Illinois legislative delegation. The results of the 1980 U.S. Census required the state to reduce its representation in the U.S. House of Representatives from twenty-four to twenty-two in time for the next biennial election. Many Illinoisans living outside Chicago argued that the legislative districts should be redrawn to reflect the city's population loss of approximately 360,000 during the 1970s, thereby awarding greater representation to suburban and downstate areas while dissipating black voting majorities in the metropolitan area. Such gerrymandering would likely elide two of the three Chicago districts that had elected African Americans to Congress, reconfiguring the First and Second Districts (threatening the congressional seats occupied by Harold Washington and Gus Savage, respectively) and bypassing the Seventh District (leaving Cardiss Collins unaffected). His tenure in the House jeopardized almost as soon as he had finished unpacking in the nation's capital, Washington vigorously led the fight for redistricting proposals that preserved Chicago's black representation in the U.S. Congress. He defended his protection of African American political influence, saying, "That is not favoritism—only simple fairness. If blacks are half of the city's population, representative government dictates that our black citizens are entitled to half the six remaining congressional seats when the remapping is completed."[65]

Bitter partisan and racial politics in Springfield failed to produce a satisfactory compromise for months, and the issue finally ended up before a three-judge panel (two Republicans and one Democrat) from the U.S. District Court. After considering and rejecting several reconfigured maps, the panel approved a plan by a two-to-one vote that preserved black electoral majorities in the First and Second Districts for the next decade. The U.S. Supreme Court approved the lower court's decision.[66]

Unable to rely on legislative redistricting to unseat Washington, the Democratic machine eagerly sought a candidate who could beat the incumbent congressman in 1982. With extravagant promises of organizational support and generous financial backing, Mayor Byrne approached a number of South Side black politicians about opposing Washington. Believing the popular legislator unbeatable, however, city treasurer Cecil Partee, state senator Richard Newhouse, state representative Gerald Bullock, and Chicago commissioner of human services Leona Cartwright all declined to run. Anticipating the machine's opposition, Washington returned home virtually every weekend during his first term to meet with constituents and to oversee the operation of his independent organization. On Saturday mornings, he or his aides held open meetings at a union hall on the Near South Side to discuss concerns in the district and solicit views on important issues; he recruited community leaders and members of various interest groups to form task forces exploring possible solutions to problems in the district. Filing the necessary paperwork to establish his candidacy on the earliest possible date, Washington submitted petitions signed by 25,000 voters (more than ten times the required number). Byrne finally gave up recruiting another candidate. Running unopposed, he won reelection with more than 176,000 votes in November 1982. Returning to the capital, having garnered the largest number of votes that year of any candidate in the nation for a seat in the U.S. House of Representatives, Washington seemed as thoroughly in control of the First Congressional District of Illinois as De Priest, Dawson, Metcalfe, or any of his other illustrious predecessors had been earlier in the twentieth century.[67]

After his 1982 reelection in a striking demonstration of vote-getting prowess, Washington was poised to return to Washington, D.C., in a position of enhanced authority and influence. An extremely hard worker and gifted orator, he had learned the nuts and bolts of politics from an early age watching his father expertly manage an important Democratic precinct. Behind the scenes, he had orchestrated political affairs in a crucial party stronghold, while Alderman Metcalfe officially represented the Third Ward at official functions. Sixteen years of training in the Illinois General Assembly had made him an effective lawmaker, skilled in the delicate political arts of persuasion, compromise, and legislative give-and-take. A progressive by temperament who chafed for years under the suffocating control of the Democratic party bosses, he had finally rebelled and established his autonomy from the Cook County machine. As a newcomer on Capitol Hill, he had immediately attracted favorable attention and shown maturity and initiative uncommon for a freshman legislator. The decision to grant him a leadership role in the fight to extend the Voting Rights Act of 1965 testified to the high regard in which he was held for a neophyte. A tough, seasoned

political operator, a staunch progressive with a strong commitment to society's unfortunates, and an impassioned advocate for racial equality, he had
established himself as one of the Reagan administration's toughest critics
in Congress. In a short time, the Chicagoan had emerged as one of the most
persistent Democratic voices in the capital, fiercely challenging an emerging conservative consensus. In 1982 Washington spoke enthusiastically
about continuing the important work he had started in Washington, D.C.
Nothing could sidetrack him from opposing the Reagan White House and
the forces of conservative Republicanism—except perhaps the possibility
of becoming the first black mayor of Chicago.[68]

2

THE PLAN AND THE MAN

On Tuesday, November 7, 1967, the mayoral victories of two African American men, Carl B. Stokes in Cleveland, Ohio, and Richard G. Hatcher in Gary, Indiana, marked a watershed in urban politics. Sweeping demographic changes in the twentieth century, in which blacks migrated from the rural South to northern and western cities and whites relocated to the suburbs, altered the composition of metropolitan America. The proportion of blacks living in cities increased from 27 percent in 1910 to 85 percent in 1980, and the African American populations of central cities more than doubled between 1950 and 1970. Especially in the industrial centers of the Northeast and Midwest, blacks constituted majorities or substantial pluralities in core cities by the mid-1960s. In the decade of the 1960s alone, the black population of central cities grew by more than 35 percent, while the white population decreased by 9 percent. After the civil rights revolution, the black residents of those cities enjoyed unprecedented legal protections, allowing them to vote in significant numbers for the first time. The passage of national laws in 1957, 1960, 1964, 1965, and 1975 (especially the Voting Rights Act of 1965) greatly increased African American voter turnout in city after city. Following Stokes and Hatcher in short order, the election of Kenneth Gibson in Newark, Coleman Young in Detroit, Maynard Jackson in Atlanta, Tom Bradley in Los Angeles, Ernest "Dutch" Morial in New Orleans, and Walter Washington in Washington, D.C., made black mayors in large U.S. cities commonplace by the end of the 1970s—but not in Chicago.[1]

Chicago lagged behind these other metropolises for a number of reasons, not the least of which was the survival of the autocratic Democratic
machine. In the late nineteenth and early twentieth centuries, the tiny
population of the Windy City's black community severely limited its political influence; blacks simply did not have the votes to compete effectively
in the electoral arena. After the First World War, as the black population
mushroomed, Democratic leaders launched a successful effort to sever traditional black ties to the Republican Party. Beginning with Mayor Anton
Cermak and accelerating with his successor, Edward J. Kelly, Democrats
used scarce local resources and much more abundant federal largesse to
recruit black voters away from the party of Lincoln. Kelly's enlightened
policies—he supported open housing and public school desegregation—and
New Deal programs that especially benefited African Americans and others
who suffered disproportionately during the Great Depression enhanced the
Democratic Party's appeal. By the time Kelly left city hall in 1947, reflecting significant changes in the philosophies and practices of the two major
political parties, African American Chicago had become a reliable source
of votes for the Democratic machine.[2]

In the course of cultivating African American support for the Democratic
Party, Kelly relied increasingly on a black politician who found his ambi-
tions thwarted by the Republican leadership on the South Side. Alderman
William Levi Dawson found his advancement in the Second Ward blocked
by a hostile committeeman and switched his party membership to join the
ascendant Democrats. As Kelly's man in the city council, Dawson became
vice chairman of the Cook County Democratic Central Committee and the
acknowledged leader of Chicago's black Democrats. He won election to the
U.S. House of Representatives in 1942 and served in Washington, D.C.,
until his death in 1970. Throughout his long career as a Democrat, Dawson
remained subservient to the local machine and shunned movements for
social change. Unlike his Second Ward rival Earl B. Dickerson, a militant
civil rights advocate, avid proponent of organized labor, and president of
the Chicago Urban League (CUL), Dawson uncritically supported party
initiatives and maintained a low public profile. In a showdown with Dickerson for South Side supremacy, Dawson prevailed and established a clear
formula for success in local black politics: support the machine at every
turn and avoid all discussion of racial inequality.[3]

Dawson's unquestioning support of the omnipotent Democratic machine, a model emulated by other self-interested black officeholders, allowed

Richard J. Daley to harvest huge vote totals from the city's sprawling South Side and West Side ghettos at very little cost. Unwilling to countenance any potential rivals within the local organization, however, he balked when Dawson attempted to expand his influence on the increasingly black West Side and summarily ostracized him from the party's inner circle. Daley openly sided with others in intraparty squabbles, denied support to Dawson's candidates in local elections in favor of black politicians loyal only to the mayor's office, and sharply reduced the congressman's patronage. In 1963 Dawson shifted his residency to Washington, D.C., devoted his attention exclusively to national affairs, and ceased involvement in local politics. The once powerful politician's self-imposed exile reminded aspiring African American politicians of the need to stifle all notions of independence. Disgruntled reformers referred to Daley's overwhelming command of the black vote as "plantation politics."[4]

Daley distributed a limited number of patronage jobs, political posts, and other emoluments to the black community and received in turn the loyal backing of self-serving African American politicians who prospered along with the machine when their precincts turned out huge Democratic majorities. Black aldermen never questioned the mayor's initiatives in the city council, regardless of the impact on their constituents, and became known as the "Silent Six." Meanwhile, the mayor kept blacks confined to overcrowded neighborhoods, maintained segregation in the public schools, and countenanced police brutality on ghetto streets. A small number of dissatisfied African Americans groused about their community's shabby treatment, but the practice continued uninterrupted year after year. After black votes accounted for Daley's narrow reelection in 1963—the incumbent lost the white vote to his opponent, Benjamin Adamowski—the mayor became more generous in dispensing resources to white ethnic neighborhoods to shore up his standing with the voters living there. Even so, in 1967 black wards voted for Daley by a seven-to-one margin. At a time when a bankrupt Republican Party in Chicago offered no viable alternative, African Americans fatalistically continued to accept machine rule as the best available alternative. Besides, toppling the Daley leviathan seemed an impossible task.[5]

Yet although predominantly black wards continued to turn out voting majorities for Daley and other machine candidates, a level of disquietude was mounting in the African American community. In 1971 black wards voted for Daley by slightly more than a two-to-one ratio, still a comfortable cushion but a considerable decrease from the seven-to-one margin four years earlier. Antimachine sentiments among blacks increased in 1972 when Democratic slate makers backed Edward Hanrahan for reelection as Cook County state's attorney in 1972. After members of his gang unit had killed Black Panthers Fred Hampton and Mark Clark in 1969, Hanrahan blindly defended their actions and became a revered symbol of law and order in the city's white ethnic neighborhoods on the Southwest and Northwest Sides— but a symbol of racial oppression to the city's African Americans. Daley's initial support of Hanrahan, even after a federal grand jury indicted the state's attorney for allegedly obstructing justice during an investigation of the shooting, outraged South Side residents. The mayor eventually selected Judge Raymond Berg to replace Hanrahan, who ran as an independent and won the Democratic primary because of huge victory margins in the white bungalow belts. In the general election, however, black votes provided the crucial margin of victory for Republican Bernard Carey in a close contest. Enough African Americans refused to vote for Hanrahan or Berg, casting their ballots for the Republican or not voting at all, to alter the outcome of the election. The pattern continued in 1975, as voters in black neighborhoods backed Daley by a ratio of just one and a half to one; moreover, voter turnout in the mayoral race from 1971 to 1975 fell 13 percent. Disgruntled African Americans were voting more often against Daley and other machine candidates or simply not voting at all.[6]

African Americans cast ballots for Daley decidedly less often in 1975 but made little of the opportunity to support a black candidate who might have mounted a realistic threat to the incumbent mayor. Seventy-four years old, the recent victim of a stroke, and burdened by a number of scandals that touched several of his close associates in the early 1970s, the mayor seemed vulnerable that year while facing his first serious intraparty challenge since 1955. Enthusiasm for a black mayoral candidate waned when Ralph Metcalfe declined to run, however, as few political experts thought that any other African American possessed the name recognition and fund-raising ability to mount a serious challenge to the incumbent. State senator Richard Newhouse, an independent Democrat from Hyde Park, made the effort but never built a large following in the black community. Newhouse struggled unsuccessfully to raise money and proved unable to unite political factions on the South Side. He lost the potential votes of left-leaning independents to Alderman William Singer, whom Metcalfe endorsed, believing that he had a better chance of beating the mayor. The influential *Chicago Defender* and the Johnson family publications *Ebony* and *Jet* endorsed Daley as well. The mayor cruised to reelection, carrying all fourteen black wards, while Newhouse trailed both Daley and Singer in all African American wards and garnered only 6 percent of the black vote citywide. The machine's hold on African American voters was wavering by 1975, but inertia, fear of the Democratic machine, years of passive repetition, and the inability of a single black candidate to attract the necessary financial and electoral support worked against a unified, large-scale political insurrection.[7]

The belief in machine invincibility suffered a serious setback the following year when Metcalfe withstood city hall's efforts to terminate his political career. Incensed with the apostate's growing independence, the Democratic organization refused to reslate him for U.S. congressman and ward committeeman in 1976. The other black committeemen remained quietly on the sidelines and declined to participate in the rebellion, but Metcalfe forged ahead, promising the "liberation of the people from the Daley plantation." Backed by a surprisingly effective grassroots coalition, the defiant legislator largely ignored the candidates selected by the Democratic organization to run against him and spent most of his time criticizing the mayor. He won both the primary and the general elections, becoming the first prominent black politician singled out for elimination to survive against the full power of the Democratic machine.[8]

By the time of Daley's death in December 1976, black restiveness was undeniably on the rise. The peremptory manner in which the city council dismissed Alderman Wilson Frost's claim to the mayoralty and elevated Michael Bilandic in his stead underscored the contempt the white-dominated Democratic Party in Chicago held for black political aspirations. In the mayor's office, Bilandic wasted little time replicating his predecessor's approach to race relations. Even before showing his disregard for blacks during the catastrophic snowstorms of 1978–79, Bilandic obstinately defended the city's police and fire departments against charges of racial discrimination in hiring and promotion. Absent any evidence of intent, the mayor argued, no discrimination had occurred, despite the gaping disparities in the numbers of blacks and whites employed in the city agencies. Harold Washington's last-minute decision to oppose Bilandic in 1977, much like Newhouse's haphazard effort earlier, foundered due to lack of resources and poor organization. Washington ran better among African Americans than

Newhouse had in 1975, but black voter turnout still remained disappointingly low, less than 10 percent in some wards. As African American voters rejected one of their own for the second time in two years, it became clear to white machine politicians, as well as to frustrated black insurgents, that an increase in black political power depended on much broader electoral participation in minority neighborhoods. Until the widespread and growing black dissatisfaction matured into concrete political action, the chances of electing an African American mayor remained faint.[9]

Such pragmatic thinking explained why, despite continued hostility from the mayor's office, no black candidate surfaced to run against Bilandic in 1979. Antimachine feelings remained high, though, and the desire to vote for a reformer rather than Bilandic led the black community to rally behind Jane Byrne. Certainly, Byrne's chances of unseating the mayor seemed minuscule at the outset of the contest, but African American voters could at least cast their ballots against the incumbent to register their displeasure with the machine. Byrne also said all the right things during the campaign to qualify as a reformer. While speaking at black churches, street festivals, block club gatherings, and public housing projects, she appealed earnestly for black votes and pledged as mayor to address the many inequities that plagued the city's ghettos. Byrne's evisceration of Bilandic and his cronies (the men she called an "evil cabal") found an especially receptive audience among African Americans, who voted for her by a three-to-two margin in the Democratic primary and reveled in her stunning victory. Feeling empowered by the role they had played in dealing the machine a shocking setback, blacks expected salutary treatment from a new administration that they had helped install in city hall.[10]

Their euphoria faded quickly. Within a remarkably short time, the new mayor repudiated her promises of reform and forged alliances with the evil caballeros against whom she had recently campaigned. At least during her first year in the mayor's office, Byrne honored some of her commitments to African Americans. She selected black men as acting chief of police (Samuel Nolan) and head of the Chicago Transit Authority (Eugene Barnes), and her designation of five African Americans and three Latinos to serve on the eleven-member board of education shifted the balance of power away from an all-white segregationist bloc. By the middle of her term, however, Byrne reversed her earlier commitment to racial diversity. She replaced Barnes at the CTA with a white man and then, ignoring her earlier statement that the city would benefit from hiring a police chief from outside the department, nudged Nolan out in favor of a white veteran of the force (James O'Grady). While the school board was grappling with a controversial court desegregation order, she replaced two black board members (Leon Davis and Michael Scott) with white women from predominantly white areas of the city (Betty Bonow from the Southwest Side and Rose Mary Janus from the Northwest Side) who spoke out against the integration mandate. She promoted a white candidate (Angeline Caruso) with less impressive credentials over the more qualified black aspirant (Manford Byrd) to the superintendency of the overwhelmingly African American public school system. Her new appointments to the Chicago Housing Authority (CHA) board shifted the racial balance from black to white at a time when black tenants accounted for 84 percent of the CHA's residential population. In 1981 Byrne and her allies forced through the city council a redistricted ward map that restored white majorities in two wards that would have achieved black majorities according to the 1980 census and redrew boundaries on the Northwest and Southwest Sides to dilute the Latino vote. Relations between Byrne and the black community soured with each of her aggressive actions in alliance with the machine regulars.[11]

By 1982, resentful and betrayed, a large and growing number of blacks adamantly refused to back Byrne in the upcoming election. The mayor staunchly defended her record on diversity, but city hall's recitations of minority hiring and promotions smacked of tokenism to her jaded critics. The elevation of a select few figureheads to symbolic positions fooled no one, charged angry African American observers. "There is not one black person in the City of Chicago that controls any budgetary unit or agency," observed Renault Robinson, who had been appointed to the CHA board by Byrne and then was subsequently forced to resign the post. The mayor may well have considered the rumblings of discontent in the Black Belt inconsequential, particularly given African Americans' long history of fealty to the Democratic machine. After all, no black candidate for mayor had been able since the death of Richard J. Daley to harness the latent political power of the city's minority population—and Byrne likely thought there was no reason that 1983 would be any different.[12]

The brouhaha over Alderman Allan Streeter's election in 1982 added to the anti-Byrne feeling among African Americans and provided another reason to doubt the machine's purported invincibility. In 1981 the mayor had appointed Streeter, a longtime precinct captain and city employee, alderman of the Seventeenth Ward when the incumbent resigned. Streeter dutifully followed the instructions he received from city hall at first but refused to vote for Betty Bonow and Rose Mary Janus when black neighborhood groups vehemently protested the mayor's proposed appointments to the school board. When a federal court ruled that a special election be held in June to select the Seventeenth Ward's alderman for the remainder of the term, Byrne sought to unseat the rebellious Streeter and supported another candidate, Jewel Frierson. The machine dispatched an army of patronage workers from the Third, Ninth, Fifteenth, Sixteenth, Twenty-First, and Thirty-Fourth Wards into Streeter's bailiwick to campaign against him, but the heavy-handed intrusion into Seventeenth Ward politics backfired. Buoyed by the support of antimachine independents and a plethora of neighborhood organizations, the incumbent narrowly won the initial election against several challengers and a runoff against the organization candidate. "There's no question but that Byrne was the issue," Streeter commented in explaining his unexpected win. "People came out to register their protest. That was the key."[13]

Determined to unseat Byrne, black community leaders decided by the summer of 1982 that Harold Washington remained the best potential candidate to win the February 1983 Democratic primary. The results of a citywide survey conducted by Chicago Black United Communities (CBUC), a new organization dedicated to electing a black mayor, found Washington to be the overwhelming choice of respondents by a ten-to-one margin. Wary after the decisive failure of his campaign in 1977, however, Washington hesitated to surrender his new position in the U.S. House of Representatives for another quixotic run for the mayoralty. He enjoyed being a legislator, reveling in the challenges of drafting bills and steering them through to passage, and believed that he was engaged in his true calling. Moreover, he had been warmly received by the House leadership and had assumed a high profile on Capitol Hill very quickly. As an unusually gifted and charismatic African American in an institution with little diversity, Washington stood out for all the right reasons. "He was treated like a rock star," remembered one of his longtime aides, Jacky Grimshaw. Washington confided to *Chicago Tribune* reporter David Axelrod: "You know what it's like to be a congressman? They treat you like a king. You can come and go as you please. No one cares. Now, mayor? That's a real job, twenty-four/seven. Lots of headaches. Lots of problems. Why would I do that to myself?"[14]

Washington told Axelrod that he would consider making the race again only if a voter registration drive succeeded in enrolling at least 50,000 new African American voters and if his potential supporters raised $500,000 for the campaign. "They'll never make those goals," he confidently informed the reporter. At a July 26 meeting at Bethel AME Church called by the CBUC to discuss the survey findings, Washington de-emphasized in his speech to black community leaders the need to identify a candidate and urged instead careful planning, voter registration, and the creation of a sound campaign organization. The key to a successful challenge of the machine, he repeated throughout his presentation, was "the plan and not the man." Such talk puzzled many of Washington's supporters, who were unsure if his comments amounted to an irreversible declination of interest or simply bespoke a healthy dose of caution. After the meeting, Washington told a delegation of potential supporters that he required a substantial cache of campaign funds (by various accounts, somewhere between $250,000 and $500,000) and reiterated his demand of 50,000 new names on the voting rolls before he would even consider running for mayor again.[15]

In 1982 dozens of organizations, including the Chicago Urban League and the Reverend Jesse Jackson's Operation PUSH, launched voter registration drives in a variety of locations throughout Chicago. African American owners of banks and McDonald's franchises, usually a cautious group that avoided any political activity that might displease customers, relaxed their restrictions and allowed the CUL to register new voters in their establishments. A coalition of community organizations named POWER (People Organized for Welfare and Employment Rights) registered voters citywide and attracted support from blacks on the South and West Sides as well as from Latino and white independent groups. The People's Movement for Voter Registration, organized by black radio personality Lutrelle "Lu" Palmer and others, sought principally to register African Americans on the South Side. Unlike in previously unsuccessful voter registration drives, in which a paucity of funds limited the scope of activity, generous financial contributions from such enterprises as Soft Sheen Products and Travis Realty allowed for the purchase of radio commercials on black-owned radio stations and other forms of advertising. Having convinced Illinois officials to permit voter registration sessions at the city's public aid and unemployment compensation offices, POWER experienced great success, enrolling indigent citizens who had traditionally failed to register and vote. Black ministers became active as well. Father George Clements of Holy Angels

Church called the failure to register a sin, for example. "If you do not have a voter registration card," he told his parishioners, "Holy Angels does not want your membership." Voter registration occurred at churches, public libraries, Cook County Hospital, fast-food outlets, government office buildings, and a host of other venues. By November, surpassing the most optimistic projections, voter registration rolls contained approximately 125,000 names of newly enfranchised African American voters.[16]

As the voter registration drive proceeded in the summer of 1982, the black community also united in protesting a popular event closely associated with the city administration. After Byrne appointed three whites to the CHA board and locked blacks seeking to protest her action out of city council hearings, dissidents looked for another way to express their outrage. They targeted Byrne's ChicagoFest, the largest and most profitable of the many social gatherings her administration sponsored during the summer. Jesse Jackson organized a boycott of the gala, a popular music and food festival held annually on the lakefront that invariably attracted huge and enthusiastic crowds. Musical headliner Stevie Wonder quickly canceled his appearance in support of the protest and forfeited his $160,000 fee; the city threatened legal action and compelled other acts to honor their contracts. Still, African Americans and sympathetic whites stayed away in droves, and the boycott easily met its goal of significantly reducing attendance and revenues. Even more important, the ability of a number of African American organizations to put aside factional differences and cooperate smoothly to reach a common goal bespoke a new unity of purpose in the black community. Coupled with the spectacularly effective voter registration effort going on at the same time, the ChicagoFest boycott attracted attention as yet another example of a robust political consciousness developing in the city's black community.[17]

The result of the November gubernatorial election that year provided additional evidence of a newfound activism among Chicago's African Americans. According to public opinion polls in 1982, Republican incumbent James R. Thompson was heading for a landslide victory over the Democratic candidate, Adlai E. Stevenson III. Thompson managed to win, but only by a few thousand votes. Stevenson's surprisingly strong showing owed overwhelmingly to his dominance of Chicago's black vote, a surprising outcome explained by the enormity of the turnout. African Americans accounted for more than three-fourths of the Democrat's 467,000-vote victory margin in the city, an eye-opening demonstration of emerging black political power. The combination of bloc voting and a much larger black electorate cast a different light on the reelection possibilities of a highly unpopular Mayor Byrne—a lesson not lost on Harold Washington. Newspaper reporters and editorial writers credited Stevenson's unexpectedly strong showing to the rejuvenated political machine under the leadership of new Cook County Democratic Party chairman Edward R. Vrdolyak. Thompson also blamed the closeness of the election on the reinvigorated Chicago Democratic organization, saying, "The Vrdolyak Express ran over me."[18] Washington strongly disagreed, exclaiming, "This has nothing to do with Eddie Vrdolyak. Ronald Reagan deserves the credit. Black people know where their interests lie, and it's not with Reagan or his supporters, like [Governor] Jim Thompson."[19]

Having flayed the Reagan White House for nearly two years on Capitol Hill, Washington ardently identified the connections between the flawed policies of a Republican administration in Washington, D.C., and the devastating economic conditions endured by black Chicagoans. Reagan's attempts to demolish the welfare-state machinery assembled during the previous half century hit poor African Americans especially hard but also hurt the vulnerable black middle class. The severe cuts in government spending engineered by Reaganomics resulted in the widespread loss of jobs by black civil servants, whose numbers accounted for as much as 30 percent of the population in some South Side wards. For the Democratic mayor of an ailing Rust Belt city, Byrne seemed to enjoy a surprisingly cozy relationship with Reagan. In a widely reported telephone call during the 1980 campaign, the Republican candidate had promised the Chicago mayor that she would "have a friend in the White House" if he were elected. Unlike many mayors whose cities were suffering under the federal cutbacks inflicted by Reaganomics, Byrne refrained from criticizing the White House and instead warmly praised the president's fiscal responsibility. Washington frequently exploited the connection by singling out the two uncaring politicians to blame for hard times in the black community, one in city hall and the other in the nation's capital. Volunteers in African American neighborhoods enticed passersby to voter registration tables with cries of "Send Reagan a message" and "Get Jane Byrne."[20]

By 1982 a number of factors had coalesced to improve the prospects of an African American running for mayor. Washington had challenged black activists to register 50,000 new voters, seemingly a very ambitious goal, and they had responded by recruiting more than twice that number. The rising tide of bitterness against an unresponsive political system, manifested by the successful voter registration drive and the recent demonstrations of black political power, indicated that the possibility of electing a black mayor had never been greater. The opportunity appeared even better in early November when Richard M. Daley, the eldest son of the late mayor, announced his candidacy. If Byrne and Daley split the white vote, the chances of a black candidate winning would seem to improve exponentially. (Roman Pucinski, alderman of the Forty-First Ward and the city's most popular Polish American politician, was also supposedly considering a run for the mayoralty at that time.) On November 10, eight days after his reelection to the U.S. House of Representatives, Washington announced his candidacy for mayor in a press conference witnessed by a large and enthusiastic crowd at the Hyde Park Hilton Hotel. Spotting Axelrod in the throng of reporters present that day, he pulled him aside and explained his decision to enter the race. "They hit every target I threw at them," he said with a shrug and a grin. "What else could I do?" Washington's speech that day explicitly addressed the concerns of the large black audience in the hotel ballroom but also dealt with a number of issues of paramount importance to other groups in the city.[21] Conveying a populist message designed to have broad appeal, he intoned:

> Chicago is a city in decline. Each year for the last decade, we have lost 11,500 jobs, 3,500 housing units, and nearly 36,000 people. Since 1955, women, Latinos, Blacks, Youth, and progressive whites have been left out of the Chicago government. Since 1979, the business, labor and intellectual communities have been allowed but token involvement in Chicago government. . . . "The city that works" doesn't work anymore.

Frequently interrupted by prolonged applause and cries of support from the enthusiastic crowd, he paused and smiled. Several times the audience chanted, "We shall see in '83." Washington continued, outlining his vision for the future:

> I see a Chicago in which the neighborhoods are once again the center of our city, in which businesses boom and provide neighborhood jobs, in which neighbors join together to help govern their neighborhoods and their city. . . . As mayor of this city, I would open the doors of City Hall. I would dig into that untapped reservoir of talented whites, Latinos, women and Blacks and unleash that ability for the benefit of this city.[22]

Washington's speech condemned the gross inequities inherent in machine politics, appealed forthrightly to the groups excluded in the past by the city's ruling clique, and extolled vital neighborhoods as the necessary counterpoint to the longtime cultivation of downtown business and political interests. A rousing call to arms intended to unite African Americans in common cause, the speech also appealed to the other have-nots in Chicago who stood to benefit from a changing of the guard in city hall. Delivering the speech to a crowd with very few whites and Latinos in attendance, Washington nevertheless repeatedly advocated a diverse coalition that touched a multitude of racial and ethnic groups throughout the city. The decision to emphasize inclusiveness clashed with the views of some of the candidate's African American supporters, who saw little chance of attracting white votes and favored a concentrated effort to squeeze every last vote out of the black community, creating a tension that never dissipated during the campaign. Nor did Washington's frequent allusions to broad reform goals always comport with the overriding interests of black nationalists and those sympathetic to their single-minded focus on racial issues; this strain persisted throughout the 1983 campaign and afterward. While the candidate insisted on leaving the door open for collaboration among several reform-minded groups, the impetus and drive of his mayoral campaign necessarily stemmed first and foremost from the energized black community.[23]

The fortuitous circumstances that convinced Washington to run again for mayor and the resultant excitement in the black community went unnoticed in the rest of the city, however, where the media and political analysts eagerly turned their attention to the impending battle between Byrne and Daley. From the outset of the Byrne mayoralty, the newspapers had been predicting an eventual showdown between the boss's son, who seemed destined in many minds to exercise his birthright and reclaim city hall for the Bridgeport faithful, and the female mayor, an interloper whose following had become fragmented and brittle. Byrne generally retained the support of the Democratic organization, but ill-tempered face-offs with the police, firefighters, and teachers' unions had sharply reduced her standing with voters. Whatever achievements the mayor compiled had disappeared in an atmosphere of unabated contentiousness complemented by what a *Chicago Tribune* reporter called "her image as a mind-changing, impulse-directed chief administrator." As well, the Daley name still resonated with many Chicagoans. The mayor accordingly did all she could to isolate the young Daley, to drive him out of the Democratic organization and into political oblivion.

When Daley had announced his intention to run for state's attorney in 1980, a move widely perceived as preparatory to seeking the mayoralty in 1983, Byrne recruited Fourteenth Ward alderman Edward M. Burke to run against him in the primary. Burke lost decisively, and, even with the mayor openly backing the Republican candidate, Bernard Carey, Daley won the general election handily. From that moment forward, Chicagoans looked to the 1983 mayoral election as the inevitable clash between the two powerful politicians for control of the Democratic machine's valuable remains. The Washington candidacy seemed largely to be an afterthought, a matter of consequence only to the degree that the African American's presence in the election would siphon more votes from one or the other of the two white protagonists.[24]

Politicians and reporters based their low regard for the Washington candidacy largely on the black community's poor track record of marshaling support for one of their own and long history of following in lockstep the dictates of the machine. The denizens of city hall figured that, based on the consistent behavior of a group noted for low turnouts at the polls, a relatively small percentage of the electorate in African American wards might opt for reform but that such a protest vote would be negated by the reliable balloting for the machine candidate. "The Organization owns a lock on a solid 20 percent of the black vote," contended Don Rose, a veteran political consultant in the city. "This is the vote the Machine would deliver for a George Wallace against Martin Luther King." Rose's fatalistic assessment seemed accurate when only one of the fifty Democratic Party committeemen voted to nominate Washington (the white committeeman of Washington's home Fifth Ward, Alan Dobry) and all but one of the black committeemen sided with Byrne. African American politicians in the Democratic machine behaved as ordered, meaning that a successful insurgency would have to result from an unprecedented and unlikely grassroots movement powerful enough to undo more than fifty years of history. Recent signs of a newfound activism in the black community notwithstanding, the prospects of an African American candidate attracting enough votes to defeat Daley and Byrne struck Chicagoans as remote.[25]

In the campaign's first few weeks, nothing transpired to contradict that narrative. Public opinion polls gave the mayor a substantial lead over Daley, with Washington a distant third. Exploiting the multimillion-dollar reelection fund she had stockpiled during the previous four years, Byrne saturated radio and television outlets with advertisements designed to challenge her image as a flighty, indecisive administrator more prone to confrontation than reasoned judgment. The mayor readily admitted to having stumbled at times, especially during her first months in city hall, but argued that she had learned from her early mistakes and become a tough, battle-tested leader. If she still came across as pugnacious, Byrne defiantly said, such combativeness served public figures well in a demanding city like Chicago, where elected officials famously resorted to unscrupulous tactics. If her bitter battles with the three public employee unions had seriously inconvenienced city residents and created a disputatious environment, the mayor argued, her willingness to face down greedy special interests had been vitally necessary to salvage Chicago's imperiled financial situation. Byrne contended that the city had been saddled with a crippling budget deficit when she took office in 1979 and that only her courageous decisions to cut services and raise taxes had saved Chicago from certain financial catastrophe.[26]

From the moment on November 22 that she announced her intention to seek reelection, Byrne campaigned extensively in every corner of the city and aggressively sought votes from the white, black, and Latino communities. Echoing her campaign slogan, "Mayor Byrne for *All* Chicago," the mayor established special subcommittees within the larger reelection committee to recruit black, Latino, and women voters. Her integrated campaign staff included a healthy number of nonwhites, and she dispatched approximately one-third of the campaign's unpaid volunteers to African American neighborhoods. Byrne and her aides readily conceded the majority of black ballots to Washington but believed finishing second among African American voters was one of the keys to winning the primary.[27]

In her appeals to African American voters, Byrne acknowledged that her standing in the black community had plummeted during the previous four years but attributed the falling-out simply to "lack of communication from my office." She strongly denied that any of city hall's actions that had drawn criticism from the South and West Sides had been intended to convey disrespect for African Americans. In fact, she argued for having made more high-level appointments of minorities than had any previous mayoral administration. Underscoring that claim, Byrne elevated a number of blacks onto city boards such as the CHA, the CTA, and the Chicago Board of Education shortly after declaring her candidacy for reelection. In the months leading up to the election, she began appearing frequently at black churches, established a temporary jobs program for the unemployed especially designed to benefit ghetto residents, improved garbage pickup and other service provisions in black neighborhoods, and bought more than forty thousand hams for distribution to public housing residents shortly before Christmas. She also persuaded Massachusetts senator Edward Kennedy, who had endorsed the mayor for reelection, to send a letter to black voters urging them to return her to office. Cynical and self-serving though her sudden rediscovery of African American concerns may have been, no one could deny the extent of Byrne's efforts to salvage a damaged relationship that had been so important to her four years earlier.[28]

Negating the mayor's use of incumbency and support from the Cook County Democratic machine, which continued to be a powerful political instrument even in its attenuated condition, offered a challenge to Richard M. Daley. In addition to possessing the illustrious surname that still evoked memories of stability and security among many Chicagoans, young Daley could also claim by the early 1980s an impressive set of credentials and indications of personal growth that could allay some fears about his suitability for high office. Believed by many Illinois politicians to have been an unimpressive and arrogant state senator with noxious interpersonal skills during his early years in the general assembly—*Chicago* magazine ranked him among the ten worst Illinois legislators one year—he had supposedly matured and become more collegial and amenable to compromise, especially after his father's death in 1976. According to political analyst Don Rose, leading Democrats attending to Daley's personal growth during his time in Springfield amounted to a process of "civilizing Richie." In the state's attorney's office, he continued to surprise skeptics by making good appointments, avoiding scandal, and compiling a sound record as a prosecutor. Although many Chicagoans found it difficult to view the son of Chicago's greatest boss as an iconoclastic outsider, Daley based his campaign to unseat Byrne on the need to clean up government and restore probity to city hall. Curiously enough, Richard M. Daley ran for mayor in 1983 as a reformer.[29]

Any hopes that Daley may have held originally about luring disillusioned black voters away from Byrne dissolved when Washington announced his candidacy. Daley could rely on the support of a few African American ministers and politicians who honored decades-old ties to his father, but many residents of the South and West Sides once firmly in the sway of the elder

Daley had long since soured on that relationship. The younger Daley recited for black audiences his accomplishments as state's attorney, emphasizing his office's record on reducing crime and hiring minorities, but shied away from discussing such topics of overriding interest to African Americans as open housing, public school desegregation, and police brutality. Like his father a lifetime resident of Bridgeport who felt constrained by Chicago's combustible tribalism, Daley saw his appeal to black voters limited by the need to maintain the support of his white ethnic base. Also like his father, he advocated increased funding for social welfare programs and expansion of other initiatives beneficial to black neighborhoods but staunchly affirmed the right of white Southwest and Northwest Side residents to bar public housing projects from their neighborhoods. He indignantly denied being a racist and lambasted Byrne for her duplicity toward African Americans but never devised an effective plan for cultivating widespread appeal among black voters.[30]

Because both Daley and Byrne hoped to attract some black votes, they refrained from leveling the kind of harsh criticisms against Washington that might have appeared racially insensitive. Throughout December and January, no doubt continuing to see the black aspirant as a minimal threat, the two white candidates took turns hurling charges and countercharges against each other—and largely ignoring Washington's presence in the race. This decision made a great deal of sense to the political experts in the Daley and Byrne camps, for Washington's campaign appeared to be spinning its wheels. His long-shot candidacy inevitably suffered from a number of serious liabilities common to all reformers but heightened for minority candidates. Widely known on the South Side but lacking the kind of name recognition throughout Chicago enjoyed by Daley and Byrne, Washington faced an uphill battle introducing himself and his platform to the metropolis's disparate voters. The two white candidates similarly began with access to much greater sums of money to underwrite their campaigns, and, as in 1977, Washington understood that fund-raising would be a daunting challenge and conceded that he could never hope to match the amount of spending by his opponents. In addition, the halting start of Washington's campaign owed to the difficulty in resolving two fundamental issues that defined the minority candidate's pursuit of executive power. Balancing the calls for reform and redistribution while also being sensitive to issues involving race and ethnicity, Washington needed both to mollify the interest

groups heavily invested in his campaign and specify the goals and aspirations of the reform effort over which he presided.[31]

Washington's 1977 mayoral campaign had been an administrative nightmare, plagued by indecisiveness, contradiction, unsure lines of authority,
and poor communication, and the 1983 effort started out much the same
way. The candidate selected Renault Robinson to serve as his campaign
manager, but Robinson floundered from the outset and had to be replaced
within three weeks. Washington then chose Al Raby, a highly respected
civil rights leader who had served as the liaison between local groups and
Dr. Martin Luther King Jr.'s national crusade during the mid-1960s. Raby
had not managed a political campaign since his own unsuccessful run for
alderman in 1975 and tried to decline the post before Washington finally
convinced him that his lack of recent political activity would not be too
much of a handicap. The candidate likely selected Raby, who was known
as a patient and diplomatic facilitator, for his ability to reconcile the competing interests of the varied groups dedicated to electing a black mayor.
From the beginning, a fissure in the campaign existed between the black
nationalists on the South Side and the integrationists downtown. Despite
Raby's best efforts, the fundamental differences in belief between the two
groups made the rift irreconcilable.[32]

The black nationalists, who called themselves the Task Force for Black
Political Empowerment, rejected the bourgeois politics of the past and called
for electoral change as a first step in the long-term goal of revolution. Having worked for years to increase political participation on the South Side,
conducted much of the voter registration, and done other preliminary work
necessary to lure Washington into the race, they felt justified in demanding
the most influence in the campaign. Under the leadership of radio commentator Lu Palmer, the Reverend Al Sampson, and academics Conrad Worrill
and Robert Starks, these ideologues saw race as the overriding issue and
devoted themselves passionately to the attainment of political power. Variously known by mainstream Washington supporters as the "Forty-Seventh
Street Crowd," the "Sound and Light Show," and the "Shadow Campaign,"
they operated independently from the official campaign headquarters and
strove to ensure that moderating forces did not dilute the aims of the black
nationalist movement. They objected to racial diversity in the campaign's
leadership, dismissed the need to enlist the support of white liberals, criticized African Americans around the candidate who espoused integration,

and saw no reason to promise "equity" and "fairness" to a wide variety of ethnic and racial groups. The black nationalists supported Washington not as a reformer bent on improving local government or as a charismatic politician capable of uniting a number of different interest groups but simply as the best available African American candidate.[33]

The black nationalists despaired when Raby moved Washington's campaign headquarters, which opened at first in a nondescript storefront on the South Side, to a downtown office building at 109 North Dearborn. The symbolism outraged Palmer and his cohorts, who characterized the relocation as "fleeing the base" in order to camouflage the candidate's race, as much as it satisfied the integrationists, who argued for a central location from which to seek votes in all parts of the city. Raby and the other downtown campaign workers, a mix of whites, blacks, and Latinos roughly proportional to citywide percentages, wore coats and ties at campaign headquarters in an effort to project respectability and professionalism. Members of the downtown staff generally kept their distance from the activities of their counterparts on the South Side, as if two autonomous campaigns existed wholly independent of each other; the two groups communicated infrequently, usually only to monitor Washington's schedule and coordinate his personal appearances.[34] Raby explained, "Downtown we had had the professionally minded campaign technicians who may not have been the city's most experienced election people, but most had some electoral experience. Then you had the crew down at Forty-Seventh Street doing their own thing, quite separate from the rest of the campaign."[35]

The tension between the two campaign staffs lingered throughout the campaign, and people in both camps grumbled about the strategy and tactics employed by the other group. Occasionally, as when task force members heckled black ministers endorsing Daley or destroyed posters for Daley and Byrne displayed in black neighborhoods, Raby downplayed the incidents in interviews with newspaper and television reporters and scrambled to practice damage control. In such cases, he and the other downtown staffers appreciated the fact that Chicago's rigid racial segregation shielded much of the task force's brazen activities on the South Side from mass-media attention.[36]

The candidate faced the problem of how to manage such an unorthodox campaign. The challenge amounted to much more than simply balancing the competing egos of ambitious political aides, adjudicating turf battles, or even finding room to accommodate like-minded advisers who agreed about the broad sweep of strategy but differed over particular tactical issues. In this case, the two competing groups disagreed about virtually every item on a long laundry list of beliefs; they agreed only about the need to pursue a single overriding objective—the election of Harold Washington. So, according to the two antagonistic groups, what exactly did it mean to elect Washington mayor? What precisely would the goals and aspirations of a Washington administration be? What message should be conveyed to voters on behalf of the candidate? The decision to cooperate exclusively with one group or the other would speak volumes about the meaning of a vote for Washington. In short, who spoke for the African American candidate to the Chicago electorate, Al Raby or Lu Palmer?

In a decision both daring and necessary, Washington allowed both campaigns to continue operating more or less independently with only a modicum of coordination. Keenly aware of the need to mobilize the African American electorate and exploit the potential political power of the black community, Washington knew that he benefited from the task force's tireless proselytizing on his behalf. He nodded at affirmations of racial pride and assented when his black nationalist supporters chided the political machine for its racist practices. Palmer and his cohorts often expressed frustration that Washington spent too much time campaigning outside of the black community and lent too much authority to the downtown integrationists, but they rejoiced when he took white city leaders to task for preserving racial inequality—which he did periodically, especially in South Side venues addressing black audiences. He singled out Richard J. Daley (and his son) for special blame on one notable occasion, saying:

> [Richard J. Daley] was a racist to the core, head to toe, hip to hip, there's no ding or doubt about it. He eschewed and fought and oppressed black people to the point that some thought that was the way they were supposed to live, just like some slaves on the plantation thought that that was the way they were supposed to live. I give no hosannas for a racist, nor did I appreciate or respect his son. If his name were anything other than Daley, his campaign would be a joke.

Such impolitic utterances, although gleefully received by the black nationalists, caused Raby and others downtown to wince in anticipation of the indignation they knew the remark would trigger throughout the rest of the city. Many whites found Washington's straightforward racial appeals for votes unsettling, as when he urged parishioners at a black church to "make it unfashionable and uncomfortable" for African Americans to vote for anyone else. Washington may not have appeased the black nationalists by making his campaign solely about racial uplift, but neither did he shy away from candid discussions about segregation and economic exploitation as a means of enhancing his support in the black community.[37]

Yet at the same time, Washington worked cooperatively with the diverse staff at the Dearborn Street headquarters and made a concerted effort to appeal broadly to a variety of constituencies across the city. Convinced that he would require votes from whites and Latinos as well as African Americans, he had no intention of limiting his appeal exclusively to one segment of the electorate. Although members of the Chicago media invariably identified Washington as the black candidate in their campaign reporting, he did everything possible to resist being pigeonholed as simply the spokesman for a single aggrieved minority. Instead, he unfailingly presented himself as an antimachine crusader with all that that characterization implied to women, lakefront liberals, workers, the poor, and other minorities, as well as to African Americans, who had been systematically excluded for decades. "The overriding issue is fairness," Washington proclaimed. He characterized both of his opponents as ignoble products of the Democratic machine and his candidacy as the only alternative available to any and all voters fed up with the kind of autocratic government that had beset the city for generations. In speeches delivered throughout Chicago, he talked about the plight of African Americans but also about the myriad other groups suffering from the economic decline and physical decay that resulted from machine misrule. He enumerated the benefits of reform available to the denizens of the white bungalow belts on the Southwest and Northwest Sides, the Latinos living southwest and west of the Loop, and the affluent whites arrayed along the lakefront north of the Chicago River. He spoke repeatedly and movingly about the need for a rainbow coalition to break the machine's enervating stranglehold on a troubled city.[38]

Washington especially pursued votes from Latinos, a group that according to the 1980 census had doubled in size during the previous decade to 14 percent of Chicago's population. With only about one-third of eligible Latinos registered to vote, the group offered great potential for any politician seeking to increase the size of a minority coalition. Emphasizing the commonality of interests they shared with African Americans, Washington reminded Latinos of how political participation could improve their lot in Chicago. They may have been officially identified as Caucasians, he told Latino audiences, but whites treated them like "niggers." Quizzed by reporters about his provocative use of language, Washington responded, "Yes, they do treat Latins like niggers. You know it. I know it. Why not say it?" Any serious challenge to the hegemony of the Democratic machine, he brashly insisted, necessitated widespread participation by historically pliant ethnic and racial groups that for the first time were demanding a new way of doing business in the city.[39]

Washington needed to reassure whites, Latinos, and other groups that his rainbow coalition would not cater exclusively to African Americans, a concern that gave rise to the related problem of defining an appropriate role in the campaign for the Reverend Jesse Jackson. The best-known African American in Chicago and a gifted public speaker with important connections in the black community, Jackson expected deference commensurate with his stature as a renowned national figure. He wanted to be consulted often about campaign strategy and looked forward to a prominent role in the campaign—all of which struck Washington insiders as disastrous ideas. As much as Jackson's intrepid civil rights crusades had enthralled African Americans, many Chicagoans viewed the activist as a publicity-hungry charlatan and inveterate troublemaker. To the city's reformers, his reputed inability to work with others and ceaseless self-promotion made him unreliable as an ally; others saw him as a dangerous radical whose uncompromising rhetoric condemning racial inequality placed him squarely outside of the political mainstream. Apprehensive whites feared that Jackson would really run the city behind the scenes in the event of a Washington victory, a possibility that the candidate repeatedly disavowed. The campaign minimized Jackson's public appearances while using his talents as an organizer and fund-raiser behind the scenes. Happily or not, Jackson went along. Tamping down the racial antagonism that Jackson's presence ignited and constantly affirming his own independence, Washington returned again and again to articulating his plans for reform.[40]

Washington's dedication to reform became clear in the early months of 1983, a commitment that the local media and many Chicagoans overlooked because of the city's preoccupation with racial politics. According to Kari Moe, a Washington aide who helped to compose the campaign's economic development platform, Washington made the decision personally to accentuate policy in his speeches and circulars. In fact, the candidate outlined a remarkably detailed blueprint for reshaping the city that was designed to serve both as a clear presentation of his position on the issues and as an outline for municipal governance in the ensuing years. Hal Baron, cochair of the Research and Issues Committee for the campaign, proposed the formation of several issue teams (representing different class, race, and neighborhood interests) to consider a variety of viewpoints and to craft position papers for the candidate's perusal. Fifteen issue teams, relying on the participation of more than 150 volunteers altogether, considered topics ranging from housing, jobs, fiscal policy, and economic development to women and senior citizens before submitting their recommendations to the Research and Issues Committee for additional refinement and then to the candidate himself for final editing. The Committee to Elect Harold Washington published the final product, *The Washington Papers*, in January 1983. *The Washington Papers* specified in broad strokes the candidate's reform design for Chicago's future.[41]

Rejecting the standard means of composing a campaign platform, which commonly entailed gathering a handful of experts and political insiders together for a brief time to draft position papers, Washington sought broader participation by teams composed of many diverse interest groups. Fully aware that the latter course would be cumbersome and inefficient, he nonetheless opted for the nontraditional approach of a "bottom-up" rather than a "top-down" orientation that contrasted sharply with the Cook County machine's mode of operation. Furthermore, the emphasis on inclusivity in formulating *The Washington Papers* reflected the document's contents and, the candidate indicated, provided a detailed preview of his approach to governance. The campaign's commitment to openness, which Washington often contrasted with the secrecy of the Byrne administration, required a new accessibility to information in government. Accordingly, the candidate pledged to issue an executive order establishing freedom of information on the first day of his administration. *The Washington Papers* promised greater local participation not only in decision making but also in policy formulation, indicating an appreciation for the support of neighborhood organizations across the city.[42]

The Washington Papers devoted an entire section to the importance of neighborhoods, not only in the 1983 election but also in the ensuing years of a Washington mayoralty, and throughout the text discussed their potential role in governance. Specifying the "energy, experience, and creativity" of its three million residents as Chicago's greatest asset, the document promised a rebirth of neighborhoods underwritten by city hall. In a straightforward declaration of intent, the document said, "The Washington program for neighborhoods is to mobilize the city's vast assets on behalf of people in the neighborhoods and organize the apparatus of city government, and other sectors, to work for them." Reporting that Chicago was spending approximately twenty million dollars in community development funds annually on land clearance for new construction, *The Washington Papers* sketched an alternative approach that entailed citizen participation in decision making and the concomitant rehabilitation of the existing housing stock and local businesses. With laudatory comments about the historical significance of neighborhoods groups, the campaign promised to consider the priorities developed by community-based organizations of all stripes. While a Washington mayoral administration would work closely with existing community-based organizations, *The Washington Papers* also proposed the creation and staffing of official neighborhood planning boards that would cooperate with municipal agencies in planning and prioritizing local development projects. These boards would participate in decisions about how to allocate Community Development Block Grant (CDBG) funds and other federal largesse, an unprecedented opportunity that had been solely a prerogative of city hall in the past.[43]

As outlined in *The Washington Papers*, the neighborhoods would also play a leading role in the crucial activity of economic development. In keeping with the traditional wisdom of the post–World War II era, Chicago's city officials and civic leaders had subscribed for decades to a series of downtown-first plans for offsetting metropolitan decentralization. Culminating with the Chicago 21 Plan, which had been sponsored by the Chicago Central Area Committee and released to widespread acclaim in 1973, these comprehensive plans recommended urban redevelopment schemes designed to protect the vitality of the Loop and frequently required the destruction of viable neighborhoods abutting downtown. At the very least, claimed reformers, the concentration of scarce resources in a limited area surrounding Chicago's core deprived the city's peripheral areas of adequate funding. Worst of all, the saturation of the central business district with redevelopment plans—and money—had produced paltry results in recent years. In scattershot fashion, noted Washington, the Byrne administration had authorized a Five-Year Capital Development Plan, a North Loop Development Plan, a South Loop Development Plan, an Enterprise Zone Plan, a Waterway Development Policy, a High Tech Development Plan, a World's Fair Plan, the (corporation counsel John) Melaniphy Study of Neighborhood Needs, and many other plans that combined to form an incoherent mélange of overlapping designs. (The black candidate singled out for special condemnation the Enterprise Zone Plan, which he described scornfully as the Chicago version of President Reagan's principal urban program.) Other than a steadfast resolve to continue subordinating the needs of outlying neighborhoods to the welfare of the Loop, Washington charged, the Byrne administration's many plans shared very little in common and had yielded negligible positive results.[44]

Besides his commitment to avoid piecemeal reform and to develop a unified economic development policy, Washington also promised a new ethos in city hall that balanced downtown and neighborhood interests. He took direct aim at the Chicago 21 Plan as a transparent attempt to gentrify areas abutting downtown at the expense of thriving peripheral communities. In 1978 Loop businesses employed only about 18 percent of the Chicago workforce, reported the candidate, yet the final Byrne administration budget allocated more than two-thirds of the funds earmarked for economic development–related capital improvements to downtown. Moreover, Byrne and previous mayors had utilized tax abatements and other inducements almost exclusively for the recruitment and retention of corporate headquarters and other firms likely to be situated downtown. In its pursuit of big corporations with hefty payrolls, the city had largely ignored small and locally owned businesses that often provided significant numbers of jobs in outlying areas of the city. In their fascination with new technological industries, both the city and the state had recently mounted expensive public relations efforts to attract companies involved in the production of such commodities. Washington cautioned against thinking of "high-tech" industries as a quick fix to the city's grave economic problems, emphasizing the speculative nature of such efforts. Instead, he recommended halting the epidemic of plant closings that plagued the city. Contrary to popular belief, he argued, many businesses fleeing such older industrial cities as Chicago did so not to stem the flow of red ink or avoid bankruptcy but rather to increase profits in already thriving enterprises for the benefit of ceaselessly avaricious parent companies. Industrial loss could be slowed if local governments provided adequate incentives for such companies to remain in Chicago—and the retention of factory jobs particularly benefited the city's far-flung manufacturing neighborhoods.[45]

The Washington Papers closely linked the ideas of neighborhood empowerment and economic development. The virtues of community-based, bottom-up development, went the argument, included greater equity, stable employment, and improved public-private relations. Increased community control over economic activity would result from local ownership, some varieties of which included small-scale community development corporations, worker-owned cooperatives, and firms owned by neighborhood residents. The support of small, locally controlled businesses also provided the opportunity to encourage minority and female ownership as an alternative to the white male-owned firms that predominated in Chicago and elsewhere. These innovative types of entrepreneurship depended on a significant amount of public subsidies, as well as a municipal government willing to bargain aggressively with businesses and other governments on behalf of local interests. Municipal agencies would likewise need to use affirmative action and set-aside programs to spur minority and female business ownership. Washington stopped well short of declaring that Chicago's economic future relied entirely on community-based development but argued that such activity could provide a critical supplement to the shopworn modes of business recruitment that had been producing meager results in Chicago for decades.[46]

A frank challenge to the manner in which the business elite and the Democratic machine had jointly been guiding Chicago's political economy, *The Washington Papers* charted a much different course for the city's future development. The political pundits who invoked Washington's previous years as a machine loyalist to question his reform credentials simply dismissed the document as meaningless good-government boilerplate or just ignored its contents altogether. Although the candidate's crusade for municipal reform entailed the usual goals of greater efficiency, elimination of waste, eradication of patronage, and transparent government, *The Washington Papers* went much further in seeking equity for a number of groups that had long been overlooked in the Windy City. In his attempt to forge a populist coalition of the have-nots and political liberals, the candidate pursued a policy of redistribution that potentially had far-ranging consequences for the city. Washington spoke of reallocating political and economic power from the elites that had long enjoyed the benefits of their favored status to the groups shut off from the societal mainstream, from the downtown to the neighborhoods, from the few to the many. His vision of redistribution prominently featured race, to be sure, but also encompassed much more.[47]

Washington's reformist campaign languished early, as both black and white voters doubted that he had any real chance of unseating the incumbent mayor or defeating the purported heir of the Democratic machine. The turning point of the campaign came with a series of four debates in January 1983 that made an immediate impact on the black candidate's status. Both Byrne and Washington had eagerly agreed to debate from the outset of the campaign, but Daley, a notoriously inarticulate public speaker, refused to participate. By mid-January, however, Daley's standing in public opinion polls was rapidly declining along with his chances of overtaking the mayor. Daley finally agreed to four televised debates—to be held on January 19, 23, 29, and 31—as a desperate attempt to rescue his polling numbers from free fall. For Washington, the debates presented the chance to obtain the television time his threadbare campaign could not afford to purchase, as well as the opportunity to reach vast audiences otherwise unavailable to him.[48]

The first debate, which attracted the largest viewership of the four, established a pattern that continued throughout the later forums. Washington ignored Daley most of the time while aggressively criticizing the mayor at every turn. "I'm running for the office of Mayor of the City of Chicago because Jane Byrne is destroying our city," he declared in his opening statement, accusing the mayor of "fighting for control of city patronage . . . and fat-cat city contracts for her cronies" at the expense of helpless taxpayers. Byrne remained composed in the face of Washington's—and Daley's— relentless censure of her mayoral record. During an extensive discussion of the city's fiscal woes, unbalanced budget, and the steps necessary for reclaiming fiscal solvency, the mayor combatively defended her record against the challengers' merciless recounting of her administration's erratic management and wasteful practices. When Byrne ruled out the need for new taxes and Daley agreed with her assessment, Washington excoriated their disingenuousness and taunted that they "can run but they can't hide" from admitting the necessity of raising additional revenue. When Byrne and Daley vacillated about the need to cut the city payroll, Washington rejoined that he relished the opportunity to wield an ax to several bloated municipal departments. The media reported that the mayor gamely held her own during the spirited discussion, and Daley surprised viewers with his calm demeanor and low-key sense of humor, but Washington emerged as the big winner. His thorough knowledge of the issues and impressive oratorical skills made Washington the dominant personality of the debate and removed any doubt (especially among black voters) about the viability of his candidacy. Suddenly, discussions of the mayoral race at water coolers, bars, and bus stops around Chicago took notice of the loquacious, self-assured African American candidate.[49]

The other three debates essentially followed the script employed in the first contest: the two challengers, Washington leading the way, pilloried the mayor for failed policies implemented during the previous four years, and Byrne resolutely defended her record. In the second debate, which focused on issues related to public safety, both Daley and Washington questioned the accuracy of statistics proffered by the mayor that purportedly showed a decline in crime during her tenure. Washington promised to dismiss police superintendent Richard Brzeczek, whom he referred to as "the top cop who's become a political prop," as one of his first acts as mayor. The third debate dealt with economic development, presenting Washington an opportunity to denounce the mayor for having expended virtually all of the city's development funds on downtown refurbishment to the exclusion of the neighborhoods. He also spoke in abundant detail about his specific plans to create five thousand new jobs in waste recycling, five thousand jobs in public works, and eleven thousand new conservation jobs for buildings that would cut energy bills by $675 million annually. The challengers' assaults on the mayor's record peaked in the final debate, an acrimonious affair frequently interrupted by outbursts from a large and boisterous crowd. In his opening remarks, Washington directly addressed the subject of race for the first time in the debates. He said, "I am running to end Jane Byrne's four-year effort to further institutionalize racial discrimination in this great city."[50] He offered a scathing assessment of race relations in the city, blaming the mayor for many of the problems. He explained:

> There are some who believe that I should avoid the race issue, but I will not avoid it because it permeates our entire city and it has devastating implica-

tions. Instead of fighting for quality education, Jane Byrne has fought to make the school board a racial battleground, despite the fact that a majority of the students are black or Hispanic. Instead of fighting to improve living conditions of Chicago's residents, Jane Byrne has made a racial battleground out of the CHA board.[51]

The four debates, watched by more than five million viewers overall, aided all three mayoral candidates to varying degrees. Mocked for four years as a flighty, emotional harridan whose impulsiveness had damaged the city's good reputation, "New Jane" appeared to be a calm, competent professional thoroughly conversant with the city's problems. Daley started haltingly but gained confidence and poise with each debate; his oratory, though far from compelling, proved to be satisfactory enough not to derail his candidacy. A consensus quickly developed that Washington, whose campaign had not yet aired a television commercial and who still remained relatively unknown to many white voters, benefited the most from the prolonged exposure. He impressed viewers with his eloquent and thoughtful dissection of the complex issues facing Chicago. His answer to a question about ways to improve the police department's Office of Professional Standards, for instance, showed his knowledge and preparation to good effect. After Byrne cursorily responded that the OPS was already working effectively and Daley blandly conceded that there was "nothing wrong with improvement in the Office of Professional Standards," Washington told the audience, "The precise question is what I would do to improve the [OPS], and when I answer it I'll be the only one to answer the question." He then elaborated on the OPS's many deficiencies, detouring to criticize the police superintendent as a "subaltern" of the incumbent mayor who had lost all credibility with the public, and enumerated specific ideas for strengthening the agency.[52]

The opportunity to stand toe to toe and hold his own against better-known adversaries allowed Washington to reassure white voters of his qualifications, noted *Chicago Tribune* political writer David Axelrod, while infusing black voters with a sense of optimism that their man had a reasonable chance of winning. Washington aide Jacky Grimshaw remembered older black women as a particularly "tough sell" on the idea of an African American candidate defeating the machine and becoming mayor of Chicago, but even that jaded demographic became less defeatist after the debates. Byrne and Daley aides admitted that the African American candidate clearly profited most from the debates but added that his impressive performance would change the minds of very few voters. Having already acquitted themselves well and exceeded expectations, the Byrne and Daley campaigns declined Washington's call for a fifth debate.[53]

Although the debates energized Washington's somnolent campaign and the results of public opinion polls moved him ahead of Daley into second place, his ascendant political fortunes failed to secure the endorsement of Chicago's two major daily newspapers. Daley's polling numbers remained very low, but both the *Chicago Tribune* and the *Chicago Sun-Times* officially backed him. On January 23, the *Chicago Tribune* issued a tepid endorsement of the state's attorney, explaining that Byrne's shoddy record and Washington's polarizing campaign left its editorial board no choice but to favor Daley. As the only candidate who offered hope to the city's concerned voters, explained the *Tribune*, Daley appeared to be the best choice by default. More positive in its support, the *Sun-Times* praised Daley's intangible leadership qualities, observed that he projected a strong image, and cited his reputation for reliability and integrity. Both papers referred unflatteringly to Byrne and portrayed her four years in city hall as an abject failure. Washington received scant mention at all. The voters seemed to be much more aware of Washington's presence in the contest after the debates, but the mainstream press still treated the mayoral race as a great drama featuring two star performers center stage in the spotlight and a lesser supporting actor barely visible in the background.[54]

While political experts and the local press continued to minimize the viability of the Washington campaign a month before the Democratic primary, an extraordinary political movement was gaining momentum in black neighborhoods. Unlike the halfhearted, lifeless campaigns of 1975 and 1977, African Americans increasingly believed in 1983 that their champion had a real chance to win the mayoralty. Once deserted and quiet, Washington campaign headquarters bustled with activity after the debates. Long desperate for help to perform mundane electioneering tasks, the candidate's staff suddenly found no shortage of volunteers eager to ring doorbells and distribute leaflets. Blue Washington campaign buttons appeared everywhere in the African American community, often among city workers who removed the buttons when they went downtown to work in the mornings and replaced them when they returned home in the evenings. Ministers and choir members proudly wore their buttons during Sunday church services, a reflection of the close ties forged between Washington and the black community's many churches. Moreover, the advocacy of the black clergy demonstrated how the Washington candidacy had taken on the trappings of a religious crusade among African Americans. Democratic-machine precinct captains reported massive defections among black voters who had earlier been rooted firmly in the Byrne camp. Best of all for the insurgent, minority voter registration continued unabated during the winter months; an additional thirty thousand blacks registered to vote after the November 1982 election.[55]

The remarkable political transformation taking place in the black community at last became evident to the entire city population after the rally for Washington at the University of Illinois at Chicago Pavilion on February 6. Still trailing Byrne in the polls with barely two weeks remaining until the primary, Washington and his advisers believed that he needed one more dramatic, well-publicized event to convince undecided black voters that the mayor's lead could be overcome. In defiance of an aphorism that campaign functions should be held in cozy, compact venues so that modest crowds would appear much larger, the campaign decided to hold a rally in the cavernous twelve-thousand-seat pavilion. On February 6 snow fell throughout the bitterly cold day, and campaign organizers expected a turnout of only about six thousand persons. To their delight, many more than twelve thousand enthusiastic Washington supporters braved the heavy snow to show support for their candidate. In what reporters covering the event likened to a religious revival, members of the happy throng responded to a clergyman's rhythmic invocation and then listened to musical performances by Curtis Mayfield and the Barrett Sisters. Members of the crowd sang, applauded, chanted, and roared their approval as a steady stream of dignitaries, including the Reverend Jesse Jackson, Senator Alan Cranston of California, Congressman Ronald Dellums of California, and Congressman John Conyers of Michigan, spoke in favor of the candidate.[56]

In the third hour of the program, an exuberant Washington finally made his way to the stage as cries of "We want Harold! We want Harold!" echoed throughout the hall. The buoyant candidate delivered a fiery speech that took aim at both of his rivals, telling the audience, "You have a right to more than choosing between Tweedledee and Tweedledum. You have a right to a real alternative." While mocking Daley as a vacuous politician hoping to ascend on his father's coattails, he saved his most barbed attacks for Byrne. Washington called the mayor a "flunky of Ronald Reagan" whose appointments showed her contempt for the blacks she had so assiduously courted four years earlier. He reiterated his promise to fire the police superintendent, prompting the crowd to chant, "Fire Brzeczek! Fire Brzeczek!" He likewise took aim at Charles Swibel, Byrne's chief fund-raiser and discredited CHA chairman, saying, "Nor will this city any longer be Swibelized by a gentleman who has lived off the fat too long. He's on the agenda to go too." The tumultuous reception he received from the adoring crowd, Washington later commented, convinced him for the first time that he would prevail.[57]

Thereafter, Washington's confident pronouncement about winning no longer sounded like the obligatory statements of unfounded optimism routinely uttered by candidates as a matter of course to reassure wavering supporters. The triumphant rally at the UIC Pavilion caused a reassessment of the mayoral election in the campaign's last days. Black businesses, previously reluctant to become involved in another ill-fated antimachine crusade, at last loosened their purse strings and donated an estimated $250,000 to the Washington campaign in February. The Byrne campaign, which had her enjoying a steady and comfortable 38 percent of the vote for weeks, looked on nervously as its 10 percentage point lead over Washington dwindled to 6 percentage points (with 10 percent undecided) in the final week. The denials from Byrne campaign headquarters about fomenting racial divisiveness notwithstanding, Democratic Party regulars began circulating through white neighborhoods to spread the word of Daley's demise and Washington's surge. The campaign printed and distributed thousands of copies of an open letter written by former Republican governor Richard Ogilvie, alerting voters that the election had become a contest between Byrne (whom he had endorsed) and Washington. Democratic precinct captains dispersed mimeographed circulars on the Northwest and Southwest Sides, warning that a Washington victory would threaten the racial homogeneity of all-white neighborhoods. Although the candidate herself refrained from overt race-baiting, she referred to Daley as a "spoiler" and warned ominously that a vote for the state's attorney could open the door to a Washington victory.[58]

On the Saturday before the primary, the covert racial appeal suddenly became explicit. Edward Vrdolyak, Democratic Party chairman and a staunch Byrne ally, addressed a large gathering of precinct workers on the Northwest Side, not knowing that a few newspaper reporters were also in attendance. The journalists reported that Vrdolyak said, "A vote for Daley is a vote for Washington. It's a two-person race. It would be the worst day in the history of Chicago if our candidate, the only viable candidate, was not elected. It's a racial thing. Don't kid yourself. I am calling on you to save your city, to save your precinct. We are fighting to keep the city the way it is."[59]

Although members of the Byrne campaign had been saying much the same thing in hushed tones for several days, hearing such bald expressions of racism from the Democratic Party chairman without the careful use of innuendo or code words immediately ignited a fierce reaction. Byrne attempted to distance herself from the sentiments expressed by Vrdolyak and disclaimed any responsibility for her compatriot's controversial remarks. Daley denounced the party chairman specifically for employing fear tactics and the Byrne campaign generally for using race to drive white voters out of his camp and into hers. Washington condemned Vrdolyak's comments and demanded that Byrne do the same. Coolly suggesting that such appeals to racism revealed an increasing desperation in the mayor's office, Washington called the party chairman's hysteria another piece of evidence indicating that he was going to win. Discussion of Vrdolyak's ill-timed comments and their impact on the upcoming mayoral primary monopolized the front pages of the city's newspapers—and other newspapers throughout the country—for the remaining days before the election.[60]

As Vrdolyak's remarks sparked angry charges and countercharges about the exploitation of race in the campaign and passions rose to new heights, Washington serenely predicted victory. Speaking at a large rally on the eve of the election, the black candidate sounded themes of racial pride and reassured the audience about the next day's outcome. He said, "We've run the course. We met the enemy on the battlefield. We fought him on his own terms. We pushed him, whipped him to his natural knees." He was right. In an extremely close race, Washington managed a victory margin of just 33,000 votes out of 1.2 million cast. He prevailed with 36 percent of the vote, while Byrne (34 percent) and Daley (30 percent) split the remainder of the ballots. An elated Jesse Jackson offered a knowing summation of the outcome with linguistic flourish: "Black people were energized. White people were traumatized."[61]

Jackson's antics the night of the election magnified the trauma for whites already troubled by Washington's unexpected win. Recognizing that many Chicago whites loathed the controversial Jackson yet desperately needing the resources and contacts available through his Operation PUSH, the Washington campaign had done a masterful job during the primary of utilizing the veteran civil rights leader's influence while keeping him out of sight. Given Jackson's notorious love of the spotlight, the local media marveled at his invisibility throughout the campaign. All that changed on the evening of February 25, however, as the election returns pointed to an upset victory for the African American candidate. Monopolizing the stage for more than an hour at the ballroom reserved for the Washington faithful, Jackson excitedly told the jubilant crowd, "We want it all! We want it here! We want it now!" Fearful that his supporter's overheated rhetoric would alarm anxious white voters, the candidate took the stage to dispel fears of a massive African American takeover and spoke soothingly of a rainbow movement. Worried about another potentially damaging outburst, Washington and his aides worked overtime thereafter to keep Jackson on a short leash. The candidate said, "I run my own stuff. That's why I make mistakes. I don't understand why people keep saying Jesse Jackson is running the campaign. Some people don't like Jesse, but why graft that onto me? I have my own [church] minister."[62]

Pilloried at the outset as a hopelessly disorganized effort, the Washington campaign never became a model operation by traditional political standards but nevertheless improved with time. Competing factions found their own niches and cooperated sufficiently with other groups for the common cause. Unbridled passion and an unrelenting optimism among an enthusiastic army of volunteers more than compensated for what the effort lacked in efficiency. The powerful momentum of the movement became evident, noted one campaign insider, when children in the public schools and public housing projects brought cans stuffed with pennies and nickels to Washington headquarters. Inmates in Cook County Jail passed the hat and contributed its meager contents as well. The frenetic activity on primary election day perfectly illustrated the campaign's strength. Busloads of college students from around the state, some from as far away as Southern Illinois University in Carbondale, arrived unannounced in Chicago to help usher elderly and infirm voters to the polls. After providing a cursory orientation, grateful campaign workers dispatched the eager undergraduates to precincts that were reporting low turnouts. "By early afternoon," remembered William J. Grimshaw, who was tracking developments at campaign headquarters, "we were getting calls from persons who had already voted, urging us to please stop knocking on their doors."[63]

A close analysis of the 1983 Democratic mayoral primary revealed that Washington won principally because so many African Americans showed up at the polls on February 22 and almost all of them voted for him. In ten black wards, Washington won every precinct. Remarkably, he received larger victories in five wards than Daley did in his home Eleventh Ward. In all, Washington carried fewer wards than Byrne—nineteen to the incumbent mayor's twenty-two—but swept the African American vote in precincts within wards won handily by his opponents. He won modest vote totals outside the predominantly African American South and West Sides—in black and Latino enclaves as well as a smattering of white votes throughout the city, especially on the North Side along the lakefront—but the registration, mobilization, and turnout of what he referred to as his base made the difference. In that regard, the work of Lu Palmer and his colleagues at the Forty-Seventh Street office had proved to be invaluable. The drive to elect Washington within the black community became a crusade, part secular and part religious, that leaders of the Democratic machine recognized very late in the contest. In the aftermath of her surprising loss, Byrne marveled, "They came out in droves. It was almost like a religious movement. I don't know how you overcome that."[64]

At first blush, the outcome of the Democratic primary seemed to ensure a Washington victory in the April 12 general election. After all, the Democratic nominees for mayor had won (usually by overwhelming margins) in every mayoral contest since 1931. In a heavily Democratic city, Chicago's Republican Party slogged along on a tiny budget and resignedly fielded long-shot candidates in election after election. The Republican candidate, Bernard Epton, had received 11,042 votes in his party's primary, while Washington amassed 415,050 in the Democratic contest. Both Byrne and Daley had pledged their support (if unenthusiastically) to the party's nominee. Party chairman Vrdolyak guaranteed that there would be "no obstructionism. . . . The Democratic party will give its full support to the Democratic candidate." Expecting the complete backing of his party, which would guarantee certain victory, Washington and his aides prepared to move into city hall. He began naming the members of a transition team charged with identifying potential appointees to executive posts and held meetings with many Chicago business tycoons to allay their fears about working with a black mayor who had spoken repeatedly about empowering neighborhoods at the expense of downtown. Accounting for the possibility of a certain number of defections from the

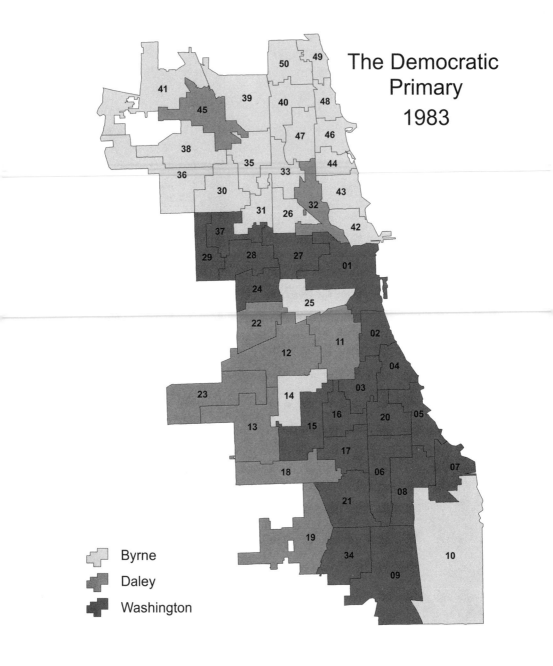

The Democratic
Primary
1983

Byrne

Daley

Washington

ranks of white and Latino Democrats and a reduced voter turnout in the anticlimactic general election, veteran political analyst Don Rose summed up the situation this way: "He might not win as big as some other Democrats have, but he should win."[65]

Yet in the days immediately following the primary, even as Washington and his close advisers were considering cabinet appointments and strategizing about the sequence of mayoral policy initiatives, the Democratic Party began splintering. Washington told reporters, "I am the nominee. I expect the support of the Democratic committeemen." He agreed to talk with party leaders, but emphasized that "there will be no deals made relative to that accommodation." Nor would he renege on the commitments specified in his campaign platform, especially his promise to dismantle the insidious patronage system that had long been the life's blood of the Democratic machine. If indeed the candidate remained faithful to his reformist rhetoric, party insiders realized, their control of jobs, promotions, contracts, and other perquisites would be jeopardized. In short, ward committeemen, precinct captains, aldermen, a multitude of elected officials, a veritable army of municipal employees, and all of the family members dependent on the machine's beneficence saw a Washington mayoralty as a genuine threat to their well-being. The wholesale defections that followed and the lengths to which the defectors went to ensure Washington's defeat resulted from the high stakes at play. As reform alderman and Washington supporter David Orr concluded, "This was a war."[66]

On February 28, Twelfth Ward alderman Aloysius Majerzyk fired the first shot in the political war when he announced his support for the Republican mayoral candidate. An eerie silence followed, as other Democratic officeholders remained mute about their willingness to get in line behind the party's mayoral candidate. Michael Madigan, Illinois Speaker of the House and Thirteenth Ward committeeman, endorsed Washington but also advised him to meet with the committeemen collectively and appeal for their support. Affronted that he should be expected to grovel in front of party leaders when their backing should be a routine matter, Washington refused. "I'm not going to kiss their asses," he said off the record. Although the candidate reported that Vrdolyak had offered his "personal assurances" of the party's unified support, other Democratic notables remained ominously quiet. Fourteenth Ward alderman Edward Burke cautioned, "There are alternatives." Several committeemen explained that, as much as they valued party unity and normally felt obligated to support the nominee, the overwhelming sentiment of their constituents against the Washington candidacy made it extremely difficult for them to do so. Washington operatives in the field reported that only two white committeemen, Alan Dobry of the Fifth Ward and George Dunne of the Forty-Second Ward, were actually campaigning for the nominee.[67]

If the machine leadership delayed and dissembled in the days following the primary, the same could not be said of white Democrats at the grass-roots level. The racial tension generally absent from the primary campaign but released at the eleventh hour by Vrdolyak's intemperate remarks carried over unbridled in late February and March. Angry residents of the white bungalow belts emphatically declared their opposition to a black mayor. They rejected Washington's declarations of comity and inclusiveness, repudiating his attempts to forge a multiracial coalition. For many beleaguered whites on the Southwest and Northwest Sides, the threat of black incursions into their neighborhoods combined with fears about the loss of patronage to make a minority mayoralty a loathsome prospect. Voters who had reflexively cast Democratic ballots throughout their adulthoods abruptly pivoted and embraced the Republican mayoral candidate. The huge number of volunteers pouring into Republican campaign offices offering their services overwhelmed the silent, empty rooms that had resembled mausoleums just days before. At first, a number of whites wore paper bags over their heads with "Unknown Democrats for Epton" scrawled on their makeshift headwear. Soon whites relinquished their anonymity and openly wore buttons and carried banners proclaiming, "Democrats for Epton." Other expressions of support for the Republican appealed brazenly to voters' baser instincts. A leaflet circulating throughout the city read: "Your vote for Mr. Epton will stop contamination of the city hall by a Mr. Baboon"; another predicted that, in the event of a Washington victory, the city would change its name to "Chicongo" and its seal to crossed chicken drumsticks. A button spotted in white neighborhoods depicted a watermelon divided in half by a diagonal slash. T-shirts urged "VOTE WHITE, VOTE RIGHT." African American police officers reported to the *Chicago Defender* that racist handbills and crude cartoons opposing Washington were being posted anonymously on bulletin boards in their precinct station houses.[68]

The curious object of the rebellious Democrats' affection, sixty-one-year-old Bernard J. Epton, had traveled a tortuous path to the Republican mayoral nomination in 1983. A native Chicagoan, World War II veteran, and senior member of the law firm of Epton, Mullin, Segal, and Druth, which specialized in insurance law, he had been active in a number of Jewish organizations and the local Republican Party for many years. He won election to the Illinois House of Representatives in 1968 from the Twenty-Fourth District, a racially mixed, heavily Democratic area encompassing Hyde Park and the University of Chicago. Because Illinois at that time required the election of two members of the majority party and one member of the minority party in each legislative district, Epton continued to win reelection, despite the paucity of registered Republicans in the area. After the state reduced the membership of the House and introduced single-member districts, essentially ensuring the election of a single Democrat in most Chicago localities, Epton announced his retirement from politics and moved his family from Hyde Park to a more affluent Gold Coast neighborhood on the Near North Side. Presupposing a win by Byrne or Daley in February and unable to find a mayoral candidate, the Cook County Republican leadership selected Epton as their sacrificial lamb—in effect, granting the nondescript veteran his moment in the limelight as a parting gift, a ceremonial last hurrah in recognition of his many years of loyal service to the party.[69]

During his seven terms in the Illinois House of Representatives, Epton had earned the reputation of a moderate Republican who usually voted in favor of good-government reforms, kept his reputation unblemished by scandal and impropriety, and studiously looked after the financial interests of the business community. He voted for legislation banning racial discrimination, contributed generously to civil rights causes, and served on the boards of several African American charitable institutions. He often introduced legislation in cooperation with Democrats from across the aisle, including Harold Washington, and consistently received the endorsement of the progressive Independent Voters of Illinois. In recognition of the experience he had gained in his legal practice, Epton emerged as the House's recognized expert in matters related to insurance. Although some liberals complained that he refused to recuse himself on matters that seemed to pose a conflict of interest with his legal firm, he voted often enough to safeguard policyholders' interests to avoid being labeled a mouthpiece for the insurance industry. On the House floor and in committee meetings, he evinced a sardonic wit, keen intelligence, and, at times, a thin skin. Political correspondents in Springfield viewed Epton as eccentric—he once boasted to the press that he possessed the highest IQ in the Illinois General Assembly—and reported that his temper sometimes flared during debate, but overall characterized him as pleasant, polite, and approachable. For the most part, they summarized, his legislative career had been wholly unremarkable.[70]

After Washington's primary victory, Epton immediately promised to take the high road during the campaign. He refused to be cast as the Great White Hope and told the *Chicago Defender* that he would "repudiate any efforts by white racist Democrats" to rally around him as the antiblack candidate. "I have no desire to win a vote because an opponent is black and I am white," he added. "A bigot is a bigot, and I want no part of it." Following on the heels of his inexpensive primary campaign, the funds for which came almost entirely from his own bank account and contributions from family members, he planned an equally low-key effort for the general election. Friends and family initially staffed key positions at his campaign headquarters; his daughter served as campaign manager, and he saw no reason to hire a media consultant. Eschewing the cutthroat politics for which Chicago had become infamous, Epton promised to refrain from personal attacks against his opponent and to devote his time to sober discussions of the issues. During his first campaign appearances, he met those lofty goals. Epton described Washington as articulate and intelligent and spoke highly of their time spent together in the Illinois General Assembly. In his lengthy and detailed discourses on the many problems facing Chicago, he presented himself as a pragmatist who recognized the need for fiscal responsibility and hardheaded business principles. In order to restore the city's good name on Wall Street, Epton argued, municipal agencies would need to live within their means. Millions of dollars could easily be trimmed from the city budget, he calculated, while expressing a willingness to reduce services and lay off workers in order to achieve the necessary economies rather than raise taxes. The Epton campaign of late February indeed resembled a didactic tutorial on municipal governance with an emphasis on moderation and fiscal retrenchment.[71]

But during the early days of March, Epton shifted gears and converted his campaign from an informal mom-and-pop affair to a slick, streamlined operation. As droves of Democrats continued volunteering for Epton's campaign, talk in Chicago turned to the possibility that a Republican might actually win the mayoralty. National officials of the Republican Party, who had ignored Epton's requests for financial aid in January and February, contacted his headquarters in March and eagerly asked what they could do for his campaign. With the national party's promise of $200,000, Epton happily reported that he suddenly seemed likely to raise much more than the $300,000 he had estimated necessary to run a credible race. James Fletcher, who had piloted Illinois governor James R. Thompson's first campaign, replaced Epton's daughter as campaign manager, and John Deardourff arrived from a high-powered Washington, D.C., political consulting firm to become media adviser and top strategist. What began months earlier as a flight of fancy with no illusions of success rapidly metamorphosed into a deadly serious quest that appeared attainable, and Epton's strategy changed to reflect his improved prospects. A harsh tone crept into the candidate's speeches for the first time. "I used to think that Harold was an amiable fellow and an intelligent one," he told a cheering crowd on the Northwest Side. "I guess I was wrong on both counts."[72]

For the final month of the campaign, Epton substituted ad hominem attacks for financial seminars. His revised strategy, explained Deardourff to reporters, primarily revolved around exposing a series of embarrassing episodes in Washington's past and portraying him as an unreliable person with a history of failing to meet his financial obligations. Believing that a great number of voters remained unaware of Washington's past legal troubles, Epton unrelentingly attacked him as a politician of questionable integrity who could not be trusted to obey the law, pay his debts, or fulfill his commitments. The idea of Washington as a candidate of dubious ethics, Epton and his aides had concluded, appeared to be his Achilles' heel. Issues fell by the wayside as the Republican painstakingly reviewed Washington's legal problems in the 1970s—having his law license suspended for collecting fees from clients and then not performing the work, serving time in jail in 1972 for failure to file federal income tax returns, and not disclosing the existence of five lawsuits against him in 1975 when he was appealing to have his law license reinstated. Campaign buttons appeared bearing Washington's Cook County Jail mug shot as a reminder of his incarceration. The assault on the black candidate's reputation would conveniently allow whites to say that they voted against him for reasons other than race. Epton seconded that notion, saying, "Harold in my opinion is not the best qualified candidate the black community can produce."[73]

During his 1977 run for mayor and earlier that winter during the primary, Washington had cursorily addressed his earlier brushes with the law but not to the satisfaction of Deardourff and others in the Epton camp. Pilloried daily about these matters by the Republicans during the 1983 general election, Washington and his staff developed an item-by-item defense to charges regarding his income tax troubles and the suspension of his license to practice law. The Democratic candidate reiterated that he had been found guilty only of failing to file tax returns for four years, not of attempting to defraud the government or conceal income. The Internal Revenue Service (IRS) had withheld from his paychecks essentially all of the taxes he owed—excepting a total of $508.05 for 1964, 1965, 1967, and 1969 combined—which he repaid along with a fine of $1,036.68; he also served thirty-three days in jail and a three-year probation. Why had Washington neglected to file his income tax returns four times? Bogged down by the pressures of legal work and legislative affairs, the discomfited candidate claimed, he simply forgot. "It's just what it was," he told reporters. "Stupid." His defenders also pointed out that the government's decision to prosecute a misdemeanor tax case, the kind of transgression that very rarely went to court and usually resulted just in the payment of a fine, caught Washington off guard. When Albert Jenner Jr., a prominent Chicago attorney and Republican counsel during the Watergate hearings, failed to file tax returns for three years at roughly the same time, the IRS declined to prosecute or levy a fine. Many Democrats believed the extraordinary action against their candidate amounted to retaliation by the Nixon administration for the congressman's role in leading the boycott against Spiro Agnew a few months before. "Well," agreed Washington, "you don't have to be a genius to put two and two together." In order to avoid the opprobrium attached to a conviction in federal court, why had Washington not contested the charges? "He just wanted to get the stupid thing over with," said one of his attorneys, "and get on with his life."[74]

Washington's admission of culpability for not filing his income tax returns left a number of questions unanswered, Epton insisted, related to issues raised by the state during legal proceedings years before. Immediately after Washington had pleaded nolo contendere (no contest) to the charges and Judge J. Sam Perry had announced the sentence in 1972, the prosecution protested the trial's outcome. James R. Thompson, U.S. attorney for the Northern District of Illinois and future governor of the state, had strongly objected to the judge's decision to impose a light jail sentence (far less than the maximum of four years allowed by statute) on an elected official who should have been held to a high standard. Moreover, Thompson asserted, his office had charged at the hearing that "not only had the defendant not filed income tax returns for the years charged, he had failed to file income tax returns *for the last 19 years* and, to our knowledge, has never filed an income tax return." Washington and his aides scoffed at the idea that he had been delinquent for so long. After all, the candidate rejoined, no statute of limitations prevented the government from filing charges in 1972 or for that matter in 1983. Why had the state's attorney's office not pursued legal remedies if any evidence existed to substantiate such preposterous charges?[75]

Washington lost his license to practice law in 1970, he explained, because of disagreements with five clients (over a period of five years, 1962–66) who claimed that he had failed to perform work for them despite accepting retainer fees ranging from $30 to $150. The clients in four divorce cases had paid only a portion of the required retainer fees, Washington explained, so he did not complete the work for them. In the fifth instance, a traffic case, the client expressed unhappiness with the result and wanted a re-fund—which Washington eventually provided. The Chicago Bar Association originally suspended Washington's license for one year but, due to the intervening issue of the federal misdemeanor conviction and several procedural delays, did not reinstate him until five years had passed.[76]

Finally, even though Washington had said that he knew of no legal actions pending against him at the time he was seeking to have his law license reinstated in 1975, he had been sued five times. The candidate continued to maintain that he had not been aware of any lawsuits, and no legal trail existed revealing that he had received summonses to appear in court. Like the trivial misunderstandings that cost Washington his law license, the five inconsequential legal proceedings involved paltry sums of money. Epton discovered as well that Washington had fallen behind on the payment of some utility bills, and the *Chicago Sun-Times* later published a story that the candidate and two others had failed to pay property taxes on an abandoned property they jointly owned. Republicans suggested that although none of these disclosures amounted to much singly, a troubling picture emerged from the sum of the cases. At best, they charged, the Democratic candidate appeared to be a careless deadbeat; at worst, his habitual legal troubles made him an arrogant scofflaw. Friends and political allies offered a more benign interpretation that emphasized Washington's notorious indifference to money and material comforts. Impervious to his own financial well-being, said his backers, the absent-minded Washington was frequently cavalier in managing his own financial affairs. The less generous view adopted by Epton accentuated a worrisome inattention to detail, irresponsibility, and disregard for the law—not the qualities most voters sought in an aspiring mayor, the Republican observed dryly.[77]

As the Epton campaign built up steam and Washington scrambled to clear his name, Byrne resurfaced to announce that she was reentering the campaign as a write-in candidate. She characterized Chicago as much too "fragile" to be entrusted to anyone else's leadership and spoke of her fear that the city might suffer a relapse under a new administration. Vrdolyak announced that the Democratic Party would take no part in her insurrection, and other party leaders echoed the chairman's sentiments. Massachusetts senator Edward Kennedy endorsed Washington and flew to Chicago to dissuade Byrne from running because of the potential damage her recklessness might do to the party nationwide. No doubt salivating at how Byrne might split the white vote with Epton just as she had done with Daley and thereby increase his chances at election, Washington nevertheless condemned her reappearance in the contest as a selfish act. The voters would surely repudiate her disregard for fair play, he added. "They like to know that when you strike out, you're out," he commented, "and you don't come back and ask for three more strikes." After receiving a number of frosty welcomes at campaign gatherings, culminating in an especially inhospitable reception at a Southwest Side nursing home, Byrne abandoned the campaign. Her comeback lasted barely a week.[78]

As they did their best to ignore the distraction briefly supplied by the mercurial Byrne, Washington and Epton met in the campaign's lone televised debate on March 21. Following what had become a familiar pattern, Epton immediately went on the offensive, unleashing a fierce attack on his opponent's integrity. Flourishing a three-inch-thick black binder that his campaign staff had assembled for the occasion and frequently referring to its damaging contents, the Republican returned again and again to the tale of Washington's "salacious" legal history. Past behavior provided important clues about future conduct, Epton commented, and then asked several rhetorical questions about his opponent: "Will he obey the law? Will he do what he promises? Will he tell the truth?" Seemingly caught off guard by the vehemence of Epton's gibes, Washington seemed nonplussed in responding that he had explained his transgressions many times before. He had made mistakes, owed up to them, and paid the price. His repeated attempts to steer the conversation away from past events toward contemporary issues invariably met with the Republican's barbs steering the conversation back to the integrity issue. When Washington spoke of enforcing existing affirmative action statutes as mayor, for example, Epton retorted, "I'm glad the congressman is going to follow the law. It would be refreshing."[79]

Between the evening of the debate and Election Day, just less than three weeks overall, the thin veneer of civility present earlier in the mayoral contest disappeared completely, as Epton vigorously questioned his adversary's fitness to be mayor and Washington responded in kind. The campaign slogan the Republican coined, "Epton—Before It's Too Late," addressed the fears of white Chicagoans apprehensive of the changes a black mayor would impose. (Disingenuously or naively, Epton maintained at the time and afterward that the slogan referred only to Chicago's financial problems.) Drawing energy from the huge assemblages that roared approval at his speeches, the Republican strayed further and further away from the moderation and restraint that had defined his political career. With the chants of "Ber-nie! Ber-nie! Ber-nie!" and strains of "Bye, Bye, Blackbird" ringing in his ears, Epton pandered to the baying crowds. He told avid North Side listeners that it would be "sheer idiocy to support a man who had been sentenced to jail." Epton suggested that Washington "bring back some brains" from an out-of-town fund-raising trip and proudly boasted, "I've done more for the black community in one year than Harold has in a lifetime." Charging that the media had handled Washington's candidacy with kid gloves because of race, he threatened to file a grievance with the federal government for violation of the fairness doctrine. "If [the media] consider this [fairness] in equal time to my candidacy," he charged, "then they should go back to Russia and learn how to do it properly."[80]

When Epton claimed to be a victim of "reverse racism" because the press downplayed his opponent's foibles, Washington accused him of "playing with fire." Epton's irresponsible charges could lead to a "race war" by inflaming passions within the black community, Washington speculated, a potentially tragic outcome made possible because Epton "doesn't know what he's doing." Epton responded with a press release, calling Washington's statement "ugly, reprehensible and dangerous" and accusing the Democrat's campaign of making race an issue. The Republican strongly affirmed that he would never condone any racial appeals made by his supporters, a curious statement considering the tenor of the campaign being waged throughout many Chicago neighborhoods on his behalf.[81]

Washington lashed back at a candidate he felt was claiming to be above reproach while simultaneously behaving hypocritically, charging Epton with suppressing his own unsavory history of ethical lapses. A study released by the nonpartisan Illinois Public Action Council stopped short of accusing Epton of illegal influence peddling during his years in the general assembly but pointed out that his law firm had received a hefty $1.3 million in fees during that time. "Epton was so enmeshed in conflict of interest so pervasive that, in effect, he sold his seat in the House to the state's insurance industry," said the council's executive director. A report issued by the Illinois Department of Insurance similarly raised damaging questions about the Republican's abuse of power in making insurance policy for the state. Supplied with an analysis of Epton's voting record compiled by his staff, Washington also took aim at the characterization of his opponent as a moderately progressive legislator during fourteen years in the Illinois House. The revised picture that emerged from staff research showed Epton to be a penny-pinching conservative out of touch with the views and values of most lakeshore liberals. Washington's campaign advertisements therefore began portraying the Republican as an unfeeling plutocrat who voted against a reduction of the sales tax on food and medicine, lower utility costs for senior citizens, the funding of rape crisis centers and domestic violence shelters, collective bargaining for state employees, and a number of other public welfare expenditures championed by Washington. In contrast, Epton voted for a repeal of the inheritance tax, cuts in Medicaid funding, and prohibitions on state-assisted abortions for women on public aid. Research also revealed that Epton had missed a strikingly high number of roll-call votes in the House, according to a Republican colleague, because of serious health issues.[82]

The Washington campaign attempted to take advantage of questions raised by the media about Epton's medical history, specifically repeating claims that the Republican had been institutionalized twice for depression and had been prescribed lithium to control his anxiety. In a clipped response to the speculation about his mental health, Epton said that he had become anguished and withdrawn in 1975 after physicians had failed for years to find the cause of his recurring abdominal pain. Tests administered in 1979 finally identified ulcers in his small intestine as the source of the discomfort, after which prescription medicine alleviated the problem. In 1978, Epton added, he had been hospitalized at Michael Reese Hospital in Chicago for migraine headaches. Thus, the candidate maintained, medical conditions that flared several years earlier were no longer problematic, and, following a checkup on March 15, 1983, his personal physician had judged his health excellent. Speculation about Epton's emotional stability resonated because he appeared agitated, prickly, and quick to anger at campaign functions. His shrill, defensive outbursts at reporters and questioners, filmed and replayed to television viewers on the nightly news, exposed a striking volatility and raised questions about his self-possession. In the later stages of an intense nine-week campaign full of innuendo and calumny, the Republican candidate's composure seemed to be fraying.[83]

Epton's heightened irritability paralleled the rising level of tension in Chicago's white neighborhoods, where a sulfuric mixture of racism and territorialism made the Washington candidacy anathema. An incident on Palm Sunday, March 27, on the city's Northwest Side provided an especially graphic illustration of the hatred unleashed by the mayoral race. When Washington and former U.S. vice president Walter Mondale attempted to attend services at St. Pascal's Roman Catholic Church, Epton supporters jeered and jostled them in full view of television cameras and newspaper photographers. The demonstrators, wild-eyed with rage, screamed "Tax cheater," "Crook," "Carpetbagger," "Go Home," and the occasional racial epithet. Next to an entrance to the church, someone had recently spray-painted the words "Nigger Die." Because of the continuing commotion outside, Mondale and Washington remained in the church briefly before retreating to their car, surrounded by the shouting mob. Around the nation and the world, film footage of the frightful incident lent stark visual images to the written reports of the racism running rampant in Chicago. In articles such as "Chicago's Ugly Election" in *Newsweek* and "Racial Brush Fires" in the *New Republic*, national magazine correspondents recounted the lurid details of racial antipathy on full view in the city's white neighborhoods. Washington's media team hastily created a series of television commercials that employed dramatic film footage of the furious crowd at St. Pascal's to illustrate the fearful tone of the Epton campaign and to urge undecided voters to renounce racism with their ballots.[84]

Already thought to be the most scurrilous campaign in Chicago's time-honored tradition of sordid politics, the 1983 mayoral contest plumbed new depths five days before the election when Washington responded angrily to charges of having been arrested for child molestation. Rumors of Washington having been apprehended on a morals charge had been circulating in white neighborhoods for weeks, but grew in intensity in early April. An enterprising television reporter traced anonymous leaflets spreading the accusation, which further alleged that the police had suppressed the evidence and the *Chicago Tribune* had refused to print the story, to one of Vrdolyak's aides. Reporters for several local news organizations investigated the claims and found them baseless, as the *Tribune* revealed in a story published four days before the election. Washington had remained exceedingly calm throughout the bitter campaign, despite having been the subject of one personal attack after another, even reacting to the St. Pascal travesty with amazing equanimity, but his composure shattered in the face of the child molestation charge. Speaking at Mundelein College on the night of April 7, he inveighed against yet another assault on his good name.[85] Directing his indignation squarely at Epton, Washington thundered, "Do you want this job so badly? Are you so singularly minded that you would try to destroy character? If that is the kind of man you are, and if these are the kinds of dogs of racism and scurrilism that you are going to unleash, I say to you, Mr. Epton, I will fight you day and night."[86]

Although Washington's outrage was no doubt genuine, the decision to confront the rumors of child molestation forthrightly rather than ignore the unpleasantness also reflected a consensus among his advisers that Epton, Vrdolyak, and their cohorts had overplayed their hand and that such tawdry political tactics would backfire against the Republican candidate. Epton had condemned some of the vile speech and behavior being employed in his name, but his periodic denunciations (however heartfelt) carried little weight as the actions multiplied and the racial tension in Chicago worsened. At least partially responsible for the degeneration of the campaign's moral tone because of his own snide comments about Washington, Epton bowed to the prejudice and hatred animating some of his supporters and found himself unable to control the worst of it. As the increasingly disagreeable campaign lurched to its conclusion, he kept an unusually low profile, tempered his remarks about his Democratic opponent, and confidently predicted victory in the upcoming election.[87]

The fixation with race in March and April, much less evident during most of the primary, and the constant need to respond to his opponents' ceaseless attacks kept Washington from emphasizing the policies constituting his mayoral agenda as he had months earlier, but his campaign revived the reform message in the final days before the general election. The thinly disguised support of Epton by Vrdolyak, Burke, and other Democratic organization stalwarts allowed Washington to accentuate his antimachine message. Especially on the last weekend, the black candidate spent most of his time in lakefront precincts on the North Side, where reform appeals to the city's largest concentration of liberal voters had traditionally paid dividends. "The battle cry of this campaign never was and never will be race," he repeated at countless stops. "The battle cry is reform." Heralding progressive politics at every opportunity, he interrupted his mayoral campaign to deliver a comprehensive critique of the Reagan administration on behalf of the national Democratic Party in a syndicated radio broadcast on March 12. As he had been doing for weeks, he tied the important issues in the Chicago mayoral election to broader reform themes prevalent throughout the country. Having roundly condemned Reaganomics and called for a budgetary shift from guns and bombs to books and jobs, his speeches at the end of the campaign dealt less often with national concerns in favor of local issues: pleas for open government, neighborhood revitalization, new economic policies that favored job growth outside of the Loop, and an end to patronage. He felt that the invocation of those ideas should entice enough white liberal and Latino votes, in combination with the expected landslide of black ballots, to win the election.[88]

The victory formula worked as anticipated, if barely. Approximately 1.3 million Chicagoans voted on April 12 as a record 74 percent of registered voters trudged to the polls. In black neighborhoods, voters began queuing up long before polling places opened their doors at 6:00 a.m. In white precincts on the Northwest and Southwest Sides, poll watchers reported massive turnouts as well. Washington won by 46,250 votes, a narrower victory than in the primary, even though Epton carried twenty-eight of the fifty wards. The victor won more than 99 percent of black ballots—all the votes "except for the accidents," quipped Epton—and 75 percent of the much smaller Latino vote, improving significantly on the 13 percent of the Latino vote he had received in the primary. He received 12 percent of the white vote, roughly the same percentage as in the primary, and a disappointing one-third of the white vote along the North Side lakefront, despite the attention lavished on the area in early April. (He won 5 percent of the vote in the white wards of the Southwest and Northwest Sides.) Only 30 percent of those whites identifying themselves as liberals in exit polls voted for the black candidate, even as Democratic candidates for other offices in those locations easily cruised to victories over their Republican opponents. Even so, Washington advisers remained convinced, the vote totals for their man would have been even lower among white liberals if not for the intense campaigning along the lakefront just before the election. Presumably because of race and the disclosures about Washington's legal travails, white voters failed to warm to the Democratic mayoral candidate, and many of those who voted for him did so unenthusiastically. "Washington is almost the last person I would vote for as mayor," groused one Hyde Park liberal, explaining his reluctant vote for the Democrat, "but Epton *is* the last."[89]

Commensurate with his behavior during the campaign, an embittered Epton accepted defeat gracelessly. At the Grand Ballroom of the Palmer House Hotel on Election Night, he spoke encouragingly to his supporters at 11:00 p.m. and promised to return when the final vote totals confirmed his optimistic projections—but later declined to speak to the expectant crowd when he received the disappointing results. As he was leaving the hotel, Epton grudgingly offered Washington good luck in dealing with the city's financial problems but added, "Maybe he'll learn to pay his bills promptly and his taxes." In an apparent allusion to the lack of votes received from African Americans and Jews, two groups that had benefited from his philanthropy in the past, he said, "I certainly will save a lot of money in the future on charitable causes." His petulance persisted. Two days later, he said, "It seems like the people voting left their brains at home" and incredibly claimed that the Chicago media "should be thoroughly ashamed of itself for finding racial hatred when it was almost non-existent."[90]

In contrast to the spite and paranoia emanating from the Epton campaign, euphoria reigned among the Washington faithful. The predominantly African American crowd awaiting voting returns on Election Night at Donnelley Hall, a printing plant on the South Side converted into a makeshift auditorium, endured some harrowing moments as the Republican's mounting vote totals cut into an early lead for the Democrat but rejoiced late in the evening when the local news outlets declared Washington the winner. At about 1:30 a.m., welcomed by cries of "We want Harold! We want Harold! We want Harold!" the beaming victor made his way through the jubilant crowd to the podium. "You want Harold?" he asked the delirious throng. "Well, here is Harold." In the following minutes, he delivered a speech that emphasized the historic dimensions of the electoral victory and returned repeatedly to the themes of unity and reconciliation.[91] He said:

> Blacks, whites, Hispanics, Jews, gentiles, Protestants and Catholics have joined hands to form a new Democratic coalition and to begin in this place a new Democratic movement. The talents and dreams of our citizens and neighborhoods will nourish our government the way tributaries feed into the moving river of mankind. We have kept the faith in ourselves as decent, caring people who gather together as part of something greater than ourselves.[92]

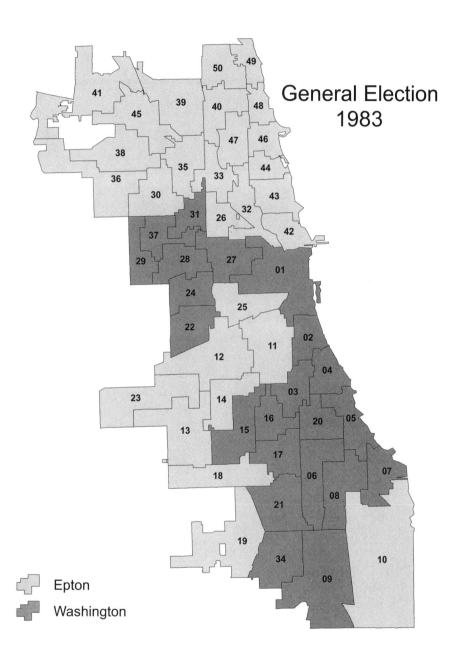

General Election
1983

Epton

Washington

Later that day, after grabbing a precious few hours of sleep, the mayor-elect attended an "ecumenical prayer unity luncheon" attended by, among other luminaries, eighteen Chicago religious leaders, Mayor Byrne, and Richard M. Daley, the state's attorney. Saul Epton, who substituted for his vacationing brother, offered generous congratulations to the mayor-elect. In his remarks to the press after the luncheon, Washington again spoke of harmony and healing. "We are now in the process of building a new city, a multi-ethnic city," he said, and promised "to reach out to every area of the city."[93]

Washington and his aides recognized that the challenge of conciliation would be considerable, but at first they understandably basked in the accolades pouring in from around the nation in recognition of their dazzling accomplishment. *Ebony* judged the election of a black mayor in Chicago as significant as Joe Louis's defeat of Max Schmeling in 1938 and Dr. Martin Luther King Jr.'s "I Have a Dream" speech at the 1963 March on Washington. The unlikely regime change in Chicago sparked excited talk of a black presidential candidate in 1984. Given the history of racial politics in the Windy City, virtually no one had predicted the election of a black mayor in 1983. Beginning with very little money and a bifurcated campaign organization—the divide between the Raby cohort and the Palmer followers never closed completely—the likelihood of engineering a successful insurgency had seemed remote indeed. Don Rose's characterization of the Washington campaign as the "most inept" he had ever seen accurately reflected the disorganization and unclear lines of authority that reporters and politicians described openly at the time, but failed to account for the positive element nurtured by the lack of structure—the creative tension, what Washington ally David Orr called the "constructive chaos." The energy and enthusiasm, the surge of voluntarism, turned a political election into a crusade and led to the phenomenal success at new voter registration, which ultimately produced the overwhelming black vote that gave Washington his victory. Yet the historic election of 1983, which ended in such remarkable fashion and seemed to portend a wholesale alteration of local politics and government, also left a radioactive landscape that threatened the possibility of healing. Winning at the polls, the proud and resourceful survivors of the Democratic machine made certain, was not the same thing as governing the city.[94]

3

THE DEVALUED PRIZE

Mayoral inaugurations in Chicago traditionally occurred in cramped city council chambers where, because of limited seating, only aldermen, assorted elected officials, and family members of the new mayor attended. On April 29, 1983, due to the historic nature of the election and the winning candidate's desire to be known as the people's mayor, Harold Washington departed from custom and held his inauguration in the spacious auditorium at Navy Pier. The four thousand guests present that day included the mayor-elect's fiancée, Mary Ella Smith, his siblings, friends, political supporters, and campaign workers, as well as the city's leading politicians, business executives, and other prominent citizens. Celebrities in attendance that day included such civil rights legends as Coretta Scott King, the Reverend Ralph Abernathy, Benjamin Hooks, and Dick Gregory. The excited crowd gave the mayor-elect a five-minute standing ovation when he entered the hall and strode confidently to the dais. After Mayor Byrne called the city council into session and Joseph Cardinal Bernardin delivered the invocation, Gwendolyn Brooks, the poet-laureate of Illinois, read a poem she had written for the occasion, and Studs Terkel read Carl Sandburg's "The People, Yes!" Judge Charles E. Freeman, Washington's friend and colleague from the Third Ward Democratic organization, administered the oath of office. When Judge Freeman completed the swearing-in ceremony, pandemonium erupted as the new mayor looked on and smiled broadly.[1]

The forty-second mayor of Chicago then delivered an inaugural address to the gathering at Navy Pier and a citywide television audience that called for racial healing, reiterated the promise of reform, and commented on the need for stringent economy measures to address the city's grievous financial problems. Alternately optimistic and foreboding, his speech struck a somber chord overall. "Racial fears and divisiveness have hurt us in the past," Washington allowed. "But I believe that is a situation that will and must be overcome." Sounding a conciliatory note, he added, "In our ethnic and racial diversity, we are all brothers and sisters in a quest for greatness. Our creativity and energy are unequalled by any city anywhere in the world." While appealing for racial comity, he called his election a mandate for reform and a cry for an end to business as usual in a city long controlled by a venal political organization. "One of the ideas that held us all together said that neighborhood involvement has to replace the ancient, decrepit and creaking machine," he told listeners. "City government, for once in our lifetime, must be equitable and fair." He pledged to open the operation of municipal government to the people, install a new level of transparency in city hall, eliminate the evils of patronage, and demand an unprecedented degree of accountability from municipal workers. "I'm asking the people in the neighborhoods to take a direct role in the planning, development and city housekeeping," he intoned, "so that our city becomes a finer place to live."[2]

The new mayor devoted a significant portion of his address to the worrisome financial situation he was inheriting from his predecessor in city hall. The gravity of Chicago's fiscal problems far exceeded what he and others in his campaign had been led to believe, Washington explained, with deficits in municipal agencies much greater than the press or public knew. He accused the spendthrift Byrne administration of accumulating a deficit well in excess of $150 million in the municipal budget, as well as $200 million shortfalls in the coffers of both the city's public education and its transportation systems. Compounding the budgetary deficiencies, the lame-duck administration had hired approximately 750 new city employees during its last days in office. To forestall financial exigency, Washington announced a moratorium on hiring, a freeze on city salaries, the release of several hundred recently hired city workers, and reductions in executive compensation. Moreover, he promised that new members of his cabinet would be employed at salaries considerably less than the amounts then being paid to Byrne officials. The grim financial reality could no longer be hidden from the public, the new mayor said, and the difficult journey back to fiscal responsibility would begin promptly the following Monday when he moved into his city hall office. Washington mused that Chicago's financial shortcomings, along with a host of other significant challenges, accounted for the "reflective and somber mood" in which he found himself at the beginning of his mayoralty.[3]

Apart from the Byrne administration's profligacy, African American mayors such as Washington came to power at a perilous moment in the history of U.S. cities. When newly elected black mayors moved into city halls, observed urban historian Jon C. Teaford, they found that whites had "carted away the wealth of the metropolis to suburban communities beyond central-city jurisdiction." The loss of population, industry, and retail to other regions of the country, as well as to outlying communities, left central cities saddled with shrinking tax bases at the same time that the demand for public services was increasing. Rising costs of welfare, law enforcement, and maintenance of aging infrastructures exacerbated the problems confronting neophyte black mayors. As University of Chicago sociologist William Julius Wilson noted, "The dilemma for urban blacks is that they are gaining political influence in large urban areas . . . at the very time when the political power and influence of the cities are on the wane." Increased reliance on federal aid, ongoing for decades, became problematic as Republican administrations in Washington, D.C., during the 1970s and 1980s practiced a "New Federalism" less generous to the cities. According to many scholars—and the new mayors themselves—historic breakthroughs in urban politics by African Americans had brought them only a "hollow prize." To be sure, the situation in Chicago by the early 1980s paled in comparison with the severity of conditions in other industrial cities such as Detroit, Cleveland, and St. Louis, among others. Still, if Harold Washington was not saddled with a hollow prize in 1983, Chicago in the throes of deindustrialization and federal disinvestment could certainly be termed a devalued prize.[4]

Sustained and substantial population loss underscored Chicago's declining fortunes. The city lost nearly 558,000 inhabitants from 1960 to 1985, a 15.7 percent decline, during a time when the surrounding suburban areas grew 58 percent in population. In part, the exodus from Chicago fed the 16 percent growth in the six-county metropolitan region of northeastern Illinois (Cook, Lake, DuPage, Will, Kane, and McHenry Counties). No longer merely an important but secondary force existing in the shadows of the dominant metropolis, the conglomeration of suburbs around Chicago was becoming instead the dominant geopolitical region in the state. By contrast, the steady drain of population from the Windy City meant a devastating loss of human capital and the surrender of political influence in state government.[5]

Having been the Midwest's major metropolis during the nation's rise to industrial prominence in the nineteenth century, Chicago became a principal casualty of deindustrialization in the second half of the twentieth century. Like so many other Rust Belt communities, the Windy City struggled to make the transition from an economy based on manufacturing to one centered on service and high technology. The post–World War II flight of industry took a terrible toll on Chicago, long the premier workshop of the nation's heartland. The uprooting of industry commenced immediately after the war, as 243 factories left Chicago for the suburbs from 1946 to 1950. The city's share of manufacturing employment in the metropolitan region fell from 71 percent in 1947 to 54 percent in 1961; by 1965 the majority of the area's industrial jobs existed outside the city limits. The exodus continued at an accelerated pace. The city lost 60 percent of its manufacturing jobs after 1960, relinquishing 123,000 jobs between 1973 and 1977 and another 150,000 between 1979 and 1983. During the 1970s alone, one-fourth of all factories in Chicago shuttered their doors. The list of factory closures in the 1980s, which included Western Electric's gigantic Hawthorne Plant, Johnson and Johnson, Campbell's Soup, the Schwinn Bicycle Company, Wisconsin Steel, and a large portion of USX's South Steel Works, collectively accounted for the loss of more than 30,000 jobs.[6]

The departure of Chicago's signature industries in particular highlighted the sweeping changes weakening the local economy. The Union Stockyards, long the symbol of the city's blue-collar prominence, surrendered advantages of scale and lost business because of changing market conditions, the truck's replacement of the railroad car as the most efficient distributor of processed food, and the rise of Kansas City, Fort Worth, and other regional meatpacking centers. The long, slow decline of the stockyards in Chicago concluded in the early 1970s when the few remaining meatpacking plants ceased their hog and cattle operations. The construction of Wacker Drive and the Eisenhower Expressway exchange sent the apparel industry, once shoehorned into lofts west of the Loop, to suburban plants and southern states. The apparel, food processing, and furniture industries, which had accounted for more than 25 percent of the metropolitan region's workforce before the Second World War, employed fewer than 16 percent by 1957. The steel industry, which expanded farther around the southern tip of Lake Michigan into northwestern Indiana to meet military demand during World War II, continued to thrive in the prosperity of the early Cold War years. By 1954 Chicago-area foundries and blast furnaces had surpassed Pittsburgh's plants as the world's leading iron and steel producers, yet signs of future decline were evident by the end of the decade. Steel companies replaced old equipment and introduced new processes sparingly and, because limited space curtailed plant expansion within Chicago, opened new facilities outside city limits on Indiana lakefill. The steel industry steadily began to lose its market share to other domestic and foreign producers, a development that accelerated in the 1970s and afterward.[7]

Economic experts attributed job loss to globalization and other inexorable international forces beyond the control of local governments, but idle workers and vulnerable families ravaged by escalating unemployment rates looked to city hall for solutions to their worsening predicament. A number of troubling questions confronted mayors and other local officials. Were large manufacturing cities such as Chicago doomed to continuing contraction? Was the loss of population, industry, and retail irreversible? Was a reduction in manufacturing inevitable, and, if so, how could cities adapt to emerging economic realities? How could cities such as Chicago best weather the transition from industrial-based to service-based economies? In the absence of a national industrial policy, could local and state industrial policies be helpful? Should municipal governments respond with planned industrial districts, technical schools, enhanced job training, and other nostrums? Should mayors concede the loss of industry and increase their reliance on the traditional progrowth agenda that emphasized downtown rejuvenation—which, in Washington's case, meant the repudiation of his campaign's call for greater attention to neighborhood development? Along with all mayors of declining Rust Belt metropolises in the 1980s, Washington faced these perplexing questions as part of the urgent need to develop an effective strategy for economic renewal.[8]

Unlike many mayors of large industrial cities who were seeking solutions to the same imposing economic problems, however, Washington approached the task lacking a unified political coalition in support of his

efforts. The tenuousness of the campaign alliance between the black nationalists and the Dearborn Street contingent never subsided, and their
different expectations for a Washington mayoralty remained a powerful
factor dividing the two groups after the election. Both factions believed
their contributions essential to the victory, saw the electoral triumph as
vindication of their ideals, expected that Washington would initiate fundamental changes in city government that established policies and practices
to their liking, and anticipated that the lion's share of the new mayoral administration would come from their ranks. The new mayor faced a dilemma
in seeking to balance the interests of two groups that occasionally agreed
on priorities but more often harbored strikingly different visions of city
government's future operation. Moreover, Washington could not afford
to alienate either the black nationalists or the mainstream integrationists
when he would doubtless need the backing of both groups in order to be
reelected in four years.

Wedded to the ideal of reform, Al Raby and his cohorts downtown appreciated the importance of the overwhelming black vote for Washington
but saw lakeshore liberal support as having made the critical difference in
the recent victory. In the extremely close contest, the decision to concentrate on the lakefront precincts during the last few days of the campaign
seemed to have paid off. Patrick Caddell, a pollster for the Washington
campaign, attributed the electoral outcome solely to the last-minute saturation of the progressive-minded North Side. Because of the decision to
rebut Bernard Epton's charges and affirm the candidate's reform credentials
one last time, Caddell insisted, Washington "snatched victory from the
jaws of defeat." Washington's genuine commitment to reform, repeated
often in a variety of venues during the campaign, articulated clearly in *The
Washington Papers*, and strongly affirmed in his inaugural address, promised an end to patronage specifically and machine rule generally. The new
administration would be open and accessible to the public and introduce
policies based on equity and fairness—all goals cheered by the Independent
Voters of Illinois, Independent Precinct Organization, Better Government
Association, and other silk-stocking organizations dedicated to cleansing
Chicago's sordid municipal government. During his first days in office, the
new mayor thrilled lakefront liberals with a series of symbolic actions that
demonstrated his commitment to efficient government. In short order, he
cut his own salary by 20 percent, traded in the mayoral limousine for a less
ostentatious Oldsmobile 98, imposed a limit on campaign contributions

from companies having been awarded city contracts, released a detailed plan for the modernization of municipal operations, and introduced computers and other new forms of technology into antiquated city bureaucracies that continued to manage municipal affairs with manual typewriters, handheld calculators, and mimeograph machines.[9]

A citywide reform crusade devoted to efficiency and honesty seemed decidedly less enthralling to many African American loyalists on the South Side. Perhaps no position taken by Washington unsettled black nationalists more than his condemnation of patronage. The mayor proclaimed his intention throughout the campaign to sign the Shakman decrees, court rulings that prohibited politically motivated hirings, firings, and all coercive actions against municipal employees. In depriving the Democratic machine of an indispensable means of ensuring subservience and installing an apolitical merit-based system, the mayor saw the reform as a vital component of his drive to open up city government. Lu Palmer and many others saw no sense in enforcing the Shakman decision, however. In hard economic times with unemployment in African American neighborhoods easily reaching double digits, the loss of patronage jobs would impose additional hardship on the needy. After white machine politicians had long hoarded a disproportionate share of city jobs and other perquisites of office, the time had come for balancing the scales. To the victor belonged the spoils, and the black community had at last emerged victorious. Denying that the time had come to make amends for past transgressions, however, Washington promised fairness rather than compensation for historical injustices. When he chuckled that "no one but no one in this city will be safe from my fairness," bewildered black supporters who expected to garner a cornucopia of political jobs and favors as the fruits of a hard-earned victory shook their heads in disbelief. "Fuck fairness!" cried Palmer. Democratic committeeman Niles Sherman put it less profanely, saying, "Those individuals who put the mayor where he is deserve more than a pat on the back." Washington said of the restlessness in the ranks of his supporters, "I've got five, ten, sometimes a dozen of my own people [in the city council] who are giving me hell because I don't 'take it all.' They're telling me I'm crazy. I know what I'm doing. But they're giving me a hell of a time. Shit, half of them would be with Vrdolyak right now, if they didn't know their wards would kick their ass for it."[10]

Many African Americans, especially the black nationalists, also expressed dismay at the composition of the Washington administration taking shape in the spring and summer of 1983. Having contributed barely more than

10 percent of the mayor's winning vote, whites composed a majority of the transition team appointed by the mayor. The pattern continued when he selected cabinet heads and other high-ranking members of the new administration. Although Washington appointed an unprecedented number of African Americans to key positions in city government—including his chief of staff, corporation counsel, press secretary, chief lobbyist, police superintendent, housing commissioner, and chairman of the Chicago Housing Authority—he stopped short of the overwhelming majority the black nationalists expected and indeed demanded. Nor, with the exception of James Montgomery as corporation counsel, did Washington select African Americans with prominent civil rights credentials. (Montgomery had earlier won an eighteen-million-dollar wrongful death settlement against the City of Chicago for the murder of Black Panthers Fred Hampton and Mark Clark by police.) The mayor appointed a number of whites to administer cabinet departments, ranging from Streets and Sanitation to Economic Development to Planning. Black critics of the nascent Washington administration objected to the presence of too many white liberals, too many bureaucrats and technocrats, and too many self-professed reformers who were much more interested in efficiency and municipal housecleaning than in exhaustive social change.[11]

Even when Washington appointed an African American to be his chief of staff, a post arguably second only to the mayor in the city hall hierarchy, the black nationalists repudiated the choice. Washington had brought Bill Ware, who had served as his chief of staff in the U.S. House of Representatives, back to Chicago to serve in the same capacity in the mayor's office. Ware had grown up in Chatham, a middle-class black neighborhood on the city's South Side, and had received his undergraduate and law degrees from the University of Chicago. Resettled in Washington, D.C., he had served as legislative counsel for the American Civil Liberties Union and director of the legislative affairs office of the U.S. Equal Opportunity Commission before going to work for Congressman Washington in 1981. A bureaucrat obsessed with efficiency in municipal government and dedicated to the professionalization of the mayor's office, Ware shunned politics and remained aloof from discussions about patronage. The black nationalists, who viewed him as a remote good-government reformer more at ease with academic theorists and white lakeshore liberals than with the South Side common folk, cared little for Ware's preoccupation with process; they wanted a more accessible chief of staff who shared their desire to rectify past injustices.[12]

Racial tension also existed among the twenty-one members of the city council who found themselves in league with the new mayor. The black machine aldermen linked to Washington by their constituents' expectations continued to suspect the motives of the independent white Democrats with whom they were suddenly allied, and the white reformers still looked askance at the progressive bona fides of their new African American compatriots. The small white minority within the Washington coalition often felt ostracized and disrespected. "It was like we were just there as adjuncts," complained Martin Oberman, independent Democrat from the Forty-Third Ward. "Like whites were just a necessary evil." When disputes arose and the white aldermen proposed reputedly color-blind reformist policies, many African Americans distrusted their motives and argued for more straightforwardly redistributionist approaches that openly benefited minorities. A lack of trust poisoned the atmosphere in coalition caucuses. It was "brutal" behind the scenes, remembered Forty-Ninth Ward alderman David Orr, where a "bullying mentality" prevailed until Washington came into the room and harassment of the white minority suddenly ceased. The mayor remained steadfast in supporting progressive measures, but some black members of the coalition expressed dissatisfaction at every turn. The uneasy situation scarcely improved with time, recalled Orr.[13]

Unable to rely on a harmonious political alliance in unified pursuit of his objectives, Washington prepared to deal with a large number of Chicagoans (nearly half of the electorate) who had voted against him and remained dubious of his ability to heal the city's wounds and govern effectively. He doubted that the opposition could be won over readily but counted on his candor, unprecedented attention to neighborhood concerns, and effective operation of city government over time to reduce the antipathy facing a black mayor in white ethnic neighborhoods. The rancor dissipated very slowly, if at all, during his first year in office. Opposition to Washington remained unyielding on the city's predominantly white Northwest and Southwest Sides, where residents feared they would lose the racial insularity maintained there for generations. Six months after the election, led by Jean Mayer of the Southwest Parish and Neighborhood Federation, eight community organizations from the Southwest Side and an equal number from the Northwest Side merged to create the Save Our Neighborhoods/ Save Our City (SON/SOC) coalition. "Blacks and Latinos have set their agendas," asserted Mayer. "It's time white ethnics did the same." At least superficially, SON/SOC and the new administration seemed to share many populist goals in common—neighborhood-based economic development, increased citizen participation in local government, and improved service delivery outside of the downtown, among others. But the fledgling organization's leaders questioned the mayor's sincerity in espousing neighborhood development and called for unified resistance to city hall initiatives.[14] "The Declaration of Neighborhood Independence," SON/SOC's founding charter, read less like a general statement of principles than like an ad hominem attack on the new mayor. It began:

> These are extraordinarily trying and dangerous times for Chicago. None know or understand this better than the predominantly white ethnic neighborhoods of our city. Instead of the order and peace which we have rightfully grown to expect over the years, a distressing politics of needless conflict and mindless vengeance has become the order of the day. Responsibility for this deplorable state of affairs rests with the current Mayor of Chicago, Harold Washington! Behind the well-crafted, public veneer of the Mayor as Charmer, Healer and Reformer, there thrives a cynical political opportunism, ready to exploit every racial fear and antagonism without regard to their dire consequences.

A number of community leaders disavowed the organization's inflammatory rhetoric, and the Office of Human Relations of the Roman Catholic Church's archdiocese sent a letter to parish priests in affected areas recommending that they keep their distance from SON/SOC. Nevertheless, membership in the organization grew rapidly after the 1983 election.[15]

In April 1984, more than one thousand people attended SON/SOC's first convention. Jammed into an auditorium at the downtown Hyatt Regency Hotel, standing-room-only crowds listened to speeches outlining relevant issues to the Northwest and Southwest Sides, viewed slide-show presentations on neighborhood preservation, and voted on a series of proposals introduced by five committees. The housing committee proposed a home-equity insurance plan that would provide residents with a hedge against depreciating real estate values, a safeguard against the expected desegregation of all-white neighborhoods that SON/SOC members feared would be unleashed by a black mayor. The economic development committee advanced a linked development plan that would levy a fee on new downtown office buildings, the proceeds from which would be allocated to the neighborhoods for investment according to the desires of the local inhabitants. The other committees introduced measures related to local real estate practices, access to Federal Housing Administration information, and public education. Convention delegates approved all of the proposals unanimously or by overwhelming margins. In the considerable coverage devoted to the gathering by the local press, SON/SOC leaders portrayed the organization's members as the "new victims" of racial politics in Chicago.[16]

In addition to the grassroots opposition he confronted in white neighborhoods, Washington simultaneously confronted a resolute group of elected officials with sufficient resources for undermining his attempts to initiate reform—or even at times for hindering the administration's ability to conduct routine city business. Attempts to disrupt the activities of the new administration began immediately after the election, as Washington complained in a letter to Byrne, with accelerated hiring and promotion within city agencies. The extent of the opposition to the incoming administration became evident during Washington's first day on the job when he found that the mayor's office on the fifth floor of city hall had been picked clean of official paperwork. Byrne had left absolutely nothing to her successor, absconding with every scrap of paper that dealt with city business—including the voluminous mayoral files, an indispensable reference for comprehending the city's labyrinthine bureaucracy. She had even carted off much of the furniture, an Oriental rug, televisions, typewriters, a video camera, and other items belonging to the city. The mayor's desk contained only a single paper clip tucked away inside an otherwise empty drawer. "I sat there and laughed for ten minutes," Washington chuckled. "I almost cracked up. There was nothing there, no personnel files, nothing." Many of Byrne's assistants treated members of the incoming administration with equal disdain. Requests for interviews went unanswered, and many exiting administrators left incomplete files in half-empty file cabinets. Rumors swirled around city hall about impromptu shredding parties in the final days of the Byrne mayoralty.[17]

A palpable uneasiness settled over the downtown buildings housing Chicago's municipal government during the first days of the Washington administration, nowhere more so than in city council chambers. In Chicago's long and storied history of boisterous politics, incidents of friction between the mayor and city council abounded. Intraparty clashes had not been uncommon, as factions within both the Democratic and the Republican Parties frequently battled over patronage and policy. But never before had the breach between the executive and legislative branches in the city been so deep, burned with such intensity for so long, or threatened so seriously to disrupt the operation of local government. The combination of the political machine's resistance to reform, the residue of an unusually rancorous election, and the toxic element of racial tension that lingered long after Election Day yielded a flammable mix that the new mayor struggled unsuccessfully to defuse. Feral opposition to Washington materialized at once, long before the city council convened to mark the start of a new mayoral administration.[18]

Four years earlier, having flayed the Democratic machine unmercifully during the mayoral campaign, Byrne quickly made peace with the party leadership after her election and cooperated easily with the "evil cabal" she had denounced so bitterly just weeks before. In 1983 a number of prominent Democrats indicated their willingness to mend fences with Washington as well, the residual tensions regarding race notwithstanding, if the new mayor forswore his antimachine animus. Race mattered less to them than jobs and contracts. "None of this would have happened if Harold had come to us the way Byrne did," Fourteenth Ward alderman Edward Burke told the mayor's representatives. Unwilling to repudiate his reformist campaign rhetoric, however, Washington reiterated his intentions of dismantling patronage and initiating sweeping changes in city hall. Recognizing the impossibility of an accommodation on the terms dictated by the machine, he refused to cut deals that would betray the principles his campaign had clearly staked out during the previous months. "I'm not going to pull a Byrne," the defiant mayor vowed, and any chance of a rapprochement with the machine leadership evaporated.[19]

On April 19, the uneasy peace gave way to open warfare when Washington informed Alderman Vrdolyak that he would be stripped of two powerful positions on the city council: the post of president pro tempore and the chairmanship of the Building and Zoning Committee. Vrdolyak quickly agreed to surrender the former but not the latter. When Washington insisted on the loss of the committee chairmanship, the alderman angrily retorted, "You're attacking my manhood," and threatened to build a coalition within the city council to block the new administration's policies. The infuriated mayor lashed back: "You supported Epton, bullshitted me, and you've been organizing from day one. Let's get it out front." In the two weeks prior to the first scheduled meeting of the city council, the two politicians worked feverishly to assemble a working majority of aldermen in the fifty-member city council. Washington began with twenty reliable votes, sixteen African American aldermen and four white independents committed to reform. (A considerable number of the black aldermen, habitual supporters of the machine who blanched at the new mayor's avowed intention of abrogating patronage, might normally have sided with Vrdolyak if left to their own devices but could not have survived politically in their communities if they opposed Washington.) The mayor thought he could achieve a majority easily by recruiting a handful of votes from two sources: the eight returning aldermen who had supported Richard M. Daley in the election and the seven newly elected whites. Vrdolyak and the other fourteen aldermen who had (openly or secretly) supported Bernard Epton, the core of the opposition to Washington, needed to capture at least eleven votes from the same group of fifteen. To Washington's surprise, he recruited only one additional supporter, while Vrdolyak succeeded in bringing fourteen of the fifteen undecided aldermen into his developing alliance. By the time of the first city council meeting on May 2, the maverick alderman's faction outnumbered the mayor's forces twenty-nine to twenty-one. The Vrdolyak Twenty-Nine, as they came to be called, lacked the necessary thirty-four votes to override a mayoral veto but possessed an adequate number to derail all of Washington's initiatives. Legislative gridlock ensued.[20]

The twenty-nine-to-twenty-one alignment in the Chicago City Council, which created a prolonged legislative paralysis, resulted from a combination of demographic, political, and personal factors. Just as in the election, race continued to be a significant part—but not all—of the story. Many members of the Vrdolyak Twenty-Nine, especially the newly elected aldermen, delayed until the last moment before aligning against the mayor. In the end, they bowed to arguments about race, political power, and self-interest. As Vrdolyak and his emissaries ceaselessly pointed out to the newcomers, the predominantly white wards represented by the hesitant aldermen had voted against Washington by considerable margins; siding with the solidly white bloc in the city council simply reflected the desires of their constituents. "Epton beat Washington six to one in my ward," commented Alderman Joseph Kotlarz of the Thirty-Fifth Ward. "I would have had a lot of grief if I'd been on the other side." Vrdolyak and his allies cynically exploited racial fear, just as they had done during the campaign, to cultivate anti-Washington feeling among the skittish aldermen. Holding the powerful office of Cook

County Democratic chairman, Vrdolyak could offer additional inducements to recruit potential allies. In firm control of the party apparatus, for instance, he could promise to help aldermen become ward committeemen. He also won over new aldermen by offering them the patronage and money associated with prestigious committee chairmanships. "You got to take who gives you the most," admitted Thirty-First Ward alderman Miguel Santiago, the only Latino among the Vrdolyak faction. Two interrelated factors—the perception that a black mayor posed a threat to white neighborhoods and the fealty to a political machine threatened by a reform administration— bound the twenty-nine renegades tightly together in rebellion.[21]

Able leadership by the tough, savvy Vrdolyak also proved to be indispensable. Having transcended his hardscrabble origins and earned the reputation of a ruthless political infighter, he never hesitated to challenge authority when advancing his own career. After growing up above his father's tavern amid the steel mills on Chicago's Southeast Side, Vrdolyak earned an undergraduate degree from St. Joseph's College in Rensselaer, Indiana, and a law degree at the University of Chicago before becoming a personal injury lawyer. Elected alderman and committeeman of the Tenth Ward by the age of thirty-four, the ambitious Vrdolyak became one of the young Democrats in the city council who openly chafed under the suffocating leadership of Mayor Richard J. Daley in the 1970s. A Croatian barred from the party's Irish inner circle, he became the most prominent of the "Young Turks" who impatiently pushed for more power and recognition. Smart, handsome, by turns amiable and abrasive, and seemingly always spoiling for a fight, "Fast Eddie" Vrdolyak reveled in his reputation as a charming rogue. Opinion in the city divided about whether the irascible Vrdolyak acted primarily out of crass racism or political opportunism—Washington publicly leaned toward the latter, once calling his adversary an "engaging rascal"—but no one denied his effectiveness in managing the rebellious coalition. An untiring cheerleader, he kept morale high by convincing his allies that they could win. He frequently called meetings to plot strategy, hosted the other members of the Vrdolyak Twenty-Nine at his home, created a buddy system to oversee the commitment of young aldermen who showed signs of wavering, and even sent flowers to his allies' wives on Mother's Day. Dissatisfied with verbal pledges to oppose the mayor in all instances, he required each alderman to sign a loyalty oath to the coalition. Vrdolyak's scrupulous attention to detail paid off, as he successfully nurtured a camaraderie and sense of purpose that kept the twenty-nine dissimilar aldermen unified in the face of challenging circumstances. Fear and intimidation played a role as well. "Name me a white guy who can cross Vrdolyak," challenged an alderman.[22]

Second in command of the anti-Washington forces, Alderman Edward M. Burke determined not to surrender the power he had accrued during a lifetime in politics. A florid orator with an encyclopedic knowledge of city statutes and *Robert's Rules of Order*, he infused city council meetings with heaping doses of hyperbole and malice. Burke ferociously debated his opponents and peppered the mayor with disruptive motions and abstruse points of order, while Vrdolyak more often maneuvered behind the scenes. The scion of local Democratic machine royalty—his father, Joseph P. Burke, had unilaterally run the Fourteenth Ward as alderman and committeeman— he served on the police force and graduated from law school before laying claim to his political birthright at an early age. At twenty-four, he became the youngest committeeman in Chicago history and, at twenty-five, the second youngest alderman. He attempted to shield his predominantly white Fourteenth Ward constituents from minority incursions, opposed gay rights, and defended policies tied to the preservation of law and order. Stylishly dressed and meticulously coiffed, self-righteous and smug, he treated his enemies with disdain and frequently questioned their honor. Burke's fervor proved to be a powerful accelerant in combination with Vrdolyak's guile.[23]

At the dramatic May 2 showdown in city council chambers, the legislative body's first meeting after the election, the aldermen greeted Washington with the standing ovation customarily afforded a new mayor. The show of goodwill ended abruptly. Aware that his supporters lacked a majority and seeking time for additional negotiations with the opposition, Washington hastily gaveled adjournment and led his twenty-one followers out of the room. Surprised but reacting swiftly, Vrdolyak hurried to the podium, called the council back into session, declared the existence of a quorum, and presided over the adoption of a series of resolutions giving his twenty-eight allies control of the city council's administrative structure. The resolutions, which passed unanimously in rapid fire, reorganized the council while enhancing its authority in local government, increased the number of committees so that virtually all of the Vrdolyak Twenty-Nine could be awarded chairmanships, and installed Edward Burke as the chairman of the powerful Finance Committee. The city council adjourned in short order, Vrdolyak and his followers having concluded what the newspapers referred to as a coup. Asked why he had not done more to offset Vrdolyak's machinations and avoid such humiliation that day, Washington blurted, "Because I wasn't going to kiss their asses."[24]

For several days following the pivotal city council meeting, representatives from the two factions privately discussed the possibility of reconciliation. Washington and Vrdolyak met in the mayor's office but failed to arrange a cease-fire. Washington canceled the next scheduled city council meeting as negotiations dragged on to no avail. On May 16, Cook County circuit judge James C. Murray heard arguments from attorneys representing the two groups and found in favor of Vrdolyak and the other aldermen who remained at the May 2 meeting. Possessing a quorum and acting legally and properly, the judge ruled, the twenty-nine aldermen had conducted council business in an appropriate manner. Murray affirmed the rules drafted and leadership appointments made by the truncated city council and denied Washington the authority to veto the actions. He also noted in his twenty-two-page opinion, however, that the mayor could veto measures funding the newly created committees. Contemplating the continued disruption of municipal affairs and chiding the city council for its belligerence, the judge urged the two sides to seek compromise in the best interests of Chicago's residents. Lawyers for the mayor appealed the ruling to the Illinois Supreme Court, which upheld Judge Murray's decision on June 27. Washington promptly vowed to file a civil rights lawsuit in federal court, charging that the actions of the Vrdolyak Twenty-Nine had illegally reduced the number of African Americans in city council leadership positions from eight to four, but later announced that he would abide by the existing court rulings. The stalemate continued.[25]

The conduct of municipal business degenerated into a sadly predictable sequence of actions on the city council floor. Frequently, the Vrdolyak Twenty-Nine passed legislation over the objection of the minority faction. Washington then vetoed the measure. When the mayor or his acolytes introduced an ordinance, the opposition defeated it by a vote of twenty-nine to twenty-one. If someone in the majority then moved adoption of a facsimile, which passed by the same count, Washington responded with a veto. After the predetermined voting concluded, another tiresome tableau played out as aldermen exchanged insults and accusations in heated debates. Members of the unruly gallery heckled the legislators, and shoving matches occasionally ensued between ill-tempered aldermen. The mischievous Vrdolyak usually sat primly in his seat, smirking at the chaos unfolding around him, although he sometimes joined in the florid verbal exchanges. Meanwhile, the city council failed to approve Chicago's two-billion-dollar budget, a new gang crime bill, and many of the mayor's appointments to important government offices. "They used to say that Chicago *wasn't* ready for reform," said Washington. "Well, Chicago is. It's the *City Council* that's not." Local comedian Aaron Freeman dubbed the bitter legislative struggle the "Council Wars," a satirical reference to the popular film *Star Wars*, and the disapproving *Wall Street Journal* reproachfully referred to Chicago as "Beirut on the Lake." In the summer of 1983, Washington saw his mayoralty mired in dysfunction.[26]

Stymied at every turn by the city council, the mayor launched new policies by executive order whenever possible and otherwise attempted to initiate reforms by any means available. Within the first three months of his administration, Washington managed to make some meaningful changes—sometimes with city council approval but most times without— that he hoped would provide a foundation for far-ranging alterations yet to come. Following through on one of his principal campaign pledges, for example, he took the first step in ending patronage by signing the Shakman decree, prohibiting the hiring of employees for political reasons. Unlike in past years, when local officials determined the next fiscal year's municipal budget behind closed doors and finalized the particulars shortly before its adoption, the mayor promised to create a decentralized budget-making process whereby residents would participate in identifying priorities and the city council would be given more time for review of the preliminary draft. He issued an executive order on freedom of information, granting the citizenry unprecedented access to local government documents and other public records. Arguing that the informal and unofficial arrangements long practiced by machine government fostered favoritism, he spurned the custom of managing labor relations with handshake agreements in favor of collective bargaining for all city employees. He created the Mayor's Task Force on the Homeless, which subsequently led to increased funding for overnight shelters and emergency food dispensaries. He also managed to change the manner in which the city utilized Community Development Block Grant (CDBG) funds awarded by the federal government.[27]

The CDBG program, created by the Housing and Community Development Act of 1974, awarded block grants to cities for housing, public facilities,

child care, and economic development, ostensibly in blighted neighborhoods. Title I of the act required cities to utilize the grants "principally
[to] benefit people of low and moderate income" but provided no means to
ensure compliance. In prior years, Chicago mayors had unilaterally decided
how to spend the federal dollars and ignored the recommendations made
at the local public hearings mandated by the 1974 law. Byrne treated the
program's guidelines so cavalierly and used the funds for such a wide variety
of purposes that CDBG awards became known locally as "Jane Byrne's Fix-It
Fund." Her plans for the largesse had openly violated federal guidelines in
spending money for activities clearly prohibited by the legislation, most notably by fattening patronage rolls and by making improvements in pockets
of affluence in Chicago rather than in the city's impoverished areas. With
the help of Congressman Dan Rostenkowski, Washington negotiated a deal
with the Department of Housing and Urban Development (HUD) whereby
the federal government would overlook the money the Byrne administration had overspent if Chicago strictly adhered to program guidelines in
the future. To allocate the $147.7 million in CDBG funds awarded Chicago
for 1983–84, which meant countermanding the budget already created by
the Byrne administration, Washington scheduled public hearings downtown to allow individuals and community groups to recommend changes
in the plans for allocation. After further revision, the proposals would be
forwarded to the city council for another round of assessment before submission to Washington, D.C.[28]

With relations between the mayor and his aldermanic foes poisoned by
the Council Wars, negotiations over CDBG funds proceeded acrimoniously.
At first, the Vrdolyak Twenty-Nine insisted on the right to approve all
federal grants and contracts. Not surprisingly, Washington refused. With
a June 1 deadline for submission of the city's application to Washington,
D.C., rapidly approaching, the two sides reached an agreement that both
gave the city council unprecedented influence over the spending of federal
funds and fulfilled the mayor's pledge to open the process to broader-based
participation. The compromise allowed the city council to disapprove any
federal grant or contract in excess of $50,000 and empowered the mayor
to shift (without council approval) up to 10 percent of the federal dollars
from one project to another. The final funding formula for 1983–84 met
Washington's goal of distributing increased sums of money to community
programs, shifting $13.5 million designated for patronage hires under the

Byrne plan to neighborhood improvements, with the stipulation that the aldermen would play a role in selecting sites for infrastructural improvements in their own wards.[29]

Fiscal responsibility had long been an article of faith for municipal reformers, and Chicago's financial predicament in 1983 reinforced the mayor's determination to halt the flood of red ink that began during the previous administration. Byrne had denied Washington's request that she cease making unnecessary last-minute appointments during the final days of her mayoralty, thereby irresponsibly increasing municipal payrolls. She disputed the incoming administration's estimate of a $168 million deficit and blamed the Daley and Bilandic administrations for the financial problems she inherited; all parties acknowledged that the city had compiled a significant debt by outspending its revenue. "Getting hold of the financial mess we inherited from Jane Byrne was something else," Washington sighed. "She ran this place like a Ma and Pa candy store, and we had to spend a lot of time straightening it out." The primary bond-rating agencies, Moody's and Standard & Poor's, had downgraded Chicago's bonds sufficiently in 1979 and 1980 to increase the city's cost of borrowing money by millions of dollars. As painful as workforce reductions and other economy measures would be, especially in less affluent minority communities, Washington recognized the necessity of restoring fiscal balance by cutting spending. Within his first year in office, he laid off approximately seven hundred municipal workers, sold several municipal parking garages, and canceled a property tax cut conceived by the Byrne administration. (Despite the city's imposition of so many exacting budget cuts, Chicago's business leaders worried that Moody's and Standard & Poor's would lower municipal bond ratings because of the persistent warfare between the mayor and the city council.) In the areas of the municipal bureaucracy outside the purview of the city council, especially in the mayor's office, Washington imposed as many economies as possible.[30]

While attempting to restore the city's financial health, the mayor also sought to stimulate economic growth. His campaign pledge to bring new businesses and jobs to the neighborhoods as well as to downtown, the commitment to divert economic development funds from the Loop to historically neglected areas of the city, aroused considerable concern in Chicago's business community. Talk of decentralized development "scared the daylights out of many of Chicago's business leaders," reported *Chicago*

Tribune urban affairs reporter R. C. Longworth, who sympathized with the concerns of the very investors "whose dollars were needed if the city is to grow." Chicago's leading businessmen anticipated difficulties communicating with the new mayor because they shared very little in common with him and knew few of the same people; Washington privately admitted that he felt uncomfortable in the presence of wealthy entrepreneurs. Pondering the consequences of an upset in the election, in a December 13, 1982, editorial titled "White Business and Black Mayors," *Crain's Chicago Business* had warned: "[Washington] has to win the support of a basically suspicious business community, which in the final analysis, is as it should be. Rep. Washington comes from a neighborhood—culturally and politically—that is foreign and forbidding to white business people. They harbor a very real fear that they will be unable to deal with Rep. Washington's administration because they don't know the territory, and they fear also that they'll be unwelcome."[31]

Chicago's economic elite had enjoyed amicable relations with the Democratic machine for decades, freely pursuing a downtown-first development agenda that few politicians of either political party ever seriously questioned. The city's giants of industry and commerce—the banks, department stores, utilities, daily newspapers, real estate developers, architectural firms, and other corporations with headquarters in the city core—had worked closely with the Daley, Bilandic, and Byrne administrations in fashioning a series of plans for the city's future growth. Organizations such as the Chicago Central Area Committee, the Commercial Club, and the Chicago Association of Commerce and Industry effectively represented the interests of these wealthy businesses as well. Suddenly, the merchant princes of State Street and the financial lions of LaSalle Street faced the prospect of dealing with the city's first black mayor, an avowed reformer with populist inclinations whose campaign rhetoric raised real questions about the path of Chicago's future economic development. Sam Mitchell, director of the Chicago Association of Commerce and Industry, put the Washington administration on notice: "If incentives to invest in downtown are removed, there is still plenty of land available in the suburbs."[32]

Washington indeed intended to invest in neighborhoods, but his philosophy revolved around a balanced development approach predicated upon the existence of a prosperous downtown. According to his design, a thriving central business district would generate sufficient revenue to enable precious public resources to be invested judiciously in neighborhoods with unfulfilled economic potential. Like his predecessors in the mayor's office, he understood the economic facts of life in the nation's third-largest city. He knew that the central business district, which measured slightly less than 1 square mile out of Chicago's 224 square miles, accounted for approximately one-third of the tax base. He also knew that downtown blocks teeming with construction portended a bonanza for the city in the form of rising tax revenues. Thus, he had no intention of curtailing a real estate boom in the urban core that began several years earlier during the Byrne administration, a serendipitous spike in investment that eventually injected eleven billion dollars into the rapidly developing West Loop between 1979 and 1986. Washington deviated from earlier mayors, however, in his determination to share a large portion of the largesse with the neighborhoods. It need not be feast or famine for comparatively small businesses situated outside the Loop, he insisted, when sufficient economic growth and reasonable distribution could produce a steady diet of financial meals for all Chicago business owners.[33]

To spearhead the development effort, Washington selected someone with the kind of background in neighborhood activism that unnerved the business community all over again. Rather than pick a successful business-man committed to the construction of large-scale projects in the central business district, he chose an academic with strong ties to community or-ganizations. He appointed Rob Mier, a professor in the School of Urban Planning and Policy at the University of Illinois at Chicago and the founder of its Center for Urban Economic Development (CUED), as commissioner of the Department of Economic Development (DED). A Vietnam veteran who had denounced the war after his tour of duty and become involved in the peace movements in Oakland and St. Louis, Mier joined the UIC faculty in 1975 to teach urban planning and community development. In 1978 he founded the CUED, a think tank that provided technical assistance and mentoring to community-based organizations. In 1982 Mier became a charter member of the Community Workshop on Economic Development, an ad hoc watchdog group that emerged to monitor the Reagan adminis-tration's identification of enterprise zones and evolved into a permanent organization devoted to neighborhood empowerment. He helped draft the economic development platform outlined in *The Washington Papers*, the crucial policy document of the 1983 mayoral campaign, and joined the administration soon after the election. Along with other activists recruited from Chicago's many neighborhood organizations, Mier and his cohorts brought to the Washington administration a countercultural sensibility and an aversion to traditional methods of economic development that made the boosters of Chicago's downtown extremely wary. "We'll try to work with Rob," said a Loop banker, "but he's going to have to prove to the business community that being populist doesn't mean being antibusiness."[34]

An iconoclast who scoffed at much of the conventional wisdom about coping with deindustrialization, Mier rejected the idea that Chicago should concentrate its efforts on competing against other cities for runaway industries. "There are 300 plant relocations per year in the whole country," he said, "and there are more than 20,000 localities chasing them." Cities and states that lured businesses away from their prior locations by offering excessively lavish financial packages achieved only short-term gains, he argued, and perpetually faced the need to increase incentives to retain firms they had enticed from elsewhere. Arguing that the increased mobility of capital in the global age created a permanent buyer's market, Mier preached retention and expansion of manufacturing rather than cutthroat competition for new industry. In that regard, he also remained highly skeptical about the recruitment of high-tech industries as a panacea for ailing cities. Such ventures, generously underwritten by state governments in California's Silicon Valley, the research triangle in North Carolina, and along Route 128 near Boston, produced disappointing job growth, he contended, and the benefits bypassed minorities and other especially needy groups. In his view, the expansion of high-tech industry would likely occur in the suburbs (not the inner city) before demand became saturated nationally. The best bet for Chicago remained small business over large industry, neighborhood enhancement over central business district aggrandizement, and jobs over real estate development.[35]

As a community activist who had always been an outsider exhorting city hall to behave differently, Mier saw government service in the Washington administration as a rare opportunity to ensure that policies embodying equity and fairness be given a respectful hearing on the inside. An unvarnished idealist, he also believed that the close proximity of residents to their local government gave city dwellers the potential to create a laboratory of democracy in which the citizenry's heightened expectations held municipal officeholders and bureaucrats to a higher standard of accountability. Mier openly admitted that the new mayoral administration possessed a social justice agenda, demanding particular attention to issues involving poverty and race, that would shape economic development as fully as any other aspect of local governance. Just as surely as economic development would emphasize job creation, a strategy based on the expansion of employment opportunities would target the needs of minorities and women. Because the supposedly unerring operation of the market had consistently overlooked the welfare of women and minorities in the past, local government could not rely on normal economic growth to rectify inequities. Improving the quality of life for the people most in need of an economic boost required not only weighing the need for development in the neighborhoods versus downtown but also balancing manufacturing- and service-sector growth.[36]

In the Washington administration, incoming cabinet members believed, corporate interests would no longer be ceded carte blanche authority to determine development policy. Chicago might continue to pursue a large number of service jobs, but Mier and his colleagues in the Department of Economic Development would simultaneously strive to limit the hemorrhaging of manufacturing employment. Unwilling to forgo the wealth created by downtown aggrandizement, the city would continue to grant tax breaks and other incentives to attract new businesses. Chicago would still offer sweetheart deals, for example, for the building of luxury hotels that provided such low-wage service jobs as maids, bellboys, and valet parking attendants—what Mier called "McJobs"—but would also demand something in return from the wealthy hoteliers. City hall would require that businesses investing in Chicago's downtown set aside a generous portion of the new jobs for retrained minorities, women, and members of other underrepresented groups. At the same time, personnel in the Department of Economic Development would work overtime to restore manufacturing in the city's sagging industrial areas and to bring small businesses to scattered, run-down commercial strips.[37]

In one of the administration's most innovative steps to foster a new kind of industrial development, the Department of Economic Development created the Local Industrial Retention Initiative to identify the industrial development organizations with the greatest potential to maintain industrial activity in a number of neighborhoods throughout the city. Rather than dealing with manufacturers individually, as city hall had always done in the past, LIRI would provide opportunities for decentralized planning and enhanced funding in a systematic fashion. Administering the program, Arturo Vazquez sought to improve relations between small businesses and the neighborhoods by ascertaining that each local industrial council included businessmen as well representatives from neighborhood groups. The local government program provided money for neighborhood industrial councils and community organizations to attract and retain manufacturing. As well, the neighborhood groups served as liaisons between city hall and relatively small businesses in their geographical areas. By the end of 1983, LIRI had awarded seventy-six thousand dollars in CDBG funds to four community-based organizations, with the expectation that the program would expand in later years. For a relatively modest expenditure, the mayor's office could monitor and respond to business needs, receive early warning signs of possible industrial flight, and assess the possibility of attracting new manufacturing firms to specific locations.[38]

As part of its effort to retain industry, the administration allied with community organizations to limit residential and commercial land use through the creation of Planned Manufacturing Districts (PMDs). Disputing the Chicago Tribune's charge that the protection of manufacturing would mean "snuffing out needed development," the mayor said that "Chicago has the opportunity to be one of the few American cities in recent years to balance massive residential and commercial development with a strengthened manufacturing base." The city could not afford to consign all industry to the South and West Sides, he continued, while preserving downtown and North Side locations where factories once existed for retail establishments, luxury apartments, and condominiums.[39]

The drive to pass enabling legislation for PMDs in the city council, which finally came to fruition after many years of effort, began with the first industrial-to-residential conversion in an established manufacturing area of the city in 1983. The conversion of an abandoned factory into fifty-seven loft condominiums that year in the North Branch Industrial Corridor, an area on the city's Near Northwest Side that included the Clybourn Avenue, Goose Island, and Elston Avenue manufacturing concentrations, alarmed activists, who feared that the replacement of industry with upscale residences, offices, and retail would eliminate high-paying factory jobs. The neighborhood LIRI group, the Local Employment and Economic Development Council, began organizing among the corridor's residents, businesses, and trade unions to forestall industrial displacement. Its efforts nurtured by sympathetic bureaucrats in the Department of Economic Development and the Department of Planning, LEED fashioned a blueprint for the Clybourn Corridor PMD. Washington approved the proposal shortly before his death, somewhat later than neighborhood activists had hoped, which became the prototype for the Goose Island and Elston Avenue PMDs that began operation in 1989. Despite a tardy and gradual commitment to the innovative planning tool, Chicago pioneered in the use of PMDs during the Washington administration.[40]

The newness of the DED, which lacked a clear mission statement, gave Mier the opportunity to establish meaningful goals in an area of local government traditionally devoid of influence. Writing on a blank slate, the Washington appointees established policies and procedures commensurate with the agency's new identity. In 1981 Richard Longworth, the *Chicago Tribune*'s influential reporter, had published a multipart series detailing the ineffectiveness of Chicago's Economic Development Commission. The following year, a major bureaucratic reorganization of local government combined units within the Department of Planning and the Department of Neighborhoods with the Economic Development Commission to form the new Department of Economic Development. In its first year of operation, the new agency spent a large portion of its thirty-five-million-dollar annual budget on making infrastructural improvements in the city's industrial areas; Mier and his subordinates envisioned undertaking much more ambitious tasks than completing street and bridge repairs. The major goal of the department, the new leadership repeatedly lectured staff members who remained in place following the reorganization, would be providing jobs for able-bodied people throughout the city. "Whatever this department does ought to be judged by the standard of creating jobs for Chicagoans who are in need of employment," Mier said simply. At a time of national economic recession with the local unemployment rate hovering around 10 percent, with racial minorities especially in jeopardy, local government would use its resources to lure businesses and create jobs.[41]

Mier and his like-minded followers discovered that the ethos of a government agency, fortified by a workforce composed largely of patronage appointees, could not be transformed overnight. Accustomed to decisions about major undertakings being brokered in a political process far removed from their offices, staff members of the Department of Economic Development and its forerunner had settled into a comfortable routine of handling small-scale projects. Mier described conditions in the department's offices when he arrived as abysmal, the workers indifferent, equipment antiquated and unsatisfactory. He recalled, "One of our favorite metaphors was that we won the opportunity to drive a 1940s jalopy in a 1980s road race. Worse yet, the pit crew was either inexperienced, working for the mayor's opponents, or often, both. [Kari] Moe was fond of saying that trying to get things done was like fighting a war with someone else's army."[42]

Duplicating the situation that existed in a myriad of Chicago's municipal offices, personnel ranks in the DED included several different groups with widely varying opinions about the new directions identified by the administration: Washington supporters eager to revise the definition of economic development, lackadaisical workers who needed to be motivated and given an appreciation for what the agency could accomplish, and political appointees allied with the mayor's enemies who continued to work sluggishly as before or, worse, sabotaged new initiatives. Believing that the transformation of a hidebound institution would take two to three years, Mier struggled immediately to impose a number of necessary changes. He fought to shift the department's focus from politics to service and to create a new respect for ideas originating in neighborhood groups. His strict adherence to equal opportunity hiring within the unit, including the establishment of goals for diversifying the workplace, reinforced the ideal of equal opportunity citywide in the pursuit of jobs. Within the calcified municipal bureaucracy, he labored to foster an atmosphere of openness and accessibility that nurtured innovation and creativity. Ideally, such changes would dissolve organizational barriers, improve communication, and stimulate teamwork within the Department of Economic Development while creating linkages to other agencies in city hall.[43]

Within six months of the 1983 election, Washington's chief of staff, Bill Ware, directed Mier to centralize and stimulate economic development by forming a subcabinet of commissioners from the various cabinet departments engaged in related activities. Acting at the direction of the mayor, who wanted to break down existing fiefdoms in city hall and create a forum for the coordination of policies, Ware sought to create a more streamlined bureaucracy where trained professionals (not politicians) could share ideas and refine programs. Mier began presiding over weekly development subcabinet meetings, which included (in addition to Economic Development) the commissioners of Planning (Elizabeth Hollander), Housing (Brenda Gaines), the Mayor's Office of Employment and Training (Maria Cerda), and Cultural Affairs (Fred Fine). Mier, Hollander, Gaines, Cerda, and Fine came to the administration from a variety of backgrounds, none related to electoral politics. The Department of Economic Development continued to lead the way, while the other cabinet departments contributed to the effort of reflecting the values and achieving the goals expressed in *The Washington Papers*.[44]

The development subcabinet existed, at least in part, to administer projects of such size and significance that no single department could manage the complex financial, political, and logistical tasks by itself. A long line of "builder mayors" in the Windy City had fashioned their legacies essentially on the strength of the large-scale construction projects completed during their time in office, a commonplace that led many Chicagoans to evaluate mayoral administrations by the size of the bricks-and-mortar footprints left downtown. William H. "Big Bill, the Builder" Thompson had eagerly taken credit for the city's construction boom of the 1920s, and Edward J. Kelly had adroitly utilized New Deal funding to complete a remarkable number of schools, roads, parks, and other large-scale projects during the Great Depression. Martin F. Kennelly had supported the construction of the celebrated Prudential Building, the first downtown skyscraper built in more than a generation, and initiated a number of projects in the early 1950s that came to fruition under his successor, Richard J. Daley. Presiding over the biggest building boom since the Great Fire of 1871 and guiding an architectural renaissance that reconfigured the city's downtown, Daley outdid all of his predecessors and set a new standard for builder mayors. His gaudy list of achievements included O'Hare International Airport, the John Hancock Building, the Sears Tower, a University of Illinois campus, mammoth high-rise public housing projects, and a massive network of multilane expressways. At the time that she vacated city hall, Byrne claimed credit for a list of expensive projects in the planning stages that included a world's fair, a new downtown public library, Navy Pier refurbishment, North Loop redevelopment, and new rapid transit lines to O'Hare and Midway Airports. The Washington administration's insistence on decentralization, neighborhood participation in decision making, and jobs rather than real estate development appeared to clash with Chicago's venerable builder tradition.[45]

Throughout the 1983 campaign and during his first months in office, Washington eschewed the need to erect massive edifices in the Loop—the kinds of structures that Mier derisively called the "monumental and grandi-ose"—in favor of small-scale "people projects" dispersed throughout the city. Such an approach allowed community participation and dovetailed nicely with the administration's philosophical commitment to decentralization. The mayor frequently expressed an aversion to spending large amounts of the city's money on a few oversize projects and only reluctantly agreed to ignore his misgivings. He found it necessary to do so occasionally, however, grudgingly admitting the need at least to give serious attention to the com-pletion of projects initiated before his mayoralty began. As commissioner of planning Elizabeth Hollander remembered, the mayor realized that he really had no choice in such instances. Washington also believed that, given the strength and durability of the "builder mayor" tradition in Chicago, the press would judge his administration a failure without some towering visual evidence of construction in the central business district. The absence of co-lossal new buildings would be seen as an inability to govern effectively. Issues concerning the venues for three of Chicago's professional sports teams—the Bears, White Sox, and Cubs—had to be settled, for example, to keep any of the franchises from departing the city for the suburbs or Sun Belt cit-ies willing to build them new stadiums. If he lost one of the city's teams, Washington told Mier, neither he nor any other African American candidate could ever be elected mayor again. DED officials looked at cooperation with urban growth coalitions in the construction of megaprojects downtown as a generally distasteful prospect and a potentially dangerous precedent, but accepted the uneasy collaboration as a necessary evil.[46]

In the early 1980s, Chicago's downtown business community united around the desire to complete one project more than any other: a world's fair the city would host in 1992. Indeed, many members of the city's economic elite had come to view the creation of a grand spectacle to commemorate the five hundredth anniversary of Columbus's voyage to the New World as an essential element in Chicago's return to greatness. The Columbian Ex-position of 1893, still widely regarded as one of the most influential world's fairs in history, had proclaimed Chicago's status as one of the premier cities of the modern age, and so another extravaganza of comparable scope and creativity could affirm its continued importance in the postmodern era. Hosting a world's fair would provide Chicago confirmation of its status as a "world-class" city. Earlier mayors had at least endorsed the idea in principle—Byrne had indicated her wholehearted backing of the project—

and Illinois governor James R. Thompson enthusiastically promised state assistance. The topic surfaced occasionally during the 1983 election, but Washington never spoke at length during his campaign about the strength or weakness of his commitment to the project. The downtown growth coalition, accustomed to having city hall's support for all such ventures in the past but already wary of the new mayor's effect on the business community's future prospects, saw his backing for the massive undertaking as absolutely essential.[47]

In addition to Washington's own well-known lack of enthusiasm for building what he called "Taj Mahals" in the heart of the city, other concerns posed by Chicagoans left his support of the World's Fair uncertain. The uneven history of world's fairs in the United States during the post–World War II decades raised questions about the utility and—most important—profitability of these enterprises. Pursuing international acclaim and downtown rebirth, Seattle (1962), New York City (1964), San Antonio (1968), Spokane (1974), and Knoxville (1982) had held expositions that razed large swaths of real estate, built massive new commercial and entertainment structures, created and landscaped new parks, and improved highway networks feeding into central business districts. In each case, public financing dwarfed the dollar amounts contributed by the private sector. Despite sunny predictions of windfall profits, the world's fairs proved to be extremely costly affairs that frequently left stockholders and taxpayers in arrears. Seattle netted a small profit, and Knoxville essentially broke even, but the other fairs lost significant amounts of money. When the visiting crowds departed and work crews disassembled pavilions and concession booths, reconfigured downtowns remained as lasting evidence of massive urban renewal. In other words, groused the unhappy residents of cities burdened with hefty debt obligations, opting for a world's fair simply became another example of the city deferring to the whims of an urban growth coalition pursuing new avenues for downtown redevelopment at all costs.[48]

The product of an alliance between Loop business interests and city hall, advocacy for the 1992 Chicago World's Fair looked very familiar to careful students of earlier expositions. In the late 1970s, a coalition of banks, corporations, architects, and planners began working with Mayor Byrne to obtain for the city the designation of 1992 world's fair host and in 1981 created a nonprofit organization to plan and manage the event. Chaired by Thomas G. Ayers, former president and chief executive officer of Commonwealth

Edison, the 1992 World's Fair Corporation consisted of representatives from
seventeen of the leading corporations representing a variety of industries
in metropolitan Chicago: energy (Commonwealth Edison); manufacturing
(Borg Warner, Inland Steel, Zenith Radio, Esmark, and General Dynamics);
communications (the Chicago Tribune Company, Field Enterprises, Johnson Publishing, and the Illinois Bell Telephone Company); banks (Chicago
Title and Trust Company, Continental Bank, Harris Bank, and the First
National Bank of Chicago); retail (Marshall Field's Department Store); advertising (Foote, Cone, and Belding); and development (Dearborn Park
Corporation). The 1992 World's Fair Corporation's original estimates of the
project's cost ranged from $885 million to $1 billion. By situating the fair
just south of the Loop in the area known as Burnham Harbor, the planners
and architects designing the project envisioned not only a generous return
on investment in the form of revenues but also the first major step in the
redevelopment of the Near South Side.[49]

The 1992 World's Fair Corporation's actions immediately generated resistance from a number of dissidents suspicious of traditional top-down,
core-centered development, opposition emanating from many organizations outside of and activists inside of the Washington administration.
Opponents of the fair balked when a series of revisions to the original
plan utilized less landfill in Lake Michigan and nudged the site westward
into existing neighborhoods. The final plan for the fair's location, which
extended from Thirteenth Street south to Thirty-First Street and from the
Pilsen neighborhood east to the lake, required demolishing large sections
of Pilsen and Chinatown to make room for parking lots. Further, the design called for the elimination of existing residences and small businesses
while at the same time featuring plans for the construction of housing for
middle- and upper-income groups seeking an attractive location near both
the Loop and the lakefront. Plans for the new upscale housing development also included shopping centers and malls for the convenience of the
new affluent residents. Because of the proposal's likely impact on Pilsen,
the city's largest Mexican neighborhood, substantial resistance developed
among members of the Commission on Latino Affairs and other Latino
organizations. Throughout the Near South Side and beyond, dissenters
objected to the possibility that world's fair development would undermine
viable neighborhoods on behalf of moneyed downtown interests. If redevelopment ransacked such lively communities as Pilsen and Chinatown,

went the argument, the fair should be relocated elsewhere—or not held in Chicago at all. Dissidents also dismissed the claim that a world's fair would generate thousands of well-paying new jobs for Chicagoans.[50]

As he had during the mayoral campaign, Washington refrained from sharing his views on the world's fair during his first months in office. His reluctance to take a clear position on the issue even confounded the city's planning commissioner, Elizabeth Hollander, who said, "It was never clear to me whether the [administration's] aim was a better fair or no fair." Caught between the avid boosters of the business community and a city council majority, on the one hand, and impassioned neighborhood activists and a vocal city council minority, on the other, the mayor issued vacuous statements nominally endorsing the fair but steadfastly maintaining that the city would not assume financial responsibility for hidden costs or disappointing attendance. Instead of providing pledges of wholehearted support, which the 1992 World's Fair Corporation doggedly sought, he procrastinated and called for additional study. Refusing to proselytize in favor of the project, Washington gave speeches to neighborhood organizations that struck a mildly skeptical tone. His appointments to the World's Fair Authority, the organization that supplanted the 1992 World's Fair Corporation, represented a wide cross-section of Chicago's economic and geographical interests instead of the customary selection of the Loop's representatives. Signals from city hall likewise remained mixed, fueling rumors of internal divisions within the administration. Officials from the Planning Department and the Mayor's Office of Intergovernmental Affairs appeared to be touting the fair behind the scenes, while Department of Economic Development personnel seemed discreetly negative. Absent city hall's usual issuance of boilerplate statements endorsing business investment and economic growth, apprehensive world's fair boosters pored over the tea leaves and feared the worst.[51]

Inactivity on the North Loop Redevelopment Project also raised concerns about Washington's purported aversion to spending huge sums of money on the refurbishment of a portion of downtown that had been in steady decline for years. The new mayor inherited the project, as the two previous mayoral administrations had done, without a clear plan for how to pay for the eradication of blight from a twenty-seven-acre site in the central business district immediately south of the Chicago River. Under Byrne, efforts at anchoring the redeveloped area with a hotel complex on one of the project's six blocks unexpectedly fell through, and progress on the entire undertaking ground to a halt. Washington publicly expressed concern about aspects of the North Loop plan but stopped short of officially ending the city's participation. He assigned the project to the Department of Planning, where the commissioner, Elizabeth Hollander, quietly explored additional development possibilities, especially Chicago's initial use of Tax Increment Financing to spearhead investment. The preliminary discussions about TIFs proceeded slowly, and, as months went by in 1983 without any announcements of progress, questions persisted about the fate of the North Loop.[52]

Members of Chicago's economic elite similarly wrung their hands over the status of another big downtown project, the conversion of Navy Pier into a tourist attraction. Opened in 1916 as Municipal Pier, the three-thousand-foot structure jutting into Lake Michigan north of the Loop originally doubled as a busy freight terminal for harbor shipping and a recreational facility. Renamed Navy Pier in 1927 to honor World War I veterans, the downtown appendage variously served as a jail incarcerating draft dodgers, a convention center, a terminus for excursion boats, a naval training center during the Second World War, and the original campus of the University of Illinois at Chicago. In 1976, following extensive renovation, the city utilized the pier's auditorium as the center of its American Bicentennial celebration. In 1980, after conducting a "highest and best-use" analysis, the city entered into negotiations with the James W. Rouse Corporation of Baltimore, Maryland, to redevelop the pier into a year-round commercial emporium containing four hundred thousand square feet of retail and entertainment space. Besides leasing public property to the corporation, the city faced the need to make public improvements costing $60 million. On July 1, 1982, the city and Rouse, the developer of Boston's Quincy Market, Baltimore's Harbor Place, New York City's South Street Seaport, and other festival marketplaces, signed a letter of intent for the $280 million project that designated June 1983 as the completion date for negotiations.[53]

With the new Washington administration still settling into city hall offices in June, both parties agreed to postpone the deadline for negotiations until December 31, 1983. At first, the mayor expressed concern about the potential impact of the project on Chicago's finances and stated that none of the city's general fund revenues would be dedicated to the project. At the same time, however, members of the administration expressed a willingness to work with the Rouse Corporation to reach a satisfactory arrangement.[54] Recalling the feeling about the project at the Department of Economic Development, Mier said:

> The Navy Pier was important because at the same time we were throwing up roadblocks in front of the World's Fair, we were engaged with this other large project, the Navy Pier. It was important to be really aggressive about the Navy Pier precisely so that we wouldn't be typecast as knee-jerk opponents to every large project. We also chose the pier for this approach because it was being promoted by the Rouse Company, and the company's managers had a reputation for being flexible.[55]

Representatives of the city and the development firm made steady progress on the specifics of the architectural designs but achieved less success untangling financial knots. Consequently, the administration asked the city council to postpone the negotiating deadline yet again to June 1984, but the city council's Joint Committee on Special Events and World's Fair and Ports, Wharves, and Bridges rejected the request for another six-month extension. In 1984, with negotiations at a standstill, the city closed the pier altogether due to its deteriorating condition and rising maintenance costs. The Navy Pier development project appeared to be yet another casualty of the Council Wars.[56]

The routine, day-to-day unpleasantness of the Council Wars, in which acerbic aldermen continued to trade insults across the aisle and to transact very little city business, gave way to an outburst of animation in October 1983 in conjunction with what the *Chicago Tribune* called "the first major political embarrassment" of the Washington administration. On October 21, 1983, the *Tribune* reported that the mayor had asked for and received the resignation of one of his top aides, Clarence McClain, a street-smart, flashy character Washington kept around to provide access to anyone being "professionalized" out of access to city hall. McClain had accumulated a number of vice convictions between 1965 and 1971 and had failed to pay thirty-one thousand dollars in back real estate taxes and water bills on property he owned. Chicago police records showed that he had been arrested and found guilty of soliciting a prostitute, pimping, and operating a house of prostitution; in addition, the courts had dropped five other charges against him during those years. The mayor and his staff discussed the matter and quickly concluded that McClain, who had served as a loyal

Washington assistant for approximately a decade, would have to be cut loose to keep the aide's disreputable past from becoming a major scandal and a lingering distraction. Washington acted swiftly, admitting that he had not required a thorough background check before hiring McClain and requesting his resignation as soon as he found out about the criminal record. But the administration's adversaries pounced just as quickly. The McClain incident raised serious questions about Washington's screening procedures for high-level appointments, intoned indignant aldermen, and also created doubt about the backgrounds of others working in and around the mayor's office.[57]

Washington's foes in the city council exploited the McClain incident with relish, calling for an investigation of the administration's hiring practices and using every opportunity to question the moral fiber of the mayor and his associates. Burke inaccurately referred to McClain as "an arrested child molester" and charged during one television appearance that city government was being "run by pimps and panderers." On a radio talk show, the acerbic alderman said, "When the Washington-Bloom-McClain political caravan comes around to your neighborhood, the mothers and fathers of Chicago children better lock them up and keep them out of the way." Vrdolyak joined in, asking how Chicagoans could trust a mayor who "surrounds himself with ex-cons, including a convicted pimp." Exploiting the media's eagerness to uncover any hint of political scandal, Washington's political enemies persisted in subsequent weeks to invoke the lone example of shoddy hiring in an administration that had been praised uniformly by the press for the high quality of its appointments.[58]

The Vrdolyak forces in the city council pressed their advantage in the last weeks of 1983 by attempting to turn the mayor's reform of the city's budget-making process against him. Each annual budget for the upcoming year had to be approved by the city council before midnight, December 31. Under machine rule, previous mayors had maintained firm control of the budget-making exercise, while the compliant city council served as a rubber stamp and quickly approved the document with only cosmetic changes. The mayor's office had traditionally drafted the budget behind closed doors and sent its handiwork to the city council for inspection in late November, leaving precious little time for participation by the legislative branch and even less for public scrutiny. Budget making had been an entirely secretive process, dominated by the mayor, with no public oversight. In 1983 Washington kept his promise to make substantial changes, introducing a new procedure largely conceived by his chief of staff, Bill Ware. Under Ware's direction, administration staffers gathered suggestions at dozens of open meetings throughout the city and then incorporated those ideas into the crafting of a preliminary budget. Next, the administration held hearings during the summer at several locations throughout Chicago on the budget draft to allow individuals and organizations to recommend revisions. Then the amended budget went to the aldermen well before Thanksgiving, weeks earlier than before, to encourage full discussion by a city council acting as a truly deliberative body. The changes introduced by Ware hypothetically paved the way for a more participatory process but also created opportunity for the Vrdolyak Twenty-Nine to make additional mischief.[59]

The 1984 budget submitted by Washington to the city council on November 14, 1983, contained a little something for everyone: austerity measures for economy-minded reformers who perceived the need to slice more fat out of a bloated municipal payroll, new soak-the-rich taxes that pleased progressives, and a new 6 percent tax on commercial leases conceived by Burke that would permit the elimination of a monthly head tax on city employees. (The *Chicago Tribune* strongly criticized the mayor's budget for excessively increasing the tax rate, especially for creating the levy on commercial leases, as a risky maneuver that the newspaper warned could drive businesses out of the city.) Three weeks later, much to the total surprise of the mayor and his council allies, the City Council Finance Committee presented its own 1984 budget for consideration. Instead of just modifying the city council's role in fine-tuning the mayor's fiscal plan, Burke and his committee cohorts broke new ground by submitting a 547-page alternative budget that resembled the original version in many ways but also differed in some notable instances. Washington's 30-page response to the city council budget objected to the elimination of specific jobs as cost-cutting measures, the proposal to slash executive salaries further, and an additional allocation of $563,000 for city council committees. The mayor especially balked at the proposed oversight authority granted the council in all municipal hiring, a change that he noted would shift personnel matters from professional managers back into the hands of patronage-starved aldermen. Most important, observed the *Tribune*, Burke's brash challenge threatened the mayor's exclusive prerogative to set the city's financial priorities.[60]

Burke and the mayor reached agreement shortly before Christmas on a compromise budget, which the Finance Committee dutifully approved, but hard-liners among the Vrdolyak Twenty-Nine refused to vote for the

measure on the city council floor. Complaining that the mayor and his followers had fared too well in the compromise, the hard-liners succeeded in
sending the latest version of the budget back to the Finance Committee
for another round of hearings. On December 27, after a historic five-week
battle between local government's executive and legislative branches, the
city council approved the 1984 budget. Both the mayor and his opponents
singled out aspects of the final document as triumphs for their side in
the protracted struggle. Washington secured wage increases for top administration executives and the reinstatement of 425 vacant jobs that had
originally been cut by Burke. The city council agreed to the creation of
eight new committees, seven of which would be chaired by the mayor's allies. The Vrdolyak Twenty-Nine gained job security for an estimated 8,000
"departmental service employees" in city government who had been hired
by previous administrations without civil service protection. The majority
bloc also succeeded in emasculating the Department of Neighborhoods,
which had long been seen as a political arm of the mayor's office, through
its reorganization as the Office of Inquiry and Information and severe cuts
in staff. "It used to be a helluva lot easier in the old days," sighed Burke in
assessing the new budget-making process, "when you got your instructions
[from the mayor's office] about what to do."[61]

In evaluating the 1984 budget, the local press railed against the new costs
to city government that partially offset the revenue increase produced by
new taxes. Higher administrative costs occasioned by the increase in the
number of city council committees and relatively fewer cuts in the municipal
workforce at a time of supposed financial exigency, chided critics, could
hardly be seen as a victory for a reformist mayor who had pledged leaner,
more efficient budgets during the recent campaign. A close reading of the
final budget, which included a roughly equal number of gains and losses
for each faction, could perhaps best be termed a draw. Overall, however,
the media portrayed the 1984 budget as a resounding victory for Washington's foes—especially Burke—who had supposedly expanded the power
of the city council at the expense of the mayor. The fact that Washington
had initiated the change in the budget-making process that made such an
outcome possible, which he still proudly defended as a means of democ-
ratizing municipal government, appeared to many Chicagoans as more
evidence that the mayor could not defeat his wily city council opponents.
Either as naive reformer or ineffective politician, the local media implied,

Washington again seemed overmatched in his struggle against the devious Vrdolyak, Burke, and their henchmen.[62]

The perception that the Vrdolyak Twenty-Nine were winning the Council Wars and subverting the mayor's attempts to implement his agenda gained greater currency during the last months of 1983 and the first months of 1984. Citing the "lack of cooperation needed to solve some of the city's fiscal problems," Standard & Poor's lowered Chicago's bond rating in September 1983 from A-minus to BBB-plus, and in March 1984 Moody's Investor Service dropped the city's bond rating from Aa to Baa1. The two financial agencies employed slightly different scales to evaluate the creditworthiness of municipalities, but they agreed that the lack of stability in Chicago's local government merited a warning to potential purchasers of the city's bonds. The statement of declining confidence by Wall Street produced several negative consequences, including increased difficulty in selling the bonds necessary for infrastructural improvements, higher interest rates for borrowing money that would cost the city millions of dollars over the course of long-term notes, and an overall weakening of the city's financial reputation that potentially created limitations on other means of raising investment capital. Washington's city council foes pointed to the lower bond ratings as more evidence of financial mismanagement in the mayor's office. As the bond-rating agencies made clear in the analyses they provided in trade publications, however, their decisions to downgrade Chicago stemmed fairly or not from the unsettled political climate in city hall and not from any evidence of incompetence or malfeasance by the new mayoral administration.[63]

By the time that Washington's first year as mayor had drawn to a close, a consensus had formed that the protracted deadlock in city hall constituted both a victory for the majority bloc in the city council and also a grave problem for Chicago. Deflecting the mayor's lofty plans for transforming local government, the intractable Vrdolyak Twenty-Nine had proved to be relentless and able adversaries. The opposition had been "more fierce than I could have imagined," Washington ruefully admitted. Moreover, the ongoing struggle for control of the municipal bureaucracy prolonged the racial friction that many Chicagoans had hoped would dissipate after the contentious 1983 election. As black alderman Clifford Kelley grudgingly acknowledged, "This fight has polarized the entire city." Unable to heal the racial wounds that continued to bedevil the city, the mayor found the goal of restoring civility in the fractious city council equally elusive. To the mayor's unending frustration, the media singled him out for the lion's share of the blame for not "reaching out to expand his constituency" and for having "blamed" his "policy failures" on his city council opposition. Even some of the mayor's allies criticized him for not achieving more amid the sound and fury of the Council Wars. Martin Oberman, one of the few white aldermen loyal to Washington, said he believed that "a more systematic effort should be made to bring about the reforms the mayor is committed to."[64]

Washington and his aides bridled at the suggestion that both sides in the Council Wars shared equal responsibility for the impasse. In the mayor's view, Vrdolyak, Burke, and their cabal acted irresponsibly in single-minded pursuit of power and patronage while refusing to allow the duly elected government of Chicago to conduct the city's business. Washington heatedly objected to the media's characterization of the Vrdolyak Twenty-Nine as some sort of loyal opposition, an imputation that he felt granted his enemies more credit than they deserved. He countered: "That's no longer loyal opposition or the legitimate political opposition. This is just an attempt to destroy, to stop things. There seems to be this hesitancy on the part of many, many people to point things out. In the main, it's the media, but not exclusively. To a great extent, but not all."[65]

The blame for any interruptions in the provision of municipal services, in Washington's view, fell entirely on the willful band of obstructionists whose delaying tactics sought to discredit the administration. In an open letter to New York City mayor Ed Koch, he elaborated further: "Yet [here] we have cynical, sometimes desperate members of the opposition who would rather see not a pothole filled, not a bond passed, not a library built, not an appointment approved and not a single step forward taken by the city of Chicago during the administration of this mayor. And who, therefore, have tried to hold the businesses of the city of Chicago as their political hostage."[66]

The administration's inability to achieve reform frustrated progressives who watched in exasperation as the promise of open government and resource reallocation crumbled under the weight of endless procedural wrangling and political gamesmanship. The mayor's failure to meet his stated objectives assumed much less importance to many Chicagoans in comparison with other shortcomings resulting from the incessant Council Wars. To the great distress of the downtown growth coalition, for example, progress on a number of initiatives conceived years earlier appeared to be stalled.

Northwestern University professor Louis Masotti voiced a common perception, saying, "A lot of projects are either on hold or falling off the edge." Just
as they blamed the mayor's lack of enthusiasm for monumental construction projects downtown, business leaders craving stability and order in the
community also rued Washington's inability or unwillingness to achieve a
working relationship with his political foes. If such fractiousness within local
government persisted, the wealthy elite worried, Chicago's credit rating and
reputation among prospective investors would worsen. Wary from the outset, State Street and LaSalle Street interests found little in the Washington
administration's first year to assuage their growing concerns.[67]

Washington likewise had made few inroads into the hostility he encountered in the white ethnic wards that voted solidly against him in February
and April 1983. Three out of four residents of the Northwest and Southwest
Sides polled by the *Chicago Reporter* agreed with the statement that the
mayor was "out to get them" (even though virtually none of the respondents
could cite an example of how they had been singled out for mistreatment).
The chairman of the Northwest Federation charged that the mayor had
consistently ignored the voices of people from white neighborhoods and
sought "revenge because we didn't vote for him." Jean Mayer of the Southwest Parish and Neighborhood Federation and SON/SOC, who blamed
the mayor's difficulties with the city council on the racial polarization his
campaign had engendered, accused Washington of "governing from a position of vindictiveness and spite." Asked by the *Chicago Tribune* to grade the
mayor's first year in office on a scale of one to ten, she responded, "I would
give Washington a zero."[68]

None of the others asked to assess Washington's first year graded his
performance as severely as had Mayer, who remained embittered long after
the 1983 election, but the results of public opinion polls could not have
provided cheerful reading in the mayor's office. In a telephone poll of one
thousand randomly selected voters conducted by Gallup Associates in the
spring of 1984 for the *Chicago Sun-Times* and WMAQ-TV, nearly one-half
of white respondents and more than one-third of black respondents believed that the city had deteriorated during the first year of the Washington
mayoralty. Merely 7 percent of whites and 11 percent of blacks saw Chicago
under Washington as "less divided racially" than during the Byrne administration. Although three-fourths of the African Americans who had supported the mayor in 1983 indicated that he should run for reelection, only

half of the whites who had voted for Washington thought he should seek a second term. The respondents provided no detailed explanations for their answers and offered no reasons for the administration's shortcomings, but their answers clearly reflected a sense of dissatisfaction. Did responsibility for the gloomy situation in Chicago rest primarily with the unscrupulous politicians controlling the city council or with the ineffectual mayor who had proved incapable yet of forging an effective governing coalition? Either way, the city's prospects seemed equally dreary to Chicagoans a year after Washington's election.[69]

4

CHICAGO WORKS TOGETHER

On April 30, 1984, Harold Washington delivered a speech as a visiting fellow at Harvard University's Kennedy School of Government. Having just concluded his first year as Chicago's mayor, Washington gladly accepted the invitation from such a prestigious institution to convey his ideas about balanced growth, redistribution, industrial retention, and enhanced citizen participation. His visit to Cambridge, Massachusetts, allowed him to address an overflow crowd in a spacious auditorium as well as to interact throughout the day with smaller groups in a variety of locations on campus. Washington was following in a long line of Chicago elected officials who had spoken at Harvard in the past, most of whom had regaled rapt students and professors with colorful tales that illustrated the Windy City's reputation for depraved politics. In one memorable instance, Mayor Carter Harrison had amused the Ivy Leaguers with the story of how, concerned that a photographer was snapping pictures in city council chambers for use in a police lineup, aldermen ducked under their desks and sprinted for the exits. Intent on using the invitation as an opportunity to correct popular misconceptions about the Council Wars and the supposed ineffectuality of his administration, Washington made no mention of outlandish behavior by comically corrupt politicians. Instead, he adopted a stern tone during his plenary talk and throughout his stay at the university. He could not pass up the opportunity to lambaste the Reagan administration, which he did by chiding the American people for electing a second-rate movie star to the nation's highest office, but devoted most of his time to criticizing the press. The mayor indicted television news programs for their reliance on sensationalism rather than substance and for their unwavering attention to racial politics while ignoring the less dramatic but essential meat and potatoes of municipal governance. In his telling, the media's fascination with racial conflict trivialized the friction between the mayor and the city council and bypassed the real issues confronting the Windy City.[1]

Dissatisfied with the popular narrative that emphasized the lack of progress in his first year, Washington hoped to shift the spotlight away from recurring city council imbroglios toward the substantive policy matters obscured by sensational headlines. He sought to revive the spirit of reform carefully nurtured during his 1983 campaign by specifying discrete goals that would flesh out his broad antimachine rhetoric. Whereas Mayor Byrne had confused Chicagoans with a plethora of overlapping city plans, he hoped to produce a single document that clearly identified the objectives of the new administration and educated the citizenry about the concrete benefits of his designs. Reflective of his mayoralty's overall approach to governance, the comprehensive plan would pay particular attention to the needs of Chicagoans long ignored by the ruling class but not deal exclusively with racial inequality. His plan for the city's future, Washington intended to make clear, included all of its residents.[2]

Washington's understandable frustration with the news media aside, the persistent focus on the Council Wars by electronic and print journalists (both inside and outside of Chicago) was easy to understand. The gridlock resulting from the clash between the city's legislative and executive branches kept the mayor from appointing his people and implementing his programs, presenting a stark contrast to the manner in which city government had operated in previous decades when the nation's last great urban political machine reigned supreme. Chicago in 1984 bore scant resemblance to Richard J. Daley's "city that works." The rich cast of characters at the heart of the conflict, the proud and unyielding mayor versus his bombastic, crafty adversaries, generated additional interest. The split in the city council almost exactly along racial lines, as well as the residue of bigotry unleashed in so many of the city's neighborhoods during the 1983 mayoral campaign, reinforced the belief that tensions between blacks and whites alone accounted for the political warfare. Voting returns provided additional evidence of a binary split in the city where African American precincts had voted overwhelmingly for Washington and white precincts had produced equally lopsided victory margins for the assorted white candidates who surfaced in the primary and general elections. From near and far, the story in Chicago appeared to be the tumult created by the election of the city's first black mayor.[3]

At Harvard University, just as he did regularly in Chicago, Washington strenuously objected to such an interpretation as reductionist and harmful. At the end of a highly disputatious year in the mayor's office, he believed more firmly than ever that his twenty-nine antagonists in the Council Wars opposed his every initiative for one fundamental reason—not primarily because of race or ideology but due to their single-minded pursuit of power. To be sure, Washington acknowledged, his foes manipulated the racial fears and animosities of their constituents at every opportunity and did so with undeniable success. Chicago's long history of racial segregation and the black population's political awakening, culminating in the successful drive to break free of the Democratic machine's control, constituted the necessary context to comprehend the dramatic events of 1983. But, the mayor believed, his twenty-nine adversaries exploited racial prejudice principally to defend their own political and pecuniary interests. Struggling desperately to keep the fraying cloth of the Cook County Democratic machine from being ripped apart altogether, Vrdolyak, Burke, and their allies sought at all costs to protect their lucrative fiefdoms. Unwilling to surrender the jobs, contracts, and perquisites that had defined politics in Chicago for generations, the unyielding survivors of the Daley machine faced off against the man whose threatening vision for the city's future jeopardized their livelihoods. The mayor firmly believed that the press somehow overlooked this elemental truth.[4]

Regardless of how the media portrayed the struggle that continued to rage in city hall, Washington remained determined to pursue a bona fide reform agenda that transcended a narrow focus on racial injustice. Beginning in January 1984, he urged the administration's subcabinet to draft a new development plan that specified exactly how the administration would reach the broad goals outlined in *The Washington Papers* during the 1983 mayoral campaign. The prompt creation of such a plan would dispel any criticism of the previous year's goals as just mundane campaign rhetoric and underscore the mayor's resolve to pursue genuine change. Moreover, the reform prospectus for Chicago would reflect the nostrums that Washington and other progressives yearned to apply on a much larger scale throughout urban America. Rob Mier remembered hearing the mayor announce on the radio one morning that a new development plan would be forthcoming from city hall in approximately sixty days. When Mier asked Washington later that day about the timetable for a plan he had never heard mentioned before, the mayor smiled sheepishly and said, "I figured you'd fill in the blanks." In a series of weekend retreats, subcabinet members assessed the progress made during the administration's first year and considered how to condense the laundry list of broad objectives enumerated in *The Washington Papers* into a much shorter, more precise set of goals. In the first stage of discussion, the commissioners distilled the contents of the original campaign document into a list of thirteen priorities while also pondering the inclusion of other aims that had surfaced during the first year of the Washington mayoralty. After additional meetings, the subcabinet members further reduced the number of goals from thirteen to five before presenting their handiwork to the mayor and others in city hall.[5]

The 1984 development plan, *Chicago Works Together*, identified five broad goals—job development; neighborhood development; balanced growth; enhanced public involvement in decision making; and a state, regional, and national legislative agenda. (The fifth goal underscored Washington's belief that such worthwhile changes at the local level needed to be part of a comprehensive reform package implemented nationally.) Unlike most comprehensive city plans, *Chicago Works Together* contained no maps, charts, graphs, photographs, or other illustrative material. Instead, the document elaborated on each of the five broad goals with a series of policies and a list of specific programs; each program outlined several measurable goals (the number of jobs to be created, the number of houses to be rehabilitated, and so forth). Echoing the administration's sustained emphasis on jobs instead of real estate, the plan highlighted employment retention and expansion. The remarkable growth in the central business district that originated in the late 1970s, resulting in the increase of both commercial office space and residential housing that began in the Byrne administration and continued during the Washington years, provided the opportunity for development in peripheral areas of the city. Private investment in downtown would allow the allocation of public dollars for housing, commercial development, and industrial retention in the neighborhoods.[6]

The title selected by the subcommittee for the 1984 development plan—"Chicago Works Together"—held special significance for two reasons. First, while reinforcing the Washington administration's dedication to inclusiveness, the title served as an ironic reminder that Chicago's reputation as "the city that works" rested on the efficient delivery of services in the Loop and in designated white enclaves only. Consigned to neighborhoods that suffered from perpetual neglect, minorities never believed that the city worked all that well for them. The plan provided yet another opportunity to repeat that Chicago should be the city that worked for everyone. Second, allusions to togetherness and cooperation singled out the disruptive forces in the city council for blame in perpetuating the administration's difficulties during the previous year. If Washington and his aides had fallen short in fostering an altruistic ethic in city government, the reason could readily be found in the obstructionism practiced by his opponents in city council chambers and hostile precinct headquarters.[7]

Chicago Works Together won accolades from urban planners nationwide who cheered the Washington administration's willingness to reject the customary top-down urban plan in favor of a genuinely more comprehensive approach that considered the needs and desires of all the city's inhabitants. Reformers contrasted the administration's document with *Make No Little Plans*, a much more traditional plan issued the same year by the Civic Committee of the Commercial Club of Chicago, which recommended revitalization of the urban core exclusively. In an exceedingly favorable assessment of the administration's plan in the *Journal of the American Planning Association*, reviewers said, "The *Chicago Development Plan 1984* [*Chicago Works Together*] is the strongest indication thus far that American cities are willing to try to harness economic development for their disadvantaged residents. It is virtually certain to be the forerunner of similar plans, especially in cities where the political power of blacks and Hispanics is on the rise."[8]

The 1984 plan received high marks in progressive circles for designing programs to benefit the unemployed, the working poor, and other disadvantaged groups in historically neglected areas of the city—and for targeting local government's resources to especially needy neighborhoods rather than directing the lion's share of funds toward the central business district and then dividing the remaining amount equally among undifferentiated corners of the city. Outsiders commenting on the promise offered by *Chicago Works Together* saw Harold Washington's Chicago as potentially becoming a liberal outpost in an America under the sway of Reagan conservatism, a city where enlightened leadership might provide a beacon of hope by improving the lives of racial minorities and the poor.[9]

The release of *Chicago Works Together* attracted relatively little attention in the Windy City, however, where the Council Wars proceeded apace. "Washington is too weak to win, too strong to lose, and too stubborn to make a deal," summed up the *Chicago Tribune*. The mayor's enemies kept up a steady drumbeat of criticism, alternately charging him and other city officials with duplicity and incompetence, and the administration spent countless hours trying to refute the allegations. Washington prodded the media and the city's voters to look beyond the political flare-ups miring civic life, keep their eyes on the ball, and consider fully the meaningful adjustments to municipal government he was pursuing. Instead, the unceasing disruptions to local governance orchestrated in city council chambers made a mockery of the phrase "Chicago works together."

In a ludicrous but revealing example of the ongoing antagonism, Vrdolyak held a press conference at a downtown site littered with trash and pointed at the mountain of debris as evidence of city hall's inability to eliminate dreadful eyesores from highly visible areas in Chicago's central business district. The inept administration could not even provide such basic services as garbage removal in the heart of the commercial district, the indignant alderman charged. According to eyewitness accounts collected in a subsequent investigation, city workers had unloaded the refuse from a Department of Streets and Sanitation truck in the empty lot several hours before reporters and television crews arrived for the press conference. The municipal employees admitted that their supervisor had ordered them to dump garbage in an area that had been thoroughly cleaned already—yet another case, an outraged mayoral aide explained in a press release, of Washington's enemies spreading outright falsehoods and attempting to sabotage city government for their own nefarious political purposes. The scandal unearthed by Vrdolyak's bogus disclosure monopolized media coverage for several news cycles until another outbreak of conflict in city hall supplanted it.[10]

Much of the continuing friction between the mayor's office and the city council in the spring of 1984 revolved around the dispensation of the year's Community Development Block Grant funds from the federal government. A year earlier, a comparable fight had ensued when the new mayor challenged the long-standing practice in the city of diverting antipoverty funds into middle-class wards. In 1983 white machine aldermen had balked when Washington insisted that Chicago conform to the CDBG's stated intention of directing aid to distressed neighborhoods; after a lengthy battle, the mayor and his city council adversaries reached a compromise that allowed the city to meet the program's submission deadline. The dispute flared again in 1984 but became more problematic because the Reagan administration had reduced CDBG funding to the nation's cities by roughly one-third. (Chicago's allocation for 1984–85 totaled only $103 million, down from $147.7 million the previous year.) New federal eligibility rules, designed to shift even more money from middle-income areas to low-income neighborhoods, also threatened to imperil cities' discretion in using redevelopment money. The Department of Housing and Urban Development, which administered the CDBG program, insisted that each neighborhood receiving federal funding must contain a majority of low-income households. Alderman Roman Pucinski of the Forty-First Ward, an affluent area with a median income that ranked second among the city's wards, recognized that he would no longer be able to secure any community development funds for his constituents under the new HUD guidelines. "There is no question that these rules [by the federal government] play right into the hands of the mayor," complained Pucinski, attacking Washington's goal of redistributing resources among Chicago's unequal neighborhoods.[11]

Washington responded that the city had no choice but to comply with federal dictates and squarely put the blame for the expected decreases in community funding on the Reagan administration's budget cuts. "It seems that some were trying to put the jacket for truncating those funds on me," he told a gathering of Democratic officials on the Southwest Side. "And the jacket just won't fit, period." Refusing to accept the inevitability of HUD's new approach, however, the city council's Finance Committee conducted three days of public hearings on the mayor's refusal to allocate funds using past practices. Although federal officials announced that the Washington administration was interpreting the new guidelines correctly and that the HUD office in Chicago would be monitoring community development spending closely that year, several aldermen persisted in arguing that the mayor was purposely ignoring alternative means of allocating CDBG funds. Those aldermen and several business organizations argued that federal funds should also be used to shore up viable neighborhoods to forestall economic decline. "Some money needs to go into good areas so they can remain healthy," contended Charles Shanabruch, executive director of the Beverly Area Planning Association. "It's foolish to say, 'You have to go down the tubes before we'll work with you.'"[12]

As in the previous year, the mayor and his opponents announced a compromise shortly before the deadline for the receipt of grant applications in Washington, D.C. The city council voted to approve most of the $103 million in CDBG funds for the neighborhood programs originally proposed by Washington. The mayor's office agreed in return to one minor concession, the transfer of a few million dollars earlier earmarked for housing and economic development in struggling areas into thirteen neighborhoods championed by the city council's majority bloc. The *Chicago Tribune* explained the compromise, in which Washington appeared to have yielded very little ground, as part and parcel of Vrdolyak's new strategy of tempering council opposition to administration proposals and allowing the mayor more latitude in governing. According to council insiders, noted the *Tribune*, majority-bloc leaders had become concerned that the public might be tiring of their continual harassment of the mayor. Moreover, the opposition leaders felt confident that Washington would falter if allowed to exercise more freedom in making policy. Give the mayor enough rope to hang himself, they had decided.[13]

The *Tribune*'s theory that the majority bloc in the city council was beginning to pull its punches against the mayor quickly evaporated, however, as Finance Committee chairman Edward Burke launched another offensive. On May 23, 1984, Burke declared at a city council meeting that Washington no longer legally held the office of mayor because he had violated a state law. An obscure Illinois ethics statute stipulated that any elected official who failed to file a statement of personal finance by April 30 each year forfeited his office, and records in Springfield showed that the mayor's staff had filed his ethics forms three weeks late that year. (Later that day came the disclosure that two top Washington aides—chief of staff William Ware and press secretary Grayson Mitchell—had also violated the law by submitting their forms late.) As some amazed aldermen stared in stunned silence and others shouted angrily, Burke announced that Vice Mayor Richard Mell, alderman of the Thirty-Third Ward, had become acting mayor. Absent from council chambers to attend a ribbon-cutting ceremony elsewhere in the city, Washington did not learn of Burke's ploy until after the city council meeting adjourned.[14]

The furor over Burke's startling power grab—what the *Tribune* called a "banana republic–style coup d'etat"—came swiftly and forcefully. "I am the mayor!" Washington thundered. Forty-Third Ward alderman Martin Oberman, an ally of the mayor, dismissed Burke's action as a "grandstand play" devoid of substance. Chicago Corporation Counsel James Montgomery flatly rejected Mell's claim to the mayoralty, noting that only a court could remove an elected official for failure to comply with a state law. Wayne Whalen, the member of the 1970 Illinois Constitutional Convention who had written the ethics law, opined that Washington had been in "substantial compliance" with the statute by filing a detailed report, even though it had been submitted three weeks late. The fact that no one in Illinois had ever been removed from office for failing to submit an ethics statement by the deadline failed to deter Burke, who filed suit in Cook County Circuit Court on May 23, seeking the mayor's immediate ouster.[15]

Montgomery and members of his staff regarded Burke's lawsuit as nothing more than a nuisance and expressed confidence that the mayor would retain his office, but Washington and others in the administration worried that the alderman's machinations might be taken more seriously by the public. Rumors that the mayor had been purged prompted a spontaneous demonstration of hundreds of the administration's supporters in the lobby outside city council chambers. Speaking live on seven radio stations that appealed primarily to African American audiences, Washington urged calm and reassured listeners that he remained in control at city hall. Alluding to the potential for violence if African Americans believed that the Vrdolyak Twenty-Nine had successfully staged a coup, the mayor charged that Burke "would like to see the city go up in cinders." Burke angrily rejoined, "I think that kind of inflammatory rhetoric is a self-fulfilling prophecy."[16]

Although it seemed highly unlikely that the legal wrangling would result in the mayor's dismissal, Burke and his claque took advantage of an opportunity to exploit a blunder in city hall for their political gain. The subsequent disruptions in the city council and debates over the ethics statute in the state legislature embarrassed the Washington administration and created yet another delay in the conduct of city business. The nature of the controversy recalled the mayor's earlier criminal convictions for failure to file his income tax returns and again raised the issue of competency. "This really brings the whole thing into focus," argued one of Washington's enemies. "It's just one more example of his slipshod approach. That is a legitimate issue." The issue, legitimate or fanciful, allowed the Vrdolyak Twenty-Nine to dissimulate for weeks while claiming that important decisions could not be made until the mayor's legal status had been fully clarified in the courts.[17]

On July 2, nearly six weeks after informing the city council of the mayor's illegal actions, Burke abruptly announced that he would not be pursuing his suit to remove Washington from office after all. The unrepentant alderman calmly said that recent amendments to the state law regarding ethics statements, which automatically granted public officials a month's grace period after the filing deadline and clarified the process for assessing fines and penalties, had resolved the issue to his satisfaction. Burke admitted that other aldermen had urged him to break the impasse and find an acceptable solution so that the normal operation of the city council could resume. The Finance Committee chairman had agreed to do so when the state legislature revised the ethics law, bringing an end to an unusually antic battle in the ongoing Council Wars.[18]

The sniping between the mayor's office and the city council persisted in July when Washington proposed a $250 million general bond issue in response to neighborhood demands for infrastructural improvements. In many areas of the city outside the Loop, residents called for long-overdue repairs and maintenance of streets, alleys, sidewalks, curbs, streetlights, and sewers, much of which had been built by the Works Progress Administration as part of President Franklin D. Roosevelt's New Deal in the 1930s. The administration argued that low prevailing interest rates and attractive debt-financing opportunities in the 1980s had created a propitious moment for taxpayers to invest in the city. All areas of Chicago would benefit from the refurbished infrastructure, suggested the mayor, none more so than the predominantly white neighborhoods of the Northwest and Southwest Sides where opponents of the administration enjoyed rabid support. Even though a quick tabulation revealed that 63 percent of the bond money in the mayor's plan was earmarked for wards represented by Vrdolyak and his allies, Washington's proposal stalled in the city council when he refused to grant aldermen total control over spending the bond funds. Even when many residents of the Southwest Side objected to the disruption of the infrastructural repairs due to what they perceived as petty political infighting, the majority bloc held firm in opposition.[19]

In a surprising moment of candor, Thirty-Third Ward alderman Richard Mell told a puzzled reporter why he and other majority-bloc members opposed a bond issue of such apparent value to the city and indeed to his own neighborhood. Yes, Mell agreed, the proposal seemed eminently fair and evenhanded. Politics dictated that he reject any measure originating in the mayor's office, however, regardless of its merits. He explained:

> But the sad situation is, in fact, it is naïve to ask why isn't this being done or why isn't that being done just because they're good-government positions. There are some who believe that to get rid of Harold Washington is good government because we simply can't take four more years of him. Maybe . . . two years of not having this [bond] is worth ten years of political stability in this city. It's a legitimate position; arguably, not voting for this bond is in the best interest of the city.

Even in the face of rising public distemper, Mell and the other white aldermen would simply not endorse any change that might redound to the benefit of the administration. "I will sacrifice a vote that probably won't be popular in my community for the good of the coalition," he admitted. The city council failed to approve the general-obligation bond issue that year.[20]

In the summer of 1984, local infighting momentarily took a backseat to national politics in the presidential election year. A vociferous critic of President Reagan since his days in the U.S. House of Representatives, Washington spoke enthusiastically in 1984 of unseating the Republican administration, installing a liberal Democrat in the White House, and altering the nation's political course by embracing a new set of domestic and foreign policies. The mayor's outspoken opposition to the president continued unabated from Chicago's city hall, where he charged that Reagan's mean-spirited and fundamentally flawed economic policies were taking a terrible toll on the nation's impoverished citizens. "None of his people know what it's like to go to sleep hungry at night," he said. "None of them know what it's like to face the Chicago winter with no roof over your head." Washington believed that the *Chicago Tribune* served as the unofficial organ of Republican conservatism and that the newspaper answered directly to the Reagan White House. He scoured the *Tribune*'s articles and editorials for fingerprints left by HUD's Samuel Pierce, Attorney General Edwin Meese, Education Secretary William Bennett, and the president himself. Washington's gibes at the Republican administration, sporadic during the first months of his mayoralty, increased in frequency and intensity when the election year arrived. As the African American mayor of one of the nation's largest cities and an outspoken, eminently quotable politician who eagerly made himself available to national media outlets, Washington determined to use his platform to advance the causes in which he believed. Formed during many years as a progressive legislator in Springfield and Washington, D.C., his positions on vital national issues generally dovetailed with the stance taken by the Democratic Party's left wing—especially with efforts on behalf of African Americans and the poor. In his public comments during 1984, Chicago's mayor urged the party to choose candidates and adopt platforms that would provide the American voter with a robust alternative to the Reagan brand of conservatism he held in such contempt.[21]

The political terrain in the United States after four years of the Reagan presidency left Washington in an unsure position with regard to the Democratic Party's selection of a presidential candidate in 1984, however, in large measure as a result of events triggered by his own victory the previous year. African American leaders throughout the nation huddled in the summer months of 1983 to consider which presidential aspirant among the Democrats offered the best opportunity to unseat the Republican incumbent. Single-minded in their determination to deny Reagan a second term, the black leaders nonetheless expressed reservations about the leading potential candidates in the party's liberal wing. Both Walter Mondale and Edward Kennedy had upset many African Americans during the recent Chicago mayoral election by shunning Washington and endorsing conservative white candidates. Many angry black voters saw Mondale and Kennedy as having acted out of political expediency rather than principle in the Windy City; leading African American politicians excoriated the two white Democrats for their disloyalty, for ignoring the unwavering support offered by the African American community in the past. At the same time, Washington's inspiring victory in Chicago had raised the political consciousness of blacks across the nation. Despite warnings that a widespread defection of minority voters might ensure a Reagan victory in 1984, many angry blacks argued for the selection of an African American presidential candidate that year. After a group of the nation's most influential black leaders met in Chicago in June 1983 and formally endorsed the idea of backing one of their own in the upcoming election, the Reverend Jesse Jackson answered the call. On November 3, 1983, he announced his candidacy for president.[22]

No less disappointed with the Democratic Party's white liberals, Washington nonetheless refused to enlist immediately in Jackson's campaign. "We do not have the political luxury to be in any campaign behind a black candidate who can't win," the mayor explained. "The task at hand is defeating Ronald Reagan." Washington said that he would refrain from endorsing a presidential candidate until the Democratic national nominating convention in mid-July and in the meantime named his own favorite-son slate of delegates. A free agent who hoped to use his endorsement as a bargaining chip at the convention, the mayor stood by during the early months of 1984 as Jackson's candidacy gained momentum and fared much better than the experts had expected. Jackson received more than three million votes in party primaries, approximately 20 percent of the total number of ballots cast, while winning five primaries and caucuses.[23]

At the Democratic National Convention in San Francisco, Washington attempted to leverage the votes of his thirty-six favorite-son delegates to obtain front-runner Walter Mondale's endorsement of a stronger jobs plank in the party platform. Instead of the plank forwarded by the U.S. Conference of Mayors (USCM), which called broadly for full employment, job training, and urban public works, the Chicago mayor offered an alternative proposal drafted by a consortium of union locals. With organized labor's backing, Washington's specific plank vowed to create one million jobs within the new presidential administration's first two years. Assured of the votes necessary for nomination and supported by a number of Democrats in the Illinois delegation, Mondale forces rejected the Washington alternative. Moreover, the party leadership denied the Chicago mayor the opportunity to address the convention because he refused to endorse Mondale. Just hours before the final roll call vote for president, denouncing the indifference with which his causes had been treated by the Mondale camp, Washington announced that he would vote for Jackson; the mayor's thirty-six delegates followed his lead. After Mondale secured the nomination on the first ballot, Washington promptly approved the choice and promised to campaign strenuously for the Democratic nominee. Despite having cast a vote for Jackson as a symbolic act of protest against the Democratic candidate's disappointing position on job creation, the Chicago mayor pledged to work hard for the party against the real enemy in the White House.[24]

Washington had hoped that the conduct of national politics in San Francisco would provide a brief respite from the constant unpleasantness of the Council Wars, but the mayor's Chicago nemeses who served as members of the Illinois delegation continued to nettle him at the convention whenever possible. A Vrdolyak aide sent all members of the Illinois delegation invitations to a breakfast purportedly hosted by the Chicago mayor, but the delegates who showed up in an empty ballroom at the appointed time found themselves victims of a hoax. Vrdolyak struck again, presenting television viewers one of their lasting images of the convention, when he manufactured a heated dispute between Washington and a television reporter. The mayor, who refused to appear in the same forum with Vrdolyak, agreed to an interview alone on the convention floor with CBS correspondent Ed Bradley. When Bradley attempted to expand the discussion by summoning Vrdolyak, who conveniently stood grinning nearby just off camera, Washington felt that he had been duped by the interviewer. Infuriated, the mayor yelled at Bradley to turn off the camera and stormed away. Taken out of context by viewers, Washington's volcanic reaction seemed exaggerated and unwarranted. For days thereafter, the *Chicago Tribune* mocked the mayor for his "snit" in front of a national audience.[25]

The ensuing presidential campaign provided Vrdolyak another chance to bait the mayor when Jackson refused to renounce the endorsement of the Reverend Louis Farrakhan. As the Nation of Islam's chief national spokesman, a charismatic and disputatious orator who addressed a variety of religious and secular topics from the church's national headquarters in Chicago, Farrakhan earned credit in the black community for speaking truth to power but often offended great numbers of people (white and black) with his bigoted remarks. In the course of several speeches in the summer of 1984, the Black Muslim minister labeled Judaism a "gutter religion" and referred to Adolf Hitler as "a very great man." His comments sparked a national uproar and left Jackson in an untenable position. Farrakhan eventually distanced himself from the Jackson campaign but not before Washington's enemies recognized an opportunity to exploit the controversy. Vrdolyak introduced a resolution in the city council calling for the mayor to denounce Farrakhan and his racist remarks. Referring to the unquestioned good relations he had enjoyed with Jews and Jewish organizations over the course of his long political career, Washington adamantly refused to sign the resolution. Instead, he impugned the sum and substance of Vrdolyak's machinations. He told his press secretary, "The whole point of this guy, his whole message, is that black politicians are getting their strings pulled by whites—bankers, corporations, the media. So I'm going to prove Farrakhan wrong by jumping up and denouncing him—because the bankers and corporations and media say I have to? Because Eddie Vrdolyak says I have to? Shit . . ."[26]

Washington no doubt refused to censure the Black Muslims for a combination of reasons, some political and some personal. He understood Farrakhan's considerable popularity among Chicago's African Americans. Not only had the straight-talking minister upbraided whites for their transgressions when other black leaders hesitated to do so, earning the admiration of the downtrodden for his resoluteness, but the Black Muslims had amassed considerable goodwill among African Americans by providing vitally important social programs in Chicago's ghettos. The church's provision of free breakfasts for schoolchildren and drug rehabilitation clinics won high marks among South Side and West Side residents. Regardless of the minister's inflammatory rhetoric, which many African Americans regretted, his church's good works in desperately poor neighborhoods starved for social services were undeniably praiseworthy. The mayor's denunciation of the Black Muslims would be highly unpopular in Chicago's ghettos, a direct affront to part of his political base—which, of course, Vrdolyak understood all too well.[27]

At the same time, Washington rejected the Vrdolyak resolution as an illogical and hypocritical gambit based on racist premises. He objected to the need to pass the kind of phony litmus test reserved exclusively for African American politicians. Why were black politicians, and not their white counterparts, expected to condemn offensive speech? Why, contrary to the persecution of Jews throughout thousands of years of European history, were only blacks being asked to purge themselves of anti-Semitism? Why were leading white politicians not being asked to condemn religious prejudice among their constituents? Was Vrdolyak being asked to answer for the attitudes and actions of his ancestors in Croatia? Washington would gladly denounce religious and racial bigotry of all stripes, he said, but saw no compelling reason to address the misguided remarks of a solitary public figure who happened to be black.[28]

Forty-Ninth Ward alderman David Orr, a staunch Washington ally, introduced a resolution whereby the mayor would unambiguously condemn anti-Semitism and all other forms of bigotry in toto. Consideration of Orr's proposal on the city council floor quickly degenerated into a lengthy discussion of racism and anti-Semitism, the colloquy degenerating into hyperbole and name-calling. From the presiding officer's perch, the mayor admonished aldermen for their incivility and the threats that followed. Orr's resolution never came to a vote. Vrdolyak's alternative measure passed several weeks after its introduction, with every white alderman voting in favor and every black alderman voting against it; Washington refused to sign the measure. The disheartened mayor told reporters that the city council's handling of the Farrakhan contretemps "will be remembered as a low point in city history." Vrdolyak and his followers let the matter drop temporarily but later resurrected their demands that the mayor repudiate Farrakhan.[29]

Just as the demand that the mayor denounce Farrakhan was intended to drive a wedge between city hall and Washington's African American electoral base, Vrdolyak and his allies sought to use recurring speculation about Washington's sexuality to undermine his relationship with the city's gay community. As a middle-aged male who had been unmarried for decades and who closely guarded the details of his private life, the mayor had frequently been the subject of a whispering campaign about his sexual preferences. Rumormongers called Mary Ella Smith, an unmarried elementary schoolteacher long identified as Washington's fiancée, merely a platonic female friend whom the administration conveniently trotted out as the mayor's companion at special functions. The mayor's foes slyly pointed out that Washington had surrounded himself in city hall with handsome single men, beginning with chief of staff Bill Ware and including several of his bodyguards. When Ware became seriously ill, the whispering campaign intensified. "They're implying I have AIDS [acquired immune deficiency syndrome]," Ware said. "I'm not the real target. This is aimed at the mayor."[30]

Personally and politically committed to gays and lesbians as full-fledged partners in his rainbow coalition, Washington could not express indignation or repulsion in denying the rumors of his own homosexuality without seeming to repudiate a portion of his alliance. Regardless of the unsubstantiated claims circulated about his love life, he continued to appear at gay-pride rallies and strongly backed a gay-rights ordinance introduced in the city council. He issued an executive order barring discrimination against homosexuals and named the city's first gay and lesbian liaison. Yet at the same time, the mayor told his second press secretary, Alton Miller, he resented the lies being spread by his enemies and wished to assert his heterosexual identity. Raised in a community with strong traditional views of male sexuality, Washington seethed privately at what he saw as character assassination. Expressing frustration at the quandary in which he found himself, the mayor exclaimed to Miller, "I'm a man, goddamnit. In *my* family, it makes a big difference." Caught between his desire to affirm his heterosexual virility and determination not to insult members of the gay and lesbian community, the exasperated Washington usually ignored the rumors and said nothing.[31]

But not always. On one notable public occasion, Washington's temper flared when goaded by the shameless Vrdolyak. Seeking permission from the mayor to speak in a city council meeting, the alderman waved his arms daintily and chirped in a falsetto voice: "To someone of your gender I should say, 'pretty please.'"[32] Washington reacted angrily, threatening to descend from the dais and pummel his antagonist, and pandemonium ensued in the chamber. For a substantial time after the blowup, Washington stopped talking to Vrdolyak altogether. The rumors about the mayor's sexuality persisted after the city council incident, occasionally surfacing in the local newspapers, but Washington remained steadfast in his resolve not to comment on the issue directly.

The flap over the mayor's sexuality, his refusal to denounce Farrakhan, the blowup with Ed Bradley at the Democratic Convention, and other ancillary stories that surfaced during the summer of 1984 diverted attention from more meaningful issues and confirmed Washington's low regard for the Chicago press. The mayor argued that his recurrent tussles with Vrdolyak and Burke over comparatively trivial matters, which he thought should have been covered briefly in sidebars if at all, had become the unhealthy preoccupation of newspapers and broadcast media enamored of politics as spectator sport. "No one wants to deal with that nitty-gritty stuff of government," he lamented. "The news is not Vrdolyak calling me a bastard and me calling him a son of a bitch." By no means, the mayor allowed, could the press ignore the bitter fighting between the two factions in city hall. But he hoped that the reporting of conflict in city government could delve into the substantive issues at play and, rather than romanticize the political clashes between colorful combatants, educate the public about the real consequences of policy making. Nothing begged for such serious treatment more, the mayor believed, than the bitter contest that raged for more than three months that year over the control of city contracts.[33]

The authority to award city contracts assumed great significance in Chicago, particularly in the years after the Shakman decisions, for a number of reasons: the potentially damaging effect on patronage, the historic racial inequity in the receipt of city contracts and the subsequent demand among minorities for affirmative action as recompense, and the distribution of power between the mayor and the city council at a time when funds still to be disbursed for the completion of public works projects totaled between $820 million and $1 billion. Many years earlier, in response to allegations of rampant corruption in Chicago's procurement procedures, the Illinois General Assembly had passed the State Purchasing Act of 1955, ending city council participation in contract awards and vesting that authority entirely in the mayor's office (leaving the city's aldermen solely an advisory role). In 1984, calling the Washington administration guilty of approving wasteful contracts and bestowing city business on preferred vendors for political reasons, the city council challenged the arrangement. Ironically, machine aldermen were charging the mayor with preserving patronage by funneling city contracts to his political supporters. In a series of compromise proposals that he said would allow the timely completion of the city's airport and mass transit projects, Washington opened the door to broader participation for the city council by allowing the Finance Committee to help draft specifications for contracts and to assess the bids submitted by companies and individuals—but not to make the final decisions on awards. Citing his intention to honor the spirit of the 1955 reform by keeping the control of city contracts out of the clutches of the rapacious aldermen, the mayor agreed to enhance the city council's oversight function but insisted that the final approval of contracts remain in his purview.[34]

The mayor's determination to retain control of city contracts stemmed in large measure from his unwavering commitment to affirmative action. A city audit in 1982 showed that white male businessmen and the firms they owned received 94 percent of the contracts awarded by the city. Between 1982 and 1984, with African Americans constituting nearly 40 percent of Chicago's population, black-owned businesses received only 7.4 percent of the contract dollars distributed by the city; with 14 percent of the population, Latinos received just 1.5 percent of awards. Shortly after taking office, Washington drafted new unofficial guidelines for city government agencies empowered to award contracts. Spurning strict quotas, he opted instead for establishing targets that would allow consistent progress toward the goal of parceling out 30 percent of the city's contracts to companies owned by minorities and women (thereby bringing city hiring practices more in line with Chicago's population distribution). In practice, that meant funneling 25 percent of contracts to businesses owned by African Americans, Latinos, and other minorities and 5 percent to firms owned by women. The mayor publicly defended the so-called 25-5 formula as a necessary countermeasure to the Reagan administration's systematic refusal to pursue affirmative action measures. Also, all projects funded by the city that created twenty or more jobs had to consult the Mayor's Office of Employment and Training as the "first source" of job referrals. His administration's new guidelines, he affirmed, would redound to the benefit of small businesses (white as well as black owned) and, along with the stated policy of favoring local businesses whenever possible, distribute more contracts to city vendors than to competitors from beyond city limits. The mayor proudly proclaimed that Chicago's city hall was "one of the few institutions in the country putting the rhetoric of affirmative action into policy." Indeed, muttered some administration stalwarts, progress on affirmative action would have been even greater except for the extreme caution exercised by Bill Ware. Intent on protecting Washington against charges of cronyism or favoritism, the chief of staff became known as "Bottleneck Bill" because his excessive scrutiny of all personnel matters subject to mayoral approval caused recurrent delays in city hall.[35]

To accelerate the hiring of minorities and women, the administration contracted management consultant James Lowry to assess the current situation and recommend new policies and practices. After an intensive investigation of city procedures that lasted eight months, the consultant concluded that the disappointing pace of the affirmative action efforts owed to inefficiency and inertia in the municipal bureaucracy. Affirming the legitimacy of the administration's goals, he presented a series of recommendations to the mayor. Lowry advised Washington to formalize the 25-5 formula by issuing an executive order and by monitoring compliance closely through the installation of new technical and fiscal accounting procedures in Chicago's Purchasing Department. The mayor endorsed the Lowry report and vowed to root out the "old boys network of city officials and business executives" that had monopolized city hiring for years to the detriment of minorities and women; he issued Executive Order 85-2, establishing affirmative action as official city policy in April 1985.[36]

Washington also applied his affirmative action guidelines to downtown commercial development. The mayor's office entered into a number of unwritten, good-faith agreements with private businesses that received low-interest revenue bonds or the opportunity to purchase city land at discounted prices; in return for accepting these subsidies from local government, the developers consented to meet the 25-5 goal for hiring in construction and postconstruction work. The set-aside program increased the number of contracts awarded to companies owned by minorities and women, but not without controversy. Because of the city's difficulties certifying and monitoring the eligibility of firms receiving awards under affirmative action strictures, millions of dollars in contracts went to front companies not owned by women or minorities. A three-month investigation in 1984 by *Crain's Chicago Business* found that the city had granted approximately one-third of the sixty-two million dollars to ineligible or undeserving businesses.[37]

Washington acknowledged enforcement problems. In the administration's defense, he pointed first to the uncooperative, inefficient bureaucracy ensconced in city hall and explained that the city council had stifled his attempt to overhaul the Department of Purchasing. "We have an inherited structure," he continued. "Some are incompetent. Others don't give a damn. What's lacking is the personnel we can trust to do the job." The mayor also noted that he had requested funds in the 1984 budget to hire twenty-one additional compliance officers but that fourteen of those positions had been lost to cuts demanded by the city council. The administration proceeded with its reform efforts nonetheless, determined not to delay the introduction of affirmative action because of imperfect compliance. "Ideally, we'd like to have had our monitoring in order, but that would have been like waiting for Lefty," he said. Casting a suspicious eye on the city council's majority bloc convinced Washington that any progress his administration made would surely be lost if he relinquished control of city contracts.[38]

Rather than attack affirmative action directly, the city council's majority bloc officially based its opposition to Washington's control of city contracts on its desire to limit unchecked mayoral power and eliminate politics from the process. "Right now, no one has the power to stop a bad or wasteful contract," argued Vrdolyak. "Right now, political support of the Washington administration is one sure way to get a city no-bid contract." While Vrdolyak took the high road in justifying the aldermen's challenge to established mayoral prerogatives, Burke disdained any pretenses of statesmanship and descended straight to the low road. Offering a more cynical explanation to reporters, he swore to oppose Washington putting "his own buddies and pals and cronies in positions that presently are held by the buddies and pals and cronies of the [majority bloc]." Vrdolyak vowed that the council would amend the 1985 city budget to provide aldermen control of city contracts, and Washington immediately promised to veto any budget containing such a provision.[39]

In yet another example of a compromise cobbled together at the last moment to avoid the cessation of important government functions, the two sides reached agreement only hours before several public works projects (most notably the repair and expansion of O'Hare International Airport) would have ground to a halt. After a stalemate that lasted thirteen weeks, the mayor's opponents essentially accepted a proposal he had proffered much earlier: the city council gained the right to review, not approve, no-bid contracts in excess of fifty thousand dollars. The frustration of the one thousand construction, engineering, and design workers then laboring at O'Hare International Airport, who complained about having been treated like yo-yos in a political game as they waited anxiously to see if they would retain their jobs, mirrored the dissatisfaction welling up throughout Chicago. Once a fascinating spectacle in a city accustomed to political intrigue, the Council Wars had settled into a predictable and distasteful pattern that no longer enthralled the citizenry. Time after time, following prolonged and rancorous argumentation, the mayor and the aldermen grudgingly reached settlements that kept the listing ship of state afloat but made few changes to improve service delivery. The city council gave every indication of turning historically mundane tasks, such as the adoption of an annual city budget, into an unyielding battle of wills designed to thwart the mayor's reform agenda.[40]

The showdown over the 1985 municipal budget proved to be every bit as contentious as the previous year's dispute. Expecting to be at loggerheads over the budget again, the mayor conveyed his draft to the city council on October 16 (roughly a full month sooner than he had in his first year) and launched an extensive public relations campaign touting the document in the local press. The city council balked immediately, Burke dismissing the mayor's early submission as a "public relations gimmick." As in the previous year, looming budgetary shortfalls made clear the need for tax increases, service reductions, or some combination of the two. No one disputed the administration's warning that federal aid would be cut again in the coming fiscal year. As Finance Committee chair, Burke accepted the need for budget cuts but disagreed with the mayor about the city services in need of trimming. He indignantly identified the city agencies in the mayor's budget that would actually enjoy increases at a time of supposed financial exigency, singling out the mayor's office and the corporation counsel's office for special opprobrium, and accused Washington of protecting his own pet agencies in the city bureaucracy from cuts during lean times. Moreover, he assured the public that any tax hikes would be the result of mayoral initiatives and none of the city council's doing.[41]

While raising questions about a multitude of line items in the detailed budget, the mayor's foes dwelled especially on the administration's suggested cuts in the police force. With the assent of the police superintendent, Fred Rice, the mayor proposed reducing the number of uniformed officers in the city from 12,000 at the beginning of 1984 to 11,500 by the end of 1985. According to Washington and Rice, Chicago's population loss, the declining number of calls for police assistance, and the reassignment of approximately 350 officers then engaged in peripheral administrative tasks to the streets more than justified the slight reduction. Moreover, they reported, a force of 11,500 men and women would still give Chicago the nation's highest ratio of uniformed police officers to city residents. Such arguments gained little currency in the city council, however, where alarmist aldermen spoke darkly about the inevitable crime wave such misguided attempts to save money would engender. Nor did the local media approve of a reduced law enforcement presence on city streets. A sprawling metropolis with a multitude of social problems could never have too much police protection, editorialized the *Chicago Tribune*, regardless of whatever favorable ratios and optimistic projections the mayor cited. A consistent defender of law and order, the *Tribune* insisted that the numbers of police should be reduced only as a last resort and then after all other city agencies had absorbed substantial cuts.[42]

Vrdolyak and Burke responded aggressively with a series of budget amendments to increase the number of police in Chicago. Speaking on behalf of the mayor's office, Forty-Ninth Ward alderman David Orr and Twenty-Ninth Ward alderman Danny Davis called the Vrdolyak-Burke amendments a "shrewdly disguised effort" to politicize law enforcement in a manner reminiscent of standard practices in Chicago before the wholesale reform of the police department triggered by the Summerdale Scandal in 1960. (After the disclosures of the Summerdale Scandal, which exposed a burglary ring operated by police, Mayor Richard J. Daley had instituted far-ranging changes in the structure and operation of the police force to reduce political influence.) In short, charged Orr and Davis, members of the city council's majority bloc were scheming to return control of the police to aldermen and Democratic Party committeemen and make the superintendent subservient to politicians. The amendments approved by the city council Finance Committee would subject decisions regarding pay, benefits, and all personnel decisions within each precinct (including promotions and transfers) to local aldermen. Most worrisome to reformers, the amendments affirmed that "no such (Police) unit or activity shall be diminished, reduced, reorganized or eliminated" without city council approval. This effort to exploit the proposed reduction in police ranks, noted Orr and Davis, simply amounted to another attempted "power grab" by Vrdolyak and Burke. Just as with the foiled attempt to control city contracts, the aldermen endeavored to gain political advantage over the mayor by seizing powers reserved exclusively for his office.[43]

On December 12, following a turbulent six-hour session replete with parliamentary maneuvering, a flurry of rejected amendments, and heated outbursts, the city council's antiadministration majority passed its version of the 1985 budget. The mayor issued a stern veto message, saying that the changes to his budget "represent illegal and improper encroachments by the legislative branch on executive functions and threaten the city's ability to operate a police department free of political influence." He roundly rejected the majority bloc's inclusion of a twenty-six-million-dollar property tax cut as fiscally imprudent but allowed that he would be willing to agree to his opponents' call for more police if additional sources of funding could be identified. Washington called the initial give-and-take on the budget a "well-organized opening salvo" and expressed optimism that further negotiations could produce a satisfactory middle ground.[44]

The mayor's rosy outlook proved to be unrealistic, however, and budget negotiations stalled in mid-December. Discarding the objectionable provisions for increasing city council control of police operations, the majority bloc made its last stand, refusing to compromise on the proposed twenty-six-million-dollar property tax cut. Advised against lower property tax levies by the New York financial firm of Lazard Frères, the administration resisted initially but then agreed to a smaller reduction subject to negotiation. The day after Christmas, the mayor's office began making contingency plans for the continued operation of city government in the absence of an approved 1985 budget by the December 31 deadline. To ensure the uninterrupted provision of vital city services, the administration prepared to provide skeleton police and fire services as well as to operate emergency kitchens and makeshift shelters for the homeless. At the same time, chief of staff Bill Ware began recruiting leading bankers and businessmen to endorse the administration's fiscally responsible approach and municipal union leaders to lobby recalcitrant aldermen. He also discussed strategies for isolating Burke from other members of the majority bloc by convincing them that he would "sell them out for his own bill."[45]

Washington, Vrdolyak, and Burke continued negotiating in city hall on New Year's Eve, with the results of their deliberations passed by the city council a few hours before midnight. The final 1985 budget included a twenty-million-dollar property tax cut and maintained police staffing at twelve thousand persons. The mayor expressed satisfaction at the deletion of language granting the city council increased control of some executive branch prerogatives and celebrated the continued independence of the police department. He characterized the inclusion of a property tax reduction as a victory for the irresponsible aldermen who willingly undermined the city's fiscal well-being to score political points with the taxpaying public. A spokesman for the nonpartisan Civic Federation predicted that expected pay increases during the coming year for firefighters, skilled tradesmen engaged in city work, and newly unionized municipal workers would demand more revenue and therefore erode much of the twenty-million-dollar tax reduction. The likely impact of the tax cut remained unclear as both sides in the Council Wars claimed victory in the latest test of wills.[46]

Washington knew that the struggle over the particulars of the annual budget mattered to Chicago's residents, who understood that decisions made about tax rates and service provision considerably influenced their daily lives. Consequently, he fully understood and—to a degree—applauded the media's decision to give the political battle extensive coverage in the last weeks of 1984. Still, he objected to the imbalance in reporting that resulted in front-page headlines for the budget battle to the virtual exclusion of all other matters related to local governance. It appeared to him that reporters and editors relegated any news not related in some way to the Council Wars, no matter how compelling, to secondary or tertiary status. Thus, he felt, the media curtailed its coverage of the budget battle only to report on the administration's unannounced removal of a holiday crèche in city hall two weeks before Christmas in response to protests by religious groups. An innocuous, hardly newsworthy event became sensational front-page news when Burke called Bill Ware "the Grinch who stole Christmas" and intimated that Washington's chief of staff had acted at Minister Farrakhan's direction. The newspapers devoted numerous column inches to the fate of a small Christmas display while ignoring much more important stories in the city. The mayor believed that inadequate coverage of the administration's fight with the Playskool Company, which began at roughly the same time as the budget battle and continued long after, constituted the perfect example of such questionable priorities. A significant episode with far-ranging implications for the administration's ability to retain industry, a test case that received considerable attention in the national press and in social science literature, the legal tug of war with Playskool slipped in and out of the local news sporadically for months and never received the coverage that Washington believed it deserved.[47]

The maker of Lincoln Logs and other popular toys in Chicago since the 1930s, Playskool employed more than 1,200 people at its Northwest Side factory by the 1970s. In 1980 Mayor Byrne had awarded a one-million-dollar tax-exempt Industrial Revenue Bond at a below-market interest rate to Playskool's parent company, Hasbro-Bradley of Pawtucket, Rhode Island. With such financial assistance, indicated Hasbro-Bradley, capital improvements could be completed to its aging factory that would allow for increased production and create 400 new jobs. In fact, rather than expanding the workforce, the company steadily reduced the number of laborers employed at the plant after the completion of renovations. On September 19, 1984, after months of repeatedly denying any intention of reducing production at the factory, Playskool announced that the Northwest Side plant would close just before Christmas, most of the 700 people still employed there would be fired, and its operations would be relocated to a new plant in East Longmeadow, Massachusetts. Arguing that the closing of the facility would devastate the neighborhood economically and that the company's decision to leave constituted a breach of public trust after accepting such a generous subsidy, a combination of community, labor, and business groups united to oppose the plant's shutdown. Frustrated in their earlier efforts to create an "early warning network" that would combat job loss created by factory closings, the activists saw the Playskool announcement as the perfect opportunity to publicize the problem and galvanize public support—and to enlist the Washington administration in the fight against manufacturing job loss.[48]

The activists found eager allies in city hall, where Washington and Rob Mier, the commissioner of the Department of Economic Development, expressed confidence that Chicago business and industry leaders would join the condemnation of Hasbro-Bradley's crass opportunism. Washington claimed that Playskool's departure would not only remove 700 factory jobs but also eliminate another 450 jobs among local suppliers and seven million dollars in area bank deposits. "This is a real case of corporate arrogance," said Mier. "This company made promises to get a cheap loan and then just walked away without a second thought." A coalition of community, business, and labor groups called for a nationwide boycott of Hasbro-Bradley toys, held rallies outside the factory, and picketed at toy stores that sold Playskool products in the Chicago area. The demonstrators evoked moving images of Playskool workers, facing imminent job loss, unable to afford purchasing toys they had themselves made for their children's Christmas presents. On December 4, 1984, the city filed a lawsuit in Cook County Circuit Court, seeking to block Playskool's departure. Judge John Hechinger denied the city's motion for a temporary restraining order but scheduled a hearing on a permanent injunction for December 14. The litigation continued into the early weeks of 1985.[49]

On January 31, 1985, the City of Chicago and Hasbro-Bradley reached an out-of-court settlement that allowed the shuttering of the Northwest Side factory but required that the company slow the pace of evacuation and make several concessions to fired workers. The negotiated agreement obligated the firm to maintain production at the Playskool site with 100 workers until November 1985 and to help 580 laid-off workers find new jobs. Hasbro-Bradley agreed to pay five hundred dollars to any company that would hire former Playskool workers and one hundred dollars to any of its former employees who found new jobs for their peers. The company also set up a fifty-thousand-dollar emergency fund to help newly unemployed workers pay medical and utility bills and pledged to work with the city for the next year to seek other possible uses for the Playskool factory that would reemploy the same workers. Washington praised Stephen Hassenfeld, chairman of the board at Hasbro-Bradley, for "[helping to] write a record of corporate responsibility that sets high standards for business everywhere."[50]

The mayor's grandiose political rhetoric notwithstanding, the aftermath of the Playskool saga turned out to be less ennobling than he proclaimed. The administration and local activist groups working in concert had successfully exposed a company's shady business practices, won the battle for public opinion, kept the guilty party from fleeing the scene undetected, and wrung several concessions from the perpetrator. In the mid-1980s, when cities seemed entirely at the mercy of untethered corporations pursuing tax abatements, subsidies, and other sweetheart deals from communities anxious to recruit new industry, local governments rarely enjoyed such success. Yet Playskool eventually left Chicago, and the Northwest Side neighborhood where its factory stood arguably never fully recovered from the loss. The job-placement program enjoyed some successes but largely overlooked especially needy low-income, African American, and Latina women workers. Hasbro-Bradley sold the 750,000-square-foot factory and the surrounding land to private interests for manufacturing and distribution uses. By 1988 the Playskool site housed fifteen companies that jointly employed 400 people, almost none of whom had worked at Playskool. The preemptive action by Washington and Mier somewhat mitigated an impending economic setback, arguably making a modicum of headway in the effort to address a very formidable problem faced by Chicago and other manufacturing cities. The settlement with Playskool fell short of a reliable antidote to deindustrialization, however, as all parties recognized. Surely the mayor was right in saying that charting the progress and evaluating the success of his job-retention efforts at the Playskool facility (and other locations) meant more than rehashing the latest high jinks in city council chambers.[51]

Shortly after the media's cursory mention of the city's deal with Playskool, a new instance of political intrigue involving the mayor and his enemies captured the headlines of the Chicago dailies. The story transfixing the reading public dealt with the replacement of Third Ward alderman Tyrone Kenner, who had been convicted in 1983 of mail fraud and extortion and been sentenced to five years in prison. At that time, Washington appointed Dorothy Tillman, the ward's Democratic committeeman, to serve in the position until a special election could be held in February 1985. The mayor endorsed Tillman, who had accompanied the Reverend Martin Luther King Jr. to the Windy City in 1966 and remained there after the civil rights leader returned to the South, to succeed Kenner; a victory in the special election would make her the clear favorite to fill the office permanently. Her principal competition came from James "Skip" Burrell, a deputy foreman in the city's sewer department and staunch Kenner loyalist. On January 30, 1985, Washington summoned Burrell to his apartment, hoping to persuade him to drop out of the election in the interest of party unity. Burrell concealed a microcassette tape recorder in his jacket pocket during the visit, secretly recorded his conversation with the mayor, and then gave the tape to Kenner. On February 20, a *Chicago Tribune* columnist, Michael Sneed, broke the story on page 1 and quoted liberally from the tape. Vrdolyak denied passing a copy of the tape to the newspaper, but Sneed reported that the alderman's associates had been spreading stories about its contents among the city's politicians for days and had eventually sent the tape to the *Tribune*. Sneed characterized Washington's candid comments as arrogant, inappropriate, and unethical, particularly his bullying attempt to force Burrell out of the race and his surprisingly caustic assessment of Tillman's abilities.[52]

The next day, the *Tribune* published the entire four-page transcript of the recorded conversation. In all, the dialogue between the two men—and the damage to the mayor's reputation—amounted to much less than the previous day's teaser had promised. Certainly, no political spin doctor could characterize Washington's comments about Tillman as flattering. He described her as "abusive and crude and insincere" and mocked her meager knowledge of how municipal government operated from the precinct level to city hall. Moreover, he belittled her reputed experience in the civil right movement and suggested that she had exaggerated her relationship with Dr. King to improve her stature in the black community. He had supported Tillman for alderman, the mayor confessed to Burrell, only because of her elevated standing among South Side community activists. Washington denied any unethical motives for backing Tillman, however, and he neither threatened Burrell nor offered him any inducements to withdraw from the race. As mayoral spokesmen insisted, the full transcript of the tape showed the meeting to be nothing more than a restrained attempt to persuade Burrell. Washington appeared less a ruthless political boss than a smooth-talking used-car salesman.[53]

At a press conference called to address the negative implications of the newspaper story, the mayor and his representatives downplayed the substance of the conversation between the two men and spoke at length about the illegality of the unauthorized electronic surveillance. Even the original *Tribune* story acknowledged that Burrell had violated the Illinois eavesdropping law. Referring to the incident as "Vrdolygate," Chicago Corporation counsel James Montgomery reminded the press that Burrell's actions constituted a felony. Washington went further, adding that the newspaper that reported the story (and by association the author of the article and the editors who authorized its publication) had been accessories to a criminal act. Tillman issued a statement denying that she harbored any hard feelings toward the mayor and pledging to work closely with him in the city council if elected later that month. The story lingered for several more days, but the conversation dealt increasingly with the journalistic ethics surrounding the decision to publish the transcript and the administration's decision not to take legal action against the newspaper.[54]

In the week following the furor over what became known as the "Vrdolyak tapes," the extent of the miscalculation by Washington's enemies became clear. In the absence of any legally incriminating remarks, the secret recording embarrassed the mayor only in revealing his lack of enthusiasm for a candidate he felt obligated to endorse. The transcript further demonstrated how frequently he sprinkled his everyday conversation out of range of microphones and television cameras with profanities, a revelation that could hardly have been shocking to close followers of Chicago politics. If anything, thought press secretary Alton Miller, learning about the contents of the tape probably caused some white voters to hold the mayor in higher esteem than they had before. In some ways, his low-key, good-humored attempt to win Burrell over made him seem more human and less threatening. In addition, the episode again highlighted the extremes to which Vrdolyak and his cronies would go to gain any advantage—and provided another challenge to the notion that the supposedly deft maneuvers of cunning aldermen against an overmatched mayor always ended successfully.[55]

The mayor's opponents likewise failed to benefit from the controversial decision not to retain Chicago Public Schools superintendent Ruth Love after her contract expired in March 1985. Appointed in 1981 by Mayor Jane Byrne, Love had clashed repeatedly with the school board over both policy and funding issues. Criticized as an imperious and inflexible administrator, she saw her reputation suffer further as student performance on standardized tests failed to improve under her leadership. After a May 1984 audit of rumored irregularities in reading-test scores unearthed worrisome discrepancies at some schools, the board of education had voted six to five not to renew Love's contract. The angry superintendent claimed to be an innocent victim of political intrigue and vowed to contest the decision in the courts. She also reported having received several telephone calls from Vrdolyak, who offered to help in her battle against the administration. Vrdolyak refused to comment.[56]

Throughout the dispute between the superintendent and her board of
education critics, Washington kept an exceedingly low profile and reiterated
his intention to maintain a healthy distance from school politics. When the
mayor declined to come to her defense, Love accused him of being involved
behind the scenes in a plot to install one of his cronies (assistant superintendent Manford Byrd) as her successor. Between tapings of a television
news program, believing that the cameras had been turned off, she called
Washington "a mess" and referred to him and Byrd, among others, as "a
bunch of gays." Love's intemperate remarks reinforced Washington's negative impression of her, an assessment gleaned from discussions with school
board members who had kept city hall informed about her periodic blunders.
The mayor regarded her as one of the weak appointments Byrne had made
in her effort to curry favor with African American voters. Whatever his
involvement in the plot to remove Love from the superintendency, he undoubtedly considered Byrd a much better choice for the important position.
Vrdolyak and others failed to find any evidence of Washington's participation
in Love's ouster, and, as much as they may have hoped that the firing of a
black woman would engender an outcry from African American community
leaders, no scandal or popular uprising ensued. The mayor survived Love's
stormy exit from Chicago officialdom without noticeable wear and tear.[57]

Indeed, by the end of Washington's second year in office, the myth of
invincibility surrounding Vrdolyak, Burke, and their followers had begun
to erode. Changing perceptions of the Council Wars at the middle of the
mayor's term in office appeared gradually in the local media. Midterm as-
sessments of Washington's record fell decidedly short of lavish praise, but
reporters and editorial writers no longer uniformly described the heavyweight bout between the mayor and the city council majority as a hopeless mismatch. Even the highly partisan *Chicago Tribune* admitted that the
unbroken string of triumphs for the Vrdolyak forces in the administration's
first year had given way to more mixed results in the second year, constituting a modest resurgence by the mayor. Among the city's progressives, the
administration's improved fortunes proved to be reason for celebration
and cautious optimism. "Washington has made some stupid mistakes,"
liberal political consultant Don Rose told a reporter, "but in context they
seem almost frivolous compared to the things Ed Vrdolyak does every day
of his life, on purpose, as a matter of policy, and as a perfect expression of
everything he stands for."[58]

To be certain, the basic math of the Council Wars remained the same. The opposition forces retained their impregnable twenty-nine-to-twenty-one advantage in the city council, as Vrdolyak and Burke firmly preserved the loyalty of the coalition's membership. Rumors surfaced occasionally of rifts within the majority bloc, and differences of opinion allegedly surfaced from time to time in their caucuses. Some hard-liners pressed for continual hectoring of the mayor, while others, more concerned about the public's potential impatience with the city council's obstinacy, cautioned against excess. Advocates of open confrontation at every juncture clashed with those who called for more covert activity plied behind the scenes. Such discord reflected dissimilar views about tactics, not any wavering from the shared objective, so the twenty-nine allies managed to mute their differences and maintain a united front. After all, the quest for power and the imperatives of race—the factors that originally animated the rebellion against mayoral authority—remained as compelling to the aldermen in early 1985 as they had two years earlier. No one doubted the effectiveness of the guerrilla warfare. Ordinances submitted by the mayor's office had perished in committees, initiatives introduced by the twenty-one administration loyalists had suffered ridicule and defeat on the city council floor, and the legislature had refused to approve fifty-eight of the mayor's appointments to various commissions and committees by April 1985. Washington continued to fight an uphill battle to govern in the face of a city council determined to foil his reform designs at every turn.[59]

The interminable strife in city hall unsettled the city's leading merchants and financiers, who yearned for a return to the civic peace and accommodating downtown-first climate they had come to expect in Chicago. Some prominent corporate executives condemned Washington and his enemies equally for the breakdowns in municipal governance and for undermining Chicago's reputation as a business-friendly city, while others blamed the mayor alone. For members of the growth coalition who saw Washington as a remote and isolated figure in city hall, confirming their fears at the time of his election, the lingering dissatisfaction with the administration revolved around the loss of access and influence. No longer could the chief executive officer of a multimillion-dollar manufacturing concern or the president of one of Chicago's leading banks, neither of whom knew Washington intimately or moved in the same social circles with him, be given an exclusive audience with the mayor or local officials on short notice. Reform meant listening to more voices, more constituencies, more interest groups. Especially powerful businessmen had enjoyed "particular access" to mayors in past administrations, and "now they feel they don't have that access," remarked deputy press secretary Christopher Chandler. "The reason is, the access has been broadened."[60]

The lack of progress on large-scale projects deemed of great importance for downtown redevelopment further troubled Chicago's business and financial leaders in the second year of Washington's term. Discussion about the 1992 World's Fair dragged on and on with no resolution, for instance, as the mayor stopped short of issuing an unequivocal endorsement and continuously called for additional deliberation. He insisted that Chicago's financial stability must not be undermined in any way, that none of the city's municipal services should be disrupted, and that the World's Fair Authority should assume all of the costs of construction and operation. Meanwhile, a number of community groups grew stronger in their opposition to the damaging effects that project would have on thriving neighborhoods, and the Mayor's Advisory Commission on Latino Affairs adamantly recommended that Washington not support the proposed fair. Another study group directly challenged the World's Fair Authority's projections of job creation. In a report released in September 1984, the Chicago 1992 Committee contended that necessary displacement would eliminate thirty thousand existing jobs in and around the fair site. The critique continued. Residents of the area, particularly women and minorities, would have virtually no opportunity to obtain the relatively small number of high-paying construction jobs. These excluded groups might well have better luck being hired for employment in tourism after the completion of the fair, but such jobs, poorly paid and often part-time, would be available for at most a year. Boosters of the fair no doubt cringed at reading the Chicago 1992 Committee's terse conclusion: "As an overall economic development tool, the Fair promotes employment in a low wage unstable industry, possibly at the expense of manufacturing industry surrounding the site, while leaving an infrastructure the utility of which is unclear and has not been subject to public debate." Absent a strong endorsement by the administration, corporate leaders felt, the publication of such damaging reports was gradually leaching away public support from what the business community regarded as a crucial element in the drive to ensure Chicago's future greatness. The city's establishment expressed shock at the mayor's apparent lack of enthusiasm for the World's Fair, remembered planning commissioner Elizabeth Hollander.[61]

Negotiations also lagged on another development project highly valued by the downtown business community, the conversion of Navy Pier into a retail and entertainment mecca. As discussions continued to proceed slowly with the Rouse Corporation in the fall of 1984, the Department of Economic Development also entered into talks with the U.S. Steel Corporation about building a new mill at its South Works location in Chicago's Calumet region. Once a steelmaking giant occupying dozens of buildings on acres of lakefront property, the South Works had been reduced to a single furnace, as U.S. Steel had laid off more than seven thousand workers in the previous six years. Both the Navy Pier and U.S. Steel projects required substantial financial contributions from the city. The DED estimated that Urban Development Action Grant (UDAG) funding from the federal government totaling approximately forty million dollars would be required in each case, but prior experiences indicated the unlikelihood of receiving two grants of such size in a single year. Because of his desire to save the local steel industry, preference for manufacturing jobs rather than low-paying service jobs, and commitment to declining neighborhoods undercut by industrial flight, Washington designated the UDAG application for the South Works project as the administration's first priority. He directed DED personnel to seek alternative sources of funding for Navy Pier, which remained a viable project on the administration's agenda, but the prioritization of South Works sent a clear and disappointing message to the business interests who preferred the pursuit of tourism and retail rather than industrial retention. In March 1985, the administration terminated its negotiations with the Rouse Corporation and formed a task force to assess the situation. The future of Navy Pier appeared unclear.[62]

The downtown-first growth coalition also questioned the administration's commitment to the North Loop project. Despite whatever misgivings he might have held, the mayor had refrained from renouncing the redevelopment plan conceived by his predecessors. Forsaking Byrne's strategy, though, Washington turned the North Loop effort over to the Planning Department, where commissioner Elizabeth Hollander and her aides devoted considerable attention to the preservation of historic buildings along with the creation of moneymaking enterprises. Working closely with historic preservationists, Hollander adopted a meticulous block-by-block approach that seemed to slow the pace of demolition and construction even further. As the first step in the administration's goal of creating a "theater row" in the northern section of the Loop, in 1984 the Planning Department arranged for the sale of the sixty-four-year-old Chicago Theatre to an investment group intending to convert the grand old movie palace into a performing arts center. Months in court to stay the demolition of the aged building, the acquisition of a UDAG to underwrite structural improvements, and the defeat of a hostile proposal by several aldermen to consign the theater to other uses slowed advancement on the project. The mayor's office vied with members of the city council's majority bloc for months over the best means of paying for improvements in the central business district before finally convincing them to employ Tax Increment Financing, a creative means of financing the renewal of blighted areas approved by the Illinois General Assembly in 1977, to redevelop the vacant block just east of city hall. Impatient investors in Chicago chafed at the glacial pace of the North Loop project, which they regarded as yet another indication of the mayor's inadequate attention to the crying need for downtown redevelopment as the spearhead for economic revitalization.[63]

Dissatisfaction with Washington's first two years in office also grew among constituencies that cared less about the gilding of the central business district than about attention to worsening conditions in other areas of the city. The inadequate provision of suitable lodging for Chicago's large and diverse population plagued the administration much as earlier mayoralties had faltered at trying to ensure adequate shelter for all residents in the private housing market. Brenda Gaines, Washington's choice for housing commissioner, had been able to reverse the net loss of housing units for the first time since the early 1970s, and her creative use of public-private partnerships leveraged multimillion-dollar grants from the federal government for the construction of new homes. Gaines also announced that the administration was making available low-interest loans for 1,500 middle- and moderate-income families that had previously been unable to qualify for mortgages. But such limited increases in the housing stock paled in comparison with the worsening public housing crisis that had made the Chicago Housing Authority synonymous nationally with corruption, malfeasance, and dysfunctionality. The second-largest public housing authority in the country with more than 145,000 tenants, the CHA had been perceived as a public relations disaster for years, owing to the shameful quality of life experienced by residents packed into the deteriorating structures and to the administrative scandals frequently erupting in the agency. Much of the criticism revolved around massive high-rise projects such as the Robert Taylor Homes, Stateway Gardens, and Cabrini-Green that had become infamous for dangerous overcrowding, inadequate service delivery, violence, and illegal drug usage.[64]

Washington harbored no illusions about the forlorn situation with the city's public housing. He referred to high-rise projects as "canyons of despair that should never have been built" and fully recognized the extent of venality at CHA headquarters downtown. "The CHA didn't have a problem," he told a top aide. "They *were* the problem." Furthermore, the despondent mayor saw no solution and seriously doubted that any reformer, no matter how honest and well intentioned, could improve the situation substantially. He said, "Nobody can make the CHA work. . . . The only solution is to just get rid of it. What you need in the meantime is someone with Renault Robinson's skills to keep it all together." Washington admired Robinson's heroism in organizing the Afro-American Patrolmen's League and had long considered him a loyal ally. He recognized Robinson's lack of managerial experience but hoped it would not prove to be a fatal flaw. Appointed to the CHA board several years earlier by Byrne and fully cognizant of the many intractable problems he would face heading the agency, Robinson spurned the mayor's offer initially but in August 1983 agreed to serve as chairman.[65]

Robinson's tenure as CHA chairman proved to be an unmitigated disaster from the beginning. Charging blindly ahead to root out the most egregious examples of improbity and mismanagement, he ham-handedly brought the CHA's simmering crisis to a boil. Without identifying a suitable alternative, he immediately canceled the exorbitant elevator-repair contract. By January 1984, in the midst of a frigid winter, fewer than 30 percent of the elevators at the Robert Taylor Homes, Stateway Gardens, and Cabrini-Green functioned at all. (The CHA eventually contracted eight elevator companies for repairs.) Equally impetuous in paring the CHA payroll to end featherbedding, he fired more than two hundred heating-plant workers—a disastrous miscalculation when pipes froze and burst that winter and tenants suffered without heat for interminable lengths of time before the remaining staff members could respond to their complaints. Residents of the projects complained that the agency's erratic service had sunk to new levels of unreliability. While poorly conceived and hastily implemented attempts at reform backfired, Robinson also faced charges of nepotism for hiring his brother-in-law (a convicted felon with no experience in housing) and for extravagant spending in his own office. In the spring of 1984, the CHA hired Zirl Smith, an experienced housing professional from Wilmington, Delaware, as executive director to handle the agency's day-to-day operations. Smith and Robinson bickered constantly over policy, however, and tensions rose between the CHA and HUD. The bureaucrat heading HUD's regional office in Chicago allied with Robinson against Smith, and Washington became convinced that HUD officials in Washington, D.C., loyal to the Reagan administration were trying to embarrass the CHA. The mayor later admitted that the Robinson appointment had been a mistake—but a minor one, he insisted, in the context of the city's enduring and overwhelming public housing crisis.[66]

Despite the jumble of problems the mayor's office faced and the determined opposition encountered in the city council, Washington believed that he and his aides had laid a sturdy foundation for change by the midpoint of his first term. The hazardous climate prevailing in city hall notwithstanding, the administration could claim some noteworthy achievements after two arduous years. Making hard fiscal choices, Washington had made inroads against the alarming financial situation he had inherited. The elimination of approximately three thousand city workers, the painful paring of city services, and two bare-bones budgets had reduced Chicago's deficit from about $168 million to a more manageable $21 million. The city's bond rating, lowered by Standard & Poor's and Moody's during the mayor's first year in office because of the turmoil in local government, held steady the second year and fortunately still remained investment grade. In 1984 alone, boasted the administration, the DED created or retained more than eight thousand jobs in Chicago. The press and good-government groups overwhelmingly gave the mayor high marks for the quality of his appointments to top-level administrative posts, ranging from Elizabeth Hollander in the Office of Planning and chief of staff Bill Ware to police superintendent Fred Rice and fire commissioner Louis Galante. The city's law office, once considered a low-powered refuge for underachieving attorneys, improved dramatically under corporation counsel James Montgomery's leadership. Montgomery had eliminated potential conflicts of interest in his office by barring all outside legal practice and regularly held seminars for city attorneys with nationally renowned lawyers and judges. In short, Washington had selected qualified professionals rather than well-connected politicians as members of his cabinet. Chicagoans accustomed to the media's periodic disclosures of waste, graft, bribery, and other illegalities in city hall noticed the absence of major scandals in the administration. Open access to government records, public participation in budgeting, and a substantive new ethics ordinance gave city government an unprecedented dose of transparency.[67]

Without question, the first two years of the Washington mayoralty had produced a number of important structural reforms that improved the quality of municipal government and demanded more accountability in city hall. Yet because of the power wielded by the city council's majority bloc, as the mayor himself admitted, the administration enjoyed much less success in achieving the far-reaching changes that he and his constituents had sought. Social reform, anathema to the political machine's old guard, required a fundamental alteration of the way municipal government worked, much greater openness and accessibility in city hall, and the redistribution of the city's resources on a more equitable basis. Progress toward achieving the goals outlined a year earlier in *Chicago Works Together*, a reiteration of the fundamental aims propounded during the 1983 mayoral campaign, still came grudgingly. The centerpieces of the Washington reform program—job development, balanced growth, neighborhood empowerment, enhanced public participation, and a regional, state, and national legislative agenda—continued to draw heavy fire from an antagonistic city council. A U.S. appellate court ruled in 1984 that the ward map redrawn during the Byrne administration had not gone far enough to end discrimination against black and Latino voters—and had indeed exacerbated the situation—but the details of redistricting were still being adjudicated in the courts. Until legal action ended racial gerrymandering and the reconfiguration of Chicago's wards provided minority residents with proportional representation in local government, the mayor's enemies in city hall would retain their majority status. The twenty-nine aldermen would still be in a position to blunt reform, if not quash it altogether.[68]

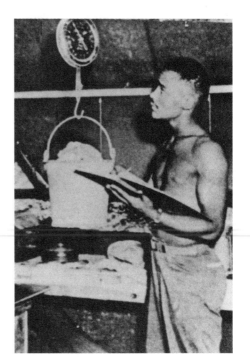

Sergeant Harold Washington, 1887th Engineer Battalion, U.S. Army, in Guam, April 1945. Courtesy of the Chicago Public Library, Harold Washington Library Center, Special Collections.

Harold Washington with three Roosevelt College classmates. Courtesy of the Chicago Public Library, Harold Washington Library Center, Special Collections.

Congressman Harold Washington with activist Lu Palmer prior to the 1983 mayoral election. Courtesy of the Chicago Public Library, Harold Washington Library Center, Special Collections.

Al Raby, Harold Washington's campaign manager, addresses campaign staff during the 1983 mayoral campaign. Courtesy of the Chicago Public Library, Harold Washington Library Center, Special Collections.

Harold Washington proudly poses with female city hall staff members, demonstrating the unprecedented number of women he had appointed to his administration. Courtesy of the Chicago Public Library, Harold Washington Library Center, Special Collections.

Harold Washington with Twenty-Second Ward Democratic Committeeman Jesus Garcia (*left*) and national labor leader Cesar Chavez (*right*), October 11, 1985. Courtesy of the Chicago Public Library, Harold Washington Library Center, Special Collections.

Harold Washington accompanies Alderman Dorothy Tillman on a tour of the Third Ward to talk with her constituents, October 9, 1986. Courtesy of the Chicago Public Library, Harold Washington Library Center, Special Collections.

Harold Washington addressing attendees of the eighteenth annual Gay and Lesbian Pride Parade, June 28, 1987. Courtesy of the Chicago Public Library, Harold Washington Library Center, Special Collections.

At the end of her unsuccessful run for mayor in the Democratic primary, Jane Byrne endorses Harold Washington in the general election, February 28, 1987. Courtesy of the Chicago Public Library, Harold Washington Library Center, Special Collections.

5

BALANCED GROWTH

Harold Washington's State of the City address, delivered on April 11, 1985, at the Palmer House Hotel to the nonpartisan League of Women Voters, marked the midpoint of his mayoral term and split neatly into two parts. In the first half of the speech, the mayor extolled his administration's accomplishments during the preceding two years, and in the second half he presented a detailed agenda for the ensuing twelve months. Virtually ignoring the resistance he had encountered during the previous two years from the city council's obstreperous majority, the mayor dwelled instead on the advances already made and the continued progress in the future that together would engineer a municipal rebirth. He pilloried Chicago's past "'facade' of the 'City that Worked,'" noting that decades of cronyism and inequality had initiated a protracted period of decline, damaging the spirit as well as the material prospects of a metropolis struggling to compete in a rapidly changing international economy. The Windy City's renaissance under his leadership would be based on the equal treatment of all citizens and unprecedented access to elected officials, resulting in the people repudiating "a government of deals and [replacing] it with a government of ideals." More than just a fanciful ideal, fairness would be the fundamental organizing principle for a diverse and productive community—"red and yellow, black and white, young and old, affluent and striving, men, women and children, pulling together in a symphony of achievement." Reform need not impede economic development, just as neighborhood improvement need not come at the expense of downtown revitalization. In fact, balanced growth would be a vital element in future prosperity—a process already commenced under the Washington administration, the upbeat mayor proclaimed.[1]

Washington proudly enumerated the unmistakable signs of Chicago's rejuvenation evident under his stewardship during the previous two years. He cited a report by the U.S. Department of Labor that the city had enjoyed a net gain of sixty-four thousand jobs in 1984 and boasted of a 12.3 percent increase in retail sales, as well as the addition of 103 more factories, the same year. Additional encouraging economic news could be found in the central business district in the form of 3.5 million square feet of new office space and the resumed use of another 3.5 million square feet that had previously stood unoccupied. Rising levels of tourism had led to the construction and planning of four thousand new hotel rooms downtown. The ongoing $1.5 billion development program at O'Hare International Airport, the largest and costliest public works project in the city's history, promised to ensure Chicago's primacy as a crossroads for international travel and trade for years to come. Finally, in a reference designed to reassure the anxious business community, the mayor spoke glowingly in his remarks of the progress made by the World's Fair Authority in planning for a blockbuster event in 1992.[2]

At the same time that he trumpeted the major public works that pleased the city's growth coalition, Washington also reaffirmed his commitment to neighborhood uplift. "It's not enough to have your head in the skyline," the mayor told his audience, "if you're walking on broken sidewalks." He listed several improvements completed outside the Loop in the past two years, most noticeably the construction, rehabilitation, and weatherization of twelve thousand housing units (a number surpassing the total of the previous four years) along with the construction or refurbishment of three public library branches. The mayor's increased attention to people living in distressed communities showed in the threefold increase of the city's funding for homeless shelters, the opening of five new senior citizen nutrition centers, and a 33 percent increase in food vouchers distributed under the Women, Infants, and Children program. To stimulate citizen participation in government, Washington had created public task forces on the steel and apparel industries, hunger, homelessness, youth gangs, crime prevention, and women's issues. Building on his predecessor's proclivity for underwriting celebrations along the lakefront and in a few select areas of the city, the mayor's office provided financial and logistical support for staging eighty-eight neighborhood festivals scattered throughout Chicago.[3]

For the year ahead, Washington proposed a series of measures in keeping with his reform vision and challenged his enemies to forswear for the good of the city the "cheap shots and the quick headlines" that had become their stock in trade. He appealed to the city council to remove the roadblocks that stood in the way of implementing his agenda fully, beginning with the belated approval of mayoral appointments that had been languishing for an extended length of time. He also urged the city's legislators to embrace the administration's commitment to affirmative action by endorsing the Minority Business Enterprise/Women's Business Enterprise (MBE/WBE) program that established the 25–5 formula as official city policy. He reiterated Chicago's urgent need to repair infrastructure in the neighborhoods, a clear reference to the general-obligation bond the city council had blocked the year before. With or without city council support, his administration would accelerate its efforts in Springfield and Washington, D.C., to lobby for a fair return on taxes paid by Chicago to those distant seats of government. The mayor pledged to continue the fight for ward redistricting that would provide equitable representation in the city council, especially for Latinos. (Not coincidentally, the mayor and his aides expected, rectification of the imbalance in the local legislature would help dismantle the numerical majority that had stifled his reform efforts.) Noteworthy for its lack of new programs and policies, the mayor's agenda dealt overwhelmingly with the completion of tasks commenced earlier and the successful implementation of initiatives held captive in city council chambers. He closed the rousing State of the City address on a positive note. "I'm here to tell you tonight," he concluded, beaming ear to ear, "the state of the city is real good."[4]

The State of the City address contained a certain amount of public relations puffery, a commonplace in any mayor's summation of his or her administration's accomplishments, but also accurately reflected Washington's real sense of achievement and genuine hopefulness for the future. Along with many others in city hall, he shared the belief that encouraging developments in recent months had signaled a clear momentum swing in the Council Wars. The administration had weathered the storm—the early successes for Vrdolyak, Burke, and their followers were not being repeated by late 1984—and even the jaded Chicago media were (often grudgingly) admitting that the mayor seemed at last to be holding his own. Hard-earned progress in the face of such determined opposition was encouraging, and the mayor was laboriously building a solid record that promised much greater results if the guerrilla operations of his political opposition could be suppressed. Even though the redistricting suit in federal court had not been won as quickly as expected, the mayor and his political strategists felt sanguine about the eventual outcome of the litigation—just as they remained confident about his reelection prospects in 1987. Slow and steady progress on achieving the goals set in *Chicago Works Together* would vindicate Washington's ceaseless calls for reform. The mayor still saw balanced growth, which entailed equity for all groups and all locations in Chicago, not just as a key element in his vision for the city's future but also as a realizable goal. Throughout his speeches, he returned joyfully time after time to the theme the "New Spirit of Chicago."[5]

Washington's buoyancy proved to be infectious, nurturing a real sense of possibility among his aides and department heads. His insatiable love of politics impressed friend and foe alike. "Politics is like shooting pool or eating Cracker Jacks," he often joked. "Once you start, you just can't stop." Chicagoans saw in their mayor a garrulous public figure, a ruggedly handsome and gregarious politician who eagerly waded into crowds of well-wishers and gamely wore sombreros and yarmulkes at ethnic celebrations. But they knew very little about the private life of the man whose days and nights seemed to be devoted entirely to public affairs. Apart from his presence at ceremonial functions that required a mayoral appearance, he rarely attended the theater, viewed a museum exhibit, took in a ball game, or dined at any of Chicago's elegant restaurants. He lived simply in a nondescript Hyde Park apartment, reading widely, watching very little television, and listening to all-news radio station WBBM-AM. He professed no interest in making money, dressed plainly in clothes more comfortable than fashionable, and frequently amused members of his staff and reporters by wearing soup-stained ties.[6] David Potter, his press secretary during the 1983 campaign, remarked:

> One of the reasons I like the guy so much is because he's a slob with a suit on. I find it endearing. He represents Everyman. He would be more comfortable in a robe and slippers than a suit. His collection of ties is ghastly, not because he doesn't have taste but just because he doesn't give a damn. He just doesn't care. He's all business. Nothing else makes any difference. . . . He is really an all-work, no-play type. I can't imagine him sitting down for ninety minutes to watch a movie.[7]

The press yearned to find out more about his private life but had to settle for pro forma accounts of his public comings and goings. He apparently spent little time with his three siblings and six stepsiblings, whom he tersely dismissed as "grass roots." Invariably courteous to municipal workers he encountered in city hall, the mayor kept even his closes aides at arm's length and formed very few close relationships with members of his administration. A handful of old friends gathered occasionally in his apartment for poker games and political gossip sessions that extended well into the night. The few visitors allowed into the inner sanctuary of his residence described a mass of reading material strewn around, including daily newspapers, city documents, biographies of historical figures such as Booker T. Washington and Henry Kissinger, and nonfiction books such as Kenneth Auletta's account of the New York City fiscal crisis. A voracious reader, he returned books lent to him by staff members in record time, prepared to discuss the major ideas developed in the volumes. Cabinet members and other officials in local government held the mayor in high esteem, which they eagerly expressed at the time and years later when reminiscing about their time in city hall, and invariably praised his intellect and compassion. Planning commissioner Elizabeth Hollander's recollections aptly summarized their views. "As a person," she said, "Harold Washington was deeply intelligent, worldly wise, widely read, kind, very personable and easy to like." Indifferent to his reclusive habits and protective of his privacy, city officials and mayoral aides admired Washington, enthusiastically enlisting in his crusade for better government, and believed that his administration was beginning to make a real difference in Chicago.[8]

The heady sense of optimism pervading city hall in the spring of 1985 stalled briefly with the news of chief of staff Bill Ware's death on May 23. Slowed for months by an undisclosed illness, Ware had become less and less of a presence around city hall as he alternated long absences with shorter and shorter appearances in the mayor's office. (Members of the administration learned after his death that he had been spending increasing amounts of time at Sloane-Kettering Hospital in New York City, seeking treatment for the malady that eventually took his life.) Newspaper obituaries cited complications resulting from pneumonia as the cause of death, but top aides in the administration attributed the thirty-seven-year-old's demise to AIDS. Washington's closest adviser since his election to the U.S. House of Representatives five years earlier, Ware had been widely praised (even by the mayor's fiercest adversaries in the city council) as a hardworking, selfless bureaucrat of unquestioned integrity whose presence had underscored the administration's commitment to good government. Like his boss, Ware never wavered in his dedication to reform principles and believed passionately that efficient business practices and sound management techniques in city hall were crucial to creating better municipal government. "Bottleneck Bill" may have frustrated others in the administration with his excessive caution and lack of political acumen, but no one questioned his devotion to municipal reform. The grieving mayor replaced Ware with Ernest Barefield, the deputy chief of staff, and vowed to continue the fight for the ideals he had shared with his deceased aide.[9]

Victory in that quest still meant prevailing in the Council Wars, however, and the administration's foes showed no signs of relenting. The majority bloc in the city council threw up roadblocks to derail or at least delay each proposal originating in the mayor's office. They fiercely battled the mayor over the O'Hare International Airport development program, which had begun during the Byrne administration, continuing the guerrilla campaign they had been waging over the massive endeavor since 1983. Month after month, critics railed that the project was proceeding behind schedule and over budget—charges that Washington consistently denied. Led by the indefatigable Edward Burke, opposition aldermen inveighed against the administration's handling of the $1.5 billion undertaking (the largest and costliest capital project in Chicago's history) and leveled a series of lurid accusations: favoritism by awarding contracts to black-owned companies that had not submitted the lowest bids, nepotism in hiring, and theft by city workers, among others. The discussion about corruption in the O'Hare project increasingly revolved around the construction of the People Mover, one of eighty separate construction projects included in the airport renovation. Critics claimed that the administration had rigged the bidding process and awarded the contract for the People Mover, a light-rail system to ferry passengers between the airport terminal and distant long-term parking lots, after opening sealed bids in secret. Corporation counsel James Montgomery's explanation that the engineering skills required for the unique project obviated the need for competitive bidding, confirmed in a ruling by circuit court judge David J. Shields, failed to persuade Burke. "The process was tainted," brayed the insistent alderman. "It cannot be rehabilitated."[10]

Righteously indignant over the administration's handling of the O'Hare development program, Burke argued against approval of the revenue bonds totaling $480 million that would allow continued funding of airport improvement in the waning months of 1985. Further, the city council Finance Committee recommended that the authorization for the project be amended to grant its chairman (Burke) a personal veto over "every payment and reimbursement, every contract and contract modification," associated with the construction. "Who does [Burke] think he is?" sputtered Washington. "Even the Mayor can't do that." After the obligatory haggling triggered by the Finance Committee chairman's demand, the factions struggled to a workable compromise: a city council vote approved the marketing of the revenue bonds, and municipal departments involved in the O'Hare project agreed to submit regular reports, detailing contract revisions and expenditures to the city council.[11]

The mayor and his enemies likewise clashed over the welfare of low-income neighborhoods through their annual battle over the disbursement of Community Development Block Grants. As it had done the previous two years, the city council in 1985 challenged the proposed budget in the administration's application for CDBG funds totaling $126.7 million. Once again, Washington charged, his council opponents had submitted an alternative budget that ignored federal guidelines, sought to use funds for blatantly political purposes, and favored relatively prosperous areas while ignoring the kinds of substandard neighborhoods for which the grants had been created. In so doing, the mayor said, his foes shortchanged the Latino community as a heavy-handed means of discouraging its growing electoral support of reform candidates. Despite sharp admonitions sent from the Department of Housing and Urban Development, which clearly delineated the types of proposals that would be considered and demanded that the city reimburse the federal government for past misuse of CDBG funding, the Vrdolyak bloc continued to argue that development money be allocated to well-to-do enclaves as well as to poor communities. Washington's adversaries pointed to his refusal to endorse aid for projects in affluent white precincts, even when the organizations purportedly seeking aid declined to submit funding proposals, as evidence that he pursued economic development funding only for minority Chicagoans.[12]

The political impasse on CDBG funding dragged on for more than two months, extending beyond the July 1, 1985, deadline for the submission of applications to Washington, D.C. The interruption of federal funding for continuing projects resulted in the layoff of thirteen hundred municipal workers, budgetary shortfalls for more than 150 social service agencies, and the suspension of work on a multitude of projects. Many of the laid-off workers staged protests at city hall, directing their ire at the city council's majority bloc. On July 9, following a three-and-a-half-hour summit meeting held several days earlier between the mayor and his opponents, the city council approved a compromise agreement that allowed for the tardy submission of the grant application. Chicago's request for a CDBG award deleted any mention of projects for ineligible areas—the administration unofficially agreed to divert municipal funds to those agencies—and the majority bloc consented to restore money for programs in low- and moderate-income areas. HUD approved the late application. Especially important, according to the mayor, the receipt of CDGB funding allowed the full implementation of the administration's new antigang program.[13]

Unceasing pursuit of reform also meant the continuation of the mayor's affirmative action guidelines, which had been imposed despite strong resistance from the administration's foes. Washington boasted about the MBE/WBE program, which established by executive order the goals of 25 percent minority and 5 percent women ownership, and the "first-source" program of job referrals, which required that city-funded projects with twenty or more new hires utilize the Mayor's Office of Employment and Training to recruit workers. Not everyone applauded the city's hiring record, however. Some community organizations complained that excessive amounts of red tape limited the programs' effectiveness in hiring minority workers, members of the business sector cited bureaucratic delays as the cause of reduced profit and a less inviting investment environment, and the city council's majority bloc charged that affirmative action programs presented a convenient subterfuge for patronage. In October 1985, Washington named a fifty-member task force composed of representatives from business, labor, and community organizations to evaluate the first-source program. Taking care to appoint members known to approve of affirmative action in principle, he expected the task force to submit recommendations for streamlining the program rather than terminating it altogether. The task force did not disappoint the mayor in its final report, heartily endorsing the continuation of the city's first-source hiring in both permanent employment and construction jobs, suggesting that the city's community-based organizations assume responsibility for referring job applicants to city hall, and recommending that compliance be encouraged through the use of both incentives and sanctions. Washington reiterated his support of first-source hiring specifically and affirmative action principles generally, a stance that resonated clearly in declining neighborhoods that had long suffered from city hall's neglect.[14]

While paying considerable attention to the substandard economic situation in neighborhoods with large minority populations, the administration also devoted a substantial amount of time to monitoring the situation in other parts of Chicago that suffered especially because of deindustrialization. Arguably no portion of the Windy City had suffered more from job loss and physical deterioration than the Calumet region in the southeastern corner of the municipality, once the thriving home of the nation's leading steel-producing complex. Obtaining iron ore mined from vast mineral deposits in Minnesota and Michigan, steel companies had erected huge rolling mills, foundries, and fabricating factories in Chicago and its environs in the late nineteenth century. The federal government had dredged and straightened the Calumet River, constructed the Calumet Harbor, and excavated the Calumet-Sag Channel. At the conclusion of the Second World War, the United States manufactured more than half of the world's steel, and facilities in Chicago and Northwest Indiana produced 20 percent of total U.S. output. Tens of thousands of Chicagoans toiled in the steel mills during the early stages of the Cold War, but declining demand, increased international competition, and continued reliance on antiquated facilities led to a calamitous decline locally that mirrored the drastic nationwide collapse in steelmaking during the 1970s and 1980s. The situation in Southeast Chicago worsened rapidly. The enormous Wisconsin Steel plant closed suddenly in 1980, while U.S. Steel's South Works and Inland Steel remained in business but steadily laid off thousands of workers during the next few years. Republic Steel halved its workforce in the early 1980s and merged with LTV Steel in 1984 in an effort to forestall bankruptcy. Once an economic powerhouse linked directly to the thriving metal industries, the region abutting Lake Calumet and the Calumet River system in Southeast Chicago was degenerating into a wasteland of deserted mills, abandoned railheads, vacant lots, and shuttered storefronts.[15]

By the time that Washington became mayor, according to the South Chicago Development Commission, the unemployment rate in the neighborhood registered a catastrophic 35 percent. With more than half of the nation's steelworkers unemployed and prime-time television news programs reporting the collapse of the industry from Buffalo, New York, to Birmingham, Alabama, future prospects for Chicago's Southeast Side were dire. Mindful of the ominous analyses proffered by economists, many of whom were predicting the eminent extinction of the steel industry throughout the United States, the mayor considered not only how to mitigate worsening circumstances for the affected population but also how best to restore economic vitality to a desiccated area of the city. Could the industry rebound from the crisis, and would the city need to provide palliatives only temporarily until the mills reopened?

Or if steelmaking could indeed no longer be a competitive economic activity in the United States, how could the industrial landscape of Southeast Chicago be converted into a viable alternative for other enterprises that would provide jobs for the community's twenty-two thousand idle steelworkers? (A young Barack Obama came to the area at the height of the crisis in 1985 as a community organizer, working to retain industrial jobs in the Calumet region.) To answer these questions, the mayor appointed a task force charged with taking the pulse of an ailing industry and a panic-stricken neighborhood. Chaired by Leanne Lachman, president of the Real Estate Research Corporation, the task force included industry leaders from steel, banking, real estate, organized labor, and academe, as well as community representatives from the Southeast Side.[16]

The Mayor's Task Force on Steel and Southeast Chicago relied heavily on the findings of a study conducted by Ann R. Markusen, who took a leave of absence from the University of California at Berkeley to serve as a staff consultant. Markusen and her research team acknowledged that the situation in both the steel industry and the neighborhood "approache[d] crisis proportions," but nonetheless perceived an opportunity for "industrial renewal." Noting that the manufacture of steel-based durable goods "still account[ed] for about 12 percent of *all* jobs in the City of Chicago," she emphasized the need to salvage as much of the industry as possible because of its continued economic benefit to the city and the Midwest. The cessation of steel production would damage a number of related employers, she warned, including material suppliers, utilities, financial services, and transportation; the negative multiplier effect would be harmful for countless workers in a variety of industries whose jobs relied on the survival of the steel mills and foundries. Her assessment directly challenged a study released in 1984 by the Commercial Club of Chicago that recommended conversion of the city into a center for financial services, banking, insurance, international business, health care, and computer software development and that totally ignored the production of steel and other durable goods. Absolute reliance on service enterprises as touted by the Commercial Club of Chicago, argued the steel task force, must not be the exclusive focus of the local economy.[17]

Markusen's conclusions, released in 1985 shortly before the publication of the task force report, optimistically addressed the prospects for the resuscitation of the region's steel industry. Southeast Chicago possessed a number of invaluable assets, including an experienced labor force, usable infrastructure, inexpensive land surrounding the existing facilities, proximity to a full complement of business services downtown, and a favorable location at the hub of the nation's multimodal transportation network. If the steel industry rebounded in the United States, mills in Chicago's Calumet region would lead the way. To remain competitive, Markusen advised, the area's steel mills needed to invest more generously in new technology, and the city's Department of Economic Development must market products more aggressively to American and international buyers. In the meantime, the mayor should exert leadership nationally by challenging the Republican administration's disastrous macroeconomic policies that were undercutting domestic producers in several key industries such as steel.[18]

The influence of Markusen's research could be seen clearly in the final report, which nonetheless stopped well short of endorsing all of her recommendations. The task force, a diverse group representing several very different constituencies, unsurprisingly struggled to reach agreement on all matters; labor leaders and academicians warmed more readily than real estate and banking executives to Markusen's analysis, for example. She observed of the real estate developers, "They just looked at the lakefront property on the Southeast Side and saw condos." She readily admitted that sharp divisions on the task force precluded acceptance of all her recommendations. In a nod to Markusen, though, the final report challenged the presumption of the steel industry's total collapse and alluded to the need for more public investment in Southeast Chicago. The publicity afforded the task force report kept alive the argument for salvaging as much of the city's manufacturing economy as possible, an important concern for likeminded officials in the Washington administration.[19]

Investigation of the steel industry's plight triggered a call for economic diversification in Southeast Chicago. In August 1985, a city government task force began studying the potential of constructing a third airport in the Lake Calumet area to complement existing facilities at O'Hare and Midway Airports. Composed of members of the Departments of Public Works, Planning, Aviation, and Economic Development, as well as representatives from the mayor's office, the task force explored the practicality of building a new airport as both a response to the region's unmet transportation needs and as an economic stimulus for Southeast Chicago. In its final report, however, the task force concluded that serious doubts about the airport's economic viability superseded any decision to proceed with further planning. The proposed project had received a "mixed reception" from such community organizations as the South Chicago Development Commission and the Lake Calumet

Industrial Commission, reported the task force, and for good reason. Due to existing landfills, wetlands, industries, and residential areas, the total cost of land acquisition, displacement of existing homes, small businesses, and factories, as well as runway construction, would be prohibitively expensive. The task force questioned the expected level of activity at an airport in the Calumet region, even with the poaching of flights from already underutilized airports in Gary, Indiana, and suburban South Chicago. In addition to the environmental concerns raised by the U.S. Army Corps of Engineers, which maintained jurisdiction over the area wetlands, the dissatisfactory results of a cost-benefits analysis indicated that a new airport should not become the economic engine sought by job-hungry residents of the Southeast Side.[20]

For the immediate future at least, the fate of the Calumet region still hinged on the steel industry—and its prospects continued to worsen. In the last months of 1985, the fate of the twenty-three hundred workers at the massive LTV Steel plant (down from sixty-two hundred workers in 1979) seemed bleak. The LTV Corporation, an international conglomerate based in Dallas, with defense, aerospace, energy, and steel holdings, was seeking to minimize losses suffered after its merger with Republic Steel in 1984. In June 1985, LTV asked for and received a reduction in Illinois state energy taxes, but the mayor denied a similar appeal to lower city taxes when the corporation refused to stipulate that those savings would be invested in the Chicago plant. The president and other top executives of LTV Steel continued to ask for tax abatements from the city, while Washington countered with offers of other investment incentives. The mayor repeatedly urged LTV to invest heavily in new technology for the Chicago plant, which he argued would be an indication of the corporation's long-term commitment to the region, but instead executives in Dallas kept bombarding city hall with requests for lower taxes.[21]

When LTV spokesmen threatened massive job layoffs beginning in January 1986, Steelworkers Local 1033 and the Calumet Community Religious Conference sought assistance from the mayor. Chicago's Department of Economic Development worked with the union and the CCRC to create a package of incentives for LTV, assembled from local, state, and federal financial contributions, to forestall additional job layoffs and the eventual closing of the mill. LTV continued to reduce work rolls during the next several months and, having filed for bankruptcy in July 1986, announced its intention to discontinue most operations in Chicago by the end of that year. The mayor viewed LTV's steady decline in Southeast Chicago "with deep regret," he announced in a press release, his utmost concern reserved for the unemployed steelworkers and their families who would be left in desperate financial circumstances when the plant closed. The city and the state of Illinois had proffered a wide array of financial and tax incentives to the corporation, Washington said, but "LTV [had] chosen to spurn [our] offers." The mayor posited that, despite his best efforts on behalf of the neighborhood's troubled residents, the financial priorities of a corporation headquartered elsewhere trumped the welfare of local workers and their families.[22]

Its efforts having come up short in Southeast Chicago, the administration won a signal victory on behalf of neighborhoods in the summer of 1985 by breaking the legislative logjam over the proposed $125 million general-obligation bond issue. Indifferent to the fact that Chicago had not repaired streets, vaulted sidewalks, and sewers in many areas since their installation by the Works Progress Administration in the 1930s, Vrdolyak and Burke refused to endorse a large-scale construction project that would provide the mayor with countless opportunities for ribbon cuttings throughout the city. Potholes on some streets had grown to alarming proportions, and inadequate runoff frequently led to flooded intersections and sizable pools of rainwater in front yards. Nevertheless, the aldermen querulously swore that no general-obligation bond issue would pass on their watch—despite the fact that 63 percent of the bond money would be spent in the twenty-nine wards (58 percent of the fifty wards) represented in the city council by the mayor's opponents. Thirty-Third Ward alderman Richard Mell, a staunch foe of the administration, admitted that his constituents favored the bond but said, "I will sacrifice a vote that probably won't be popular in my community for the good of the coalition." Equally determined to prevail, Washington and his aides kept the issue alive for months, believing that the eventual outcome of the struggle potentially held special importance in the battle over public opinion. Provision of substantive improvements in all of the city's neighborhoods would underscore the administration's nonpartisan, fair-minded commitment to reform. Accordingly, the mayor appointed an ad hoc strategy team composed of members of the development subcabinet and representatives from the press office to pursue a solution.[23]

While the mayor and several aides were touring Italy and Israel that summer, the strategy team devised an ingenious plan to marshal public opinion against the recalcitrant aldermen. City hall organized a media bus tour of select neighborhoods where collapsed vaulted sidewalks, rutted streets, and unpaved alleys dotted the cityscape—and where obstinate aldermen had refused to support repairs underwritten by the bond issue. Detailed articles in the city's dailies and minicam reports on evening newscasts made the deplorable situation impossible to ignore. When the mayor returned from Europe, he gleefully assumed the role of tour guide. White residents on the Southwest Side, with discomfited aldermen and ward committeemen in tow, joined the mayor and reporters when they exited the buses and walked through the targeted neighborhoods. Washington and his political foes kept up a good-natured banter during the excursions as large numbers of onlookers voiced their growing interest in the proposed improvements. Meanwhile, mayoral aides circulated through the crowds, distributing pamphlets that described the significant upgrades obtainable with only a $12 annual increase in property taxes. Resistance vanished in short order, and the city council Finance Committee quickly added $40 million worth of new projects to the administration's original proposal. Even Burke, the most vociferous opponent of the measure the previous year, issued a press release declaring his sudden change of heart. Having prevailed at last in a long-running battle with his opponents, the mayor triumphantly intoned, "With this bond issue the City is keeping its commitment to invest in the neighborhoods."[24]

The administration continued its efforts at neighborhood enhancement—and at the same time sought to cultivate better relations with residents of the white bungalow belt—by endorsing several policies propounded by the Save Our Neighborhoods/Save Our City coalition. After the organization's April 1984 convention, at which its members first proposed home-equity insurance, linked development, and other innovative measures, SON/SOC representatives aggressively lobbied the mayor's aides on behalf of their suggestions for decentralized economic development. The administration provided $90,000 in federal funds for the group to conduct a research project on home-equity insurance, a program designed to curb blockbusting in all-white neighborhoods. The measure provided that property owners would pay a small annual fee to a special fund for the protection of real estate values in the event of sudden racial change, which purportedly would eliminate the financial need for panic selling. Despite concerns among some of his aides that the idea of home-equity insurance sprang from the notoriously racist climate in Chicago's bungalow belts—and specifically constituted a plan for protecting white home owners from racial desegregation efforts—the mayor agreed to divert federal funding to SON/SOC to permit further study of its pet project.[25]

Washington also expressed a willingness to work with SON/SOC on another of its favorite schemes, linked development, an idea that he found intriguing. The mayor's development subcommittee noted the growing popularity of the reform, which had been utilized with some success on a limited basis in Boston and San Francisco, but also knew about the campaign against the idea being mounted by Chicago's business community. Fearing that opposition forces in the city council might introduce an ordinance and thereby "create friction and possibly stalemate and dilute your efforts on linked development," the subcommittee recommended to the mayor that he create an advisory committee to study the matter. "We believe this will maintain your leadership role on this issue," counseled the subcommittee, "and allow you to mediate a potential dispute before it breaks." In September 1984, Washington had attended SON/SOC's second annual convention and agreed to appoint an advisory committee to investigate downtown linkage. The adversarial relationship between the mayor and SON/SOC, which had from the outset of Washington's mayoralty openly dismissed his commitment to neighborhood development as meaningless political rhetoric, improved somewhat—especially after he appointed Joseph Crutchfield, one of the organization's leaders, to the fact-finding advisory committee on linkage created that year.[26]

The original linked-development proposal advanced by SON/SOC, which called for a levy of $5 per square foot on all downtown commercial development in excess of one hundred thousand square feet, immediately met implacable resistance from bankers and real estate agents. The administration's representatives on the committee and other city officials, committed to the concept of linked development in principle but unsure about the particulars, split over the advisability of making the policy mandatory. Doubtful that the real estate market in the central business district could always afford to underwrite linkage in such generous fashion, some members of the administration preferred voluntarism or at least utilization on a project-by-project basis. Members of the Department of Planning and the Department of Economic Development increasingly spoke in favor of voluntarism, which many neighborhood activists viewed as an abject surrender to business interests.[27]

The deliberations of the Advisory Committee on Linked Development never led to the wholesale adoption of the new program, because competing interests failed to reach agreement on the details. Neither the preliminary recommendations submitted to the mayor in September 1985 nor the final report completed almost a year later produced a clear consensus on how linked development could be implemented to the mutual satisfaction of neighborhood groups and downtown spokesmen. Composed equally of representatives from a number of interest groups—SON/SOC and other neighborhood organizations, civic and philanthropic institutions, city officials, and businessmen involved in banking and real estate—the committee moved at a glacial pace because its carefully crafted political balance lessened the chances of achieving consensus. According to many of its members, the group suffered from constant infighting and lack of leadership. Crutchfield and other community activists accused the development faction of negotiating in bad faith, charging that the bankers and real estate agents quibbled incessantly and seemed to care only about minimizing the extent of linkage eventually required by the city. Representatives of neighborhood organizations also complained that members of the administration, particularly officials from the Department of Planning, too often sided with the business clique in committee discussions. The developers appended a minority report to the preliminary document prepared in 1985 that called mandatory linked development in any form inimical to downtown investment and continued thereafter to maintain a stance in favor of voluntary linked development only. The approach of the 1987 mayoral election eventually left the issue in abeyance, and Chicago never formally approved a linked-development policy during the Washington administration.[28]

The city's failure to adopt linked development as a means of stimulating economic recovery in the neighborhoods underscored the difficulty of bridging the yawning gap between community activists and downtown financial interests. SON/SOC members roundly dismissed the value of voluntary linkage, viewing the advocacy of such a policy by bankers and real estate agents as just a temporary expedient to forestall meaningful change; neighborhood activists saw voluntarism as a fig leaf for the avoidance of mandatory linkage and felt betrayed by the mayor's refusal to back their position unequivocally. In truth, many members of the administration mistrusted the intentions of the SON/SOC rank and file and suspected that the racism expressed by the organization in 1983 still lingered just beneath the surface. Wary mayoral aides, never wanting to provide a lightning rod for business resistance to the mayor, feared how the imposition of a mandatory linked-development plan would be perceived in the Loop. They believed that unlimited backing of decentralized economic development, no matter how attractive to true believers in the neighborhoods, would doubtless trigger a backlash within the city's business and financial leadership at a time when the mayor was trying hard not to alienate those groups. Washington remained firmly committed to linked development on a project-by-project basis, even as he still worked to demonstrate that the neighborhoods could be bolstered without crippling the downtown—a delicate balance he struggled to achieve throughout his time in city hall.[29]

The mayor also frequently found himself attempting to mediate between business interests and community activists in discussions involving the venues for Chicago's professional athletic teams. In order to safeguard their investments, owners of the sports franchises sought public support (especially funding) for the operation and maintenance of the stadiums where the teams played. The owners and executives of the ball clubs justified their demands by arguing that the games stimulated spending in the surrounding neighborhoods and indeed throughout the city; local residents, suburbanites, and visiting out-of-towners spent lavishly on parking, food, alcohol, lodging, and souvenirs, the teams argued, contributing significantly to Chicago's tourist income. At the same time, owners cited the immeasurable benefit the teams provided casual fans as well as die-hard supporters by fostering a sense of community and civic pride. These teams became part of the metropolitan fabric, they contended, and no city could be considered "big league" without professional athletics. A lifelong sports fan who understood the importance of professional teams to the city's identity, Washington recalled his keen disappointment in 1960 when the Chicago Cardinals (the South Side's professional football alternative to the Bears) relocated in St. Louis. He remembered the radioactive political fallout from that move and vowed not to allow a professional sports team to abandon Chicago during his mayoralty.[30]

The mayor also kept in mind that "balanced growth" entailed more than simply protecting the financial investments of the city's sports moguls. He understood that the invasion by thousands of strangers on designated days could disrupt the placidity of a neighborhood and that the building of a new stadium might well demand the widespread displacement of existing residences and businesses under the rubric of eminent domain. Individuals and organizations living in the shadow of mammoth entertainment palaces complained about noise, litter, drunkenness, vandalism, inadequate parking, and a host of other inconveniences that accompanied the games. Having established himself as the guardian of neighborhood interests and a proponent of community empowerment, Washington could hardly give wealthy franchise owners carte blanche authority to alter urban environments at their whim. Nor could he blithely order the destruction of modest but stable neighborhoods in order to construct gleaming new sports venues, justifying wholesale disruption and dislocation with vague references to civic pride. At the very least, in making decisions that affected the quality of life in the neighborhoods, the Washington administration was obligated to create forums for the consideration of community concerns along with the interests of profit-seeking sportsmen.[31]

Three stadium issues commanded the attention of the Washington administration because of their projected impact on Chicago neighborhoods. The Cubs aimed to make structural changes to Wrigley Field, whereas the White Sox and Bears had become convinced that only the construction of new stadiums could sufficiently address the inadequacies of their existing ballparks. In each instance, the mayor attempted to give community representatives a voice in the deliberations and to avoid the impression that decisions were being made behind closed doors by big business in collusion with city hall. He recognized the importance of keeping the Cubs, White Sox, and Bears in Chicago and believed that the teams could be mollified without alienating his support among neighborhood groups. He found the task extremely challenging and ultimately achieved mixed results.[32]

The White Sox desperately desired a new stadium to replace superannuated Comiskey Park, their home on the South Side since 1910 and the oldest ballpark in Major League Baseball, and the Bears likewise wanted to play their games in a new stadium instead of in timeworn Soldier Field. Initial discussions between the two teams and the city centered on the construction of a single domed stadium that could accommodate both baseball and football games. City officials and team representatives considered several possible locations, principally on the West Side because of the abundance of unused land there, but the talks soon dissolved over a number of unresolvable problems. The two teams could not agree on the optimal size of the new facility, the logistical details of sharing the same space, or the resolution of scheduling conflicts. Most important, the Bears wanted to own their own stadium, while the White Sox wanted to lease space in a facility built with public financing. When Washington hesitated to pledge city funds for a new baseball stadium, the White Sox announced that they would leave Chicago for a site in the western suburbs and purchased a 140-acre tract of land in Addison, Illinois. Addison voters failed in an advisory referendum to approve the construction of the stadium, however, and Illinois governor Jim Thompson subsequently disavowed the move. The principal White Sox owners, Jerry Reinsdorf and Eddie Einhorn, then announced that other cities outside of the metropolitan area, especially St. Petersburg, Florida, and Denver, Colorado, had replaced suburban Chicago as the likely new home of the franchise.[33]

The "Save Our Sox" campaign that quickly formed, a grassroots effort among the team's loyal fans, identified two goals: keeping the White Sox in Chicago and preserving historic Comiskey Park. Excoriating Reinsdorf and Einhorn as bloodless carpetbaggers interested only in turning a huge profit, the "Save Our Sox" membership appealed to the city for assistance and tried to accentuate the ties between the team and the surrounding neighborhood. Although equally interested in retaining one of the city's two Major League Baseball teams, the Washington administration did not share Sox fans' romantic attachment to the aged stadium at the corner of Thirty-Fifth and Shields. Policy makers in city hall, immune to the nostalgia that drove the traditionalists' crusade, saw only sparse amenities in an antiquated edifice wedged into a working-class neighborhood with inadequate parking in adjacent blocks. Unlike quaint, cozy Wrigley Field with its ivy-covered outfield walls, the picturesque centerpiece of a tony North Side neighborhood, Comiskey Park lacked charm and attracted more of a blue-collar fan base on the gritty industrial South Side. The mayor hoped to save the Sox, but not Comiskey Park. A task force appointed by Washington, charged with discovering the best means of retaining the White Sox, recommended the construction of a new stadium on a South Loop site at the intersection of Roosevelt Road and the Chicago River. The recommendation immediately generated determined opposition from the nearby residential community of Dearborn Park and from developers intent on converting uninhabited buildings into lofts and constructing middle-class high-rises; neither group welcomed the noise, acres of parking lots, and chaotic traffic jams a huge stadium would bring to the gentrifying area. Moreover, the administration balked at the cost of building a stadium in the South Loop, opting instead for a location in the vicinity of the old ballpark where existing expressways, mass transit, and public utilities would reduce the expense of constructing a new ballpark.[34]

In 1986 the Illinois General Assembly passed a measure authorizing funding for a $120 million baseball stadium, with the White Sox as sole tenant, across Thirty-Fifth Street from Comiskey Park. Construction of the new ballpark stalled as Washington and Governor James R. Thompson vied for control of the Illinois Sports Facilities Authority, the state agency created to issue bonds and supervise construction of the stadium. Further delay ensued as the mayor held up appointments to the ISFA until the governor consented to a more vigorous application of affirmative action principles in hiring for stadium construction jobs. Meanwhile, not entirely satisfied with the generosity of the Illinois legislation and disappointed that the proposed new stadium would occupy virtually the same uninspiring site as the old one, Reinsdorf and Einhorn continued to negotiate with St. Petersburg officials for more favorable terms. The predominantly African American residents of the South Armour Square neighborhood immediately south of the original ballpark, many of whom would be uprooted to clear land for the new stadium, protested the destruction of their community. Economic development director Robert Mier informed the mayor that most homes in South Armour Square remained in good condition, that many of the displaced residents would be elderly longtime residents of the community, and that crime was very low in the area. "It is," Mier reported, "an old, es-tablished community with strong bonds." In short, he advised Washington, the city must proceed in a "sensitive and sensible" manner in order to be as humane as possible if demolishing the neighborhood proved necessary to retain the baseball team in the same area.[35]

Final arrangements for the new White Sox stadium, originally called Comiskey Park but renamed U.S. Cellular Field in 2003 when the telephone corporation purchased naming rights, came after Washington's death. With a less powerful mayor to represent the city's interests and Governor Thomp-son determined at all costs to keep the team in Chicago, Reinsdorf and Einhorn eventually negotiated a much better deal with the state legisla-ture. The Illinois General Assembly increased stadium authorization from $120 million to $150 million, agreed to void the ball club's rent obligation if season attendance fell below 1.2 million during the twenty-year lease, and mandated that the ISFA purchase as many as 300,000 tickets annually if season attendance fell below 1.5 million during the last ten years of the lease. Despite the best efforts of community residents, who organized the South Armour Square Neighborhood Coalition to protect as many homes and community institutions as possible, the devastation of the targeted area abutting Thirty-Fifth Street proceeded inexorably. An attorney representing the SASNC filed a lawsuit against the ISFA, the White Sox, and the City of Chicago for racial discrimination, but in 1996 a federal district court found in favor of the defendants in *Dorothy Laramore, et al. v. Illinois Sports Facilities Authority, et al.* Powerless to deflect the wrecker's ball without an effective advocate in the mayor's office, many members of the SASNC believed that the ISFA would never have run roughshod over the vulnerable neighbor-hood if Washington had lived.[36]

The interaction between the Washington administration and the Chicago Bears seemed to confirm that view, at least among African American community leaders on the Near West Side. Eager to vacate musty Soldier Field, which opened for business in 1924, and disenchanted with their landlords there, the Chicago Park District, the National Football League franchise was aggressively seeking sites for a new stadium by the mid-1980s. After the possibility of sharing a venue with the White Sox collapsed, the Bears briefly flirted with the idea of moving to a western suburb in DuPage County but soon resumed consideration of potential locations within Chicago. Buoyed by their recent success on the field—the team compiled the best record in the National Football League during the 1985 regular season and routed their Super Bowl opponents, the New England Patriots, in January 1986—the Bears had become the city's most successful professional sports franchise. At the peak of popularity in the sports-crazy city, the football team expected full cooperation from Chicago in its efforts to build a better stadium in a more propitious location.[37]

The Bears favored the proposal by the Chicago Central Area Committee to build a new seventy-five-thousand-seat stadium on the lakefront near Soldier Field, and Washington endorsed the idea as well. The mayor's vision entailed demolishing Soldier Field, erecting the new stadium just north of that site, and further developing the land around the Field Museum of Natural History, the Adler Planetarium, and the Shedd Aquarium to create a museum campus. A host of influential civic groups, including the Metro-politan Planning Council (MPC), the League of Women Voters, and Friends of the Parks, immediately objected to the despoliation of the lakeshore that would ensue at that location. The *Chicago Tribune* joined the opposition, citing potential environmental problems, and concurred with one of the mayor's Democratic foes who labeled the city's proposed deal with the Bears a "lakefront land grab." In the face of concerted political opposition to the lakefront plan, Washington created a three-person ad hoc site-selection committee—Mary Decker, executive director of the MPC; Walter Netsch, president of the Chicago Park District; and mayoral aide Al Johnson—to conduct a careful study and recommend the best possible location in the city for a new football stadium.[38]

The Mayor's Stadium Review Committee scheduled two public hearings, which presented a number of options and allowed time for questions and

comments from the audience, to discuss site-selection criteria. The committee considered a number of possibilities suggested by civic organizations
and developers: on abandoned railroad property west of Soldier Field, on
railroad land northwest of the Loop, on the South Loop site where the
two-sport domed stadium had previously been considered, and on a site in
the heart of the Near West Side. At the same time, Michael McCaskey, the
president of the Bears, specified the requirements the team had compiled
for the new stadium. Rejecting the idea of a domed facility, McCaskey said
that the team wanted to play outdoors, even though harsh weather always
remained a possibility in the season's later months. "Football is not a parlor
game," he asserted, "and our fans share that conviction." The facility's "foot-
print" would cover between twenty and thirty acres, with space needed for
fourteen to fifteen thousand on-site parking spaces; the games would also
require an additional five thousand off-site parking spaces. Most important,
McCaskey emphasized, the new facility should be completed quickly, given
the rapid deterioration of Soldier Field.[39]

Seconding the team's stated choice, the mayor's committee endorsed
the Near West Side site. McCaskey had expressed a willingness to accept
the lakefront site, but clearly preferred the West Side location, where he
felt that any community concerns could be resolved by the city and the
Bears. Locating the stadium west of the Loop would take advantage of
good transportation access, considerable space for parking, and relatively
inexpensive land-acquisition costs, noted the committee, but would also
present serious challenges related to housing loss and the city's responsibility to aid uprooted neighborhood inhabitants. "All planning for the West
Side site must take community needs foremost into account," stated the
committee, "and include community residents and organizations in the
planning process."[40]

Ravaged by decades of industrial loss, high unemployment, and population decline, the West Side had become one of Chicago's most sorrowful
areas by the 1980s. The catastrophic 1968 race riot following the assassination of Dr. Martin Luther King Jr. left the primary shopping district on
Madison Street and surrounding residential areas in smoldering ruins; a
generation later, empty lots and unrepaired buildings remained as a testa-
ment to neglect and capital flight. Rising unemployment followed after the
massive International Harvester plant closed in 1969 and Sears, Roebuck
moved its international headquarters to the Loop in 1974; unable to obtain
insurance in the aftermath of the rioting, many small businesses had fled

as well. An increasingly impoverished African American population remained, many residing in inhospitable public housing projects such as the
Henry Horner Homes and others occupying substandard housing units on
crime-riddled streets. A handful of underfunded community organizations
struggled valiantly to revive the neighborhood, desperately seeking with
little success to attract jobs and improve housing quality in the yawning
expanse west of the Loop.[41]

Determined to avoid the difficulties the administration had encountered
with South Armour Square residents over the new Comiskey Park, Mier
urged great care in dealing with the many Near West Side institutions and
community organizations seeking influence in the selection process. Eager to
foster investment and create jobs, some West Siders saw the football stadium
as exactly the kind of large-scale building project that could anchor a bleak
cityscape starved for redevelopment. Rush-Presbyterian–St. Luke's Medical
Center, a large health care complex immediately south of the proposed site,
drafted plans to build a sports medicine facility connected to the stadium and
became a staunch proponent of the project. On the other hand, the Interfaith
Organizing Project demanded full community participation in decision making and consistently counseled skepticism about the stadium's potential to
trigger an economic revival. A coalition of Chicago-area clergymen, the IOP
denounced all supporters of the project (including the mayor) for peddling
false hopes to a naive population. The Midwest Community Council (MCC),
led by veteran activist Nancy Jefferson, assumed a neutral "wait-and-see"
position, held a week of open forums to assess the stadium's likely impact
on the neighborhood, and ultimately issued a conditional endorsement of
the proposal. The administration held numerous meetings with the various
groups, and Washington conferred with approximately thirty home owners
in a Near West Side resident's house to discuss their views.[42]

Satisfied that a rapprochement could be reached with community groups,
Washington appointed the West Side Development Committee in September 1987 to finalize arrangements. (The cochairs of the fifteen-member committee included the MCC's Nancy Jefferson; Ernest Barefield, the mayor's
chief of staff; and two prominent local businessmen, Barry Sullivan and
Barry Cole.) The accord drafted by the committee and approved by the administration pledged to use revenue from luxury seating in the new stadium
to compensate uprooted residents fairly, paying the cost of equal or better
housing in another location, and to improve the Near West Side neighborhood by building a new library and park nearby the new structure. After

Washington's death, however, the Illinois General Assembly rejected the agreement. James "Pate" Philip, the conservative Republican leader of the state senate, said of the legislature's decision: "This deal is dangerous. If we pass this, it's going to set up a precedent that we can't live with elsewhere." In other words, according to Philip, the city had been far too generous to community groups seeking compensation for the jarring disruptions and partial destruction of neighborhood life. Later negotiations involving Washington's successor stalled, and the Bears remained unhappy tenants of Soldier Field until extensive renovations in 2003 gave the outmoded football stadium a thorough facelift.[43]

The controversy involving the Chicago Cubs dealt with the team's desire to add approximately eight thousand seats and light standards to Wrigley Field, the latter amenity allowing the team to play night games for the first time at the storied ballpark. The stadium's small seating capacity and the inability to play night games limited attendance, especially during the spring and fall when school kept youngsters away from the ballpark during the daytime, and cost the Cubs millions of dollars in revenue annually. In 1984 the team owner, the Chicago Tribune Corporation, threatened to move the ball club to another location outside the city (suburban Schaumburg) if the issue could not be resolved to its satisfaction. A coterie of activists in the Lakeview neighborhood surrounding Wrigley Field, an upper-middle-class enclave of well-educated home owners and locally owned businesses, vigorously opposed the introduction of night baseball to the quiet residential community; they feared increased traffic, litter, rowdiness, and an influx of automobiles where the absence of parking already constituted a serious problem. A number of community organizations, principally the Lakeview Citizens Council and CUBS (Citizens United for Baseball in the Sunshine), aggressively lobbied at the local and state levels for legislation prohibiting night baseball at Wrigley Field. The city council voted overwhelmingly against the installation of lights, with Alderman Vrdolyak in the forefront flamboyantly defending community interests.[44]

Reflecting his populist predilections and bowing to the political pressure he felt from his city council enemies, Washington vowed at a number of public appearances in Lakeview to support the neighborhood's position. Increasingly, however, he and his aides explored the possibility of a compromise with community leaders that would allow the Cubs to remain in Chicago. The Department of Economic Development and Cub management jointly conducted a neighborhood survey, the results of which showed a lack of unanimity on the lighting issue among Lakeview residents. The joint study found that more than 60 percent of people living within a half-mile radius of Wrigley Field accepted night baseball as the price of keeping the team in Chicago. With the *Chicago Tribune* publishing a steady stream of editorials justifying its demands and the newspaper's lobbyists ratcheting up the pressure on state legislators, community leaders indicated in 1985 that they would countenance the use of temporary lights for postseason (playoff) night games but not permanent lights for the regular season. Instead of simply restating his unqualified support for the neighborhood position, the mayor began asking what conditions community leaders would accept to mitigate the impact of lights added to the ballpark on a limited basis. At the same time, he urged Cub executives to bargain in good faith to reach a compromise with Lakeview residents that would achieve a balance between neighborhood and citywide interests.[45]

Negotiations between the Cubs and Lakeview community leaders proceeded unsurely under the supervision of city officials. Director of planning Elizabeth Hollander, who oversaw the talks, called the "neighborhood planning process on this issue . . . the most confrontational one in which I participated." Opponents of night baseball vituperatively attacked the ball club for its indifference to quality-of-life issues and denounced the mayor for selling out to corporate interests. As Hollander explained, "Supporters of Harold Washington felt abandoned, and opponents took maximum advantage of the controversy to put him in a bad light." Still, after nearly two years of dickering, an acceptable compromise emerged. The Lakeview Protection Plan, approved by the city council and eventually implemented under Washington's successor, limited the number of night games per season to eighteen, mandated early starting times, imposed a curfew for alcohol sales at the ballpark, and established strict parking restrictions around Wrigley Field. In subsequent years, even the most vocal opponents of night baseball conceded that the plan had produced a workable compromise that kept a beloved civic institution in Chicago at an acceptable cost to most neighborhood residents.[46]

In the sensitive and protracted negotiations over stadium deals, Washington attempted to strike a balance between the concerns of professional sport franchises and community activists. These clashes, he believed, reflected a tension between citywide and neighborhood interests that often developed over real estate transactions. Because the mayor had made the protection of neighborhoods a central component of his political appeal, community leaders expected him to defend their position unquestioningly. Yet his ongoing cultivation of business leaders and his strong aversion to losing one of the city's coveted professional teams kept him from siding uncritically with the champions of local autonomy. He sought in each case to avoid indefensible past practices (backroom deals cut downtown with little or no regard for powerless residents) and to ensure a real voice in the deliberations for Chicagoans who would be affected directly by the finalization of multimillion-dollar business deals. By their own admission, members of the administration improved their performance over time after a flawed beginning dealing with the White Sox ownership. If the outcomes never entirely pleased the mayor's grassroots supporters, at least the provision of community forums and the creation of broadly representative task forces forced critics to acknowledge that Washington had taken steps to open a historically secretive process to broad public scrutiny.[47]

As Washington and his aides spent considerable time on a variety of neighborhood issues—more so than previous administrations, according to local reporters and editors—they simultaneously felt the need to dispel rumors of hostility toward big business. Although the mayor remained no less determined to cultivate goodwill among the city's mercantile and financial elites, progress remained frustratingly slow and uneven. His attempted rapprochement with the downtown-based growth coalition became no less difficult after the collapse of the effort to stage a world's fair in Chicago, long considered the main priority of the commercial class. Planning for the 1992 event ended with action taken in Springfield, not in Chicago, but the business community and other boosters of the fair blamed the mayor for his tepid support of the project. Without exception, accounts of the prolonged struggle over the 1992 World's Fair saw the outcome as an unlikely triumph for neighborhood dissidents and an unprecedented defeat for a unified business community that had devised and successfully championed many such endeavors in past decades.[48]

From the outset of his mayoralty, Washington's insistence that agreements about the World's Fair be reached openly and that the city's liability be severely limited in the event of financial shortfalls produced standoffs with the World's Fair Corporation and the World's Fair Authority. Economic development commissioner Rob Mier reported to the mayor that the authority resisted all forms of accountability and demanded that the city levy a property tax increase to pay for increased service costs at the fair. Perhaps most troublesome, reported Mier, the authority refused to comply with the city's equal-opportunity provisions. As an independent body, the authority insisted on its freedom to ignore job set-asides for Chicago residents, economically disadvantaged people, minorities, and women. The mayor continued to laud the World's Fair as an "unsurpassed opportunity" for Chicago and issued a series of optimistic public statements reaffirming his desire to reach a workable agreement with the authority. He invariably added, however, that the city must be reimbursed for the construction, operation, and demolition of the fairgrounds. The costs of relocating residences and businesses dislodged by the fair must be borne by the authority as well, he said, and local affirmative action policies must be followed. Accustomed to more munificent treatment from city hall in the past when mayors and other elected officials reflexively blessed each and every civic project conceived downtown, the elites comprising the World's Fair Authority stubbornly refused to bargain away any of the conditions in their plan.[49]

Rising opposition to the World's Fair from different quarters no doubt reinforced the administration's resolve not to yield any ground to the authority. In addition to the resistance from neighborhood groups that would be affected directly by the razing of houses and small businesses, a coalition of good-government organizations, university professors, and urban planners objected to what they saw as a thinly disguised effort to impose an urban redevelopment project for the Near South Side. Opponents referred to the fair design, which included plans for the eventual construction of a residential housing development, shopping centers, and malls, as "Master Plan Number Two," in reference to its similarities to the earlier Chicago 21 Plan. Critics also cited a feasibility study published in May 1985 by a leading consulting firm, Arthur D. Little, Inc., predicting that the fair's financial losses could reach $350 million with unfavorable interest rates and the failure to obtain federal grants.[50]

The proposed 1992 World's Fair finally perished at the hands of the Illinois state legislature. Before committing state funds to the project, Speaker of the House Michael Madigan (Democrat, Chicago) appointed a blue-ribbon advisory committee to assess the World's Fair Authority's proposal. Under the leadership of former U.S. senator Adlai E. Stevenson III, the committee produced a report that dismissed the proposal as "fatally flawed in its treatment of theme, the environment and site configuration," concluding as well that it "is not financially sound." The State of Illinois,

which was being asked to contribute $278 million and to sell bonds total-
ing another $220 million, would not recoup any of its investment until all
private investors had achieved a profit. On June 20, 1985, Madigan strongly
advised against the provision of the necessary state funds for the fair, which
he termed a "bad risk" for state taxpayers. The withdrawal of the Speaker's
support promptly led Governor Thompson, a passionate advocate for the
proposition from the beginning, to announce dejectedly that "the fair is
dead." Washington issued a statement regretting the negative result after
much hard work and planning by a number of private and public interests,
even suggesting that the legislature might still revive the issue in a later
session. In fact, though, the Illinois General Assembly's decisive action kept
him from having to make a choice between the fair's ardent boosters and
its equally determined opponents. Indeed, Madigan later told planning
director Elizabeth Hollander that he hoped the mayor was grateful to him
for resolving that dilemma.[51]

The expiration of the campaign for the 1992 World's Fair came suddenly
and unexpectedly. Following three years of unabashed boosterism by the
local press, generous financial backing from the city's powerful downtown-
growth coalition, the avid support of the Illinois governor, and at least
the nominal support of city hall, most observers expected a very different
outcome. The local media immediately pronounced the failure to breathe
life into the project a monumental defeat for Chicago's old guard and a
striking victory for neighborhood-based reformers. Many people held the
mayor responsible. Washington's public pronouncements, though generally
appreciative of what a world's fair could do for the city, always demanded
accountability on behalf of taxpayers, flatly refused for the city to assume
any hidden costs that might emerge later, and stopped well short of unqualified endorsement. When the project's proponents argued that the city
needed the fair to burnish its tarnished image, the mayor shot back: "We
don't need a fair or anything else to sell the city of Chicago. We have one of
the greatest cities in the world." When the bad news came from Springfield,
state legislators commented that they had never received clear, unambigu-
ous signals from Chicago's city hall that the administration strongly wanted
the fair. In short, concluded director of planning Elizabeth Hollander, "The
demise of the World's Fair was a real shock to the traditional business community and a serious challenge to their leadership."[52]

Bewildered and disappointed with the unexpected end to their dreams of
a world's fair in Chicago, downtown merchants also lamented the desultory

pace of redevelopment in the blighted North Loop. Resisting pressure to level dilapidated structures pell-mell, Hollander paid particular attention to the large number of buildings with historic or architectural significance situated within the targeted redevelopment area. She hired several engineering firms and design teams suggested by the Chicago Chapter of the American Institute of Architects to make recommendations before authorizing the sale of land and the commencement of demolition. Rather than raze such venerable structures as the Oriental Theatre, the Chicago Theatre, and the Reliance Building, Hollander investigated federal grant programs to which the city could apply for historic preservation funding. In some instances, the wily planning commissioner exacted contributions from developers to subsidize the preservation of deteriorating landmarks. The city's decision to utilize Tax Increment Financing to generate capital in the North Loop paid off handsomely, yielding $11 million annually that state law mandated had to be invested exclusively in the seven blocks designated as the TIF district. Regrettably, grumbled impatient downtown businessmen, very little activity ensued as the mayor seemed satisfied to let TIF funds accumulate. In his detailed study of the North Loop Redevelopment Project, Ross Miller concluded that "the Washington administration spent four . . . years accomplishing next to nothing."[53]

Lingering questions about the fate of Navy Pier further unsettled the growth coalition. The negotiations between the administration and the Rouse Corporation, which proposed the creation of a festival marketplace as a tourist attraction on the historic pier, concluded unsuccessfully in March 1985. According to economic development commissioner Rob Mier, the city had sought a more favorable deal than the Rouse Corporation was willing to accept. Washington appointed an eighteen-member task force, chaired by eminent attorney Robert Newman and composed of other influential businessmen and public officials, to consider a range of development options for the site. In the ensuing seven months, the task force discussed a number of possible uses for Navy Pier, including a gambling casino, luxury housing, office towers, retail outlets, and other moneymaking ventures, before recommending that the site be developed for a variety of public (rather than private) uses. Taking its inspiration from New York City's Art Park, San Francisco's Fort Mason Park, and Toronto's Harbourfront, the task force proposed an urban park that included museums, educational institutions, recreational facilities, and venues for cultural exhibits, entertainment, and community activities.

To avoid a sweeping renovation of the entire pier that required an initial public investment of millions of dollars, the task force called for incremental development lasting several years, with financial support from philanthropic, corporate, state, and federal sources. In keeping with the administration's emphasis on citizen involvement, a public meeting held on September 23, 1985, offered the public an opportunity to evaluate the draft report. Owing to the extensive public support expressed at the meeting and afterward, the city council unanimously authorized $15 million for renovation to be included in a general-obligation bond issue.[54]

The Navy Pier Task Force presented the mayor with the final copy of its report, "Window on the Future," on January 17, 1986. Specifically dismissing the development of private office space, residential properties, and a casino as inappropriate uses for such a prized historic site, the task force recommended the creation of a park that could be utilized for a multiplicity of public purposes. According to the task force, Navy Pier's central location would make its cultural and recreational offerings accessible to people scattered throughout the city. Thus, its downtown location notwithstanding, the reconfigured Navy Pier would become a community center for all Chicagoans. Washington concurred with the recommendation, especially praising the view of the site as a "landmark public facility" rather than just "a piece of real estate." In 1986 Chicago reopened the pier for public use, and, even as work began on an extensive list of renovations, more than three hundred thousand people attended more than eighty events held by municipal agencies and other organizations that year. The city estimated that more than five hundred thousand people would attend events at Navy Pier the following year.[55]

In 1986–87, the administration proceeded with its plans to transform Navy Pier into a public space serving the cultural and recreational needs of the entire city. The mayor's office announced an agreement with the first anchor tenant of the development project, the Chicago Maritime Society, which was beginning preparations that year to open a 10,000-square-foot museum. Meanwhile, discussions proceeded in the administration about creating a nonprofit development corporation, patterned after the Baltimore Inner Harbor Development Corporation, to develop and manage the rebranded Navy Pier. Even then, however, the Rouse Corporation announced (and some members of Chicago's business elite applauded) its continued interest in developing the site as an investment opportunity downtown. After Washington's death, subsequent mayoral administrations' commitment to the task force's vision wavered. Mayor Richard M. Daley and Governor Thompson concluded a political deal whereby Chicago shared ownership of Navy Pier with Illinois in a new public corporation, the Pier and Exposition Authority, and the state financed $150 million in improvements. In 1995 the new Navy Pier reopened as an entertainment site, replete with shops, restaurants, exhibition spaces, and performance stages. Quickly, it became Chicago's leading tourist attraction and the "#1 leisure destination in the Midwest"—a resounding financial success and a popular gathering spot, especially for visitors to the Windy City, but a far cry from the public center envisioned by the Washington administration.[56]

The commercialization of Navy Pier reinforced Chicago's long-standing position as a popular tourist destination and convention site. At a time of rapid change from a manufacturing- to a service-based economy, proclaimed the downtown-growth coalition, the city should exploit its advantages in location, transportation, and facilities to ease the pain of deindustrialization. In 1960 the opening of McCormick Place on the lakefront just south of the Loop, with its 320,000 square feet of exhibit space, had immediately established the Windy City at the forefront of cities competing for major national conventions and trade shows. After a fire destroyed the structure in 1967, local officials wasted no time building a larger McCormick Place (with more than 825,000 square feet of exhibit space) at the same location. Despite the sizable expansion, by the mid-1980s competition from New York, Las Vegas, Atlanta, Washington, D.C., and other cities that were building or expanding their own exposition centers threatened Chicago's status as the nation's leading convention city. In 1984 the Illinois General Assembly authorized the construction of an annex to the lakefront building at a cost of $252 million, financed by new state sales and hotel taxes. The completion of McCormick Place North in 1986 brought the facility's total capacity to 1.8 million square feet of exhibit-hall space, an impressive figure that kept the city competitive for conventions and trade shows until the completion of larger facilities in other cities persuaded Chicago's government to add McCormick Place South in 1996 and McCormick Place West in 2007. The mayor's acquiescence in the 1986 expansion, noted planning commissioner Elizabeth Hollander, provided the administration with some respite from the pressure from developers, the business community, and the press to build downtown.[57]

Washington and his aides remained acutely aware of the growing frustration among Chicago's leading businessmen with what they perceived as city hall's languor in downtown redevelopment. Especially because of the disappointing outcomes on the World's Fair and Navy Pier projects, noted development commissioner Rob Mier, many members of the commercial elite continued to question the mayor's interest in large-scale construction projects. Mier recalled that the need to assuage those fears spurred the administration to intensify its efforts to refurbish the Loop. At a retreat at the O'Hare Hilton Hotel in late 1985 or early 1986, he remembered, the mayoral cabinet reaffirmed its commitment to address the business community's concerns by launching big building projects in the central city—in particular, by making the construction of a new central library a top priority in the coming months.[58]

The lack of a suitable downtown library had plagued Chicago for decades, a local embarrassment that became a national headline in 1978 because of the scathing remarks by Librarian of Congress Daniel J. Boorstin. Speaking at the Chicago Public Library Cultural Center at an American Library Association reception, Boorstin called the city's lack of a great central library "scandalous" and "a public disgrace." Housed temporarily (since 1975) in the Mandel Building, a cavernous warehouse tucked in behind other structures on North Michigan Avenue near the Tribune Tower, the main library faced eviction when its lease expired in the mid-1980s. Public library commissioners, board presidents, and civic-minded residents decried the predicament and tried to elicit enough public indignation to spur government action. Mayors Bilandic and Byrne expressed a willingness to address the problem and named study groups to consider possible locations for a new library, but years of inaction ensued.[59]

In 1983 Mayor Byrne finally sought to rectify the situation when she had the city acquire the former flagship Goldblatt's Department Store on South State Street at a cost of $10 million; she intended to renovate the unoccupied structure as a cheaper alternative to purchasing downtown real estate at exorbitant prices and erecting a new building on vacant land. Almost immediately, however, the Better Government Association and other civic organizations challenged the site selection, and the *Chicago Sun-Times* joined the opposition with a barrage of negative editorials. Dissidents questioned the proposed library's load-bearing capacity and charged that cost estimates had been set unrealistically low. Saddled with a controversy bequeathed him by his predecessor, Washington initially noted the considerable amount of money the city had already invested and seemed resigned to construction of the library at the Goldblatt's location. "Let's go ahead and make the best we can on a bad deal," he said. The furor intensified among good-government groups, architects, and preservationists, and the mayor expressed his willingness to consider other Loop sites. The administration formed the Library Policy Review Committee, composed of Library Board members and other municipal officials, and the Ad Hoc Citizens Committee to represent a host of constituencies throughout the city. The open process of selecting a site and building a new library under the mayor's leadership won praise for inviting broad citizen participation. At the same time, though, the laborious shift into yet another stage of development forestalled the completion of a highly anticipated downtown redevelopment project. Members of the growth coalition voiced their exasperation again.[60]

The real estate development community registered its extreme displeasure when the administration agreed to the imposition of a commercial lease tax as part of the city's 1986 budget. First suggested two years earlier by Alderman Burke, the measure won favor with the city council in December 1985 as a means of plugging a $78 million shortfall in the coming year's $2.1 billion budget. (Having championed the commercial lease tax at first, Burke later deserted the majority bloc and voted against what he then sought to portray as a misguided initiative of the administration.) The downtown business community erupted in outrage at the proposed tax, which imposed a 6 percent levy on any commercial business lease of more than $12,000 per year, and urged Washington to veto the bill. The mayor, who favored the retention of a property tax but declined to use his veto, regretted that "Chicago has been stuck with a Commercial Lease Tax that no one wants." Alternately blaming Burke and Washington, a number of developers sued successfully in circuit court to block enforcement. After months of litigation and negotiations between the city council and the mayor's office, a new tax package replaced the commercial lease tax. Chicago's desperate search for operating funds had forced the mayor to rely on any and all potential sources of revenue, he reminded the business community, including an ill-conceived tax that originated with his aldermanic foes.[61]

The administration's efforts to improve the downtown as well as the neighborhoods, the mayor repeatedly explained to his constituents, depended to a great extent on the resources made available to Chicago by the federal government. A recurrent critic of the Reagan administration, Washington intensified his censure of Republican policies in 1985–86. Federal funding for urban America had been decreasing for several years, he reminded Chicagoans, and the industrial cities of the Northeast and Midwest were shouldering most of the reductions in aid. The application of supply-side economics, a colossal miscalculation that saddled the nation with staggering deficits and the greatest national debt in history, had left Chicago with an untenable 8.5 percent unemployment rate and a stalled recovery from the 1981–82 recession. The investment stimulus supposedly provided by massive tax cuts had failed to materialize, and annual growth in the gross national product crept upward at a disappointing 2.2 percent. Continued increases in military outlays were diverting federal dollars from domestic spending, especially shortchanging social welfare programs, and the number of families living in poverty was growing at an alarming rate. Inflated defense spending, which dwarfed the combined allocations for Community Development Block Grants and Urban Development Action Grants by a ratio of twenty-four to one, also significantly hampered urban redevelopment. Altogether, city officials estimated, Chicago had lost close to $1 billion in federal funds since Reagan's election. Washington maintained that the president was indifferent to the welfare of aged industrial cities like Chicago, leaving them "to sink or swim if they can."[62]

Reagan's budget for fiscal year 1986 portended even greater hardship in the immediate future for urban America in general and for Chicago in particular. The budget submitted to the first session of the Ninety-Ninth Congress by the president in 1985 pared $192.2 million from the previous year's allocation for the Windy City, a reduction of 29 percent. The Chicago Transit Authority, a separate legal entity, would lose 69 percent of its federal funding as well. The impact of such draconian cuts, Washington averred, would not only "strike at the heart of Chicago's development plans" but also force the city to slash basic services to needy residents. Downtown and neighborhood alike would suffer as infrastructure went without maintenance, housing would continue to deteriorate without necessary rehabilitation or replacement, construction of homes and business buildings would cease, and the number of jobs would decline. He vehemently denied that the objections to the president's budget by cities like Chicago amounted to "the concerns of a 'special interest' group," as Reagan charged, but rather represented an articulation of the public interest. He spoke, the mayor affirmed, for the commonweal and not for profit-making concerns. Sometimes operating under the aegis of such national organizations as the U.S. Conference of Mayors and the National League of Cities and sometimes acting alone, Washington spoke vigorously against the federal policies he considered potentially disastrous for his city and others.[63]

In 1985–86 Washington took to the highways of Illinois on behalf of his "fair return" campaign. Meeting with mayors, elected officials, union leaders, and community luminaries in the Quad Cities, East St. Louis, Champaign-Urbana, Rockford, and Springfield, he sought political support for his contention that the federal government was denying Illinois a fair return on the tax dollars the state sent to Washington, D.C. He excoriated the Reagan administration for having ravaged cities through the imposition of unconscionably steep budget cuts and underscored the similar damage experienced by communities of all sizes in Illinois. "It's a common problem," he contended. "Chicago is no different than other cities in Illinois—just in the same boat." Subject to comparable cuts in financial aid that left all communities vulnerable to worsening economic conditions, Washington told receptive audiences throughout the state, public officials should work in tandem against the pernicious revival of social Darwinism led by the administration. After the mayor delivered his message in scripted speeches to public audiences and informally to smaller groups across the state, his aides distributed petitions imploring the U.S. Congress to restore funding cuts for municipalities.[64]

In particular, Washington's "fair return" campaign concentrated on blocking the impending elimination of general revenue sharing funds. Created in 1972 by the Nixon administration, general revenue sharing originally enjoyed bipartisan backing in Congress as a reform measure; that is, federal funds would purportedly be delivered more efficiently to cities by combining several federal programs in one aid package. Moreover, mayors and other elected officials envisioned general revenue sharing as a means of granting local governments greater autonomy in the use of federal funds. In subsequent years, however, Republican presidents exacted steep reductions and rescissions in general revenue sharing allocations to urban America, thereby reviving liberal Democrats' fears that the reputed reform had actually been a covert means of reducing federal aid to the cities. Both Congress and the White House had indicated that general revenue sharing would be discontinued altogether when the extension of the enabling legislation expired in the fall of 1986. Disputing the need to end the federal program, the Chicago mayor called for cuts in other federal programs—especially for curbing the runaway growth of military spending. Since he left the U.S. Congress in 1983, Washington said, the annual defense budget had ballooned from $160 billion to more than $320 billion.

"You're looking at Mr. Patriotism," he said. "I stick the flag in my BVDs at night." Yet unquestioningly granting the Pentagon a blank check year after year was decimating the federal budget and often with disappointing results. Such boondoggles as the Strategic Defense Initiative ("Star Wars") exacerbated the problem, allocating massive sums of money for untested, visionary programs. Scientists at the University of Illinois ridiculed the Star Wars initiative, urging mayors throughout the state to support a boycott in funding, and Washington happily complied.[65]

The mayor's "fair return" campaign targeted the redistributive practices of the Reagan administration whereby the federal government sent disproportionate shares of tax revenue to the suburbs and the Sun Belt at the expense of Rust Belt cities and states. Washington argued that Illinois and its communities were suffering unfairly, dispatching huge sums of tax revenue to the federal treasury every year while receiving a much smaller amount back in the form of federal aid. He explained:

> These funds are not a give-away. They are a fair return on the taxes we send to the nation's capital. Illinois ranks 47th in the nation in the return on our federal tax dollar. In 1984, out of $35 billion sent to Washington, D.C., from Illinois, we received back only $24 billion. With the loss of federal programs, this imbalance will only get worse. Chicago is losing $206 million in federal dollars in 1986, and faces the loss of $526 million in 1987. How is this budgetary hole to be filled?[66]

Determined to make "fair return" an issue that resonated outside the borders of Illinois, Washington traveled widely throughout the nation to share his views. He took his case for the cities to the nation's capital, where he lobbied U.S. senators and congressmen from Illinois and representatives of large Chicago-based corporations to oppose reductions in federal aid. He distributed copies of *Chicago Federal Agenda: Legislative and Budgetary Issues, 1986/87*, a fifty-six-page booklet outlining the importance of preserving general revenue sharing, maintaining CDBG funding at the fiscal year 1985 level, retaining the UDAG program, and salvaging as many dollars as possible for low- and moderate-income housing. The mayor conferred privately with Congressman William Gray, chairman of the House Budget Committee; Congressman Mickey Leland, chairman of the Congressional Black Caucus; and Matthew Martinez, chairman of the Hispanic Caucus, to urge resistance to more budget cutting. After his whirlwind trip to Washington, D.C., he flew to Puerto Rico to preach the gospel of "fair return" at the annual meeting of the U.S. Conference of Mayors; the organization's membership overwhelmingly approved a resolution endorsing his petition. Washington returned to Chicago and presided at the National Fair Return Petition Rally at city hall.[67]

Washington's unstinting efforts to protect the cities from further aid reductions garnered considerable attention nationwide, even though his efforts fell short against the antiurban policies of the Republican administration's New Federalism. Congress allowed general revenue sharing to expire, impervious to pleas by the nation's beleaguered mayors. By the time Reagan left office, UDAGs had been eliminated; funding for CDBGs, mass transit, job training, and public service employment had been significantly reduced; and overall federal assistance to cities had been lowered by 60 percent. Reagan's New Federalism took its greatest toll on the nation's largest cities. Federal aid to municipalities with a population of more than 300,000 decreased from $5.2 billion in 1980 to $3.4 billion in 1989, a 35 percent reduction. In 1980 these large cities received 22 percent of their funding from Washington, D.C., as compared to 6 percent by 1989. Despite the strenuous efforts of the Chicago mayor and others, federal aid to the cities continued to be a prime casualty in the Reagan administration's war on domestic spending.[68]

His attempt to ease the financial pressures on the cities blunted by the partisan opposition in Washington, D.C., the mayor held out hope in the last weeks of 1985 that at least the local political situation would soon be improved—that is, that the gridlock in the Chicago City Council would be broken by judicial fiat. The Seventh U.S. District Court had found in favor of the mayor, agreeing that ward boundaries had been gerrymandered to reduce black and Latino representation, and the U.S. Supreme Court's refusal to hear the appeal of the city council redistricting case in June 1985 left the lower court's ruling unchanged. The federal court redrew the boundaries of five wards and mandated that seven special elections be conducted to choose aldermen in the wards reconfigured by its action. Alderman Burke confidently called the chances of special elections before the 1987 mayoral contest "slim to none," but on December 30, 1985, Judge Charles R. Norgle of the U.S. District Court ordered special elections held on March 18, 1986 (concurrent with the regular primary election), in the Fifteenth, Eighteenth, Twenty-Second, Twenty-Fifth, Twenty-Sixth, Thirty-First, and Thirty-Seventh Wards. If Washington-backed candidates won at least four of the seven special elections, his opponents' control of the city council would at last be broken.[69]

Tempering the exciting news for Washington of a potential breakthrough in the Council Wars, however, the front pages of Chicago newspaper filled with the details of an emerging political scandal that threatened to reach the mayor's office. On December 26, 1985, four days before Judge Norgle announced the date for the special aldermanic elections, the *Chicago Tribune* broke the story of an undercover Federal Bureau of Investigation inquiry (Operation Incubator) that had ferreted out corruption among several aldermen allied with the mayor. The FBI had videotaped one of their agents, who posed as a local businessman seeking political influence in order to receive government contracts, surreptitiously slipping payoffs to four African American aldermen (Perry Hutchinson, William Beavers, Clifford Kelley, and Wallace Davis Jr.) and an official in the city budget office (John Adams). Questioned by the media, the FBI investigators confirmed that the successful sting operation, which they had launched the previous year, was proceeding under the guidance of a federal grand jury and that they expected criminal indictments to follow. The bad news for the mayor worsened on December 30 when the *Tribune* reported the involvement of Clarence McClain, the discredited former member of the administration, in the alleged bribery and influence peddling.[70]

Since having been exiled from city hall in 1983, McClain had unsuccessfully run for Democratic ward committeeman and opened a consulting firm that catered to black-owned businesses. He portrayed himself as a former insider in the Washington administration who knew how to navigate around local government's abundance of red tape. Boastful of his connections to the mayor and other leading city officials, McClain cultivated the impression that his clients would enjoy special privilege in their dealings with municipal agencies. For months before the FBI sting became public knowledge, the local newspapers had been regaling their readers with stories of how the well-connected hustler was profiting from his friendship with Washington and implying that he still secretly toiled as the mayor's bagman. The linkage of McClain's name with the bribery scandal—he allegedly introduced the FBI's undercover agent to the aldermen and city official in exchange for a fee of thirty-five thousand dollars—appeared to lend credence to the rumors of his continued presence behind the scenes at city hall. While no evidence seemed to exist connecting the implicated aldermen directly with the mayor or members of his staff, McClain's involvement in the sting operation allowed critics to speculate about any role that Washington or others close to him might have played in the tawdry affair.[71]

Washington denied having had any contact at all with anyone implicated in the scandal, claiming that the media were sensationalizing what he curtly dismissed as "schoolyard foolishness," but the pressure mounted for the mayor to denounce McClain again. In calling for McClain's repudiation, the *Chicago Tribune* reported that two of the mayor's staunchest allies (Forty-Ninth Ward alderman David Orr and Fifth Ward alderman Larry Bloom) were also advising him to take such action to salvage the political support of white liberals. Given the role played by the FBI, the mayor believed that Operation Incubator could be traced ultimately to the Reagan administration. Eager to divert attention from a series of scandals involving Republican agency heads in Washington, D.C., and smarting from the Chicago mayor's persistent attacks on the president's policies, Washington reasoned, "the Reagan mafia" had targeted him for retribution. The mayor also saw no coincidence in the media's fascination with what he considered a comparatively modest transgression at the exact moment that his chances of seizing control of the city council looked so encouraging. He bristled as news coverage of the scandal continued in the first months of 1986, the melodramatic treatment of the story implying that the peccadilloes of a handful of Washington loyalists symbolized an administration rife with lawlessness. Grudgingly recognizing that such a characterization of city hall deportment and ethics would raise questions among voters in the March special election, he again publicly denied any connection between McClain and city hall. He also ordered an investigation of the affair by the independent Office of Municipal Investigations and an administrative review of the Revenue Department, the Comptroller's Office, and the Purchasing Department. For good measure, he issued an ethics executive order in place of the ordinance he had introduced into the city council months before that had vanished in a committee chaired by Vrdolyak.[72]

The newspapers continued in February and March 1986 to report the latest developments in the bribery scandal but devoted increasing numbers of column inches to the special aldermanic elections. The outcome of the contests in the seven redrawn wards would determine whether Vrdolyak and his followers kept control of the city council or, if the candidates loyal to the mayor prevailed in at least four of the contests, the administration would enjoy a working majority for the first time. (In the event of a twenty-five-to-twenty-five tie, the mayor would cast the deciding vote.)

Washington loyalists won in the Fifteenth Ward (Marlene Carter), Twenty-Second Ward (Jesus Garcia), and Thirty-Seventh Ward (Perry Giles), while candidates aligning with Vrdolyak won in the Eighteenth Ward (Robert Kellam), Twenty-Fifth Ward (Juan Soliz), and Thirty-First Ward (Michael Santiago). Thus, control of the city council depended on the outcome in the Twenty-Sixth Ward, a largely Puerto Rican enclave on the Near Northwest Side, where the discovery of uncounted ballots soon after Election Day left the final tally in doubt.[73]

Luis Gutierrez, a housing activist and stout Washington ally, appeared to have won in the Twenty-Sixth Ward by a razor-thin margin over Manuel Torres, a Vrdolyak protégé and Cook County Board member, after the initial vote count. Almost immediately, however, additional votes for Torres began appearing in scattered precincts throughout the ward. Two weeks later, election officials announced that they had discovered (under highly suspicious circumstances) an overlooked cache of write-in votes that raised questions about the accuracy of the final count. The chairman of the Chicago Board of Election Commissioners, a machine loyalist appointed years before by Mayor Michael Bilandic, judged the results in the Twenty-Sixth Ward tainted and ordered a run-off election for April 29. Gutierrez indignantly declared himself the rightful winner and complained that his opponent was attempting to steal the election, a charge echoed in city hall, but meanwhile Washington partisans began tuning up the election machinery for a brief, intense round of campaigning.[74]

The initial aldermanic campaign between Gutierrez and Torres had been vitriolic, but the runoff raised the enmity to new heights. With control of the city council at stake, both sides worked frenetically and spent freely in pursuit of victory. Precinct captains and veteran campaign workers from around the city descended on the Near Northwest Side, and the lavish spending on campaign literature and media advertising made the Twenty-Sixth Ward contest the most expensive aldermanic election yet in Chicago history. In the spirit of desperation manifested by their sponsors, both candidates resorted to personal attacks, rumors, and innuendos. Gutierrez accused Torres of being a criminally negligent father who had fallen far behind in child-support payments to his former wife; Torres characterized his opponent as a dangerous radical with connections to FALN, an extremist Puerto Rican nationalist organization, and assorted terrorist groups. On the last weekend before the election, a host of Democratic worthies (Vrdolyak, Jane Byrne, Richard M. Daley, and Forty-Fourth Ward alderman Roman Pucinski, among others) canvassed the ward, urging a vote for Torres. Washington matched their energy, indefatigably tramping door to door on behalf of Gutierrez and decrying the forces arrayed against his administration. "They stole the last one," he bellowed at a rally just hours before the polls opened. "We're going to get so damn many votes this time they won't be able to steal it from us."[75]

Whatever electoral legerdemain transpired on April 29, Gutierrez defeated Torres with 53 percent of the vote. For the first time in the Washington mayoralty, Vrdolyak and his allies would not enjoy the ability to paralyze municipal government. Subdued and contemplative in victory, Washington acknowledged that the decision of the U.S. District Court to redraw the city's ward map had been the crucial turning point in giving his administration the upper hand in municipal affairs. At the same time, he identified the outcome of the special ward elections as a sign that Chicagoans had at last cast an unmistakable vote for reform. Given the opportunity to repudiate Washington's vision after two turbulent years, the voters had instead opted to stay the course. With a working majority in the city council, the mayor continued, his first priorities would be the confirmation of his appointments to sixty-three city commissions and boards still sidetracked by the council majority, adoption of a comprehensive ethics code for local officials, and passage of a city budget of his own design, free of council interference. Not for the first time in his mayoralty, but with a newfound conviction, he exalted, "The city's Democratic machine is dead."[76]

The outcome of the special elections, the satisfied mayor told his aides, significantly transformed the political landscape of the city and the state in the spring of 1986. Not only would the altered composition of the city council give his administration the unfettered ability to advance its reformist agenda for the first time, but prospects for his own reelection in another year brightened considerably with the dramatic victory in the Twenty-Sixth Ward. He had prevailed in a showdown with his enemies that the local media widely portrayed as a dress rehearsal for the following year's mayoral election. Washington also foresaw several other fortuitous developments at the time. Gradually exposed in the Council Wars as an unprincipled agitator interested more in personal aggrandizement than effective governance and discredited as a political leader by a series of electoral setbacks, Vrdolyak seemed doomed as Democratic Party chairman. Similarly unmasked as an unscrupulous contrarian, Burke could finally be replaced as city council Finance Committee chairman. With the diminishment of Vrdolyak's and

Burke's influence and the changed arithmetic in the city council, the solidarity of the administration's opposition there seemed likely to splinter further. The defeat of Republican governor James R. Thompson in November 1986 by venerable Democrat Adlai E. Stevenson III, who had lost to Thompson by only five thousand votes four years earlier, would create a much more salubrious environment for the principal city of Illinois. Finally, the end of the two-term Reagan presidency in 1988, preferably with the election of a progressive Democrat, would similarly benefit Chicago and other large U.S. cities. Tired of listening to his enemies gloat that "29 is greater than 21," the mayor viewed the great political victory in April 1986 as legitimizing the causes he had been championing the previous years. The Chicago electorate had endorsed the fundamental idea of balanced growth instead of business as usual. Washington looked to the future with a newfound optimism in the spring of 1986.[77]

6

IN SEARCH OF A MANDATE

Washington prepared for his reelection campaign with the knowledge that he had yet to remove all doubts about the efficacy of his reform program. Because of the setbacks suffered during his first term in office—caused by the incessant guerrilla warfare in the city council that had frequently stymied his initiatives—the mayor had been able to enact very few of the changes he promised the electorate in 1983. A nightmare of contentiousness and obstructionism had obscured his lofty vision. He had continued to articulate progressive principles in a variety of forums and attained a national profile as an eloquent defender of the Democratic Party's core values, but critics charged and supporters reluctantly admitted that the number of substantive breakthroughs remained frustratingly small. In short, as Washington and his closest aides understood, his administration had not yet demonstrated to Chicagoans or to other elected officials in cities around the country that his design for rehabilitating ailing industrial cities would work. In order to validate a strategy of industrial retention, balanced growth, redistribution, and increased citizen access to local government, the Windy City's mayor would need to win another four-year term, establish a productive relationship with the city council, and wield power effectively to affirm that Chicago could indeed work together for the common good of its diverse population. Despite the encouraging political victories in the 1986 aldermanic elections, the most important work for Washington and his allies remained to be completed.

The final results of the special aldermanic elections came just one year before the 1987 mayoral election and a mere ten months prior to the Democratic primary. With the need to begin campaigning well in advance of the primary, a crucial activity that would consume much of the time and energy of Washington partisans inside and outside of city hall, the administration possessed only a few months to put the finishing touches on the mayor's first-term record. After an unceasing, three-year struggle against Vrdolyak, Burke, and their followers, the new city council majority relished the opportunity to set agendas and make policy but would enjoy only a limited time to complete unfinished business and perhaps launch a few new initiatives before the election. The mayor's allies looked forward to dislodging legislation bottled up in city council committees, approving mayoral appointments that had been sidetracked by hostile aldermen, and advancing progressive measures first enunciated by Washington in 1983 but left fallow during the ensuing Council Wars. His reform agenda blunted for so long by a ruthless and unyielding opposition, the mayor would be able at last to demonstrate the plausibility of his soaring reform rhetoric. Moreover, control of the city council would allow the administration to demonstrate that the lack of progress in some areas owed to the exertions of unscrupulous aldermen and not to its own lack of proficiency. Demonstrated mastery of city hall would show the voters how a competent local government could translate the mayor's plans into a reality that benefited all Chicagoans, regardless of social class, race, ethnicity, or gender. The anticipated breakthrough in 1986–87 depended, of course, on the loyalty and discipline necessary to sustain the razor-thin majority in the city council—and the necessary unity among the mayor's supporters proved questionable at first.[1]

Uncertainty within the new majority's ranks surfaced immediately as the mayor set out to reorganize the city council, reducing the number of committees from thirty-seven to twenty-eight and transferring leadership positions from enemies to supporters. Rather than exact retribution wholesale against his opponents, as many mayoral loyalists advised, Washington steered more of a middle course. Seeking reconciliation instead of revenge wherever possible, he took action against Aldermen Vrdolyak and Burke but held out an olive branch to other members of the erstwhile majority bloc who agreed to cut their ties to the discredited coalition. The mayor hastily abolished the Neighborhood and Community Affairs Committee, which deprived Vrdolyak of his only committee chairmanship. Speaking for many of her African American colleagues in the city council, Dorothy Tillman insisted that the mayor divest Burke of the Finance Committee chairmanship as well. "Why show a racist like Burke an ounce of sympathy or respect?" she asked heatedly. Washington effected a compromise by creating the Budget Committee, complete with nearly absolute control of the city's fiscal affairs, and allowing his nemesis to remain in charge of a Finance Committee shorn of its authority. Burke kept most of his perquisites (the continued use of a city limousine and bodyguard, for example) but lost the considerable power he had wielded the previous three years. Fourth Ward alderman Timothy Evans, the mayor's trusted city council floor leader, assumed the chairmanship of the influential new Budget Committee.[2]

On May 9, 1986, at a special city council meeting called soon after the aldermanic elections, the mayor's supporters wore buttons bearing the inscription, "25 + 1." Eager to break ties with his decisive twenty-sixth vote, Washington strode cheerfully into council chambers while spectators in the gallery stood and applauded. After clarifying a number of procedural issues and dispatching Burke's perfunctory motion to adjourn the meeting, the mayor commenced the process of confirming the sixty-three nominees who had been denied appointment to city posts by his enemies. By adjournment time that day, the new majority had approved twenty-five of those nominations to a variety of municipal agencies that included the Chicago Housing Authority, Chicago Transit Authority, Chicago Park District, Urban Renewal Board, Zoning Board of Appeals, Chicago Plan Commission, and Chicago Regional Port Authority. On May 30, Washington canceled votes on the confirmation of the remaining nominees, including the appointees who would have given him majority control of the Chicago Park District, when two aldermen expected to vote with the mayor inexplicably vanished during the council meeting. The mysterious disappearance of Marian Humes of the Eighth Ward and Perry Hutchinson of the Ninth Ward without informing the mayor's floor leader jeopardized the outcome of the vote, triggered speculation about the loyalty of the two aldermen, and raised questions about the ability of the new majority leadership to control its members.[3]

Humes evasively said that she had personal business to conduct during the meeting, and Hutchinson attributed his absence to unspecified health concerns. Their vague explanations did nothing to quell the uproar in the African American community, which demanded unwavering fealty to the mayor. Now that Washington at last had a working city council majority, his supporters would not countenance the idea of betrayal by disloyal black politicians. Washington partisans picketed Humes's ward office, and Hutchinson reported receiving threatening telephone calls at home. The Reverend Jesse Jackson railed against the irresponsibility of African American public officials who had won elections with his help and then failed to appear at crucial city council meetings. Duly chastised, the two aldermen affirmed their loyalty to the mayor and promised to vote for all of his appointments. Driven to the next city council meeting in an ambulance, Hutchinson cast his votes for the mayor's nominees while seated in a wheelchair with an IV drip attached to his arm; with less spectacle, Humes attended and dutifully voted for the Washington slate as well. The new majority approved the remaining nominees to city posts, including the crucial appointment of a new Chicago Park Board member.[4]

The fight for control of the Chicago Park District, an autonomous municipal agency with a $145 million budget and a workforce of approximately sixty-five hundred full- and part-time workers, assumed special significance for the mayor because the superintendent (Ed Kelly) had consistently sided with Vrdolyak and Burke in the battle for political control of the city. Lord of the vast parks empire and committeeman of the Forty-Seventh Ward, the voluble Kelly had called the mayor a racist and opposed his reform measures like clockwork. His autocratic rule of the park district, command of an enormous patronage army, and influence in local party affairs made him, according to political pundits, a real threat to Washington as a potential Democratic Party chairman, mayor, or both. A venal man presiding over a government agency allegedly rife with corruption—the Better Government Association had published a number of exposés over the years, uncovering kickbacks, favoritism, and payoffs in the park district—Kelly comported himself much like the swaggering political bosses who ruled the city in decades past. A *Chicago Sun-Times*/BGA investigation revealed that Kelly had for decades allowed parks in minority neighborhoods to decline while simultaneously beautifying parks in white middle-class areas of the city. The *Sun-Times*/BGA probe also found more park-district workers employed in the "Fighting Forty-Seventh" than in all of the African American wards combined.[5]

The city council's approval of a new Chicago Park Board member, architect Walter Netsch, at last created a pro-Washington majority in the governing body. Rather than wait for the three remaining years on Kelly's contract to expire or remove him from office, the newly constituted board rewrote the park-district charter to create the position of executive vice president. Investing the new post with broad administrative and fiduciary power, the commissioners stripped the superintendent of virtually all authority and appointed Jesse Madison, the mayor's former commissioner of consumer services, executive vice president. Michael J. Hennessy, the general attorney for the park district, instructed all department and division heads to ignore any directions from Netsch and Madison, forcing the new executive vice president to assume firm control of the agency only after threatening to fire Hennessy for insubordination unless he rescinded the order. Kelly filed a lawsuit to block the move, challenging the legality of Netsch's appointment and claiming that the park board lacked the statutory power to amend the charter, but lost in Cook County Circuit Court. At first refusing to report to the executive vice president, the superintendent soon resigned. The removal of a Democratic-machine stalwart once considered impervious to cries for accountability in municipal government constituted a signal victory for reform.[6]

With the mayor's forces ostensibly wielding a majority in the city council, Chicago's local government faced an immediate crisis over unresolved financial issues. According to city budget director Sharon Gist Gilliam, the loss of $45.3 million in federal revenue sharing funds, pension-fund increases, anticipated pay raises for city workers, and the need to settle several legal judgments against the city accounted for an $80 million deficit in the budget for fiscal year 1986. The budget approved by the city council in December 1985 essentially dealt with the shortfall by imposing a $79.9 million property tax increase, but the Cook County Circuit Court had ruled the action illegal. Following the court ruling, city officials failed to revise the long-overdue budget as they considered a series of alternative revenue sources. By the summer of 1986, well into the fiscal year, Chicago was operating without an official budget. (At the same time, city hall functionaries were already gathering data for the preparation of the 1987 fiscal year budget.) The reconstituted city council thus was forced to stem the flow of red ink quickly through some combination of spending cuts, tax increases, and higher user fees. The necessity of raising taxes less than a year before the 1987 mayoral election would give Washington's critics ammunition to use against him, allowing them to claim that the mayor's spendthrift policies had created the financial shortfall. Now in control of the city council, Washington's enemies said, he could not avoid the responsibility of solving the crisis—and would likely have to do so by calling for unpopular tax increases.[7]

After weeks of legislative give-and-take, Washington, his aides, and city council Budget Committee members consented to a new property tax package that they felt confident would pass judicial muster. But some aldermen in the mayor's camp, most notably Burton Natarus of the Forty-Second Ward and Marion Volini of the Forty-Eighth Ward, warned that pressure from tax-weary constituents in their wards might keep them from voting for the measure. Expecting property tax increases to be an explosive issue when she ran for reelection the following February, Volini urged the administration to opt instead for a jet-fuel tax on aircraft using O'Hare International Airport. The mayor rejected the jet-fuel tax, and Volini grudgingly agreed to support the property tax increase—but Natarus continued to voice concerns publicly. Natarus had been one of the twenty-one aldermen in the mayor's camp from the beginning, and, although unpredictable and difficult to deal with at times, he had always voted along with the Washington loyalists. Not so on September 12, however, when he became the lone holdout whose negative vote kept the administration's measure from passing.[8]

Faced with the first crack in his tenuous city council working majority, Washington intensified his efforts on several fronts to pass the property tax increase. The city press office revived its public relations campaign on the need for a tax increase, which had been halted the previous December after the city council originally approved the fiscal year 1986 budget. Blanketing the local media with print and electronic advertisements and showcasing endorsements from such good-government groups as the League of Women Voters and the Civic Federation, the administration emphasized the dire consequences that would accrue without the additional revenue. The mayor warned that he would be forced without the tax increase to impose 40 percent across-the-board cuts in all city departments, resulting in layoffs affecting eleven thousand employees and including roughly half of the city's police officers and firefighters. The outcome of the legislative struggle also threatened the city's financial reputation, he informed the public, because Standard & Poor's had recently issued a press release scoring the city council's failure to pass a new tax levy and had criticized the city for failure to devise "permanent financial solutions" for chronic budgetary problems. The bond-rating agency delayed issue of a revised bond rating for Chicago pending the municipality's ability to pass the tax increase that year, making the fate of the legislation all the more important. Meanwhile, the mayor and his aides met with a number of aldermen (huddling with Natarus repeatedly) in a frantic effort to find the single vote needed for passage of the tax increase.[9]

The determinative city council meeting on September 24, a raucous affair that included bomb threats and required the sergeant at arms and local police officers to separate short-tempered aldermen, stirred unpleasant memories of the Council Wars' chaotic early days. The mayor's opponents delivered lengthy speeches extolling fiscal responsibility but also decrying the impact of more taxes on Chicago's overburdened citizenry; Washington's backers recited the need to avoid service disruptions, debilitating personnel cuts, and bond-rating reductions. Still wavering, Natarus requested the delay of the vote for yet another week so that he and his colleagues could explore additional revenue sources. The mayor refused and called a recess. Finally, following a long telephone conversation at the council rostrum with an unidentified interlocutor, the recalcitrant alderman consented to resolving the matter immediately. After the city council passed a bill to impose $27 million in aviation and motor-fuel taxes to abate part of the property tax increase, the roll-call vote to raise property taxes by $79.9 million passed, with Natarus and Washington casting the deciding votes. Disgruntled and angry, Burke fumed, "It's a fraud and a hoax. The [aviation and motor-fuel taxes] will never, never be the subject of abatement." Natarus explained that he had supported the tax increase with a "heavy heart," knowing that "there are going to be many people who are sore at me." He left city council chambers that day surrounded by a twenty-four-hour police guard. The mayor had prevailed in an important showdown, but the episode did little to assuage concerns about his new governing alliance's cohesiveness—or, critics were quick to point out, its ability to manage the city's precarious finances effectively.[10]

Washington once again reminded Chicagoans that such fiscal crises, which needlessly imperiled the delivery of vital city services, owed in large measure to the unconscionable diminution of federal funding in recent years. With the devastating impact of the Reagan administration's cutbacks in urban funding evident at every turn, the Republican White House continued to prepare budgets that stanched the flow of federal largesse to the nation's cities year after year. The president's 1987 budget, the mayor warned his constituents in 1986, included yet another series of reductions that would cut allocations to Chicago by approximately $440 million—including $238.8 million less for transportation, $72.4 million less in general revenue sharing, $49.2 million less for community and economic development, $46.7 million less for housing, $20.1 million less for job-training placement, and $14.4 million less for health and human services. Early in 1987, Washington took aim at Reagan's proposed budget for 1988, under which Chicago would receive 9.1 percent less for health and human services, 20 percent less for community and economic development, 43.8 percent less for transportation (in conjunction with a 62.4 percent reduction for the independent Chicago Transit Authority), and 100 percent less for housing. The mayor condemned the recurrent barrage of reductions, most of which targeted especially vulnerable groups such as the elderly and indigent, in order to underwrite "bloated and wasteful appropriations to the military and to questionable adventures in foreign lands."[11]

Washington similarly berated the Reagan administration's embrace of ill-conceived budget-balancing schemes, which he contended only worsened the plight of the nation's cities while failing to improve the federal government's financial soundness. The Balanced Budget and Emergency Deficit Control Act of 1985, popularly known as the Gramm-Rudman-Hollings Act, established declining annual deficit targets, leading to a completely balanced national budget by 1991. The imposition of mandatory cuts each year would devastate cities like Chicago, warned the mayor. No one questioned the need to bring the nation's runaway budget deficit under control, he said in testimony before the Budget Committee of the U.S. House of Representatives, "but it must not be balanced on the backs of our urban centers." He told the committee that strict adherence to the Gramm-Rudman-Hollings time line would, at best, leave Chicago without the wherewithal to maintain the already inadequate delivery of essential city services. "The president's recommendations and Gramm-Rudman[-Hollings] would tear the guts out of local government," Washington concluded. The modest adjustments to the budget-reduction formula contained in the Balanced Budget and Emergency Deficit Control Reaffirmation Act of 1987 (Gramm-Rudman-Hollings II), the best Democrats could do to mitigate federal funding cuts, offered little hope to worried local officials.[12]

Just as the harmful effects of dwindling federal financial assistance on the city budget had become a serious concern for a mayor preparing for reelection, so too had the expressions of dissatisfaction with the administration by various Latino groups in Chicago. After giving Washington only 13 percent of their votes in the 1983 Democratic primary, Latino voters had awarded the victorious mayor 75 percent of their ballots in that year's general election. In the close final tally, the significant increase in the Latino vote proved to be crucial in the narrow defeat of Bernard Epton. Rudy Lozano, Jesus Garcia, Juan Velázquez, José Jiménez, the Reverend Jorge Morales, and other Latino activists reported that the winning candidate's progressive campaign rhetoric that year and his promise to form an alliance of historically powerless groups had captivated many residents in their neighborhoods. At the same time, Latino progressives felt that the mayor's triumph legitimized their own reform agendas, enhanced their status citywide, and promised to give them unprecedented access to city hall. As vital contributors to Washington's victory in 1983, Latinos anticipated reaping the benefits in terms of government appointments, jobs, and political recognition. When the mayor spoke about his unwavering devotion to affirmative action in the pursuit of social justice, Latinos expected that his administration's beneficence would extend into their communities as well as into African American neighborhoods. In no small measure, the pivotal victories of Jesus Garcia and Luis Gutierrez in the 1986 special aldermanic elections elevated the expectations of Washington supporters in Latino communities as well.[13]

Without hesitation, Latino leaders acknowledged in 1986 that the city's Mexican, Puerto Rican, Cuban, and tiny Central American populations had enjoyed more economic progress and received more appointments to local government posts in the previous three years than they ever had before. The comparison between the Byrne and Washington years in city hall showed this disparity clearly. Latinos accounted for 7 percent of new hires under the former, 11 percent under the latter. Washington appointed twenty-seven Latinos to "decision-making positions" in municipal government, according to a government watchdog group, compared to Byrne's total of three. Moreover, business awarded Latino contractors by the city increased tenfold between 1982 and 1985. Latinos received fully 20 percent of the mayor's appointments to local boards and commissions. Washington had spoken at fund-raisers for prominent Latino politicians and signed two executive orders that received high praise from a Latino community concerned about immigration matters—one that eliminated the need for job applicants to identify their citizenship unless required to by federal law, an especially important consideration for immigrants seeking to obtain taxicab licenses, and another that shielded city employees from having to cooperate with federal immigration officials unless ordered to do so by a court order.[14]

Perhaps most significantly, Washington broke new ground in local government by creating the Mayor's Advisory Commission on Latino Affairs (MACLA). Granting the minority group an official voice in municipal affairs fulfilled a 1983 campaign pledge and provided an aura of legitimacy to the views of Latino community leadership. Yet the commission's creation came after a delay of many months and only after repeated reminders that the promise had yet to be honored. Latino activists chafed at what they perceived to be delaying tactics employed by some of the mayor's aides, especially chief of staff Bill Ware, who said he feared the surrender of control to a "runaway commission," and resented what they felt to be a decided lack of enthusiasm for an enhanced Latino presence in city hall. Further, Latinos complained that top mayoral aides Ernest Barefield and Jacky Grimshaw made no effort to include the commission in important city hall policy discussions. Starting with no budget, office, or staff, members of MACLA struggled to establish a niche in city hall. Maria de los Angeles Torres, the executive director of the fledgling city agency, successfully resisted the commission's consignment to a subordinate position within the Commission on Human Relations and demanded autonomy for her bailiwick within the municipal bureaucracy. With persistent effort, Torres won the right to hold monthly meetings with all city commissioners present and received regular access to the mayor. Yet despite the struggles launching the new agency, Latinos viewed its creation as an important milestone. When others in the administration questioned the need for MACLA and called for its dissolution, Torres said, the mayor never wavered in demanding its retention.[15]

Washington remained a staunch advocate for MACLA throughout his mayoralty, even when he suffered criticism for defending the commission and when tensions flared between Latinos and other local officials. Lobbying unabashedly for the hiring of more Latinos in municipal agencies, MACLA published an annual assessment of the administration's record on affirmative action—an appraisal that candidly scrutinized performance and frequently called for greater progress. The release of the reports invariably triggered a negative reaction among some African Americans, who resented the implied criticism of the mayor and condemned the agency for publicly calling attention to the administration's deficiencies. Latinos in city hall acknowledged the audacity of what MACLA was doing and gave the mayor high marks for allowing the agency's criticism of his administration to persist in such open fashion. Torres spoke often of her genuine affection for Washington but also felt that she paid a price for speaking truth to power. She said, "Whenever I said something nice about the mayor I would get these pleasant phone calls from him. But whenever we went public with the Latino hiring reports, I couldn't walk into the mayor's office for three months. When the mayor was accused of not being fair, he did take it personally."[16]

By the administration's fourth year, the feeling had become widespread in the Latino community that African Americans had fared much better in Chicago's nascent black-brown coalition. Although the record of the Washington mayoralty clearly showed advancement, growing Latino inquietude resulted from the failure to meet rising expectations. Consequently, the mayor's issue of another executive order in 1985 extending the life of MACLA elicited only subdued praise in the Latino community. The rising expressions of disgruntlement among Latinos owed to a widely shared feeling that, despite the evidence of measurable progress, so much more had seemed possible.[17] Torres explained:

> There's no doubt the black-Latino coalition has been a remarkable success. We're more inside [city hall] than we've ever been, that's clear. But mostly [the coalition] has been a success politically. It's the policy side—what we're getting, or not getting from this administration—that's the problem. We're really not participating as full partners commensurate with our numbers. Ultimately, the political coalition will suffer if a fair agenda is not pursued.[18]

Most often, friction between Latinos and the administration revolved around hiring policy. "Results for addressing black under-representation have been excellent," commented Torres in a MACLA press release. "For Latinos the results have lagged far behind what was expected and what is considered equitable." When Byrne left office in 1983, African Americans accounted for approximately 40 percent of the city's population and held about 25 percent of city jobs. Even more underrepresented in the municipal workforce, Latinos numbered around 17 percent of the population and possessed fewer than 4 percent of the jobs. Yet in 1985 and again in 1986, Latinos composed only 11 percent of city hires. The numbers for the two minority groups seemed to indicate that the mayor's frequent paeans to affirmative action redounded disproportionately to the benefit of black Chicagoans. Administration officials explained the disparity as a result of the much larger black hiring pool and the paucity of qualified Latino applicants for city employment, assertions that Torres strongly disputed based on her three years at MACLA. The city simply passed over qualified Latino applicants while hiring African Americans and others, she asserted. Some city agencies such as the Department of Economic Development compiled excellent records of hiring Latinos, Torres noted, while others such as the Corporation Counsel's Office made no effort to comply with Washington's injunction. "There are people [in the administration] who don't seem ideologically committed to translating the mayor's words into deeds," concluded Alderman Jesus Garcia.[19]

In addition to hiring practices, city hall's record seemed to be coming up short in other ways as well. Despite an increase in representation at lower levels of city employment, very few Latinos occupied positions in the highly visible upper echelons of the Washington mayoralty. The noticeable absence of Latinos at weekly cabinet meetings underscored the fact that only African Americans and whites administered the budget, law, housing, police, fire, economic development, planning, cultural affairs, and aviation departments. Torres found that Latinos composed just "7 or 8 percent" of the city's commissioners, directors, and first deputies. Only Ben Reyes, the surprise choice of the mayor's office to serve as liaison to the Latino community and an unpopular figure among many Mexican and Puerto Rican reformers, held a midlevel post in the administration. Improvement seemed real but frustratingly slow, more widespread in Latino neighborhoods than in city hall.[20]

The situation appeared no better with regard to low-income housing, a serious concern for Latinos as well as for African Americans. Despite the shortage of suitable lodging available to them in the private housing market, Latinos occupied only 2 percent of public housing units. "The Housing Department tends to think of housing as a black problem," said a local housing activist, and officials in that agency blithely commented that Latinos and other minorities would simply have to place their names on the Chicago Housing Authority waiting list—a list that had been closed for two years because of a huge backlog created by the overwhelming demand for government-subsidized accommodations. No Latinos served on the CHA board, despite repeated pleas that the mayor address the omission. After the special aldermanic elections in 1986, Latinos hoped that Jesus Garcia or Luis Gutierrez (both of whom had been housing activists before pursuing elective office) would be named chairman of the city council's housing committee. Instead, the post went to an African American woman, Dorothy Tillman. Progressives lamented the fact that public housing remained a racial issue rather than a poverty issue, much to the detriment of the Latino population.[21]

Latinos also bristled at what they perceived to be the administration's indifference to issues of particular significance in their communities. The mayor, they felt, seemed to be less attentive to problems in Pilsen or Little Village than to comparable concerns in North Lawndale or Englewood. Latino community organizers complained about working hard to assemble sizable crowds for public meetings at churches and public schools, only to have Washington appear inexcusably late or arrive unprepared to address pertinent issues. Such cavalier behavior seemed indicative of a *falta de respeto* (lack of respect) that Latinos strongly suspected was not being repeated in African American neighborhoods. Administration officials assured Latino activists that the mayor's chronic tardiness simply resulted from an overbooked schedule. "Any mayor who's on time just isn't doing his job," Washington said in his own defense, but the feeling lingered among Latinos that problems in their neighborhoods were receiving less than the full attention of the administration.[22]

Garcia, Torres, Gutierrez, and many other Latino activists who were closely identified with the mayor continued to defend his commitment to a true rainbow coalition but believed that not everyone around him shared those sentiments. Embittered from a long and painful history as the city's largest racial minority, many African Americans evinced little empathy for the deprivation visited upon smaller but rapidly growing population groups such as Latinos. The editor of an African American weekly newspaper said, "A lot of blacks cannot help but feel that we've been fighting hard for a long time, and that as soon as we got our foot in the door here come the Hispanics, pushing that door open and trying to run in ahead of us." Many African Americans in city hall questioned the depth of Latinos' loyalty to Washington, suspecting that self-interest alone accounted for their support of the mayor. Unconvinced that a multiracial alliance could transcend ethnic and racial mistrust in Chicago, black activist Lu Palmer thought conflict between African Americans and Latinos inevitable. "Our communities are in competition for political advancement," he said. "We both want to make up for past abuses. You have to make up your mind who comes first." Washington knew that his supporters among the black nationalists agreed with Palmer, and he understood the potential for jealousy and avarice to disrupt the brittle equilibrium prevailing among his supporters. He faced the difficult task of balancing the desire for redistribution and recompense among impatient allies convinced of their just claims for redress of grievances.[23]

Faced with growing unrest in Latino communities, Washington publicly counseled patience, strongly defended his administration's record, and remained true to his concept of affirmative action. Behind the scenes, revealed his press secretary, Alton Miller, the mayor sometimes chafed at Latino demands for more rapid progress. The requests for more jobs and contracts emanating from Mexican and Puerto Rican wards struck him as old-fashioned angling for political patronage with little thought for the broader welfare of the minority coalition. To counteract the divide-and-conquer tactics used by the remnants of the Democratic machine, he believed, squabbles between blacks and Latinos should be handled internally—within the "family." When Latinos pushed for quicker results, he said privately, "They're mau-mauing us, and I'm getting tired of it." To the call for a revision of the administration's 25–5 hiring formula to establish a 15 percent goal specifically for Latino hires, Washington refused to set a separate target for particular racial or ethnic groups. The goal of his administration, the mayor wrote a DePaul University business professor, continued to be an increase in the number of jobs and contracts secured by minority and women overall—not a competition among and between these groups for such awards. He maintained that, despite the ardent resistance from many quarters, the numbers had been rising for all such groups and that his allegiance to affirmative action remained as strong as ever. To ensure fairness in the allocation of city jobs, he welcomed the formation of a Latino business oversight commission that would monitor his mayoralty's achievements in affirmative action. The mayor proudly touted his administration's record on minority hiring, especially at a time when drastic reductions in federal aid had increased the pressure on a shrinking municipal budget, as one of the signal achievements of his first term.[24]

Disenchantment among Latinos and the possible loss of their votes continued to be significant concerns among the mayor's aides, but a movement to make mayoral elections nonpartisan in Chicago appeared by the summer of 1986 to be the greater threat to Washington's reelection. Since July 16, 1985, when the irrepressible Jane Byrne had declared her candidacy well in advance of any other potential aspirants, a replay of the 1983 Democratic primary seemed highly possible. That is, the mayor could be reelected with an overwhelming black vote as other white candidates split the remaining ballots. Although early polls showed state's attorney Richard M. Daley to be the biggest threat to Washington, Byrne campaigned energetically for months as the only declared candidate and refused to step aside. As a latecomer, Byrne and her supporters speculated, Daley would run the risk of being a "spoiler" whose candidacy caused the white vote to be divided. Meanwhile, the mayor coolly surveyed the political landscape and refused to announce whether he would run in the Democratic primary or seek reelection as an independent. Political experts noted that an independent candidacy virtually assured Washington of running against two white candidates in the general election, the winners of the Democratic and Republican primaries. Washington and his aides later revealed that he never seriously considered deserting the Democratic Party, which he considered the indispensable vehicle for the articulation of his reform principles at the state and national levels, and that his talk about an independent candidacy amounted solely to political gamesmanship. At the time, however, his evasiveness left the status of the Democratic primary highly ambiguous and thereby obscured the electoral picture for other potential mayoral candidates.[25]

As a solution to the political predicament in which he found himself, Daley and his supporters proposed changing state law to do away with primaries and make Chicago mayoral elections nonpartisan. Windy City reformers had been suggesting the change for decades as a means of undermining the power of the Democratic machine, and ironically the descendants of the machine were resurrecting the idea in 1986 as a means of unseating a reform administration. Under the proposition advanced by Daley and his surrogates, the top-two vote getters in a nonpartisan election would face each other in a runoff if no candidate received a majority in the initial balloting. In the case of the impending 1987 election, under the Daley proposal, Washington would almost surely be obligated eventually to run one-on-one against the most popular white candidate regardless of the number of other politicians in the race. Diligently traipsing through wards on the Northwest and Southwest Sides, Daley partisans gathered signatures on petitions advocating the procedural change for mayoral elections. By the August 18, 1986, deadline, they easily exceeded the number of signatures necessary (140,000) to place the issue before the voters in the November 4 general election.[26]

Chicago newspapers and some reformers backed the law change as a means of ensuring that the mayor would be elected with a popular majority. *Chicago Tribune* political reporter Steve Neal wrote that Washington himself had previously introduced a nonpartisan election bill as a state legislator, championing a "reform" measure that suited his political purposes at an earlier time, but in 1986 suffered a convenient loss of memory and opposed comparable legislation that would endanger his reelection. Other journalists and politicians, including influential U.S. congressman Dan Rostenkowski, matter-of-factly repeated the assertion of Washington's self-serving flip-flop. The mayor disputed the charge and angrily dared anyone to "find any record of any such bill with my name on it." Radio and television journalist Bruce DuMont accepted Washington's challenge, investigated thoroughly, and controverted Neal's claim. Nevertheless, the story continued to circulate as an example of the mayor's hypocrisy.[27]

Meanwhile, Washington scathingly condemned Daley's maneuver on a number of fronts. Making such an important change so soon before the election, he maintained, unfairly changed the rules in the middle of the game. How could election laws be altered on such short notice in a manner that directly affected incumbents? Strongly suspecting that Daley's followers had relied on traditional machine practices in circulating the petitions, the mayor questioned the authenticity of the signatures they claimed to have gathered. Most offensive to the mayor, the timing and circumstances surrounding the suggested change removed any doubt in his mind that the proposal was both personal and racial. He told a number of journalists in October 1986:

> Everyone in this room knows that the motivation for nonpartisan mayoral elections in 1987 has nothing to do—not even indirectly—with a desire for election reform in Chicago. It's targeted on me, personally, we all know that, most of its proponents freely admit it. . . . You can't write about my motives for fighting this move, with every means possible, without taking into full account that basic, primal matter of fact—no man is going to stand idly by while someone menaces him with a baseball bat.[28]

Washington served notice to the journalists that, reformer or not, he had no intention of standing idly by when menaced by enemies brandishing weapons. Given the nature of the personal attack he faced, neither would he shy away from mounting an equally devious counterattack. An obscure Illinois statute prohibited any community from submitting more than three binding or nonbinding referenda to voters at one time, whether their presence on the ballot had been secured by city council ordinance or petition. On July 29, Washington's city council allies introduced three nonbinding referenda—expansion of the Chicago Board of Education from eleven to fifteen members, authorization of legalized gambling, and reduction of natural gas charges—which passed twenty-six to twenty-five, with the mayor casting the decisive vote. "Who's kidding who?" cried Burke after the referenda passed. "Why are you so afraid of having the people vote?" But he smilingly added, "I must compliment whoever thought of it." Although the Daley partisans submitted their petitions bearing 211,000 signatures by the August 18 deadline, the three referenda passed by the city council had been sent already to the Chicago Board of Elections days earlier. Washington admitted to reporters that he had no idea how the election board would rule.[29]

The Chicago Board of Elections voted two to one to place the nonpartisan mayoral election question on the November ballot, and the mayor immediately challenged the ruling. Estimating that his enemies had forged fully half of the signatures in favor of Daley's referendum, Washington also announced that a small army of volunteers authorized by the city would be scrutinizing the eighty-one hundred petition sheets to ascertain their legality. The volunteers, a cross-section of Chicago voters selected by the administration because of their antimachine credentials, quickly discovered an abundance of falsified signatures. Congressman William Lipinski, a Daley loyalist and sponsor of the petition drive, lamely defended the blatant signature discrepancies with the offhanded observation that in Chicago, "normally petitions are 10 to 15 percent forged. . . . [M]aybe this, since it is so large, will go 20 percent." Unmoved by the congressman's bizarre defense, the Chicago Board of Elections reversed its earlier decision and canceled consideration of the nonpartisan mayoral election in November. On September 16, circuit court judge Joseph Schneider upheld the election board's reversal, a decision confirmed on October 1 by the Illinois Supreme

Court. Congressman Lipinski pledged to keep the issue alive in the future, but the Illinois Supreme Court's ruling finally settled the matter for the 1987 mayoral election. Democratic and Republican candidates would vie for their party's nominations in February, and the winners of those primaries would face each other in the April general election—just as they had four years earlier.[30]

As Washington's first term wound down, despite the possibility of candidates splitting the white vote, the 1987 election promised no shortage of mayoral aspirants. The relatively narrow margin of the mayor's 1983 victory virtually ensured a spirited challenge four years later, as did the racial unease that lingered in Chicago. The wear and tear of the Council Wars could be interpreted differently—many critics assessed blame indiscriminately and disparaged the mayor for a dearth of accomplishments, while Washington's supporters praised the administration for achieving as much as it had given the persistent opposition—but Chicagoans agreed that the unseemly political feuding of the previous years had limited progress and besmirched the city's reputation. Financial distress continued to hound Chicago, just as the same lethal economic forces plagued other industrial U.S. cities in the treacherous 1980s, and Washington's indictment of the Reagan administration for its antiurban animus echoed the laments of other big city mayors. Hamstrung by a number of limiting factors and prevented from acting decisively on his own agenda, Washington had been unable to compile an impressive record of achievement. He seemed vulnerable to many Chicagoans, friends and foes alike. Still smarting from the mayor's unexpected electoral triumph, the survivors of the powerful Democratic machine eagerly sought the opportunity to prove the 1983 outcome an aberration. Washington would still enjoy overwhelming African American support, they calculated, but perhaps enough votes could be wrung out of white and Latino wards to tip the scales in their favor. Jane Byrne thought so. She declared her candidacy for the mayoralty well in advance of any other competitors.[31]

After relinquishing office in 1983, Byrne had wasted very little time before hinting at a comeback. Although purportedly considering a new career as a television commentator, political consultant, or educator, she quickly hired a press secretary and quietly began to assemble a campaign staff for another mayoral run. Determined to improve her standing with Latino voters, she began taking a Berlitz course in Spanish and filmed a television commercial for a popular Mexican restaurant. Appearing frequently at Latino fiestas, parades, and religious celebrations, Byrne worked to create an image as Chicago's Evita Perón. The official announcement of her mayoral candidacy came in a sixty-second television advertisement broadcast nineteen months before the Democratic primary. Having silently observed the shortcomings of the Washington administration for too long, Byrne explained, she could no longer remain passive as the lives of everyday Chicagoans worsened. Lacking the endorsements of powerful local Democrats and possessing only a tiny political war chest, she mounted an underdog campaign critical of both the mayor and her old ally Alderman Edward Vrdolyak. A voluble politician who skillfully manipulated the media, she exploited her status as the only declared candidate for months by monopolizing newspaper political columns. Byrne conducted an intense grassroots campaign, meeting with mostly white and Latino groups in neighborhood homes, churches, and small businesses, criticizing Vrdolyak's leadership in the city council and Washington's inept stewardship of the city's dwindling resources. Relentlessly hammering away at unacceptably high crime rates, rising taxes, poor municipal housekeeping, and other purported failures of the administration, she urged voters to join her crusade to restore the glory Chicago had recently enjoyed during her city hall tenure.[32]

Political pundits conjectured that other leading Democrats would enter the February 1987 primary as well. Certainly, Alderman Vrdolyak's starring role in the Council Wars and his powerful position as chairman of the Cook County Democratic Party made him a logical choice to square off against the mayor. Since his early days in the city council years before when he precociously challenged Mayor Richard J. Daley's authority, Vrdolyak had made no attempt to conceal his ambition of becoming mayor someday. In an election in which race promised to play an important role again, the Tenth Ward alderman's sterling reputation among racist whites remained unsurpassed. "Given the racial situation in the city," commented a Democratic committeeman, "there is no way anyone can 'outwhite' Eddie." Still, Vrdolyak recognized the danger in splitting the white ethnic vote with Byrne and repeating the decisive error of 1983. He announced in December 1986 that he would run for mayor in the general election as the candidate of the Solidarity Party, the makeshift political organization cobbled together earlier that year by Adlai E. Stevenson III for his gubernatorial run. (Oddly, Vrdolyak remained Cook County Democratic Party chairman while running for mayor at the head of another party ticket.) To demonstrate his resolve to beat Washington at all costs, Vrdolyak promised to lend Byrne two thousand workers during the primary campaign and suspend his third-party effort until the spring.[33]

Speculation also swirled around the potential candidacy of Cook County assessor Tom Hynes, the Nineteenth Ward committeeman, former president of the state senate, and a close Daley ally. Known as an intelligent and thoughtful politician with a reputation for unimpeachable integrity, Hynes enjoyed great popularity among voters on Chicago's Southwest Side. With endorsements from influential Congressmen Dan Rostenkowski and William Lipinski, he potentially provided a formidable obstacle to Byrne for the city's white vote and announced his intention to run in the February contest. When Washington declared that he would run as a Democrat rather than as an independent, however, Hynes bowed out of the primary. Later, he resumed his candidacy and created the Chicago First Party as the vehicle for the April general election. Washington derided Hynes's indecisiveness, saying, "I gather he wasn't ready to fight, so he had to pull out and get himself together. The Democratic primary is no place for people with no courage. He had to get out. He didn't belong there."[34]

Washington formally announced his candidacy on August 13, 1986, at a lavish Palmer House Hotel fund-raising reception where an estimated four thousand guests paid $150 each to jump-start the campaign. In his brief remarks to the partisan crowd, the mayor recited his administration's achievements and emphasized the importance of reregistering two hundred thousand voters who had cast their ballots for him in 1983. He unveiled a new campaign slogan—"Chicago Working Better than Ever for Everyone"—and reaffirmed his commitment to reform. Obviously enjoying himself, he contentedly reminisced about how he had at last vanquished his foes in the city council's majority bloc and playfully pretended to have forgotten Jane Byrne's name. In a separate ballroom reserved for affluent invitees who had contributed large sums of money to attend, he scornfully mocked Daley for his unsuccessful attempt at altering the mayoral election to improve his own chances of winning. With Daley, Vrdolyak, and Hynes all remaining on the sidelines, Washington looked forward to running against Byrne alone in the Democratic primary.[35]

As Washington prepared for the one-on-one confrontation with his lone white opponent, the issue of race again dominated political discourse in

Chicago. His opposition's convoluted exertions to settle on a winning candidate reminded the mayor of the desperate search for a Great White Hope to defeat heavyweight boxing champion Joe Louis several decades earlier. Washington's supporters disagreed about the role race should play in his reelection effort. Convinced of racial pride's importance in the victory four years earlier, the black nationalists argued that Byrne's vulnerability in that area should be exploited as the best means of duplicating the fervor of the 1983 crusade against machine bigotry. The issue would also be crucial in mobilizing African American voters again, they asserted. Others in city hall counseled against a repeat of the earlier campaign, arguing instead for a color-blind strategy that highlighted Washington's sustained professionalism and statesmanship in the face of mean-spirited opposition during the ensuing years; his closest advisers also urged persistent references to Byrne's past failures in city hall. Speaking for the latter group, deputy campaign manager Jacky Grimshaw commented, "Our approach this time is more intellectual than emotional." Washington agreed. Having earlier condemned Mayor Richard J. Daley as "a racist from the core," he offered a decidedly less hostile appraisal in the midst of the 1987 campaign. "He was not a perfect man," Washington observed a decade after the elder Daley's death, "but he was as perfect as you can be in an imperfect world."[36]

Lu Palmer and other black nationalists fumed as Washington carefully avoided the topic of racism in the weeks before the primary election. They also bridled at the mayor's strategic choice of running mates to create a balanced ticket with broad appeal. Having acquiesced to the candidacy of Cecil Partee (a proven black vote getter) for city treasurer, Washington selected Gloria Chevere, a Puerto Rican with strong appeal in Latino neighborhoods, for city clerk rather than Bill Walls, an African American the mayor had fired the year before from a low-level position in the administration. (In fact, Washington and his aides had hoped to run with a white candidate for treasurer to form a true multiracial ticket, but judged that the influential Partee would be too difficult to dislodge.) When Palmer's Black Independent Political Organization quarreled with the inclusion of a Latino on the ticket, the mayor condescendingly dismissed its objection. "BIPO-Shmipo," he mocked.[37]

Despite the best efforts of Washington and his staff to de-emphasize race, comments by two of his African American supporters kept the issue alive. In the first instance, speaking at an Operation PUSH gathering on the South Side, Judge Eugene Pincham told the audience that "any man south of Madison Street who casts a vote in the February 24 election and who doesn't cast a vote for Harold Washington ought to be hung." Pincham's remark immediately drew criticism from the Committee on Decent Unbiased Campaign Tactics, or CONDUCT, a new silk-stocking organization monitoring the election to discourage character defamation based on race, ethnicity, religion, or gender. The chastened judge rejoined that his remarks had been taken out of context and explained that he had intended to say that anyone living on the South Side who failed to vote should be hung. Byrne demanded that Washington repudiate Pincham and labeled his campaign bigoted when he refused to do so. She quickly aired a television commercial that highlighted the Operation PUSH remarks and accused the partisan jurist of trying to intimidate black voters.[38]

In the second instance, Third Ward alderman Dorothy Tillman raised the issue of racial bias in a speech before a group calling itself "Women Embarrassed by Byrne." After lauding the mayor's sparkling progressive record—signing the Shakman decree, balancing the budget, imposing an ethics ordinance by executive action, and more—the alderman surmised that only the color of their skin could possibly induce lakefront liberals to vote for Byrne. Even after a furor ensued over her statement and the mayor disavowed any direct racial appeals to voters, Tillman refused to apologize for her remarks. Byrne again pounced quickly, citing Tillman's remarks as more evidence of the racially divisive campaign being run by the mayor—even though neither Pincham's nor Tillman's controversial utterances could be linked in any way to the Washington campaign office.[39]

Attempting to distance herself from the racial polarization that she claimed was being fostered by the Washington campaign, Byrne preached forbearance and understanding. "Love. Unity. Pride. Sharing. Hope. I want Chicago to smile again," she cooed to the camera in one notable television advertisement. As the campaign heated up in January 1987, Byrne increased the intensity of her attacks on the Washington administration. She chartered a city bus, filled it with local journalists, and then conducted a special tour of Chicago that stopped at unfinished construction projects. Lingering at a padlocked gate in front of Navy Pier and at a closed rapid-transit station, she denounced the mayor for his inability to complete bricks-and-mortar work. He was a talker, Byrne told the journalists, but she was a doer. She promised to resurrect ChicagoFest, which Washington had canceled, as part of her quest to revive the central business district and rekindle the city's spirit. Repudiating the administration's claims of fostering diversity in municipal government, Byrne claimed that both women and Latinos had fared better during her years in city hall.[40]

By the end of January, public opinion polls indicated that the kinetic Byrne campaign had turned a lopsided contest into a close race. With barely three weeks remaining before the primary, reported the *Chicago Tribune*, Washington's comfortable lead over the challenger had dissipated. Calling the race a toss-up, *Chicago Sun-Times* columnist Vernon Jarrett attributed Byrne's remarkable surge in the polls to her successful courting of white independents in the affluent lakefront wards. The possibility of Byrne attaining an even greater bonanza of votes in lakefront precincts rose on Sunday, February 8, when a violent winter storm paralyzed much of Chicago. Gusting sixty-mile-an-hour winds producing fourteen-foot waves dumped water from Lake Michigan onto Lake Shore Drive; the spillover froze into ice, two feet thick in places, and closed the major north-south thoroughfare from Hollywood Avenue on the north to Sixty-Seventh Street on the south. Floodwaters spilled into basements farther inland, toppled trees, and deprived many residents living near the lake of electricity. City crews worked frantically, breaking ice and piling sandbags, to clear Lake Shore Drive for the next morning's rush-hour traffic. Having been elected mayor eight years earlier because of an unpredicted meteorological disaster, Byrne reacted enthusiastically to another apparent case of divine intervention. At a hurriedly called lakefront press conference with the wind and surf surging behind her, she excoriated the administration for reacting tardily to the storm. Byrne asserted that the ability of the city's work crews to unblock the crucial transportation artery by morning, a seemingly impossible prospect at the apex of the storm, would serve as an accurate barometer of Washington's capacity to govern Chicago.[41]

By late Sunday, the situation looked hopeless for the city. Film footage of Lake Shore Drive buried under thick layers of ice and drifted snow seemingly confirmed television reporters' fatalistic predictions of protracted immobility. Yet John Halpin, the veteran commissioner of streets and sanitation, doggedly issued optimistic projections and vowed that he and his men would win the tense battle against the clock. "I would have had my people out there to suck the water up with straws if I had to," he later commented. Halpin added city workers from other municipal departments to his streets and sanitation detail and oversaw an around-the-clock operation that pulverized gigantic blocks of ice, cleared miles of roadway, and coated pavement with sand and salt. Traffic was moving steadily along the roadway by 5:45 a.m., with only a few troublesome patches remaining atop on- and off-ramps and under viaducts. Normal conditions prevailed along the length of Lake Shore Drive by 8:30 a.m. The extraordinary efforts of Halpin and the municipal workforce averted a major catastrophe, keeping Chicago working against heavy odds and depriving Byrne of a resounding public relations triumph. City hall partisans breathed a huge sigh of relief.[42]

Fortunately avoiding the kind of cataclysmic event that would have provided the challenger an eleventh-hour boost, Washington adroitly relied on the advantages of incumbency in the last days before the primary. Unlike in 1983, when he labored indefatigably to raise money, the mayor luxuriated in a steady flow of campaign contributions from Chicago and elsewhere; he outspent his opponent in the Democratic primary by an estimated two-to-one margin. The Byrne campaign pushed aggressively for a debate, but Washington's aides found a number of pretexts to stall negotiations. The mayor understood that only an underdog challenger would benefit from a face-to-face verbal exchange, and he avoided squaring off against Byrne in that format. He also enjoyed the endorsements of all the city's daily newspapers, which alternated qualified approval for his leadership under trying circumstances with harsh recollections of the Byrne mayoralty. Hardly effusive in praising the mayor, the mainstream press still foresaw after the conclusion of the Council Wars a greater chance for sound management and civic peace with Washington than with his unpredictable opponent. The *Chicago Tribune* opined, "Though it is not easy to assess Mr. Washington's record as mayor, the same cannot be said of Jane Byrne. She was terrible. And although she cannot seem to remember all the terrible things she said and did, we can."[43]

Washington prevailed in the Democratic primary, but typically in Chicago not without controversy. Election judges in a number of primarily black wards mistakenly provided Democrats who intended to vote for the mayor with the Solidarity Party ballot, an error that necessitated a lengthy postponement in reporting the vote totals. The tense delay notwithstanding, Washington prevailed with 54 percent of the votes. Chicagoans went to the polls in large numbers, and nearly 98 percent of the voters cast ballots in the Democratic primary. The mayor carried twenty-six of fifty wards, ac-

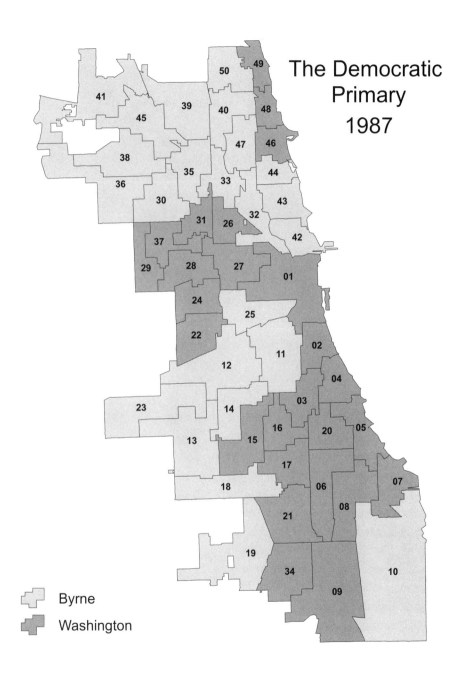

The Democratic
Primary
1987

Byrne
Washington

cumulating huge vote majorities in 78 predominantly black precincts. As they had four years earlier, Chicagoans voted overwhelmingly along racial lines. Byrne failed to attract a single African American vote in 31 precincts and captured only one in 110 others. Altogether, Washington won approximately 99.6 percent of African American ballots. The mayor did slightly better among white independents than he had four years earlier, going from 42 percent to 44 percent of the vote in the six north lakefront wards, but made few inroads into white ethnic neighborhoods on the Northwest and Southwest Sides. His winning percentage in the four principal Latino wards, the Twenty-Second, Twenty-Fifth, Twenty-Sixth, and Thirty-First, roughly approximated his winning margin citywide. In a striking contrast to 1983, Byrne graciously called for Democratic Party unity after her loss and later endorsed the mayor in the general election.[44]

Largely overlooked in the frenzy of the Democratic contest, the Republicans conducted their own primary in relative obscurity. Bernard Epton, the party's standard-bearer four years earlier, resurfaced to announce that he would run again to reclaim his good name after the unfortunate events of the last mayoral race. Unable to collect enough signatures on a petition to secure his name on the primary ballot, however, Epton retired from the race in mid-January, showing none of the petulance he exhibited in 1983. His exit left only one viable Republican candidate: Donald Haider, an erstwhile Democrat and professor at Northwestern University's Kellogg School of Management. The former city budget director in the Byrne administration, Haider hoped to parlay his financial expertise and bipartisan reform appeal into victory over whichever professional politician prevailed in the Democratic primary. Largely ignored by the press and the public throughout January and February, the good-government Republican issued a number of position papers that propounded such structural reforms as low taxes, spending reductions, the privatization of city services, and the reorganization of municipal agencies. Erudite and witty on the stump addressing tiny audiences, he won favorable notices in the press while easily coasting to victory. While more than one million Democrats cast ballots in February 1987, Haider won the Republican nomination for mayor in a primary with slightly more than eighteen thousand participants.[45]

Having survived a demanding electoral battle against a determined opponent struggling to salvage her foundering political career, Washington next faced three candidates (Haider, Vrdolyak, and Hynes) in the six weeks prior to the general election. The mayor's foes in Chicago rued the possibility of his opponents splitting the white vote, producing a replay of the 1983 outcome when Byrne and Daley divided the Democratic total, and all three took turns urging the other two aspirants to withdraw from the race. Each of the candidates claimed to be the best bet to defeat Washington in a one-on-one race, and all of them swore to remain in the contest until the end. Whether running as members of the Republican, Solidarity, or Chicago First Party, all three former Democrats essentially competed for the support of the same constituency. Each of the three white candidates claimed to be reformers—to be sure, their understanding of the appellation differed quite a lot from the mayor's concept of reform—but their fight for control of the critical white ethnic vote seldom addressed the fine points of political ideology, economic development, or social welfare policy. As in 1983, the outcome of the election seemed likely to boil down to race, political mobilization, and voter turnout.[46]

The challengers all argued for a series of debates with the incumbent, but Washington countered that he felt no obligation to appease candidates who had shunned the opportunity to define the issues within the Democratic Party. "Why should I debate them?" he asked rhetorically. "These three men ran out on their party." Instead, the mayor agreed to participate in a single ninety-minute debate on March 31. Televised by the local public television channel, the debate attracted the station's highest viewership ever for a public affairs program. In restrained fashion, Washington presented a well-reasoned defense of his administration steeped in statistical detail and generally avoided engagement with the other debaters. Like the mayor, Hynes and Haider soberly discussed municipal policy in measured tones; both men promised capable leadership and a return to civil discourse after four years of tumult. Typically pugnacious, Vrdolyak directed barbs at Washington and Hynes (while generally ignoring Haider) and blamed the administration for the city's racial unease. The mayor had shirked his moral obligation to condemn racism by all groups, the alderman charged, allowing acrimony between whites and blacks to fester during the previous four years.[47]

The press found the event unenlightening and largely blamed the rigid format for the absence of meaningful dialogue among the candidates. Uncharacteristically subdued, Washington seldom stirred to address criticism aimed his way and seemed out of sorts for much of his time on camera.

Clutching a bulging briefing book in hand, he responded by rote to questions he had been grilled by aides to expect. His usual spontaneity dulled
by too much preparation and a determination to avoid contentiousness,
Washington came across as well informed but lifeless. "My own campaign
did something to me that Vrdolyak could never do," he later told his press
secretary. "They cut my balls off." The mayor's desultory performance notwithstanding, the news media proclaimed Hynes the big loser. He looked
ill at ease, agreed reporters, and his cautious comments delivered in an
unvarying monotone left the audience visibly uninspired. He clearly failed
to elevate himself above the other debaters.[48]

Prior to the general election, Hynes split his time between portraying
Vrdolyak as unelectable and condemning Washington as a mayor undeserving of reelection. Increasingly frustrated by their inability to force Vrdolyak
from the race, Hynes and his aides grew more brazen in their allegations
against the Tenth Ward alderman. Hynes partisans first accused Vrdolyak
of stubbornly remaining a candidate despite having no chance of victory
because of a secret pact with Washington that would ensure the incumbent
mayor's reelection in exchange for a number of unspecified political favors.
Late in the campaign, the Hynes camp contributed to (and may have initiated) a Chicago Sun-Times story linking Vrdolyak with a leading Mafia don.
The aggrieved alderman denied the charges and threatened to sue Hynes
and the newspaper. Predictably, Vrdolyak defiantly remained in the race.[49]

Hynes also sought to fashion a stark contrast between his and the may-
or's administrative backgrounds—between his unruffled capability in the
county assessor's office and Washington's disputatious tenure in city hall.
Presenting himself as a judicious, low-key public servant, he promised the
voters a municipal government so quietly competent that "you won't even
know I'm there." A charming television advertisement for Hynes showed
his young son drifting off to sleep as his father droned on and on about the
potential virtues of greater government efficiency. Returning to the theme
of Washington's hostility toward downtown business interests, Hynes characterized the "first-source" hiring program as a thinly disguised affirmative
action effort detrimental to Chicago's economic growth. He further accused
the mayor and his cabinet of dishonesty in financial reporting and of mishandling federal aid, especially funds to address the city's worsening public
housing problems.[50]

More than the other two challengers, Hynes hammered away at the
uninterrupted flow of bad news regarding the Chicago Housing Authority

in late 1986 and early 1987. The embattled housing authority reeled from one crisis to another that winter, involving funding shortfalls, intramural factionalism, escalating violence, and poor leadership. The CHA lost a seven-million-dollar federal grant to remodel and improve security at the Robert Taylor Homes because of its failure to submit the required contracts by the December 31 deadline established by the U.S. Department of Housing and Urban Development—despite already having been granted several extensions by the federal agency. Hynes attributed the embarrassing oversight to CHA chairman Renault Robinson and called for his removal from office; Robinson blamed CHA executive secretary Zirl Smith, who resigned on January 7. The mayor accepted Robinson's resignation on January 16, ending the chairman's controversial three-year tenure as head of the beleaguered agency. Twenty-Seventh Ward alderman Wallace Davis, a Washington ally, called for the entire CHA board to resign after two children fell to their deaths in a high-rise public housing project with broken elevators. Crime statistics released by the Chicago Police Department in January 1987 for the previous year showed that violent crime had increased by 31 percent in public housing projects, more than doubling the citywide increase.[51]

The avalanche of inflammatory newspaper headlines left the mayor scrambling to defend his administration's record on public housing at a most inopportune moment. Despite being hamstrung by his inability to recruit top-notch personnel to run the CHA, Washington maintained, he had made "immeasurable progress" in solving the manifold problems inherited from his predecessors. Decades of mismanagement, winked at by previous mayors and countenanced by HUD regional supervisors, had left a quagmire of astounding proportions. Washington pointed out that Chicago's egregiously underfunded housing agency received just one-third of total state expenditures for public housing, even though Chicago operated more than half of the low-income projects in Illinois. The nation's second-largest public housing authority, the CHA had never placed higher than twelfth in the rank order of HUD funding. The reduced flow of federal dollars owing to the Reagan administration's imposition of a New Federalism had exacerbated the problem. "I inherited one holy mess," the mayor asserted. "I'm going to straighten it out. I'm on the road to doing so."[52]

Hynes and other critics of the mayor questioned his capacity for solving the CHA conundrum and called for external control of the floundering Chicago agency as the only hope for the city's 145,000 public housing residents. Alderman Burke suggested that the U.S. District Court should place the CHA in receivership. HUD officials were seriously considering a federal takeover of Chicago public housing, but the mayor vowed to oppose the threatened intervention. Fearful that the Reagan administration would demolish vast tracts of low-income housing and privatize what remained without taking care of the dispossessed residents, Washington continued to defend his administration's ability to reform the CHA. Charges and countercharges about the CHA's fate flew back and forth between Chicago's city hall and HUD headquarters in Washington, D.C., throughout the mayoral campaign, but the fate of the housing agency never became a leading issue prior to the election. In large measure, the mayor's opponents spent relatively little time assailing city hall about the CHA because Byrne and others associated with her administration (specifically Vrdolyak and Haider) had all been complicit earlier in public housing's worsening predicament. Only Hynes could criticize Washington's handling of the CHA with impunity.[53]

Washington hit back against Hynes, asserting that his opponent's squeaky-clean reputation belied a long history of legal work completed during a period of public employment that clearly amounted to conflict of interest. "He should be the last person in the city to question the integrity of anyone," countered Hynes. "His history and his record are one of sleaze." Such heated rhetoric failed to interest an electorate apparently immune to ad hominem attacks, as evidenced by the challenger's lagging poll numbers. With no last-minute signs of growing support among white ethnic voters, Hynes finally withdrew from the race less than forty-eight hours before the polls opened. "I love Chicago enough not to be mayor," he declaimed.[54]

Fully expecting to be the principal beneficiary of Hynes's withdrawal, Vrdolyak praised his erstwhile rival for "putting the best interests of the city of Chicago before any personal ambition" and immediately sought to capture as many newly available Democratic votes as possible in the little time left before the election. Most Hynes supporters likely swung into the Vrdolyak camp, but many prominent Democrats followed Daley's lead and declined to endorse any of the remaining candidates. In the last thirty-six hours before the election, Vrdolyak campaigned feverishly around the city and repeated the themes he had been emphasizing in the preceding weeks—only with greater gusto. He openly questioned Washington's integrity, exhuming the scandals related to the mayor's personal finances that had surfaced years before. He mocked Washington for having accomplished so little during four years in office (conveniently forgetting the major role he and his compatriots had played in limiting those achievements) and for lacking a coherent vision for Chicago's future. He questioned the mayor's competence, saying, "He doesn't have a clue what the job is about. He doesn't have the faintest idea of how to run a government." The brazen alderman even excoriated the mayor for ignoring the well-being of the city's African American population. Washington eagerly raked in a mountain of votes from black precincts in 1983, Vrdolyak jeered, but then turned a deaf ear to the needs of his constituents after Election Day.[55]

Vrdolyak spoke often during the campaign about the issue of Chicago's unacceptably high crime rates, which he compared unfavorably to the figures during the Byrne administration. The city had become a markedly more dangerous place during the Washington years, he asserted, in large measure because the mayor had imposed draconian cuts in budgetary items related to public safety. "The mayor is basically antipolice," he charged. The alderman further claimed that the city was using the Chicago Intervention Network, a multimillion-dollar antigang program launched in 1984 after the murder of a local high school basketball star, Ben Wilson, as an extension of the mayor's reelection campaign. When CIN failed to solve all of the city's gang problems within six months, critics blamed the mayor for relying on street-intervention workers, neighborhood watches, alternative youth programming, and victim assistance, while stubbornly holding the line on police department allocations. Vrdolyak's aides also circulated a broadside that prominently displayed a photograph of the Reverend Jesse Jackson, who was supposedly acting cooperatively with Washington, at the Cook County Jail, registering inmates to vote. The new voters included murders, rapists, drug addicts, and child molesters, the alderman lamented. The pamphlet explained that the incidence of crime was rising "because Harold Washington is more interested in registering criminals to vote than in arresting them!" Vrdolyak straightforwardly accused the mayor of being soft on crime and cast himself as a true sentinel of law and order.[56]

While the press closely followed the antics of the always quotable Vrdolyak and debated whether Hynes would remain in the race, Haider cheerfully tramped around the city in what he proudly termed the city's first walking mayoral campaign. He unexpectedly demonstrated a real flair for stump speaking. At ease addressing crowds in a variety of settings, the professor-technocrat openly joked about his long-shot status and appeared sincerely to be enjoying himself. He spent much of his time exhorting third-party candidates to withdraw and, citing his many years as a management professor and his stint as the city's budget director, discussed at length a list of ten proposals for improving Chicago's financial future. Starved for news coverage in a race that pitted him against glib, experienced politicians, Haider demonstrated a quirky sense of humor and engineered a number of stunts designed to attract media coverage. The day after St. Patrick's Day, for example, he rode a two-and-a-half-ton elephant (on loan from the Shrine Circus) across State Street. The image of the distinguished academician astride the symbol of the Republican Party, captured by television news cameras and newspaper photographers, interrupted the other candidates' monopoly on media coverage—at least for a single news cycle. "We told you we expected something big from the Republican National Committee," Haider quipped, "and this exceeded all our expectations."[57]

In fact, Haider received scant support from the Republican National Committee. Judging his chances of victory farfetched in a field crowded with proven Democratic candidates, the Republican National Committee provided just $5,000 for the campaign. Nor did party officials in Illinois and Cook County provide the needy candidate with much sustenance. With only $800 in his campaign coffers after the primary victory and facing limited prospects for additional fund-raising, Haider canceled plans for volunteer organizations, neighborhood campaign offices, and phone banks. He spent most of the $800 on red jackets with the words "Don Haider for Mayor" stenciled on the back and then distributed them to onlookers at his campaign stops around the city. His lack of funds remained an insurmountable problem throughout the campaign.[58]

In contrast, the mayor never suffered from a serious shortage of funding. Despite having imposed a $1,500 limit on contributions as part of a campaign-finance ethics ordinance he signed earlier that year, Washington experienced little difficulty in raising money. A March 30 fund-raiser at the Conrad Hilton Hotel attracted an estimated four thousand guests who paid $150 apiece, for example, raising $600,000 for the campaign's final week. Washington welcomed several leading national political figures to Chicago, including Massachusetts senator Edward Kennedy, Missouri congressman Richard Gephardt, and former Virginia governor Charles Robb, for their endorsements. He also received the backing of the four Chicagoans who were serving in the U.S. House of Representatives at the time (Gus Savage,

Charles Hayes, Cardiss Collins, and Sidney Yates) and Democratic U.S. senator Paul Simon of Illinois. Both major daily newspapers endorsed Washington, as did the Chicago Teachers Union (CTU) and the United Auto Workers. Jane Byrne delivered a stirring endorsement of her own in the closing days of the campaign, after which the mayor released a television advertisement of her advising voters that "it's time to unite behind Mayor Washington." More surprisingly, two stalwarts of the Vrdolyak Twenty-Nine in the city council (Bernard Hansen and Eugene Schulter) deserted their former leader in favor of the mayor, and several other Democratic aldermen hinted that they might do the same after the election.[59]

Unburdened by grave financial worries and possessing impressive endorsements from prestigious Democrats, Washington presided over a campaign that by all accounts operated much more effectively than the 1983 operation. The reelection drive smoothly took shape as a grassroots endeavor noteworthy for its careful attention to mobilizing voters. Never forgetting the need for minimizing complacency and maximizing turnout in African American wards, the reelection machinery directed by Kenneth Glover and Jacky Grimshaw painstakingly canvassed neighborhoods on the predominantly black South and West Sides. The mayor issued Executive Order 86-2, which mandated that all facilities operated by the city provide space for voter registration. At the eight city colleges, full- and part-time faculty, volunteer members of the Student Government Association, members of the Cook County College Teachers Union, and members of the Local 1708 Federation of College Clerical and Technical Personnel for City Colleges registered voters. In addition, members of the American Federation of State, County, and Municipal Employees and the City Wide Voters Registration Coalition did the same at other locations. Campaign workers combed Chicago Housing Authority projects to register new voters, a task assumed by Washington and the Reverend Jesse Jackson on the last weekend before the election. David Axelrod replaced Don Rose, the venerable political consultant who had run afoul of the mayor during the campaign, and produced the effective television advertisements that highlighted Washington's achievements in office.[60]

The mayor's campaign team cautioned him to maintain a dignified stance befitting the city's chief executive, avoid negative campaigning, remain above the fray, and ignore the taunts (especially from Vrdolyak) hurled at him and his administration. Washington did so, for the most part, but could not always refrain from ridiculing his opponents. He bristled at the desperate search among Democrats for a white candidate to defeat him, grousing, "Singles, doubles, triples—and if they can find a fourth person, I will run against him too." Having derisively dismissed his three opponents as Wynken, Blynken, and Nod prior to the general election, the mayor had more fun when informed that Hynes had dropped out of the race. "Guess who dropped out?" he chortled. "It was Nod. Nod dropped out. Nobody was surprised by that." His lighthearted ridicule of the three challengers reinforced the impression of a Brobdingnagian figure effortlessly dispatching a scurrying band of Lilliputians who were futilely trying to tether him.[61]

Washington playfully chided his opponents at times but devoted most of his speech making to a serious recitation of the previous four years' achievements and the promise of continued advancement. He recounted how his 1983 victory and the changes imposed by Chicago's new and improved brand of government had dealt the legendary Democratic political machine a lethal blow. Under his guidance, reformers in city hall had eradicated the shopworn, discriminatory, and inefficient practices that had held the city back for so long. Returning repeatedly to his campaign theme of "working together," he regaled audiences with paeans to cooperation, fairness, racial comity, and justice. He promised to continue along the same reform path if reelected—to safeguard neighborhood interests, to enhance citizen access to government, to retain industry, to curtail the influence of real estate, and, as he emphatically told *Crain's Chicago Business*, to promulgate affirmative action (albeit with some refinements to address technical problems). After an uncertain and contentious beginning, Washington exalted, the fruits of reform were at last ready to be harvested by his administration.[62]

As he had during the previous four years, the mayor insisted that his capacious style of reform allowed for unprecedented attention to neighborhood needs and downtown redevelopment simultaneously. By no means, he insisted, did the two activities need to be mutually exclusive. He announced an ambitious goal for the next five years, a two-billion-dollar neighborhood program that would follow the improvements made possible by the 1985 general-obligation bond issue. His neighborhood platform, "Fairness Works," detailed a generous spending plan, including the repaving of another 250 miles of residential streets; sidewalk, bridge, streetlight, and sewer- and water-line improvements; rehabilitation and construction of affordable housing; financial assistance to small businesses, especially minority- and women-owned concerns; job-training and -placement programs; public transportation improvements, most notably the construction of a southwest transit line; and grants to expand cultural programming and facility renovation. He reminded Chicagoans of the struggles his administration had faced in channeling funds to the neighborhoods, saying, "I was elected to office on a neighborhood development platform, but I've had to fight every step of the way to get the money out here. I fought political obstructionists in the City Council, along with federal cutbacks choking our programs. But I still got your money to you. And I vow to continue the fight."[63]

The mayor's public orations also prominently mentioned his considerable efforts to enhance Chicago's central business district. Foregrounding the exemplary efforts of planning commissioner Elizabeth Hollander, Washington asserted that the city had finally made progress on the North Loop redevelopment effort that had stalled under previous administrations. A list of the city's achievements in its quest to revitalize the North Loop included the restoration of the historic Chicago Theatre, the execution of five redevelopment agreements in Blocks Sixteen and Seventeen, and city council approval of a fifty-eight-million-dollar Tax Increment Financing bond issue. The downtown area immediately south of the Chicago River might not yet look appreciably different, Washington assured voters, but these preliminary advances would soon give way to ground-breaking and ribbon-cutting ceremonies. In his second term, promised the mayor, city hall would continue to strengthen the downtown by building a new main public library and by cultivating innovative plans for the development of the South Loop and the River North areas. Even the *Chicago Tribune*, a fierce champion of the city's progrowth coalition that had often pilloried the administration for its lagging attention to business interests, noted approvingly in its endorsement of the mayor that shabby areas north, south, and northwest of the Loop had shown improvement during the previous four years.[64]

On April 7, 1987, Washington won reelection with 54 percent of the vote. With approximately 72 percent of eligible voters casting ballots, he beat Vrdolyak and Haider by almost 132,000 votes. Fewer voters cast ballots in white precincts than in the primaries two months earlier, a disastrous outcome for the mayor's opponents, whose only chance for victory rested with large turnouts in those areas. Washington won twenty-seven wards

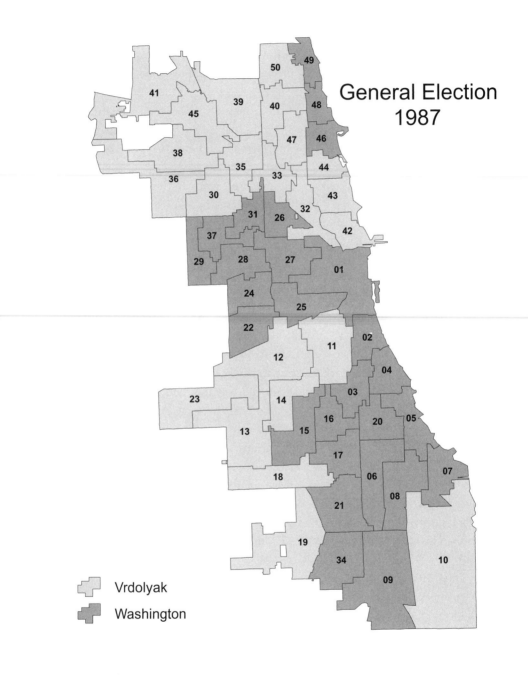

General Election
1987

Vrdolyak
Washington

(one more than in the primary) and again carried the African American vote by landslide proportions. He won ten black wards with more than 99 percent of the vote and another six black wards with more than 90 percent. He carried the four primarily Latino wards, increasing his victory margins slightly from the primary election. Vrdolyak won the remaining twenty-three wards, most situated in the Northwest and Southwest Sides of the city.[65]

Having finished second with 42 percent of the vote, Vrdolyak generously congratulated the mayor on his reelection and expressed satisfaction at his own showing. Ruefully pondering the plausibility of an even better outcome if Hynes had exited the race sooner, he still accepted defeat without recrimination and wished Washington success and good health in the next four years. He declined to discuss his political future or his standing in the Democratic Party. (Five months later, he made his break with the Cook County Democrats official and became a member of the Republican Party.) Haider accepted his predictable third-place finish with good-hearted resignation. Despite receiving only 4 percent of the vote and failing to carry a single ward, he called his campaign a useful political exercise and expressed satisfaction in his ability to educate voters about the issues. He pledged to keep a close watch on city hall during the next four years, saying, "[Washington] has it all, he can't push the blame for things on other people. He will be held accountable."[66]

During the Election Night revelry at Navy Pier, Washington celebrated his victory with an ecstatic crowd of two thousand supporters. The giddy mayor warbled "Chicago, That Toddlin' Town" off-key and, relating how his celebrity had reached the farthest corners of the globe, shared with the audience how Chicagoans traveling abroad were constantly being asked, "How's Harold?" The assembled multitude cheered when Washington declared his intention of being mayor for the next twenty years, a whimsical comment he had made many times before during his first term. (Impressed by Richard J. Daley's longevity as mayor, reported press secretary Alton Miller, Washington enjoyed speculating that he might someday become known as the "Sepia Daley.") In a more serious moment, he addressed the broader meaning of his victory. He said, "We celebrate tonight not the victory of one candidate, but a mandate for a movement. We celebrate the politics of partnership, the triumph of Democratic tradition. In four short years, our movement has taken hold, has moved from the margins to the mainstream of politics here in Chicago."[67]

Yet for all of Washington's confident talk on Election Night of possessing a mandate, privately he expressed frustration about the real lessons of the vote count. The mayor had expected a bigger victory margin. To his genuine surprise and disappointment, in 1987 he received fewer votes overall than he had four years earlier. Washington felt that, despite much politicking in strategically important areas and a praiseworthy record in office, he still garnered lower vote totals in white ethnic wards and along the lakefront in 1987 than in 1983. After Hynes withdrew from the race, aides in Washington campaign headquarters expected a large number of progressive lakefront residents to spurn Vrdolyak and turn (however reluctantly) to the Democratic nominee. Instead, Haider's dismal vote total indicated that the preponderance of white liberals had swung to Vrdolyak instead. Along with the voters in the white ethnic neighborhoods who presumably would stop short of turning city hall over to a scoundrel like the Tenth Ward alderman, went the Washington campaign's thinking, their candidate's addition of the lakefront voters formerly committed to Hynes would push the mayor's total to 60 percent or more. In the days leading up to the election, the mayor's pollsters called for his winning 30 percent of the white vote citywide; newspaper polls predicted that he would garner 16 percent of ballots cast on the Northwest and Southwest Sides. In the final tally, Washington received just 12 percent of the white vote in Chicago and 5 percent in the bungalow belts. After four years of municipal government that presented a highly favorable contrast to the Democratic machine, many of Chicago's white voters still could not bring themselves to vote for a black candidate. "We have to face it," Washington said bitterly. "We've leveled off at 53, 54 percent. That's about all we're going to get."[68]

Subsequent to a thorough perusal of the ward-level data, the mayor admitted being demoralized by the voting behavior of Chicago's white population. A Washington pollster had reported during the campaign that "whites appear to be much less hostile at the notion of another four years with Harold Washington as mayor." Others in reelection headquarters agreed, saying that they had detected less hostility toward the mayor emanating from brick two-flats and bungalows in white working-class neighborhoods. If so, that wellspring of goodwill seemed to have deserted voting booths in white ethnic precincts. Washington fulminated about the voters' preference for Vrdolyak, whom he considered a scamp and a shameless opportunist, rather than himself or Haider. Even on the lakefront, supposedly the home of the city's most enlightened voters, the mayor's appeal fell short of his expectations. Emblematic of the racial bigotry that apparently still held sway in affluent white enclaves, the residents of the tony Forty-Third Ward voted for Vrdolyak by a wide margin. Long an antimachine bastion and home of progressive Alderman Martin Oberman, the ward gave Vrdolyak 52 percent of the vote to Washington's 29 percent and Haider's 19 percent. By his own calculations, Washington had spent 70 to 80 percent of his time campaigning in white neighborhoods in 1987, yet failed to register even modest vote gains there. "He kind of smiled wanly," remembered David Axelrod, "and said, 'Ain't it a bitch to be a black man in the land of the free and the home of the brave.'"[69]

Still, the Chicago electorate had returned Washington to city hall—and with a slightly more generous governing margin in the city council due to favorable outcomes in a few key ward elections. After seventeen candidates allied with the mayor won election in February, another ten prevailed in the fourteen runoff elections held two months later. Washington loyalists won in three crucial elections in April: Incumbent Anna Langford defeated state senator James Taylor, a disreputable machine politician and longtime enemy of the mayor, in the Sixteenth Ward. Washington allies beat hostile incumbents in two other key contests, Raymond Figueroa outpolling Miguel Santiago in the Thirty-First Ward and Helen Shiller edging Jerome Orbach in the Forty-Sixth Ward. Although the final lineup of aldermen remained uncertain immediately after the April 8 general election—one race remained too close to call, and two newly elected independent Democrats remained noncommittal about their allegiance to the administration—the mayor's majority governing coalition would be increasing to at least twenty-seven and possibly to as many as thirty. In addition, several members of the Vrdolyak bloc acknowledged the futility of continued resistance and spoke openly about making peace with Washington in order to improve the operation of municipal government. The 1987 election for Washington shaped up as a qualified success, but a success nonetheless. "He'll now have a chance to prove himself out as a programmatic reformer," said political consultant Don Rose. "It's the opportunity he should have had the first time."[70]

7

THE FINAL MONTHS

Even though he privately confessed to considerable disappointment at the closeness of his 1987 reelection, Washington remained excited about a number of opportunities the victory provided. In particular, he anticipated that his continued presence in city hall would engender positive results beyond the municipality's borders. The mayor felt gratified at having defeated archnemeses Jane Byrne and Edward Vrdolyak, of course, and looked forward to applying his administrative skills in a much more inviting political environment. With the nightmare of the Council Wars finally over and with firmer control of a governing majority in the city council, Washington eyed Chicago's future with a sense of newfound optimism. Best of all, he would have the opportunity to implement his agenda for Chicago and showcase solutions to the troubles plaguing his city on the national stage. His reelection provided a pulpit that would invest his pronouncements with a legitimacy he could not have claimed as a one-term mayor who failed to secure reelection. Washington's office in city hall would become a command center from which he could continue to nurture and enhance the policies introduced during his first term. In so doing, he would fend off attacks on Chicago's autonomy launched in Springfield, lead a national crusade of city officials against the "flawed and suspect policies" of a Republican administration that had been spearheading a "federal attack on the cities," and marshal Democratic forces to install one of their own in the White House the following year. Fully confident in the efficacy of his leadership for Chicago, he expected his reforms in the Windy City to serve as a blueprint for the rebirth of the nation's struggling metropolises.[1]

Washington wasted no time summoning his mayoral colleagues to battle. On April 28, sixty mayors convened in Chicago to compose a national urban policy statement that would be submitted for adoption at the annual conference of the U.S. Conference of Mayors in Nashville on June 13–17. As the organization had been doing in past decades, the USCM planned to present the urban policy statement to each presidential candidate and to the 1988 platform committees of the Democratic and Republican Parties. In his opening address to the assembled mayors, Washington delivered a fiery oration, demanding the preparation of a manifesto that "must go beyond the traditional draft of polite recommendation." He derided the Reagan administration's claims of rebuilding the nation's economy and restoring pride to the American people. Indicting the Republicans' love affair with global adventurism and the bloated military spending it required, he decried the White House's willful disregard for the poor, the unemployed, the elderly, and other disadvantaged groups. Chicago and many other cities of necessity had introduced innovative programs that made the most of fewer and fewer resources, he noted, but desperately needed the resumption of the federal aid ruthlessly pared by uncaring Washington, D.C., bureaucrats. "We are wasting our time," he told the audience, "if we shrink from the fact that the Federal government is laying waste [to] our cities." Fortunately, the solution to grievous national problems could be found in cities that had served effectively as proving grounds for social welfare experimentation. "Just as we have changed the way we do things here in Chicago in the last four years," Washington concluded, "we must change the way we do things across urban America in the next four years."[2]

One week later, the mayor touched on many of the same themes to an audience of eight thousand persons at Grant Park in his second inaugural address. More magnanimous toward his political rivals than he had been four years earlier, observed the Chicago press, Washington devoted much of his second inaugural to the challenges facing the city from external forces. (The *Chicago Tribune* reported that the mayor had eliminated remarks about the perfidies of previous mayoral administrations from his prepared remarks, thereby softening the tone of the speech.) "Although our greatest problems are truly national in origin and national in scale," he said, "nonetheless they are local in their impact. And though we must take a role in the grand strategies laid in Washington, we are the ones who will have to carry the fight here, in the trenches, on the front lines, in our cities." A hostile federal government had eliminated general revenue sharing and severely reduced the direct aid, grants, and tax relief that had been subsidizing social services and economic development in the cities for decades. The fruitful partnership between municipal governments and Washington, D.C., having been terminated, the cities were being treated like failed industries—discarded and left to struggle for survival in a harshly competitive economic environment. Assaying his city's role in the national predicament, Washington said, "Now, more than ever, Chicago is challenged to take the lead. Just as we are finally able to leave local petty political bickering behind us, the new Spirit of Chicago is aroused to greater trials, perhaps the most important challenges our generation will face."[3]

Opportunities for more success in meeting the Windy City's imposing challenges abounded because Washington's reelection produced a decisive shift in the balance of power at city hall. Vrdolyak's loss in the mayoral race and the defeat of Democratic politicians aligned with him in the aldermanic elections served as an epitaph for the city council insurgency that had dominated local government for most of Washington's first term. (No longer a member of the city council, Vrdolyak resigned the Democratic Party chairmanship and announced his intention to run for county office as a Republican.) Former members of the Vrdolyak Twenty-Nine, including antimayoral stalwarts such as Richard Mell of the Thirty-Third Ward, Fred Roti of the First Ward, and Bernard Hansen of the Forty-Fourth Ward, deserted the unraveling alliance and made peace with the administration. A vote to replace Edward Burke as Finance Committee chairman passed forty to nine, a harbinger of more changes to come. Led by the unreconstructed Burke, nine hard-liners continued to wage a futile guerrilla war against the administration. The *Chicago Tribune* sniffed that the mayor would no longer have city council obstructionists to blame for city hall's deficiencies and that previously patient reformers and members of Washington's base on the South Side would henceforth be demanding better results. With enhanced opportunity and the elimination of effective opposition came elevated expectations, the newspaper warned Washington and members of his administration.[4]

Privately, the mayor, his department heads, and other aides evaluated both the achievements and the insufficiencies of the first term. The press and the political opposition had enumerated the administration's affirmative action and social welfare policies in great detail, the inhabitants of city hall believed, but largely ignored the substantial advances in downtown redevelopment during the previous four years as part of their attempt to portray Washington as antibusiness. The mayor had tried to address such inaccuracies in perception during the recent campaign, but never felt entirely successful in bringing the conversation around to the inroads his administration had made in Loop refurbishment. As his second term began, therefore, Washington vowed to clarify what he felt should already have been evident to Chicagoans—that new construction and rehabilitation downtown launched under his direction were "transforming this area into one of the nation's most dynamic central business districts."[5]

On July 16, along with economic development director Rob Mier, planning director Elizabeth Hollander, and comptroller Ron Picur, the mayor guided local newspaper, radio, and television reporters around downtown and surrounding development sites. Struggling to be heard over the sound of rivet guns and jackhammers at numerous construction sites, he reminded his guests that Standard & Poor's recent upgrade of Chicago's bond rating from B+++ to A-constituted a clear endorsement of the administration's fiscal policies. (Moody's, the other major bond-rating agency, raised the city's designation from Baa1 to A in October.) The four-hour bus tour proceeded from one carefully chosen stop to another, each destination designed to illustrate "the faith and confidence that Chicago's business community have in the city." Highlights of the excursion included Marshall Field's flagship store on State Street, where large-scale expansion and renovation projects were proceeding at a cost estimated between $75 and $90 million, and the Dearborn Park residential development south of the Loop that would soon contain 1,500 new townhouses for middle-class Chicagoans. The mayor explained that each of the projects owed their success to public-private partnerships, a clear indication of his administration's eagerness to cooperate with the business community for the good of the city.[6]

On the same day as the tour, the mayor's office distributed to the press a packet of fact sheets that offered quantitative evidence of recent downtown revitalization. The real estate boom, which began in the late 1970s and accelerated during the Washington years, had confirmed Chicago's position as one of the nation's leading office, hotel, and retail centers. Between January 1979 and July 1987, according to the mayor's office, investment in downtown real estate included $6 billion in completed projects,

$2.2 billion in ongoing projects scheduled for completion by 1989, and $7 billion in proposed projects. During the same years, businesses had added 33.7 million square feet of new office space, commenced construction of 7.9 million square feet, and planned another 30 million square feet. Hotels reported having more than 2,300 new rooms under construction, the renovation of 7,400 rooms within existing structures, and plans for 3,300 more rooms. After years of declining sales, during which time downtown retailers saw many of their customers depart for suburban shopping destinations, the mayor's office reported that the flight of retail dollars at last was being reversed. Despite the closing of several department stores on the State Street Mall in the previous decade, total retail sales in the central business district had risen 17.6 percent between 1982 and 1986. The Loop's leading department stores, Marshall Field's and Carson, Pirie, Scott, were investing heavily in improving their facilities, and Neiman Marcus, Bloomingdale's, and other elite retailers were completing new outlets on North Michigan Avenue's Miracle Mile. The reopening of the beautifully refurbished Chicago Theatre, the first step in transforming a large part of the North Loop into a theater district, would bring more people downtown in the evenings and benefit neighboring restaurateurs, bar owners, and other merchants who catered to theater patrons.[7]

The creation of a theater district, along with other entertainment options in the vicinity, constituted part of the effort to foster a lively nightlife downtown. Like many other large cities that had been undercut by metropolitan decentralization, Chicago had experienced a loss of vibrancy in the central business district. When commuters finished their workdays, they routinely deserted the banks, office towers, and government buildings where they worked and promptly departed for their suburban homes. Dark, deserted, and widely believed to be unsafe at night, the Loop had taken on the visage of a ghost town after five o'clock. Hoping that the presence of a population that considered the downtown its neighborhood would augment efforts to bring "18-hour vitality" to the streets, the administration sought to encourage the development of residential housing in the urban core. The mayor's office reported the completion of 15,482 living units between 1980 and 1987 in the area bordered by North Avenue on the north, Halsted Street on the west, Roosevelt Road on the south, and Lake Michigan on the east. With 1,600 units under construction and proposals for another 8,105 units under consideration, city hall referred confidently to an increas-

ing demand for downtown apartments and condominiums that offered all
the advantages of urban living. Although builders were completing units
mostly for middle- and upper-income residents, maintained the mayor, the
administration's creative use of federal, state, and local housing programs
in recent years had "resulted in development of a stock of rental units of
considerable breadth."[8]

Even though the administration appreciated the importance of a lively
and prosperous downtown, attention to the housing needs of all social
classes reinforced the commitment to the full panoply of ethnic and racial
groups living in neighborhoods throughout the city. Washington continued to affirm the importance of a new kind of economic development that
emphasized industrial retention, neighborhood business investment, and
recruitment of small-scale enterprises instead of competition for gigantic
corporate facilities that would settle downtown. City hall could do nothing
about the fact that opportunistic multinational corporations would vacate
Chicago and follow the flow of capital as soon as it became expedient to do
so. With his aides, the mayor spoke often about creating jobs particularly
for African Americans, Latinos, and other minorities in distressed neighborhoods and about economic empowerment for groups traditionally cordoned
off from the socioeconomic mainstream. Looking ahead, he envisioned the
successful implementation of his economic policies contingent upon the
attainment of political influence beyond the city's borders. Washington intended not only to consolidate his power in Chicago but also to seek greater
control of the regional forces that he believed would play an increasingly
important role in Chicago's future.[9]

Convinced that Washington's sweeping, long-term designs for the city's
future depended on an expanded political influence throughout the region,
administration officials affirmed that "the Mayor must be re-elected in 1991"
and began planning for that outcome immediately. A detailed notebook
submitted by staffers to Washington in July 1987 presented a year-by-year
blueprint of what steps needed to be taken to burnish the administration's
reputation and ensure the mayor's reelection in four years. Annual goals
included the consolidation of the political organization in year 1; the establishment of the mayor as an important local, state, and national leader
in year 2; marketing his performance as a man who delivered on campaign
promises in year 3; and planning and implementing his reelection campaign
in year 4. (The proposal adopted the state board of election's calendar, with

each year extending from July 1 to June 30.) The plan called for Washington to exert strong leadership in the state through the selection of Democratic candidates (especially in the gubernatorial race) for the March 1990 primaries and through preparations for a proposed referendum on the calling of an Illinois constitutional convention. Further, indicated his aides, the mayor should play a leading role at the 1988 Democratic National Convention in the selection of a presidential candidate, and he should ensure that his urban agenda be featured prominently in national campaigns prior to the 1988 and 1990 elections.[10]

In August 1987, after a task force had supervised nearly two years of spirited public discussions and countless revisions, the administration released *Chicago Works Together II*. Despite the original document's many virtues, naysayers had termed the absence of direct public participation in the drafting of the plan a significant flaw. Accordingly, the revised design reflected extensive involvement by dozens of neighborhoods and interest groups. Community organizations and reformers affirmed the basic themes and policies of the 1984 plan but changed two of the five goals presented in *Chicago Works Together*. The task force retained three goals (increased job opportunities, balanced growth, and assistance for neighborhood development) and excised two others (enhanced public involvement in decision making and state, regional, and national legislative agendas), while adding two new ones (the promotion of artistic and cultural development as part of economic development and the improvement of public education as an important component of economic development). Although the overall schematic changed minimally, registering only a shift in emphasis here and there, the much more elaborate planning process utilized for the revision allowed the administration to dispel criticism of inadequate citizen involvement and claim popular support going forward.[11]

While task forces and the mayor's staff busily prepared elaborate plans for the future, the administration still had to deal with the day-to-day problems of running a metropolis that faced several weighty challenges. No issue commanded more attention in city hall in the summer and fall of 1987 than the worsening predicament at the Chicago Housing Authority, which arguably had become the greatest crisis in public housing's fifty-year history in the city. The administration had been lauded nationally for giving public housing residents a voice through the creation of Resident Management Corporations, especially a well-publicized RMC at Leclaire

Courts, where tenacious tenants demonstrated remarkable financial acumen and administrative skills in the defense of their communities, but overall the plight of public housing in the city remained worrisome. Even as U.S. Department of Housing and Urban Development secretary Jack Kemp singled out the intrepid residents of Leclaire Courts for special praise, the CHA administration reported alarming financial deficits as well as a chronic shortage of resources that made routine upkeep impossible. Moreover, tenant complaints of inadequate maintenance, high crime rates, rising levels of gang infestation, and unresponsive lower- and midlevel management in the projects were increasing in frequency and intensity.[12]

Already a cause of considerable concern for the administration during the mayoral campaign, the predicament at the CHA worsened after Election Day. Washington believed that HUD was conducting a vendetta against the CHA at the behest of the White House and that the *Chicago Tribune*, a stout defender of President Reagan and no friend of the mayor during the previous four years, was covering the contretemps between the local and national housing bureaucracies with uncharacteristic zeal. In the mayor's view, the Chicago situation presented an opportunity for the Republicans in Washington, D.C., to seek retribution against one of the president's most vociferous critics and at the same time strike a blow against public housing as part of a broader ideological war to reduce the reach of the federal government into local affairs. Although he readily acknowledged the persistence of grievous problems at the CHA, Washington attempted to shift most of the blame elsewhere. He singled out for culpability the persistent warfare conducted against his administration during the previous four years, recited statistics detailing the federal government's unconscionable reduction of housing funds during the Reagan years, and asked rhetorically why HUD officials had been uninterested in the city's worsening problems during previous mayoral administrations in Chicago when the accumulating difficulties should have been addressed.[13] In his 1987 State of the City address, he said:

> For two generations we have watched this tragedy play out, all across the nation. And if the CHA has suffered under two decades of complete mismanagement during the sixties and seventies, and if the CHA board participated in the accumulation of nearly a billion dollars of deferred maintenance, the question must be raised: where was the exercise of oversight and the authorization on the part of HUD during those years? Who allowed the board to practice its mismanagement, to run the CHA into the ground?[14]

Ignoring Washington's lamentations, federal officials pronounced the evidence of mismanagement in Chicago's public housing bureaucracy overwhelming. In 1979 HUD had placed the CHA on a list of big-city housing agencies receiving failing grades for effectiveness and reported finding scant improvement in subsequent years. In fact, commented HUD undersecretary Carl Covitz in 1987, "CHA's overall condition appears to be getting worse." Covitz responded to Illinois senator Alan Dixon's expression of concern about the dearth of federal funds for Chicago public housing by pointing out that the CHA had received a generous one hundred million dollars for rehabilitation (in addition to the usual annual operating subsidies) from 1980 through 1986. Such financial support should have been more than adequate with sound management, the undersecretary added, something the CHA sorely lacked. Moreover, HUD's request for an operational improvement plan identifying problems and detailing strategies for amelioration had gone unanswered by the Chicago agency. As much as Washington sought to portray the city's public housing difficulties as part of a larger systemic failure at the national level, HUD administrators insisted that the lion's share of the problem rested with slipshod management practices in the local authority.[15]

Washington responded in 1987 with a management shakeup at CHA headquarters. Following the resignations of executive director Zirl Smith and chairman Renault Robinson, the mayor had installed Brenda Gaines as interim executive director of the troubled agency on January 7. A respected housing professional who had worked at HUD for thirteen years prior to joining the Washington administration, Gaines had previously served as the city's housing commissioner and acted as the mayor's deputy chief of staff. She brought impressive credentials and a no-nonsense attitude to the herculean task of balancing the books, providing reliable services to residents, and improving damaged morale throughout the system. The situation turned out to be even worse than she expected. The previous CHA administration had ignored a lacerating 1982 HUD report that called fourteen of the agency's nineteen project managers "incompetent." The CHA's somnambulate leadership had repeatedly failed in recent years to request funding for which the authority was eligible. Gaines found the CHA's financial accounting virtually indecipherable and faced a situation in which irate contractors who had not been compensated for work completed in the past—the amount of unpaid bills to vendors totaled an estimated seventeen million dollars—spoke ominously about terminating vital services to public housing projects. Recurring revenue shortfalls owed to the practice of using operating funds to pay for capital programs, while inadequate modernization and an absence of scatter-site development resulted from what Gaines deemed an unsustainable cash-flow crisis. Kept financially viable largely through creative accounting, the CHA was waiting for the outcome of a formal review by the federal government's General Accounting Office that had commenced on March 30, 1987. Not without cause, maintained a host of federal bureaucrats in Washington, D.C., HUD threatened a federal takeover of the local housing authority.[16]

The mayor fought back, lambasting Chicago's low-income housing as a tragic debacle from the very beginning. He called much of the city's public housing projects "obscene" and "an abomination" that "should never have been built in the first place." The myriad problems his administration confronted began with the flawed decision to build high-rise projects for families, a policy choice made by federal bureaucrats who later blamed cities for the regrettable consequences. He enumerated the critical mistakes made by housing officials in Washington:

> No parent is going to be able to supervise kids from twenty stories up. No rest rooms, no place to play. They built those elevators exposed to the elements up the side of the building, the elevators are going to break down, and so the kids are going to relieve themselves in the hallway; so the buildings stink. There's never enough money for maintenance; talk about community pride, even professional managers can't keep them in repair. It's custom made for gang recruiting. They're horrible, horrible.[17]

The only long-term solution, the mayor believed, required obliterating the high-rises and replacing them with some form of low-density, low-rise housing. Equally important, any such massive redistribution of population must include adequate relocation costs for displaced public housing tenants. In the meantime, he flatly rejected the idea of turning the operation of Chicago's low-income housing over to an uncaring, penny-pinching federal bureaucracy that had time and again showed its indifference to the plight of vulnerable inner-city populations. As well, the mayor reminded Chicagoans, the extent of corruption unearthed at President Reagan's HUD under the leadership of Secretary Samuel R. Pierce Jr. in the 1980s far surpassed the comparatively modest defalcations uncovered at the CHA.[18]

Complicating the power struggle between the Washington administration and HUD, professional, political, and personal differences between public officials exacerbated tensions and minimized the opportunity for compromise. From agency headquarters in Washington, D.C., James E. Baugh, HUD's acting assistant secretary for public housing, was engaged in a turf war over control of the CHA situation with Gertrude Jordan in Chicago, HUD's regional administrator of six midwestern states, including Illinois. Baugh routinely bypassed Jordan, a persistent critic of the Chicago mayor and a longtime protégé of Illinois governor James R. Thompson, and communicated directly with Gaines and other CHA personnel. The Reverend B. Herbert Martin, an influential minister and community activist the mayor had appointed to succeed Renault Robinson, allied with Jordan and publicly feuded with Gaines, other members of the CHA board, and the press. Exchanging insults in the local newspapers, Gaines charged Jordan with undermining negotiations by leaking information ("a blatant breach of confidence"), while Jordan accused Gaines of "immaturity" and belittled her achievements in dealing with HUD. Chicago officials complained bitterly about the treatment they received in meetings from the imperious Baugh, who they claimed seemed more intent on bullying than negotiating. Exasperated at the inability to reach an agreement and ignoring the harmful divisions within the CHA leadership, Washington defended his appointees and lashed out at the federal bureaucracy. "HUD is not Mt. Olympus," he railed to the press. "HUD is people. HUD is politicians."[19]

In their determination to retain control of the CHA, the mayor and his aides accelerated their efforts behind the scenes in 1987. Based on their unwavering premise that the best possible outcome would leave the city's 145,000 public housing residents under local jurisdiction, they rejected HUD's proposed solution of turning the administration of the CHA over to a private entity supervised by the federal agency. The mayor's representatives submitted a series of counterproposals to national housing officials in Washington, D.C., that sketched out new organizational structures and management plans. Washington simultaneously enlisted the state's leading Democratic politicians in the U.S. Congress—Senators Alan Dixon and Paul Simon, Representative Dan Rostenkowski, and others—to intervene with Secretary Pierce on behalf of the CHA's reorganization plans. When both Pierce and Baugh remained unpersuaded, Washington upped the ante. On July 7, he met secretly at the White House with Vice President George

H. W. Bush and lobbied for more time to reform Chicago's floundering housing authority. Illinois attorney general Neil Hartigan urged Pierce to continue negotiating in good faith with Washington's representatives to avoid litigation, which he warned the HUD secretary would inevitably be lengthy, expensive, and injurious to both parties. Hartigan pointedly reminded Pierce that a prolonged judicial proceeding would inevitably address "HUD's long-standing tolerance of the problems which the CHA has historically encountered and [HUD's] more recent intolerance after the Mayor of the City of Chicago and the present Board began taking very positive steps to remedy these problems."[20]

For weeks HUD officials withstood the political pressure applied by Chicago's mayor and insisted on a solution that included a federal takeover of the CHA. Pierce and Baugh demanded a negotiated settlement, explicitly laid out in a memorandum of understanding, that included the following set of conditions: the CHA would relinquish its powers under Illinois law and cede all authority to the federal government; HUD would exercise exclusive control over all spending, including the selection of contractors for repairs and new construction; and the CHA would be allowed an advisory role in decision making, but HUD would make final determinations in all matters. Further, federal officials rebuffed the mayor's requests for additional funding to augment operations, development, modernization, and other programs. The mayor flatly rejected HUD's terms, denying that the CHA possessed the power to abdicate authority granted by the state and arguing that control over local building contractors must remain in city hall.[21]

Washington's representatives and HUD negotiators finally reached an agreement, which the CHA board approved on September 15 and Secretary Pierce signed on September 23. Averting federal takeover of the local agency, the pact called for another detailed management study and outlined a complex arrangement by which a HUD liaison would work cooperatively with the CHA's managing director superintending all public housing matters; the agreement also created an arbitration panel to resolve potential disagreements between the federal government liaison and the local housing executive. The two sides agreed on Republican business tycoon Jerome Van Gorkom, who had previously served as undersecretary of state for management in the Reagan administration, as the new CHA executive director. (The selection of Van Gorkom allowed Gaines, who had served in the post for nine months, to return to city hall as the mayor's deputy chief of staff.)

Although the compromise made no mention of more housing dollars for Chicago, local officials suggested hopefully that the resolution of the conflict would clear a path for enhanced federal funding. Both Gaines and mayoral chief of staff Ernest Barefield, who had served as the administration's chief negotiator with HUD, intimated that the CHA could rightfully expect to receive more largesse from Washington, D.C.[22]

The mayor hailed the September 1987 housing accord as a resounding victory for local government that produced a "workable arrangement" for Chicago public housing. Relieved to have avoided a federal takeover and an acrimonious court battle, he predicted: "I think what is going to happen is you're going to have a slow but incremental improvement in the Chicago Housing Authority's delivery of services." Washington's optimism about the agreement proved unfounded, however. No doubt sensing a lack of urgency, the housing authority never completed the new management study. Van Gorkom resigned five months later, complaining of continuing administrative ineptitude in the local public housing bureaucracy and ruing his inability to work with the CHA board. Unconstrained by a murky memorandum of agreement short on specific requirements, HUD failed to increase funding levels for Chicago. The CHA crisis passed, at least for the moment, but even the mayor's staunchest partisans admitted that the public housing conundrum still awaited a comprehensive solution. "No one can convince me that things didn't improve under Washington," said Gaines, although she conceded that the mayor could—and should—have done much more when the public housing nightmare cried out for wholesale changes. At the same time, though, she found credible the mayor's suspicions that Republicans at HUD and in the White House were targeting Chicago for special scrutiny. Having previously served for thirteen years as a regional administrator for HUD, Gaines found the agency's treatment of Chicago uncharacteristically antagonistic. Rather than attempting to help find a solution for a troubled local housing authority, as federal officials had typically done at other locations in the past, Pierce, Baugh, and their subordinates consistently maintained an adversarial relationship with the Washington administration.[23]

The months after the April 1987 election also saw increased scrutiny of another beleaguered city agency, the Chicago Board of Health. Many of Washington's supporters, who had hoped that a reform administration would invest public health with an innovative, community-centered approach especially suited to confronting problems in poor minority neighborhoods, stifled their disappointment with the health department in the early months of 1987 to avoid censure of the mayor during his reelection campaign. These progressives became more vocal after the election, however, citing statistics that conveyed a negative picture of public health in Chicago. With one-fifth of the population lacking health insurance, the poor continued to receive inadequate care from the city's thirty understaffed public health clinics. An alarmingly high incidence of infant mortality, rampant food poisoning due to lack of inspection in restaurants and grocery stores, rising rates of AIDS, and elevated levels of other communicable diseases all pointed to an acute public health problem in Chicago. The mayor's political enemies, policy analysts, and the local media directed much of their ire at the embattled health commissioner, Dr. Lonnie Edwards. A former administrator at Cook County Hospital who had been appointed commissioner by Washington in January 1984, Edwards had quickly become known as a cautious bureaucrat, hesitant to challenge time-honored practices and determined to avoid controversy whenever possible.[24]

A competent medical professional but a political novice, Edwards as health commissioner clashed with a number of important constituencies both inside and outside of city hall. His loyalty to administration policies came into question, especially by chief of staff Ernest Barefield and Kari J. Moe, the mayor's liaison in the cabinet for health policy. Rather than subordinate his own views and fall in line behind administration programs, Edwards often continued to advance his own nostrums even after official policies had been announced. When Washington launched an infant mortality initiative in 1986, for instance, the disappointed health commissioner publicly complained about his own proposals having been disregarded in city hall. Edwards balked at following administration directives to terminate the employment of all health department employees who were violating city residency codes mandating that all municipal employees reside in Chicago; he pointed out that strict enforcement of the regulation would harm the city by summarily firing many physicians who lived in affluent suburbs. During his tenure as commissioner, Edwards railed incessantly about the health department's inadequate budget and complained about the administration's failure to hire more public health nurses, food inspectors, and lead-abatement investigators. Edwards maintained that the shortage of medical personnel to assist physicians in public health clinics necessitated the transferal of field nurses to the clinics from crucial outreach programs, thereby undercutting the important goal of providing care to homebound indigent populations. He unleashed a particularly impolitic dissection of mayoral priorities at an October 1987 city council budget hearing, saying, "There is no national priority for health, there is no state priority of health, and this has been translated to the local level. No one ever thanks you for not getting tuberculosis, or diphtheria, or polio. They do praise you for tree trimming, new curbs and garbage removal."[25]

Administration officials condemned Edwards as a political opportunist who was self-servingly presenting himself as a scrappy idealist nobly battling an uncaring bureaucracy in city hall. The health commissioner also became the target of gay and lesbian organizations for his failure to devote adequate attention to the growing incidence of AIDS. Activists complained about the paltry sums devoted by the health department for the treatment of AIDS sufferers. Edwards's response that the decidedly inadequate allocation for AIDS programs was being supplemented by money taken from budget lines for maternal and child health care failed to mollify critics, who condemned the inadequacy of the funds diverted from other programs to address the crisis. Gay and lesbian groups successfully lobbied in August 1987 for the firing of Dr. K. T. Reddi, the physician Edwards had appointed deputy commissioner of medical affairs, leading the incensed commissioner to announce that he would resign on March 1, 1988. Washington brusquely accepted the resignation without comment at a forty-five-minute news conference, seemingly confirming the rumor that the administration welcomed the change it was preparing to make. "This is a very important move by the mayor to show that he wants AIDS taken more seriously," commented Paul Varnell, research director for the Illinois Gay and Lesbian Task Force. The newspapers reported the ouster of Edwards as a "major victory" for Chicago's gay community, members of which praised Washington but regretted that "it [took] so long to get rid of [Edwards]." As a lame-duck administrator for six months, Edwards continued to disagree with the mayor's office in public discussions about health care policy. The press reported that the rudderless health department floundered during those months, rife with internal political battles and uncertain about important future policy directions.[26]

Many of the mayor's backers grumbled about the administration's lack of success in improving the quality of public health and low-income housing, two areas of city life ripe for reform and natural targets for a progressive mayor dedicated to aiding Chicago's underprivileged residents. Issues such as infant mortality and unsafe housing projects resonated especially in poor minority neighborhoods, and Washington's efforts to address those concerns had come up short. In both instances, mayoral appointments to lead the key city agencies had floundered and become political liabilities who had to be replaced. As in the case of the CHA, Washington ascribed the board of health's deficiencies to inadequate funding—and again singled out the massive revenue cuts to cities by state and federal governments as the principal problem. Even when housing and public health budgets had been spared in Springfield and Washington, D.C., argued the mayor, the need to trim expenditures elsewhere in shrinking municipal budgets had resulted in fewer jobs and reductions in human services across the board. Washington constantly affirmed his intention of reforming the public health and public housing bureaucracies, but worsening situations in the agencies made the tasks seem as imposing as ever in 1987.[27]

Problems with another important Chicago institution, the city's chronically underfunded and underperforming public education system, flared again in 1987 as well. Teachers went on strike at the beginning of the new academic year in the fall, the ninth work stoppage closing the public schools in eighteen years. Washington blamed his mayoral predecessors for creating the problem, first by piecing together a number of financially unsound settlements with "paste and thumbtacks" to end school strikes and second by arranging quick fixes rather than addressing fundamental problems in public education. Mayor Richard J. Daley had presided over a series of unusually generous settlements with the teachers' union in the 1970s, creating a large and growing financial hole that led to a funding crisis in 1979–80 and state intervention to forestall bankruptcy. Washington accused Mayor Jane Byrne and Governor James R. Thompson of using "funny money" to resolve labor disputes and pledged that he would not be a party to such financial shenanigans in 1987. Insisting that the mayor should appoint members to the board of education but not set educational policy or meddle at all in school affairs, a stance that both pleased reformers and allowed him to keep a healthy distance from the controversy, he announced his intention to avoid taking sides in the dispute. Nor, Washington pledged, would he cooperate in any budgetary sleight-of-hand that manufactured a stopgap solution at the cost of a later financial reckoning. The school board and the unions should negotiate in good faith and arrive at a responsible agreement without outside interference, the mayor intoned.[28]

The 1987 strike began after the board of education adopted a budget in July for the upcoming academic year that imposed a 1.7 percent pay cut for teachers and others who worked in the public schools—a far cry from the two-year contract sought by school employees that included a 10 percent pay raise the first year and a 5 percent increase the second year. The 29,000-member Chicago Teachers Union approved the walkout by a margin of ten to one, and 23,000 members of twenty other unions who worked in the schools (custodians, clerical workers, security personnel, and so forth) approved the September 8 strike date by comparable proportions. Superintendent Manford Byrd flatly denied that public school coffers contained the $150 million needed to pay for the desired two-year pay raises and asked the unions to join him in lobbying the state legislature for additional educational funding. Because the school board had made the same arguments so often in the past only to find the necessary funds after teachers conducted effective work stoppages, union members openly questioned management's credibility. CTU president Jacqueline Vaughn scoffed at Byrd's mention of the school system's financial woes, insisting that fairer teacher compensation simply ranked low on the list of the board of education's spending priorities. Vaughn decried public education's top-heavy salary structure, suggesting that the attenuated payroll included too many overpaid assistant superintendents, coordinators, curriculum designers, desegregation monitors, staff training specialists, and clerical personnel—and too few classroom teachers. She caustically suggested the elimination of bloated administrative salaries as a panacea for the reputed funding shortfall.[29]

The strike dragged on for weeks while impatient parents demanded the resumption of classes for the 430,000 students in Chicago's 594 public schools. Meanwhile, as the press reported in detail, the animosity escalated between board superintendent Byrd and the eleven members of the school board, on the one hand, and CTU president Vaughn and 52,000 union members, on the other hand. The standoff descended into a nasty test of wills. "The point is [Byrd] lost face," crowed Vaughn. "A black man in a black community lost face to a black woman. That's the issue." Asked if Byrd intended "to get you," she replied, "No question." Frustrated parents and teachers demanding that Washington intervene marched outside city hall and chanted, "We want Harold. We want Harold." The mayor remained in his office rather than speak with the marchers—and declined direct participation in the bargaining while urging the opposing sides to reach a compromise. He met separately with the two negotiating teams on September 19 at board of education offices to urge reconciliation, but steadfastly refused to become involved directly in the talks or dictate terms of a settlement. Instead, he blamed Governor Thompson for refusing to countenance more spending on public education and the state legislature for not overriding the governor's veto of a budget bill that provided more funds for the schools.[30]

The five-week school shutdown, which became the longest teachers' strike in the city's history, concluded on October 3 with a tentative agreement for a two-year contract that the CTU membership ratified the following day. The contract mandated a 4 percent pay increase the first year, another 4 percent raise the second year if adequate funds could be found, and the reduction of class sizes by two students for kindergarten through third grade. Funding for the $43.8 million package would be generated by firing 1,700 school employees, primarily classroom teachers with the least seniority, low-level administrators, and support personnel. The mayor happily announced the end of the strike and praised the tireless work of the negotiators in finding a mutually satisfactory middle ground. He again denounced Byrne and Thompson for having failed in the past to deal with inequities in a public school system with 85 percent minority enrollment and 45 percent of the student population from impoverished families.[31]

In the aftermath of the long and acrid strike, Washington resorted again to a populist framework in explaining the travails of the city's public schools as a function of inadequate resources provided by malign forces beyond Cook County's boundaries. The suffering residents of Chicago could find the principal villains in Springfield, he repeatedly declared, especially Governor Thompson and the members of the downstate-dominated general assembly who hoarded the state's education dollars and refused to pass needed legislation to appropriate more. The notoriety of the lengthy teachers' strike gave the mayor an opportunity to address the local public education conundrum. Reflecting upon the recent turmoil, he said:

> Never have I seen such tremendous anger and never have I seen a stronger commitment on the part of people. They are simply not going to tolerate

this meandering kind of educational system. I'm talking primarily about parents, but I'm also talking about professional people, poor people living in the housing authority [projects], people in my administration. They are just fed up with the system that is obviously flawed.[32]

The mayor attributed the stark deficiencies in Chicago's public schools to the powerlessness of the board of education, which he said wielded scant effective political influence in the county or the state. Few of "the movers and shakers" in local or state government had attended public schools, he observed, instead having matriculated in Roman Catholic schools and other private academies; their progeny typically did the same. With no direct interest in maintaining the high quality of public education, such state and local leaders simply ignored the plight of an inner-city school system with crippling funding shortages and few prospects of raising adequate revenue from a low-income population. Perhaps, Washington wondered aloud, parents and reformers outraged by the recent strike would channel their anger into a drive for meaningful change. The rancor that surfaced in 1987 might become the engine of reform. The mayor promised to lead the effort, beginning with a forum in mid-October for parents, educators, labor officials, business leaders, and other interested parties to lay the groundwork for change. He announced that members of the board of education and the CTU had signed a statement pledging cooperation in achieving the goals identified at his upcoming educational summit. He talked generally about the decentralization of educational policy making through the creation of local school councils that would invest neighborhoods with an element of control over curriculum and personnel. Such changes, along with other reforms, would be implemented by the start of the 1988–89 school year.[33]

On October 11, Washington presided over a daylong educational summit held on the University of Illinois at Chicago campus that attracted an estimated one thousand participants. Superintendent Byrd, board of education members, teachers, city aldermen, state legislators, and parents attended thirteen workshops sandwiched in between two three-hour plenary sessions. During the course of freewheeling discussions that recounted a number of problems and proposed potential solutions, the speakers at the forum slowly reached a consensus: reform should focus on two specific goals—increasing the achievement level of students and reducing the dropout rate of 43 percent—to be accomplished through the joint efforts of teachers, administrators, pupils, parents, business, and the community.

Summit attendees rejected perpetuation of the status quo and agreed on the need for a complete overhaul of the system. The mayor enthusiastically pledged his support, saying, "I'm not going to turn around until it's resolved." City hall pledged to conduct community discussions on public education in neighborhoods across the city during the coming months. Within two weeks, he vowed, his administration would select fifty members to serve on a parents' advisory council that would meet within 120 days to draft proposals for consideration by the public. The momentum for reform, sparked serendipitously by the teachers' strike, should not be squandered.[34]

The initial burst of enthusiasm ebbed somewhat when U.S. secretary of education William Bennett, in Chicago to speak to a business group on November 6, proclaimed the city's public schools the worst in the nation. "If it's not the last, I don't know who is," said the education secretary. "There can't be very many more cities that are worse. Chicago is pretty much it." Bennett cited the elevated dropout rate and the dismal performance of students on the American College Test as evidence of systemic failure. Solving the problem required reducing the swollen bureaucracy—"Explode the blob!" he exhorted—and grant parents more choice in determining which schools their children attended. In short order, he reverted to lobbying for one of his favorite ideas, the use of educational vouchers. Chicago Board of Education president Frank Gardner conceded the accuracy of Bennett's data but countered that the wheels had already been set in motion to improve the regrettable circumstances. "We hope the impact of [Bennett's] statements do not further demoralize teachers," he commented.[35]

Washington responded to Bennett's strident remarks with less restraint. The angry mayor said he found the education secretary "in no position to throw stones" as an envoy of the Reagan administration, which had presided over the "systematic dismantlement of public school systems throughout the country." The day after Bennett spoke in Chicago, the mayor convened a meeting at city hall of the fifty-member citizens' council on education and promised the group, "We're going to turn Mr. Bennett's statement around." Under Washington's direction, the council scheduled a series of neighborhood forums to be held in November and December to solicit ideas for school reform. According to their timetable, a list of specific proposals completed in February would be submitted to the general assembly in Springfield in time for the start of the next year's legislative session. The mayor also continued to assert that improvement of Chicago's schools

depended on the state living up to its constitutional responsibility for providing Illinois residents with high-quality schools.[36]

In confronting the excruciating problems in low-income housing, community health, and public education, Washington believed that he detected
a common origin for Chicago's increasingly precarious position—a "power
grab" whereby Republicans and (to a somewhat lesser extent) his enemies
within the Democratic Party were scheming to transfer authority historically vested in cities to the state and federal governments. Unable to beat
him at the polls, Washington suspected, his political enemies were conspir-
ing to dismantle (or at least limit the mayor's influence over) important
local administrative units. HUD's attempted takeover of the CHA became
the most obvious example of the strategy, and hostile forces in Illinois and
Washington, D.C., were moving on several other fronts at the same time.
Secretary Bennett's scalding remarks reinforced the argument that local
officials had proved incapable of managing the public schools and provided
ammunition to those calling for closer state supervision of the Chicago
Board of Education. Another plan called for the replacement of the school
board appointed by Washington with an elected panel, which purportedly
would result in enhanced accountability to the public. The mayor's removal
of Ed Kelly and capture of the park-district bureaucracy led to calls from
Springfield for greater control of the patronage-rich administrative unit.
Senate Republicans sponsored a bill that empowered two county officials,
state's attorney Richard M. Daley and Sheriff James O'Grady, to ignore
jurisdictional boundaries in establishing Cook County police patrols in
some outlying Chicago neighborhoods. City residents could petition Daley
for inclusion in the sheriff's patrol coverage, the program to be financed by
diverting state motor-fuel tax money earmarked for Chicago street repairs.
Governor Thompson and his legislative allies also conspired to assume control of several public authorities in Chicago that had historically fallen under
the suzerainty of local government. In the mid-1980s, legislation surfaced
in the general assembly to wrest control of the city's airports, McCormick
Place, Navy Pier, and other public authorities from the mayor.[37]

After failing to pass a bill that protected the tenure of park-district superintendent Kelly, Republican legislators representing the northwest suburbs
introduced measures in the general assembly in 1986 and 1987 for seizing
control of O'Hare International Airport (as well as Midway Airport and
Meigs Field) from the city. Citing a study conducted by the Illinois Depart-

ment of Transportation that recommended increased flight capacity in the Chicago metropolitan region, the lawmakers contended that the need for a third major airport, aviation safety concerns, worsening automobile traffic congestion, and a high incidence of noise pollution made a strong case for a regional authority that represented suburban interests. Although squarely situated within Chicago's corporate limits, legislators argued, O'Hare Airport's location far from the city's downtown and its proximity to several suburbs argued for a shift in administrative control. The proposed legislation created a fifteen-member airport authority with only four members chosen from Chicago and the remaining eleven members selected from suburban Cook County and adjacent collar counties. The new authority would be responsible for guiding O'Hare planning and expansion, as well as the potential construction of a new airport in the metropolitan area, a sharp departure from the unilateral control exercised by the city since Mayor Richard J. Daley had acquired the land for airfield expansion thirty years before.[38]

Washington fought to retain control of Chicago's airports. State representative Carol Moseley Braun, the mayor's floor leader in the Illinois House, led the opposition in Springfield to suburban takeover of the airports. In curtly stating the city's position, she cautioned against the tail wagging the dog. "The airport is not next to the suburbs, the suburbs are next to the airport," commented Braun. "Most of those suburbs would not be there if not for the economic overflow from the airport." Chicagoans in the general assembly argued that despite its location far from the central business district, O'Hare served a vitally important economic function for the city's many corporations that transacted business nationally and internationally. A spokesman for House Speaker Michael Madigan called the proposed airport authority an unnecessary level of bureaucracy, and a representative of Philip Rock, the Senate majority leader, concurred. In a predominantly partisan vote, with a handful of Chicago-area Democrats joining Republicans, the measure passed the Senate but narrowly failed in the House.[39]

Illinois Republicans also set their sights on acquiring control of McCormick Place, the nation's largest convention complex and a traditional source of income and jobs for the city. The original exhibition hall and its annex, which had been completed in 1986, attracted approximately 1.5 million conventioneers to Chicago annually and generated millions of dollars in tourist income for local coffers. After a sixty-million-dollar state bailout of the financially troubled Metropolitan Fair and Exposition Authority in 1985, the Illinois General Assembly created a new twelve-member board to manage the affairs of McCormick Place, Navy Pier, and other public authorities under the purview of the agency; both the mayor and the governor appointed six members to the new governing body. Washington and Thompson vied for mastery of the twelve-member board by demanding the power to select the chairman. (Chicago's mayor had appointed the administrator of McCormick Place since its opening in 1960.) The standoff between the state's two highest elected officials continued for more than three months in the summer of 1987 as the board deferred all decisions until the naming of a chairman. Washington applied additional leverage in the political contest of wills by refusing to approve Thompson's appointment for chairman of the Illinois Sports Facilities Authority, the agency created by the state legislature to build the new stadium for the Chicago White Sox; Thompson countered by vetoing a bill that allowed the city to establish its own system for collecting parking fines.[40]

While leaders of the city's convention and hotel industries bemoaned the "drift" that was allowing marketing and maintenance of McCormick Place to suffer during the political impasse, the mayor swore that he would not allow the governor to "blackjack" his way into control of the convention facility. Further, as White Sox management and fans worried about meeting a 1990 "play-ball deadline," Washington affirmed his intention to link the fate of the two policy-making agencies. He doggedly pledged to defend the mayor's prerogatives against outside forces seeking to curtail the city's autonomy. The resolution of the issue came in late October, with Thompson accepting the appointment of Washington's candidate, Charles A. Tribbett III, as chairman of the Metropolitan Fair and Exposition Authority and the mayor dropping his opposition to Thomas Reynolds Jr. for chairman of the Illinois Sports Facilities Authority.[41]

Convinced of the need for constant vigilance to thwart attacks from partisan groups striving to usurp his authority, Washington increasingly sought not only to solidify his political influence within the city but also to extend his power beyond the borders of Cook County. According to mayoral aide Timothy Wright, Washington based his endorsements for the 1988 state and national elections on a desire to solidify the Cook County Democratic organization and weaken the political alliances threatening Chicago. On November 18, 1987, the mayor announced a slate of candidates balanced along racial, ethnic, and factional lines—his so-called dream team—to seek county offices in the coming year. His decision to slate Richard M. Daley for state's attorney; Aurelia Pucinski, daughter of one of his most persistent city council foes, Roman Pucinski, for circuit court clerk; and Carol Moseley Braun, an African American administration loyalist, for recorder of deeds represented a call for unity among feuding Democratic factions against outside enemies. Emphasizing his desire for harmony, the mayor said that the party ticket "tells people we have gone too far with this acrimony, this negativism, this inability to get along." Wary of the reception that his diverse slate would receive among some politicians in the African American community, he firmly announced, "If you don't support this ticket, then you are no friend of mine."[42]

In contrast to the mixed reception afforded the "dream team" in black neighborhoods, Washington's decision to endorse the Reverend Jesse Jackson in the upcoming presidential race elicited an overwhelmingly positive response among his African American supporters. Unlike the situation four years earlier, when some black voters had criticized the mayor for withholding his endorsement from Jackson in favor of Walter Mondale, he threw his unqualified support to the Chicago civil rights leader more than a year before the November 1988 election. On September 8, 1987, with Jackson standing by his side, Washington made the announcement at a labor rally in suburban Cicero. In front of an estimated 1,400 sheet-metal workers at a General Electric Hotpoint factory, which was rumored to be the impending target of 1,250 layoffs when the corporation severely reduced local operations, the mayor told anxious and angry laborers and their families that the nation needed brave leadership to combat plant closings and workforce reductions.[43] He continued:

> I've looked over the entire country and seen how the candidates are responding to these cries of help from within our cities, and none of them are doing the kinds of things that they should do. . . . We need someone in that [Oval Office] whose voice is loud and clear like a clarion call that can reach to every depth in this country . . . and I call upon everybody in these United States to join with me in supporting the [Democratic] front-runner for president, the Rev. Jesse Louis Jackson.[44]

The decision to announce the endorsement at the Hotpoint plant in Cicero, a grimy industrial community where an overwhelmingly white blue-collar population struggled to overcome the corrosive effects of deindustrialization, served several important functions for Jackson and Washington. For the candidate, the gathering attracted two important groups (white ethnics and trade union members) necessary to broaden his electoral appeal and ensure the type of "rainbow coalition" he had failed to piece together four years earlier. Washington approved the location as a symbol of the crippling economic problems afflicting urban areas in the Rust Belt; he saw the Jackson endorsement as an opportunity to inveigh once again against the indifference of the nation's powerful policy makers to the suffering cities. For Chicago's mayor, the Jackson candidacy represented another chance to revisit common themes associated with fairness, redistribution, and social welfare and to condemn the rampant selfishness and materialism legitimized by the Reagan administration.[45]

Washington understood that the candidate he endorsed had no realistic chance of winning the Democratic nomination for president—the mayor indicated to press secretary Alton Miller that Jackson had promised him and other influential African American politicians that he would withdraw from the race at their request—and he fully intended for the good of the party to support the eventual nominee. In the meantime, however, Jackson's campaigning would serve a useful purpose in providing a platform for the full discussion of the most important issues facing the nation. The candidate from Chicago could infuse the 1988 presidential campaign with the kind of humane, progressive agenda that otherwise might be absent from the hustings. Chicago's mayor intended to continue that effort in the coming year and throughout his second term.[46]

In the last months of 1987, in the midst of the usual preparations of an annual budget for the approaching year, the public discussions of educational reform, and the ill-tempered caviling between HUD and the CHA, among other matters, members of the mayor's staff were preparing end-of-year reports on the administration's accomplishments and lists of issues to be prioritized in 1988. Anticipating that local news outlets would be announcing their own evaluations and projections, press secretary Alton Miller wrote the mayor that "at the very least, this summary we're preparing will keep them honest." Perhaps the most salutary development of the summer had been the elevation of the city's status in the municipal bond market by the two major bond-rating agencies, Standard & Poor's rating rising from B+++ to A- and Moody's rating from Baa1 to A. Listing matters to be addressed promptly, Miller devoted special attention to the educational forums scheduled for the following week and the need to develop a comprehensive health policy by mid-December. The next month would also be an excellent time to return to the important topic of balanced economic development, he suggested, perhaps with an op-ed piece written under the mayor's byline in the *Chicago Tribune*. Movement on several fronts would begin soon after the Thanksgiving holiday, often in highly publicized events intended to draw favorable media attention to the administration's continuing reform efforts.[47]

Members of the mayor's staff expected plaudits from the press, for example, following the announcement of an important November 30 deadline in the process of constructing a new main library downtown. Washington had put planning commissioner Elizabeth Hollander in charge of the Library Policy Review Committee, which included Chicago Public Library Board members, the library commissioner, and several key members of the mayor's staff. (The mayor also created an ad hoc citizens' committee, the members of which were charged with providing the administration with the views of their constituents.) The committee selected a new site for the library, the square block bordered by State Street, Van Buren Street, Plymouth Court, and Congress Parkway, an area that had been left undeveloped by the Byrne administration and functioned then as a parking lot. The committee announced on October 16, 1987, that the city would proceed with an international design-build competition, whereby teams of architects, contractors, and builders would compete to build the project according to a prearranged timetable for completion in January 1991 and a budget of $175 million. Competitors would submit by November 30 a list of their qualifications—experience, staff expertise, and commitment to equal opportunity, primarily—and agree to abide by the goals set by the administration for Minority Business Enterprises (25 percent) and Women Business Enterprises (5 percent). The committee would select as many as five finalists by January 15, 1988.[48]

The mayor insisted on broad-based participation in the building of a new main public library, a process of citizen involvement that would begin in earnest with the scrutiny of proposals submitted by the five finalists. On May 23, 1988, the five competitors would make elaborate presentations of their proposals (with drawings, scale models, photographs, and slides) in open public forums. Thereafter, the city would place the five plans on public display and encourage Chicagoans to examine the proposals and submit their evaluations. (Approximately thirty thousand people ultimately visited the exhibit, eight thousand of whom submitted written comments to city hall.) The press would provide extensive coverage, and the local public television station was preparing a program on the innovative selection process. After pouring over the copious written material and consulting with the city's technical experts, a citizen jury would make its recommendation to the committee and the mayor. Reflecting Washington's demand for diversity, the jury he selected included an African American historian, an African American librarian, a Latino artist, a Latino developer, a Chinese businessman, a local architectural historian, an architect from another city, and a library board member; a Chicago businessman, Norman Ross, chaired the jury. The mayor agreed, and the city council passed the necessary ordinance, to vest all decision-making powers in the Library Policy Review Committee and the jury. Washington put his stamp on the solution to a long-festering problem in the city, a hopeful signal of greater progress in a number of areas during the coming months.[49]

The promise of Washington's second term ended abruptly, however. At 11:00 a.m. on the morning of Wednesday, November 25, 1987, the day before Thanksgiving, Alton Miller sat in the mayor's office perusing a list of the day's appointments when he heard "a rattling, or rasping sound" coming from across the desk. He looked up from his notepad to see Washington leaning forward motionless, his head resting on the desk. Finding no pulse in the inert body, Miller hastily summoned the mayor's security detail from the outer office and ordered a secretary to call for medical assistance. Washington's bodyguards applied cardiopulmonary resuscitation but elicited no response. Fire Department paramedics arrived five minutes later and telephoned an emergency room physician at Northwestern University Memorial Hospital. Under the doctor's direction, the paramedics administered a series of medications and electric shock. When the patient failed to revive, they carried him on a stretcher through a crowd of reporters and city workers into an ambulance and then sped to the hospital emergency room. Dr. John Saunders, a heart surgeon and chief of the medical staff, took charge of the unsuccessful final efforts to save the mayor's life. Dr. Sanders officially pronounced Washington dead at 1:36 p.m. and informed the press that the mayor had expired of cardiac arrest.[50]

An autopsy performed later that evening confirmed the cause of death: cardiac arrest triggered by obstruction of a coronary artery. Medical examiners found other arteries surrounding the heart, which was swollen to three times its normal size, 90–95 percent blocked. The autopsy also suggested a likely cause of the mayor's heart attack—obesity. Stocky but robust when he had become mayor in 1983, Washington saw his weight rise to nearly three hundred pounds during the ensuing four and a half years. A lithe athlete in his youth who had won sprinting medals in local track meets, the middle-aged mayor wisecracked that he "couldn't run around a dime." Reporters and politicians surmised that too many banquets, an insatiable fondness for fatty foods, job-related stress, and a relentless schedule that allowed scant time for exercise accounted for the mayor being more than one hundred pounds overweight at the time of his death. Washington clearly relished consuming heaping samples of ethnic cuisine as an important part of retail politics, devouring barbecued ribs in African American neighborhoods, pierogies at Polish street fairs, and tacos at Mexican celebrations. On the other hand, city official Jacky Grimshaw argued that the pundits attributed too much importance to Washington's supposedly unhealthy eating habits as the sole cause of death. She felt that his obesity owed more to the sedentary regimen required of a big-city mayor than just to gluttony. Prior to becoming mayor, Washington had been very physically active, Grimshaw remembered, customarily walking everywhere on the South Side rather than driving. The opportunity for regular exercise vanished after 1983, however, and the busy mayor ignored warnings voiced by physicians about his steady weight gain. An exercise bicycle, the gift of a friend concerned about Washington's sedentary habits, sat unused and gathering dust in his apartment. Whatever the precise explanation—stress, overeating, inactivity, genetics, or some combination of these factors—Chicago's newly reelected mayor died abruptly at age sixty-five.[51]

The suddenness of Washington's death, with no forewarning of declining health, stunned Chicagoans—no more so than in the black community, where the mayor enjoyed a special bond with the citizenry. The depth of sadness among so many African Americans reflected his unique status as the city's first black mayor and as the charismatic hero who had delivered his people from decades of political servitude. Noticing Washington's picture displayed everywhere on the South Side—in living rooms, barbershops, beauty parlors, shoe repair shops, dry cleaners, grocery stores, and other public and private spaces—young community activist Barack Obama observed that African

Americans related to the mayor with the familiarity and affection usually reserved for close relatives. Some bewildered and suspicious African Americans discussed the likelihood that the mayor had been assassinated. The brisk sale at black nationalist sites of cassette tapes entitled *What Really Happened to Harold Washington* testified to the lingering misgivings in the black community about the actual cause of death. The sincere devotion showed in the outpourings of grief as a steady stream of hushed mourners filed by the bier in city hall where the deceased mayor lay in state for four days prior to the elaborate funeral.[52]

On November 30, dozens of national elected officials and big-city mayors, including Atlanta's Andrew Young, New York City's Ed Koch, Detroit's Coleman Young, Philadelphia's Wilson Goode, and Washington, D.C.'s Marion Barry, squeezed into Christ United Temple on the South Side alongside local residents to attend the two-hour amalgam of prayer and politics. Governor James R. Thompson, who had clashed frequently with Chicago's mayor, said with a smile that "[Washington] gave new meaning to rhetoric. When you were denounced by Harold, you were denounced." The Reverend Jesse Jackson, city council floor leader Timothy Evans, and others offered lavish eulogies, and Pastor B. Herbert Martin followed with a rousing sermon that joyously remembered Washington as a man who "loved people—black, white, brown, red, green, whatever color." After the funeral services, braving a cold mist, tens of thousands of (mostly black) mourners lined the nine-mile route from the church to Washington's final resting place in Chicago's Oak Woods Cemetery. Overlooking the praise afforded Dr. Martin Luther King Jr. a generation before, the *Chicago Tribune* reported that "no other black leader in the nation has inspired such a farewell tribute."[53]

Well before the delivery of the eulogies in Christ United Temple, Chicago's political brokers were frantically preparing for the battle of succession. In the event of a mayor's death, municipal statutes prescribed that the city's fifty aldermen select one of their own to serve as acting mayor. Recent electoral outcomes and the makeup of the city council seemed to reduce the hopes of a white alderman receiving the necessary votes to become acting mayor, but surviving members of the Vrdolyak Twenty-Nine intended to exert influence commensurate with their reduced, but still substantial, numbers. Vrdolyak, Burke, and former CHA chairman Charles Swibel met a few hours after the mayor's death to discuss how they could influence the upcoming city council vote. One fervid white opportunist, Richard Mell, considered his candidacy viable if he could recruit enough votes from Latinos, white independents, and dissident blacks. Washington's aides present at the time of his death felt that Mell, acting on unconfirmed rumors of the mayor's hopeless condition, moved with unseemly haste and enthusiasm to round up support even before the official death announcement at the hospital. He immediately telephoned Latino aldermen, thinking that they would provide the crucial swing votes in a political showdown. Desperate to obtain their backing, Mell promised to appoint a Latino chief of staff, offered control of the park district, and proffered appointments to other influential municipal positions. He courted white reformer Lawrence Bloom by pledging to name him corporation counsel. Seeing a rare opportunity in the chaos, Bloom explored the possibility of his own mayoral candidacy but concluded that he lacked the votes citywide. Many of the white aldermen favored Terry Gabinski of the Thirty-Second Ward but likewise doubted that he could win.[54]

Finally convinced that they would be unable to elect one of their own, the white aldermen intent on reasserting their authority decided to rally behind an African American they could manipulate. The man they chose, the reticent, unimposing Eugene Sawyer of the Sixth Ward, appeared to be the most malleable of the black aldermen. Assuming that they could control the painfully reserved Sawyer in the coming months, the members of the white faction were also thinking ahead and contemplating how their actions could divide the black electorate in the future. After a brief Sawyer interregnum, they calculated, Timothy Evans would undoubtedly run for mayor in the next regular election and thereby split the African American vote. Ironically, the racial politics of 1983 could be repeated with the roles reversed. Instead of Byrne and Daley splitting the white vote and allowing Washington to win, Sawyer and Evans would perform the same function in paving the way to victory for a fortunate white candidate.[55]

Uncertainty reigned among the blacks, Latinos, and few white progressives who made up the suddenly fragile city council majority. The Reverend Jesse Jackson flew back to Chicago from a Middle East peace mission as soon as he heard of Washington's death to participate in the selection of the mayor's successor. Shortly after arriving at O'Hare International Airport, he met with key Washington loyalists and agreed to back Timothy Evans as the next mayor; reporters interpreted the decision to afford Evans the privilege of eulogizing the mayor at the memorial service as clear evidence of his favored status among most African Americans. But not all. As Washington's city council floor leader, Evans had served as a lightning rod for disaffection with administration policies and had made more than his share of enemies (black and white) during the previous years. Some of the old-line African American pols who continued to rule their domains as personal fiefdoms and never fully embraced the administration's reform ethos, venal ward heelers such as William Henry, Bob Shaw, and William Beavers, saw no advantage in continuing along the same path and explored possible alliances with white former cronies in the Democratic machine. The more liberal black aldermen and the few white independents (David Orr, Lawrence Bloom, and Helen Shiller) regarded Evans's conversion to progressive politics during the Washington years as genuine but harbored some doubts about his work ethic and his dependability—in sum, his leadership capabilities. They clearly favored Danny Davis, a reliable ally with impeccable progressive credentials whose political views closely mirrored the deceased mayor's. But Davis's attractiveness to the guardians of the Washington legacy made him anathema to white and black Democrats with less altruistic visions of the future.[56]

As the political maneuvering intensified in advance of the decisive December 1 city council meeting, accusations of shady deals arose and latent racial resentments resurfaced. At a memorial service at the University of Illinois at Chicago Pavilion on the evening of November 30, an overwhelming majority of the estimated nine thousand persons in attendance favored Timothy Evans for acting mayor and strongly condemned the rumored behind-the-scenes maneuvering on behalf of Eugene Sawyer. As soon as the television cameras turned on their lights, the overflow crowd began chanting, "No deals. No deals. No deals." When Evans arrived in the midst of the ceremonies and triumphantly made his way down the center aisle to the front of the auditorium, the assemblage chanted, "Evans, Evans, Evans" and "We want Evans." *Chicago Sun-Times* columnist Vernon Jarrett attacked Sawyer and the African American aldermen who supported him as traitors to the Washington legacy. "Treat those black enemies like you treat the Ku Klux Klan," he bellowed. "If we don't do something about them, they will destroy us before the white man can get to us." An emotional Jarrett left the podium in tears. Third Ward alderman Bobby Rush accused Sawyer's supporters of "spitting on [Washington's] grave." Twenty-Sixth Ward alderman Luis Gutierrez exhorted the crowd to march from the pavilion to city hall the next day in protest of the plot to install Sawyer as acting mayor. No less passionate than Jarrett, he yelled, "We will surround City Hall because it is ours. We are not giving up City Hall. . . . Tomorrow we have destiny in our hands. Let's not give up the throne." When Gutierrez concluded his tirade and left the podium, the Reverend Jesse Jackson said to him, "You should be more careful about what you say." Unruffled and speaking calmly, Jackson advised members of the crowd to temper their emotions and act deliberately; he suggested that Washington loyalists gather outside city council chambers the next day and demonstrate in an effort to delay the selection of a successor. Jackson led the crowd in chants of "Harold lives," and the rally concluded with the singing of the civil rights anthem, "We Shall Overcome."[57]

The duty of presiding over the December 1 city council meeting fell to the vice mayor, David Orr, who had been serving as interim mayor since Washington's death. One of the city council's few consistent voices for progressive policies and a close confidant of Washington for many years, Orr had inconspicuously held the honorific title of vice mayor since the 1987 council reorganization and then quietly performed the largely ceremonial tasks assigned to the interim mayor. In chairing the city council meeting that would choose Washington's immediate successor, he found himself suddenly thrust into the media spotlight—and into an uncomfortably delicate position squarely between two warring camps. Supporters of the Evans and Sawyer factions aggressively pursued favorable rulings from the chair, and many Washington loyalists expected preferential treatment from a longtime ally who shared their values and aspirations. Orr took the job description of presiding officer seriously, however, and attempted at all times to be impartial and to give all parties their say. Considering the recent resurfacing of personal and racial animosities and the high stakes involved that day, he found the attainment of those seemingly modest aims a formidable challenge.[58]

The December 1 city council meeting began at 10:00 a.m. with a series of fulsome tributes to Washington, many uttered by aldermen who had previously slandered the late mayor and opposed him without restraint. Edward Burke and Roman Pucinski, two unrepentant leaders of the Vrdolyak Twenty-Nine, delivered flowery eulogies that praised Washington's character and accomplishments in office. Another of the mayor's bitter opponents, George Hagopian, gazed skyward and said, "I loved you like a brother."

Richard Mell came to the meeting sporting a Washington campaign button pinned to his lapel. The nostalgic recollections continued throughout the session as aldermen drifted in and out of city council chambers; in city hall corridors, several of the aldermen supporting Sawyer told members of the press that their lives and the well-being of their families had been threatened. Black alderman William Henry, who had been designated as the point man for the Sawyer candidacy, showed reporters the bulletproof vest he was wearing at the suggestion of the police. The meeting adjourned at 3:00 p.m., the florid paeans to the late mayor finally having concluded but no progress toward the selection of an acting mayor having been made.[59]

Heeding the Reverend Jackson's call from the previous evening, an estimated five thousand protesters descended on city hall to register their concern. Demonstrators jammed the corridors outside city council chambers, and the massive overflow crowd fanned out along LaSalle Street and brought traffic to a halt. Some members of the gathering carried placards indicating their displeasure at the political wheeling and dealing imagined to be occurring inside at that moment. The crowd alternated chants of "Uncle Tom Sawyer" with "Sawyer, Sawyer, you can't hide / You're committing suicide." As events inside proceeded at a snail's pace and daytime turned into evening, the size of the demonstration outside remained constant or even increased slightly. Police reported having to intervene in several scuffles but made no arrests.[60]

Although the meeting was scheduled to resume at 5:30 that evening, Orr delayed gaveling the city council back into session until shortly after 9:00 p.m. During the intervening hours, factions congregated in aldermanic offices, conference rooms, vestibules, and even public restrooms scattered throughout city hall. Burke marshaled the forces fighting for the selection of Sawyer, whom the remnants of the Vrdolyak Twenty-Nine judged to be the best choice among the African American aldermen. "He's going to play ball more with these [white guys] than Evans would," quipped a Northwest Side resident. While Evans welcomed the possibility of becoming mayor, a clearly uncomfortable Sawyer wavered in the face of the imposing challenge. A self-effacing, diffident man whose willingness to sail along with the prevailing political winds had defined his long public career, Sawyer spoke so softly that other aldermen frequently could not hear his comments on the rare occasions when he orated in the city council. Neither an innovative legislator nor an inspirational leader, the Sixth Ward alderman was a devout Christian known for avoiding controversy and confrontation. Concerned that day about the volatile crowd milling around outside and the possibility of violence in black neighborhoods, Sawyer met with Orr and others during the long recess and discussed the wisdom of delaying the vote until passions cooled. Orr suggested that he announce the lack of a quorum at 9:00 o'clock and adjourn until a later date. Sawyer agreed.[61]

But then Burke interceded, convincing Sawyer that he could not renege on his commitment. Television cameras captured images of the red-faced Burke jabbing his finger at Sawyer's face, seemingly intimidating the flinching alderman into submission. When the city council reconvened, angry onlookers in the gallery and outside in the streets resumed their taunting of the Sawyer faction. Intimating that Sawyer had been bought off by the white aldermen, the spectators chanted, "How much, Gene? How much?" and "Sawyer's in a Cadillac, driving for Vrdolyak." Several protesters in the gallery threw coins at Sawyer supporters. Bowing to the pressure from their constituents, who berated them as "Uncle Toms" and "Oreos," half of the twelve black aldermen who had declared their support for Sawyer switched to Evans during the course of the evening. And then Sawyer changed his mind again. Speaking with Mary Ella Smith, Washington's fiancée, on the city council floor, he broke down and murmured, "I can't do it. This is not what Harold would have wanted." Sawyer fled city council chambers with Burke, who had successfully called for another recess, in hot pursuit. Having cornered the reluctant candidate in a remote section of the building, Burke berated him at the top of his lungs in front of several other aldermen and a few reporters. Yet, after huddling with his pastor, the humiliated Sawyer remained adamant in his refusal to have his name placed in nomination. Burke and his cohorts hurriedly looked around for an alternative but without success.[62]

Broadcast live by all five local television stations, the city council brouhaha raged into the early-morning hours of December 2. Chicago viewers witnessed a garish spectacle of epithets, smears, charges, and countercharges, with combative aldermen stopping just short of brawling on several occasions. Both sides hurled accusations of unethical behavior at their adversaries and threatened retribution for offenses real and imagined. Two aldermen restrained William Henry from slugging Dorothy Tillman, who had been mocking him as a traitor to his race. Gesturing at an Evans supporter, Mell screamed, "You're dead! You're dead!" and slammed an ashtray down on a desktop so forcefully that he cut his hand. Sparring verbally with a group of spectators, Anna Langford grew furious when they accused her of base motives for not voting for Evans. When a quarrelsome observer scolded her for betraying the Washington movement, she rejoined, "Oh, fuck the movement. These are politicians."[63]

Amid the chaos, Evans took the measure of his opponent and sensed victory. He held an impromptu press conference and told reporters that Sawyer lacked the resolve to be mayor; the timid Sixth Ward alderman simply did not have what it took to lead the city. Watching Evans's remarks on television during a prolonged absence from the city council chambers, Sawyer sprang from his chair in anger. Stung by the condescension of his adversary's comments, he changed his mind one last time. Sawyer declared his willingness to be nominated and returned to the city council floor, where he remained for the duration of the proceedings. When the reluctant candidate reappeared, Mell jumped onto his desk and yelled, "We did it, we did it!"[64]

Members of the Evans faction utilized a succession of parliamentary maneuvers to forestall any decisions but lacked the votes to secure adjournment. Orr allowed the delaying tactics briefly but would not countenance an all-night filibuster. Contrary to the wishes of many of his allies, the interim mayor permitted the presentation of nominating speeches beginning at 1:50 a.m. Proper procedure and fairness called for as much, Orr believed. Astonishingly, according to the A. C. Nielsen rating service, televisions in 480,000 Chicago households remained tuned to the live coverage in city hall at 2:00 a.m. Aldermen nominating Sawyer touted their man as a respected, evenhanded politician, a man of "courage and compassion" who would reach out to all groups and ensure tranquillity in the grieving city; those opposed to Sawyer invoked the memory of the late mayor and spoke of their opponents in terms of betrayal and ignominy. In her fiery speech on behalf of Evans, Dorothy Tillman said, "When Abraham Lincoln signed the Emancipation Proclamation, some blacks didn't want to be free. They didn't understand freedom. They went to their masters and said, 'I don't want to be free.' Well, I don't want to go back to the plantation."[65]

The speechmaking ended shortly before 4:00 a.m., and the balloting began. Twenty-three white and six black aldermen voted for Sawyer, forging a solid twenty-nine to nineteen majority. (Evans supporters numbered twelve African Americans, all four Latino aldermen, and three white independents.) The meeting promptly adjourned at 4:16 a.m., bringing to a close the most extraordinary legislative session in the city council's long and discordant history. Observed closely by multitudes of rapt television viewers, what came to be known as the "living room coup" staggered to a conclusion that cheered Sawyer partisans and devastated Evans loyalists. Having survived eighteen hours of impassioned rhetoric, several improbable twists and turns, and much low comedy, Chicago at last emerged with a successor to Harold Washington.[66]

What kind of administration would emerge to follow the historic Washington mayoralty? What could his allies and his foes expect from Sawyer, who had attracted very little notice in the city council since his election in 1971? Chosen by Mayor Richard J. Daley to represent the Sixth Ward, a solid Democratic bastion for years on the African American South Side, Sawyer had been a reliable foot soldier for the Cook County machine who delivered votes, dispensed patronage, voted the right way in the city council, and never said anything newsworthy. Liked by his peers, he graciously listened to all points of view, kept his own judgments to himself, and avoided inflammatory discussions about race. Yet when Washington announced his candidacy in 1983, Sawyer had been the first black alderman to endorse him and had remained faithful to the administration without exception thereafter. Improbably ensconced in the mayor's office after the tumultuous events of December 1–2, 1987, Sawyer repeatedly tried to assure Chicagoans of his desire to continue Washington's policies in all regards. He had become a firm believer in his predecessor's vision, Sawyer assured the people, and he intended to move forward with an administration devoted to the principles delineated in *Chicago Works Together II*. Most important, he vowed to dispel the bitterness and bring the warring factions together after the impassioned succession battle. "We can overcome our differences and heal the wounds," Sawyer said. "The sacrifices of our late Mayor will not be in vain."[67]

For all of Sawyer's ingenuous reassurances, though, a nagging restiveness remained about the city's reluctant mayor. Thanks to the extensive television coverage afforded the living room coup, Chicagoans knew all about the unwilling candidate's vacillations that evening. The belief persisted that, as Jacky Grimshaw later commented, Sawyer was "browbeaten" into accepting the job—and that realization provoked concerns about both the new mayor's commitment to the position and his obeisance to the powerful aldermen responsible for his selection. Deeply suspicious and dismissive of Sawyer's soothing rhetoric, Grimshaw quickly exited the administration; for a variety of reasons, several other devoted Washington aides such as Ernest Barefield, Alton Miller, and Brenda Gaines soon followed. Some high-level administrators, including Robert Mier, Elizabeth Hollander, Judson Miner, and Kari Moe, decided to serve under the acting mayor for the remaining sixteen months left in his term. Many Chicagoans hoped that, burdened with few expectations and assumed simply to be fulfilling a caretaker function until the next mayoral election in April 1989, the patchwork Sawyer administration would provide an uneventful transition to the expected election and lengthy reign of Richard M. Daley. Order would be restored to the universe, at least in the minds of Chicagoans who had grown accustomed over several decades to a very different polity overseen by the elder Daley. With a stunning finality, the Washington mayoralty was over.[68]

8

HAROLD WASHINGTON
AND CHICAGO

Beginning with Harold Washington's death on November 25 and concluding with the selection of Eugene Sawyer as acting mayor on December 2,
the jumble of events left Chicagoans shocked and disoriented. The city's
political order spun wildly out of control during the fateful week, dashing
expectations about an administration just getting its footing after years of
crippling opposition. The vitriol permeating the city council floor on the
tumultuous night of December 1–2 brought back unsettling recollections of
the Council Wars, just as televised images of a furious Edward Burke hectoring a cowering Eugene Sawyer into becoming mayor scotched any chance of
a seamless transition of power. Irate protesters inside and outside of city
hall suspected the worst during the frequent recesses that punctuated the
long day and night. Convinced that sinister alliances huddled in dark city
hall corners were plotting successfully to subvert the selection process,
they braced for the worst. The frail governing coalition held together the
previous few years by a charismatic leader was fraying under the weight
of power politics, racial distrust, and personal ambition. Progressives who
had just a few days before been eagerly anticipating the further advances
of a daring reform agenda were suddenly pondering an uncertain future
with a bifurcated city council and an unwanted mayor.

The public could not believe that the laconic, undistinguished Sawyer,
one of the longest-serving members of the city council but an inscrutable

presence with no discernible influence among his peers, had replaced the larger-than-life Washington at the head of Chicago government. Even those persons who quickly pitched in to help the acting mayor expressed bafflement at his selection. Monroe Anderson, the Midwest bureau correspondent for *Newsweek* who agreed to serve as Sawyer's press secretary, remembered muttering after the surprise selection, "Sawyer. I can't believe it. Mayor Sawyer." Apparently, Sawyer found the change in his status equally confounding. During his first month in office, he refused to use the mayor's desk and instead worked at a coffee table while seated in an overstuffed chair draped in black. He still referred to the deceased Washington as "the mayor" and listlessly shuffled around city hall with his head down, murmuring to himself. Reporters began referring to the timorous, uncommunicative Sawyer as "Mayor Mumbles."[1]

Although the new mayor continued to profess his loyalty to the principles and goals of his predecessor, Washington loyalists remained deeply troubled by the events of December 1–2 and even more so by Sawyer's association with the political coterie that engineered the so-called living room coup. Second Ward alderman Bobby Rush and Third Ward alderman Dorothy Tillman led the way in questioning Sawyer's legitimacy, claimed that the mayoralty had been stolen from Fourth Ward alderman Timothy Evans, and openly began laying the groundwork for an Evans candidacy in 1989. Many of the new mayor's aides urged a thorough housecleaning in the city council, seeking to replace the malcontents and likely saboteurs at the head of important committees with more trustworthy aldermen, but Sawyer waited more than seven months before taking action. Even then he did so only at the relentless prodding of an impatient city council majority. On July 13, 1988, aldermen aligned with Sawyer stripped eight of the mayor's critics, including Evans, Tillman, Lawrence Bloom of the Fifth Ward, and Danny Davis of the Twenty-Ninth Ward, of their committee chairmanships. At one point in the stormy session, Tillman almost came to blows with Sawyer supporter Marlene Carter of the Fifteenth Ward after taunting her as "one of my Uncle Tom sisters."[2]

In Chicago's political tinderbox, Sawyer's prospects for election looked dim. Forced to rely on a white majority in the city council in order to govern but also striving to construct the essential electoral base among African American voters, the mayor needed time to mend fences within the black community. He endeavored to circumvent the state law that mandated a special mayoral election in 1989 and argued for a postponement until 1991 to coincide with the next regular round of municipal elections. Loath to allow the mayor more time to solidify his standing among black voters and eager to force the issue while memories of Washington and the living room coup remained fresh among African Americans, Evans filed a lawsuit to mandate the scheduling of a special election in 1989. After lengthy legal wrangling in the Chicago Board of Elections, the Illinois Board of Elections, and the Cook County Circuit Court, the Illinois Supreme Court ruled in favor of the earlier date. On September 18, 1988, well in advance of the Illinois Supreme Court ruling, Fifth Ward alderman Lawrence Bloom declared his candidacy for the February 1989 Democratic mayoral primary; Evans announced on October 30, followed by Cook County state's attorney Richard M. Daley on December 5 and Sawyer on December 11.[3]

Although political pundits expected Evans to be a potent force in the Democratic primary, his campaign never gained traction. His fund-raising efforts floundered from the outset, hampering his ability to purchase radio and television advertising, and without a sound political organization, the Fourth Ward alderman did little more than portray himself as the true heir to the Washington legacy and dispute the mayor's authority. In avid pursuit of the African American vote, Evans and his allies attacked Sawyer mercilessly. Dorothy Tillman's reference to Sawyer as "a shuffling Uncle Tom" at a large campaign rally provoked a stern reprimand by the Reverend B. Herbert Martin, Washington's former pastor and the executive director of the Chicago Commission on Human Relations. The Reverend Jesse Jackson spoke out as well, decrying the vituperation of the campaign speeches and urging one of the African American candidates to withdraw from the primary to avoid splitting the black vote. Evans answered Jackson's call for "unity in the community," announcing on December 29 his decision to give the mayor a "clean shot" at the Democratic nomination. He also promised to run in the April general election at the head of a new Harold Washington Party. In the meantime, Evans vowed to husband his resources, accelerate his fund-raising activities, and endorse no one in the Democratic primary.[4]

Sawyer told Chicago Democrats that, despite the diversions and personal attacks he had endured, his administration had functioned competently, adhered to the spirit of the Washington reform ethos, and completed several of the projects begun by his predecessor. In a single year, the acting mayor boasted, he had presided over the passage of several contentious items of legislation by a balky city council, including a sixty-six-million-dollar tax increase needed to maintain fiscal solvency and a measure to dissolve the city's taxicab monopoly. He managed to negotiate a labor settlement with the firefighters' union that forestalled a potential strike and reached agreement with investors to initiate private development in areas surrounding O'Hare International Airport. His heralded choice for chairman of the beleaguered Chicago Housing Authority, Vincent Lane, had started the challenging process of reorganizing public housing in the city. Bringing the painstaking work of Washington and his aides to fruition, Sawyer completed an agreement for the installation of light towers at Wrigley Field that allowed the first night game in the stadium's storied history to be played in 1988. With deference to the careful preparation by the preceding administration, he helped steer through the city council a human rights ordinance that guaranteed equal treatment for gay and lesbian citizens in housing and employment. Indeed, with little fanfare, "Gentleman Gene" had compiled a number of noteworthy achievements in the mayor's office during a brief time.[5]

A year of accolades also brought a number of negative newspaper headlines that besmirched the mayor's image of quiet dignity and probity, however. First came a report that in 1978, Alderman Sawyer had accepted thirty thousand dollars from an attorney under questionable circumstances; the mayor identified the gratuity as payment for work he had performed on a real estate transaction, but critics called the money a payoff for the alderman's vote on zoning deals. Charges also surfaced that the mayor had funneled more than two hundred thousand dollars of municipal funds to Erwin France, an influential African American consultant and controversial political fixer, for unspecified work related to city policy making. Critics demanded an item-by-item accounting of the services rendered by France that merited such generous remuneration. In the most damaging incident, Sawyer's mishandling of a scandal involving Steven Coakley, an administration liaison to the African American community, raised pointed questions about anti-Semitism in city hall. After Coakley unleashed a series of outrageous charges against Jews—alleging that Jewish physicians were secretly inoculating African American children with the AIDS virus, for example—the mayor delayed interminably before demanding his controversial adviser's resignation. Even then Coakley dissembled and delayed before finally leaving several days later. Sawyer appeared weak and vacillating during the life of the controversy, and Coakley's belated exit from city hall after a week of devastating publicity came too late to stanch the public relations hemorrhaging. The affair seriously damaged the mayor's standing in Chicago's Jewish community and undermined his reputation among many independent voters. Newspaper reporters and columnists cited what became known as the Coakley Affair as a prime example of Sawyer's questionable judgment, compounded by his maddening indecisiveness.[6]

Meanwhile, Daley fine-tuned his campaign machinery, assembled a first-rate staff, and raised money at a record pace. Having conducted a flawless campaign and easily won a third term as Cook County state's attorney in 1988, he bowed to the clamor for mayoral restoration rising from the Northwest and Southwest Sides where white ethnic voters still found magic in the Daley name. Determined to avoid the political mishaps that had doomed his mayoral campaign six years earlier, Daley offered the electorate a very different image in 1989. Under the tutelage of two highly regarded political operatives, campaign manager David Wilhelm and media consultant David Axelrod, he tried to broaden his appeal to include lakefront independents as well as his traditional base in the white ethnic wards. His selection of Avis LaVelle, a respected black city hall reporter for WGN radio, as press spokesperson sounded a note of inclusiveness to minority voters and lakeshore independents. "My hiring her sends out a message that the bickering and arguing has ended," he boasted. As well, he spoke at length in minority neighborhoods and promised to continue Mayor Washington's efforts to enhance diversity in municipal government. Striking a much different tone than he had in 1983, Daley presented himself as a healer who could restore peace in city hall after years of turmoil. He forswore any plans to reanimate the vaunted Democratic machine, which his father had dominated for so long, and denied having aspirations of becoming a political boss. In fact, Chicagoans who listened closely to Daley's speeches detected unmistakable echoes of the reform rhetoric that had long been the staple of Harold Washington's oratory. Without specifically addressing racial inequality or the city's long history of residential segregation, Bridgeport's favorite son spoke feelingly about the need for equity and inclusiveness.[7]

A long-shot candidate from the outset, Bloom never presented much of a threat to Daley or Sawyer. Admired in the city council for his keen intellect and for the eloquent advocacy of his progressive ideals, Bloom had been a consistent Washington ally and an admired upholder of the proud Hyde

Park reform tradition. Not so in the Democratic mayoral primary, however, where he often seemed arrogant and condescending in his attitude toward the other candidates. In the only televised debate, he sounded haughty and overbearing in constantly mocking Daley's lack of intelligence. Hobbled by a dearth of campaign funds and unable to rise in the public opinion polls, he withdrew from the race two weeks before primary Election Day. He endorsed Sawyer before fading altogether from the public view.[8]

The Republican primary campaign proceeded peacefully without bestirring the interest of Chicago voters—until the belated entrance of Edward Vrdolyak, who had turned down the nomination in December when the party offered it to him. The political maverick entered the contest as a write-in candidate on February 23, just five days before the primary election, as an alternative to the choice of the Republican establishment, Dr. Herbert Sohn. In contrast to the plodding Sohn, who had been campaigning with a decided lack of energy and enthusiasm, the colorful, quotable Vrdolyak enlivened the contest for the few days of his short write-in candidacy. The press speculated that Vrdolyak's chances of winning the Republican primary depended on attracting a sizable number of crossover votes from disgruntled Democrats; luring those white ethnic votes away from Daley would then allow Sawyer to prevail in the other primary. In the general election, Vrdolyak hoped to win by splitting the black vote between Sawyer and Evans.[9]

Public opinion polls in the first weeks of 1989 forecast a landslide victory for Daley in the February 28 Democratic primary, and Chicago voters behaved as expected. Reporters noted an absence of canvassing in the days leading up to the election, and poll watchers observed a dearth of last-minute electioneering. Benefiting from a low voter turnout, Daley won with 56 percent of the votes and defeated Sawyer by more than one hundred thousand ballots. Sawyer ran more than two hundred thousand votes behind Washington's 1987 winning total. The African American candidate managed only to win wards with predominantly black populations, albeit in much smaller numbers than in the Washington years, and failed to carry a single Latino or independent lakefront ward. Never assured of a unified base, Sawyer had spent an inordinate amount of time in African American neighborhoods attempting to shore up his support there and had rarely ventured into other areas of the city—with unfortunate consequences that became evident in the primary election. Daley predictably did best in the

Northwest and Southwest Sides but also made noteworthy inroads into other precincts where he had stumbled in past elections. His campaign, which reached out to diverse groups of voters in a variety of neighborhoods, seemed to pay off in broad electoral support throughout Chicago. Vrdolyak carried only seven of the fifty wards, but he won the Republican primary as a write-in candidate by a slim margin of eleven hundred votes out of approximately twenty-two thousand votes cast.[10]

Sawyer accepted his defeat placidly, offered Daley congratulations in typically courteous fashion, and told his followers that he would continue to work for racial reconciliation in Chicago. His equanimity in relinquishing the office of mayor did not extend to forgiving Evans and his allies for the way they had treated him in the previous sixteen months, however. In his role as Evans's campaign manager, the Reverend Jesse Jackson announced that he would undergo a three-day fast to "bring an end to this war and strife in the Harold Washington coalition." A steady stream of blandishments from African American community leaders, praising the acting mayor's selfless service and calling for racial unity to forestall a Daley or Vrdolyak victory, continued while Sawyer spoke of possibly undertaking a write-in campaign. At a city hall news conference three weeks before Election Day, Sawyer finally announced that he would neither run himself as an independent nor endorse any candidate.[11]

Evans publicly shrugged off the acting mayor's declaration of noninvolvement, but his campaign clearly needed the kind of boost a rapprochement between the two principal black political factions would have provided. Jackson's plaintive cries for "unity in the community" went unheeded, as many of Sawyer's supporters blamed Evans for the Democratic primary loss. Limited by the absence of campaign funds at his disposal, Evans found it impossible to counter the bitterness and defeatism mounting within the African American electorate. Unable to launch a planned media initiative in mid-March because of inadequate funding, his campaign increasingly relied on loans from family members and friends. The flailing candidate managed to retain the support of many white progressive survivors of the Washington coalition, receiving the endorsements of Lawrence Bloom, Forty-Ninth Ward alderman David Orr, political consultant Don Rose, and others, but achieved very little success at voter registration efforts. Considering his campaign's glaring deficiencies and the convincing outcome of the Democratic primary, Evans found it difficult to dispute the inevitability of Daley's election.[12]

Indeed, the Daley electoral steamroller looked no less formidable rumbling toward the April 4 general election than it had in the primary. At the same time that campaign aides were publicly talking about their expectations of a tough, hard-fought election, they quietly admitted that Daley was already preparing to govern the city. A full month before the election, the confident Democratic candidate announced the members of his mayoral transition team. Local organizations and influential individuals lined up to support the expected winner; both the *Chicago Tribune* and the *Chicago Sun-Times* lavished praise on Daley and awarded him glowing endorsements. The city's leading institutions and individuals applauded the tonic effect of his conciliatory rhetoric and temperate policy prescriptions, suggesting that the mature Daley had done well to emulate the best of Harold Washington's legacy, and speculated that his election would be the healthiest outcome for the city's troubled racial climate. Even Ron Brown, the African American National Democratic Party chairman, jumped on the Daley bandwagon immediately after the primary. Brown had been an adviser to Jackson's 1988 presidential campaign, but he never wavered in backing the official candidate of the Cook County Democratic Party. Picketed by blacks at a party function in Chicago and called an "Oreo" by Congressman Gus Savage, Brown affirmed his endorsement and confidently forecast a solid Daley victory.[13]

In the face of the Daley juggernaut, the Vrdolyak insurgency seemed hopelessly overmatched. As irreverent and impudent as always, the Republican candidate scoured the city in search of votes but found little cause for optimism. The Cook County Republican Party provided him with no campaign funding, and Governor Thompson proved similarly unhelpful; wealthy Chicago-area party members turned their backs on what they regarded as a futile undertaking. Running on a shoestring budget inadequate to purchase television advertising, Vrdolyak relied solely on stump speeches and news releases. The highlight of his threadbare campaign came in the only televised mayoral debate, in which Daley declined to participate, where he put his impressive rhetorical skills on full display. Attacking Evans on a range of issues and pitilessly mocking the front-runner for refusing to appear at the event, the Republican candidate reminded Chicagoans why his command of the forensic arts had made the Council Wars such grand theater. But political observers viewed Vrdolyak's oratorical virtuosity at the lone debate, followed by two weeks of relative quietude before the election, as his last hurrah.[14]

The April 4 election brought no surprises. Daley amassed votes "from the bungalow to the condo," his victory margin even surpassing his advisers' optimistic projections, and he prevailed with 56 percent of the vote. Winning the same thirty-one wards he had carried in the primary, Daley defeated Evans by nearly 150,000 votes. Having garnered financial contributions with ease, Daley outspent Evans in the election by a ratio of ten to one. In a contest where 94 percent of white and black Chicagoans voted along racial lines, Evans suffered the same fate that had befallen Sawyer in February: African American voter turnout fell disastrously short of the number needed to make the race competitive. The lingering Evans-Sawyer split clearly exacerbated an already fraught situation. Vrdolyak limped home a distant third, failing to carry a single ward and winning only 2 of the city's 2,911 precincts (both in his home Tenth Ward). Daley's victory margin owed in part to his ability to attract voters from Latino and independent lakefront precincts; an exit poll showed that 30 percent of the winner's votes came from Chicagoans who had cast their ballots for Washington in 1987.[15]

Daley's victory, hailed as a regal restoration in some quarters of the city, brought hope that the belligerent politics that had recently prevailed in Chicago was ending. The mayor-elect certainly encouraged such sentiments, saying, "We've run a campaign that will be remembered not for its angry words, but for the hand of friendship that was extended." Vigorously denying that his election signaled the return of unsavory machine politics, Daley promised a mayoralty devoted to good government, professional management, and accountability. The press and political experts agreed that the new mayor would be a consensus-building, open-minded manager rather than an autocratic boss. "Richie Daley is what he says he is," commented former alderman and influential attorney William Singer. "He is interested in healing this city." At the same time, many African Americans and political independents unpersuaded by such soothing pronouncements bemoaned the venomous racial divisions still afflicting Chicago and took small comfort in the return of a politician named Daley to the mayor's office. They feared the substitution of a modernized, streamlined political organization for the city's decades-old Democratic machine, the emergence of a "pin-striped machine" fueled by real estate investors, attorneys, and financiers in the Loop to replace blue-collar precinct captains sequestered in far-flung ethnic neighborhoods.[16]

Following his resounding triumph in 1989, Daley won reelection five times—in 1991, 1995, 1999, 2003, and 2007—before declining to seek a seventh term in 2011. His record twenty-two years as Chicago's mayor surpassed the previous standard for longevity established by his father. Voters obviously approved of his brief two-year "audition" (1989–91) and thereafter awarded him comfortable and sometimes overwhelming victory margins. After winning 56 percent of the vote in 1989, he tallied 68 percent in 1991, 60 percent in 1995, 72 percent in 1999, 78 percent in 2003, and 71 percent in 2007. A political colossus whose skillful coalition building undercut potential challenges from minority candidates in an increasingly diverse city, Daley dismembered any remnants of the alliance that twice carried Washington to victory in the mid-1980s. In 2003, for example, he received nearly 60 percent of the African American vote and carried all twenty predominantly black wards. Because of his recurring electoral successes in one of the nation's largest cities, he received widespread acclaim as an influential advocate for urban interests. He earned high marks for navigating his city less perilously than many of his counterparts in other metropolises through the shoals of deindustrialization and economic reconfiguration, securing Chicago's place among the small, exclusive list of global cities. He managed to survive a number of embarrassing scandals, many of which implicated family members and close friends, and remained extraordinarily popular with Chicagoans. When Daley chose not to seek reelection in 2011, no groundswell of opposition demanded his removal from office; no viable opponent preparing a challenge at the polls could be identified as the reason for the mayor's decision to retire that year.[17]

At the beginning of his pathbreaking mayoralty, during which Chicago underwent significant changes, Daley refrained from canceling all of the programs and policies introduced by Washington. In a few instances, the new mayor chose not to tamper at all with his predecessor's popular initiatives that were clearly working well. On his first day in office, for instance, he signed executive orders continuing the affirmative action plan for hiring underrepresented groups and the minority contracting program; in subsequent years, he increased the commitment to funnel city contracts to business firms owned by minorities and women. Honoring Washington's commitment to more openness in city hall, he retained the freedom-of-information initiative. Daley's repair of long-neglected parks in poor areas of the city completed plans devised during the Washington administration following the ouster of Ed Kelly. In 1990, reversing his earlier stance, he approved the Planned Manufacturing District in the Goose Island/Clybourn

Corridor and assented to the creation of two new PMDs. Moreover, he signaled an openness to the possibility of more industrial planning by appointing Donna Ducharme, a well-known advocate for Planned Manufacturing Districts and coauthor of *The Washington Papers*, as deputy commissioner of planning for industrial development.[18]

In relatively short order, however, Daley veered away from the Washington approach in matters related to urban redevelopment. Convinced that downtown enhancement assumed primacy for attracting investment in a global economy, he increasingly bypassed the neighborhoods and fixed his gaze resolutely on the Loop. Daley's drive to lure corporate headquarters from the suburbs and other cities to Chicago's downtown attracted Boeing, Exelon, Archer Daniels Midland, RR Donnelly, United Continental, and Hyatt, among other multinational enterprises. Enthusiastically joining the ranks of Chicago's builder-mayors, he oversaw the completion of nineteen of the thirty tallest buildings in the central business district. He utilized Tax Increment Financing to underwrite Loop building projects so often that critics accused him of turning the central business district into a "TIF district slush pool." The completion of Millennium Park, the redevelopment of Navy Pier as a festival marketplace, and extensive lakefront beautification under his direction secured the downtown's status as a premier tourist destination. In 1995 he dismissed Ducharme and Valerie Jarrett, another noted champion of decentralized economic development, from his administration. With the mayor's increased attention to downtown real estate, especially with high-end residential and commercial properties, interest in industrial planning subsided in city hall. In 1991 Daley merged the Department of Economic Development, a consistent advocate for community development under Washington, with the Planning Department to create the Department of Planning and Development. Although the DPD ostensibly sought economic growth everywhere in the city, attention to the neighborhoods diminished in the new arrangement.[19]

So did the commitment to openness and broad citizen participation. As Daley's hold on municipal government solidified, his dominion over a subservient city council made possible the single-minded pursuit of his vision for Chicago as a global city. He sought that goal with steely political calculation and, reminiscent of his father's dominance of the city's polity in the 1950s and 1960s, warmly embraced the city's progrowth coalition. Emboldened by his repeated electoral successes and the national and international acclaim he received as an urban visionary, the mayor became impatient with political opposition and ruled autocratically. Fully formed, the Richard M. Daley administration advanced purposefully and left little room for dissent.[20]

Rahm Emanuel, the "new Democrat" who succeeded Daley in 2011 and won reelection in 2015, pursued the same goal of gilding the urban core—but arguably with even more vigor. Unabashedly determined to sustain and enhance Chicago's status as a global city, Emanuel made no apologies for the courting of corporate titans as the key element in his unswerving attention to downtown redevelopment. At the same time, he presided over the largest mass closing of public schools in the nation's history, shuttered half of the city's mental health clinics, and failed to stem the rising incidence of firearm murders that threatened to make Chicago the homicide capital of the nation—in each instance drawing criticism for indifference to worsening conditions in poor African American and Latino neighborhoods. At the close of 2015, the violent deaths of several black residents at the hands of local police officers led to mass downtown demonstrations, calls for Emanuel to resign, and discussion in Springfield of new legislation permitting mayoral recall. As the murder rate in 2016 surpassed the previous year's gruesome tallies, dissidents complained that the administration was paying inadequate attention to the violent outbursts punctuating the incessant economic decline on the South and West Sides. The contrast with the Washington years could hardly have been starker.[21]

By the second decade of the twenty-first century, obscured in the penumbra of the Daley and Emanuel administrations, the political movement of 1983 and the eventful Washington mayoralty that followed in 1983–87 seemed like distant memories. Recalling the promise of that historical moment, reformers nostalgically detailed the positive developments that accrued and rued the changes cut short by the mayor's tragic death. "If only Harold had lived" became a plaintive refrain echoing often in some quarters of the city. Close friends and cohorts of the mayor, many of whom saw themselves as loyal keepers of the flame, still pondered the possibility of a progressive renaissance. Others saw the Washington phenomenon as a fleeting interlude during which an extremely able politician enjoyed an unexpected rise to power and attempted with limited success to alter the foundations of Chicago politics and government. For all of the energy expended by the administration—and by those in fevered opposition—no permanent multiracial alliance survived the 1980s. The overwhelming power of the city's downtown-growth coalition remained largely undiminished, relegated to a less prominent role for a short time but fully prepared to reassert its dominance when a traditional business-friendly administration reclaimed city hall. In that regard, how much did Washington's talk of fairness, open government, neighborhood empowerment, and redistribution affect the city at the time, and have there been long-lasting consequences? Did the city's residents benefit appreciably from his four and a half years at the head of local government? Does the Chicago of the twenty-first century, even with the temporizing influences of Daley and Emanuel, still bear the imprint of Washington's ideals? Given the example of the Washington mayoralty, can Chicago or any big city effectively implement policies that balance the downtown-first growth coalition with sufficient care for neighborhood concerns? Indeed, what do we make of Harold Washington and his abbreviated mayoralty?[22]

Washington was, undeniably, a preternaturally gifted politician whose granular knowledge of the city, oratorical prowess, and love of retail campaigning made him a formidable candidate for public office. Immersed in politics from an early age, he enjoyed the process as much as the outcome and spent most of his waking hours thinking and talking about the competition between electoral rivals. An electrifying public speaker, Washington both educated and entertained his audiences with an artful mix of passion, erudition, sober analysis, lighthearted banter, and lacerating censure. His declamations could be eloquent or coarse, usually delivered in a unique turn of phrase. He often varied his approach depending on the makeup of the audience, but always spoke bluntly and purposefully. Grayson Mitchell, the mayor's first press secretary, admiringly called him a "New Age politician who never met a microphone he did not like."[23] The devout following he enjoyed in the African American community owed in no small degree to his effectiveness as a communicator, and his supporters and enemies alike credited Washington with responsibility for the successful political movement that developed in 1983—the former praising his adroitness and the latter condemning his demagoguery. He held the tenuous multiracial coalition together by force of personality, a considerable achievement particularly in the early years of his mayoralty when prolonged stalemate in the city council stifled expectations held by black nationalists and reformers alike. Washington's political enemies, media critics, and wary urban scholars have grudgingly acknowledged his political dexterity, an unavoidable conclusion given the enormity of his achievement in winning the 1983 election against steep odds, but have frequently awarded him low marks for a reputed lack of administrative acumen in city hall.

Much more so than from his own inadequacies as an administrator, though, Washington's difficulties as mayor resulted from the dismaying economic and political obstacles arrayed against him. Subject to hazardous financial conditions throughout the entirety of his mayoralty, he scuffled to maintain the Windy City's solvency at a time of continued population and job loss. Adding to the financial instability for Chicago and other large industrial cities, an antagonistic Republican administration in Washington, D.C., continually reduced the federal support of urban programs that had become indispensable for balancing attenuated municipal budgets. Prevailing in a series of political skirmishes with Democrats in Congress, President Reagan managed to eliminate altogether or substantially slash funding for Community Development Block Grants, Urban Development Action Grants, general revenue sharing, the Comprehensive Employment Training Act, low-income housing, and other forms of government aid. Throughout his fifty-five months in city hall, Washington played an aggressive leadership role on behalf of a nationwide urban agenda and continually advanced harsh criticism of the Reagan administration's supply-side economics and social Darwinistic ethos—what he called "the new selfishness." Indeed, during his mayoralty, he emerged as one of the foremost advocates for America's shell-shocked industrial cities. Closer to home, Washington battled with an implacable opposition in the city council and uncooperative civil servants in the calcified municipal bureaucracy for most of his time in office. Critics tired of Washington and his defenders mentioning these factors to explain his administration's failings, but any objective assessment of his mayoralty would have to consider the powerful impediments to reform erected by the opposition.[24]

Similarly, the frequent censure of Washington's administrative ability bears careful scrutiny. Muscular opposition to the mayor's programs and policies often accounted for delayed action. The dilatory pace of decision making in city hall owed not to the mayor's indifference or ineptitude but to his temperament. An avid student of management principles and an ardent reader of books on public administration, Washington took considerable interest in the minutia of municipal governance. He surrounded himself in city hall with such policy wonks as Bill Ware and Ernest Barefield, frequently poring over case studies and flowcharts with them in the quest to streamline the urban bureaucracy. In policy meetings, he often sat impassively while encouraging everyone around the table to speak; his approach created an environment in which a wide variety of ideas surfaced and lengthy colloquies ensued without the mayor's presence inhibiting debate—but lively, far-ranging discussions often delayed the resolution of disagreements. The mayor knowingly sacrificed efficiency for exhaustive analysis and debate. The frustratingly slow pace of decision making at times in the mayor's office stemmed not from Washington's inattention to government business, said press secretary Alton Miller, but instead to his meticulous consideration—and reconsideration—of every decision that awaited his imprimatur. On contentious matters such as the World's Fair, linked development, and Planned Manufacturing Districts, the mayor often procrastinated and avoided specificity in his public remarks rather than rush to judgment. "The greatest mistake you can make is to move too fast," he said. "I'm not an off-the-cuff decision maker by nature." Compliant Democratic-machine operatives accustomed to enacting their marching orders from city hall with rapid-fire regularity puzzled at the deliberate pace of governance adopted by Washington, who made no apologies for the delays caused by the democratic processes his administration mandated.[25]

The local newspapers lauded Washington's appointments of municipal experts rather than payrollers to high-level positions in the administration, and he took great pride in choosing technocrats who drafted management-by-objectives plans and cared little about politics. He freely promised them autonomy within their own areas of expertise and, according to their testimony, kept his word. Washington commanded the loyalty and affection of those who worked closely with him in city hall. He demanded hard work and long hours, often fomenting competition among his aides to spur greater creativity in problem solving. A knowledgeable administrator with high standards, he demanded accountability and held his cabinet members and top aides to a high performance standard. He refused to micromanage, deputy chief of staff Brenda Gaines remembered, instead establishing realistic policy goals, setting clear lines of authority, and allowing his subordinates to control their own bureaucratic units. Cabinet members and others in the administration spoke often of a camaraderie they shared in working toward worthy objectives; they reveled in being part of a movement to introduce a greater measure of democracy into the political process and to improve the quality of government in Chicago. Gaines said that she admired and respected Washington. She and other members of his staff believed passionately in what he was trying to do. "He was a good administrator," she concluded. "More important, he was a *leader!*"[26]

As a strong leader with a worshipful following, a fervent opposition, and an unsteady electoral mandate, Washington fought tenaciously for four and a half years to remake Chicago along the lines he had specified. He gloated often during those years of having slain the hated Democratic machine—"The Machine is dead, dead, dead. I killed it! I danced on its grave!" he exalted in mock celebration—but he acknowledged in more serious moments that that victory constituted only the first step in the arduous process of improving the city's ailing fortunes. No doubt he confidently declared his intention of being mayor for twenty years because he realized a sobering but inescapable truth: the fundamental changes planned for Chicago under his leadership would have taken at least that long. During the 1983 campaign and throughout his administration, Washington liberally condemned his mayoral predecessors (Daley, Bilandic, and Byrne) as agents of what he disdainfully called the "ancient, decrepit and creaking machine" that had undercut Chicago's growth and development. As a corrective to the inequities and inefficiencies of machine politics, he offered a version of reform based on fairness, redistribution, and broader citizen participation in government. Broadly sketched in *The Washington Papers* and fleshed out more completely in *Chicago Works Together* and *Chicago Works Together II*, his plan for Chicago's adaptation to a postindustrial economy required a significant break with the self-serving practices of the prevailing political regime.[27]

Washington's vision of Chicago's future also called for a modified relationship between the central business district and the neighborhoods, requiring an adjustment in resource allocation that necessitated somewhat less attention to the former and more nurturing of the latter. He benefited from the increased building activity in and around the Loop that began earlier in the decade and continued throughout his stay in city hall. In his second inaugural address, he proudly claimed that economic activity in the downtown commercial district had grown at the rate of a billion dollars a year during the 1980s. Often neglecting to mention that work on projects completed during his tenure had begun during the Bilandic or Byrne administrations, he cheerfully cut ribbons and posed for photographs at dedication ceremonies throughout the urban core. Although he evinced de-cidedly little innate interest in erecting monumental structures downtown, Washington recognized the need to do so for political reasons. He realized the economic importance of the central business district and the need to maintain infrastructure that served the hub of the metropolitan region.[28]

As well, he understood the need to cultivate good relations with the business community and to provide support for investors based in Chi-cago and elsewhere. He and his minions fiercely denied any animus in the administration against the entrepreneurial class and attempted whenever possible to improve relations with powerful State Street and LaSalle Street interests. They cited a number of large-scale projects designed to bolster the central city begun or completed during the Washington mayoralty, includ-ing the expansion and improvement of O'Hare International Airport, the extensive reconfiguration of Navy Pier, the construction of a new central public library, the enlargement of McCormick Place, significant progress on the renewal of the North Loop, the city's first designation of a TIF district, and preliminary discussions about the development of the River North area and the South Loop museum campus. Denying that his emphasis on industrial retention and neighborhood renewal had damaged the city's financial prospects, he said, "We have been a partner with the development community in fostering an unparalleled track record of so called 'yuppie' development in former manufacturing areas—the South Loop/Dearborn Park area, River North, the near West Side, and now the Chicago Dock and Canal area."[29]

But the mayor and many of his aides also believed that developers re-flexively swarmed to downtown sites and that local government needed to do very little to encourage investment in the shadows of skyscrapers. "Downtown grows itself," Washington often said. By contrast, city hall had to work much harder, clearly demonstrating a potential for profit, to stimulate economic development in the neighborhoods. Aggressively led by Rob Mier, assigned a clear directive by the mayor's office, and awarded as much funding as possible, the Department of Economic Development made an unprecedented effort to attract and retain small businesses and factories in locations scattered throughout the city. In order to foster de-centralized economic development, Mier and his colleagues strengthened ties to community-based organizations, dispelling much of the mistrust that existed between neighborhood groups and municipal bureaucracies, and funneled modest sums of money via the Chicago Capital Fund to small local businesses, allowing them to remain solvent in their infancy. Results were mixed, successes limited, setbacks not uncommon. In the administration's most publicized attempt to stem the flight of business, swift action in the Playskool case won a few concessions but failed to keep the factory in Chicago. The creation of a few Planned Manufacturing Districts fell short of triggering a larger citywide movement. Critics pointedly asked whether such modest achievements dispelled doubts about a bankable strategy of "jobs, not real estate," for the city's future economic development. As in many other respects, a notable lapse in activity following the mayor's death raised questions about the efficacy of decentralized development and emphasized the political difficulties in sustaining the grudging progress made by 1987. At the very least, questions about Washington's approach remained unanswered. Again, reformers said in defending the ponderous beginnings of the new approach to economic development, "If only Harold had lived."[30]

Greater attention to neighborhood concerns included more than economic development, of course, and Washington repeatedly affirmed his interest in improving service delivery in all corners of the city. Municipal housekeeping had been egregiously unequal for generations, with city departments supplying some neighborhoods with reliable day-to-day services and regularly shortchanging others. During the Washington administration, African Americans residing in some of Chicago's poorest precincts reported seeing city snowplows and road graders rumbling down their streets for the very first time. The general-obligation bond issue of 1985, a landmark maintenance initiative, divided funds among the fifty wards so that all areas of the city benefited and the neediest enclaves received an equitable share, regardless of race or politics. In many instances, as in the case of the 1985 bond issue, the strongholds of the mayor's staunchest enemies gained the most from city hall's evenhanded disbursement of resources. Altogether, the administration spent more than three hundred million dollars on infrastructural improvements in the neighborhoods. "There are never enough city services," the mayor told one of his ward superintendents. "Your job is to ensure that everybody gets some of that 'not enough.'"[31]

Neighborhood empowerment also went hand in hand with decentralization of government, greater access to city hall, and a more broadly based participatory politics. Decrying the Democratic machine's secret operations, avaricious backroom deals, and customary practice of hoarding information,

Washington issued an executive order granting open access to all public records and named a freedom-of-information officer to guarantee compliance.
He established more than fifty task forces, noteworthy for the diversity of
their membership, charged with studying the city's problems and proposing
solutions. In perhaps his most important innovation designed to stimulate
broader citizen involvement in government, he revolutionized the city's
budget-making procedure by holding community forums at the outset of
the lengthy annual process. In all, more than six hundred neighborhood
organizations spent time with the mayor and members of his cabinet discussing the allocation of Chicago's resources before the city council received
a preliminary budget. Cabinet members testified to the stamina required
to survive the grueling all-day sessions, at which spirited discussions about
spending priorities occasionally escalated into verbal attacks on the administration, but agreed that the singular effort paid off as they witnessed the
increasing engagement of a lifeless polity. A comparable process operated
for the writing of Community Development Block Grant proposals, which
had previously served as a political tool of the mayor's office. In response
to charges of inadequate citizen involvement in the preparation of *Chicago
Works Together*, the city's 1984 development plan, the administration appointed a fifty-nine-member task force that labored for two years on a revision. After implementing changes suggested in a public forum attended by
several hundred people, city hall issued *Chicago Works Together II* in 1987.[32]

As a form of redistribution, neighborhood empowerment dovetailed
with the drive to balance the scales in favor of those groups traditionally
ignored or mistreated by the despotic political machine. In explicit recognition of long-standing racial and gender inequity, Washington issued
executive orders creating several new agencies of local government: the
Mayor's Advisory Commission on Women's Affairs, the Mayor's Advisory
Commission on Latino Affairs, and the Mayor's Advisory Commission on
Asian-American Affairs. In addition, he named the city's first gay and lesbian
liaison, supported a gay-rights ordinance in the city council, and became
Chicago's first mayor to address a gay-pride rally. When members of his
coalition carped about the undue attention afforded some minority groups
at the potential expense of others, Washington reminded them that "civil
right and human rights had to be protected in all quarters."[33]

To correct the damage inflicted by decades of patronage and discriminatory hiring, Washington steadfastly advanced the cause of affirmative

action—both as a matter of fairness and as what he insisted was a healthy and effective way of doing business in the public sector. Rather than seeking ways to circumvent the Shakman decrees, he embraced them. The mayor delivered a rousing defense of affirmative action as a pillar of Democratic Party ideology and pointed to his city as a real-life example of how the policy could be implemented effectually. He cautioned that the Reagan administration was "working overtime to kill affirmative action," famously making his case to a national audience when he opposed the president's nomination of Judge Robert Bork to the U.S. Supreme Court in July 1987. The confirmation of Bork would mean that "affirmative action is doomed, doomed, doomed," Washington warned in explaining his ferocious opposition to Bork's nomination. He took great pride in Chicago's pacesetting record of affirmative action hiring under his leadership. Having inherited a city workforce in 1983 that was 27 percent black and 68 percent white, he reported, four years of amelioration had brought the numbers (31 percent black and 63 percent white) more in line with private-sector employment. Applying the same approach to the 913 administrative positions in municipal government, the mayor altered the racial breakdown during the same time from 25 percent black and 71 percent white to 36 percent black and 56 percent white.[34]

Washington also alluded proudly to his administration's new method of allocating city contracts. Once more following a path of remediation, he established goals of 25 percent for Minority Business Enterprises and 5 percent for Women Business Enterprises. In the mayor's last year in office, the city awarded 27 percent of total city procurement to MBEs and 8 percent to WBEs. Further, the city awarded minority financial firms an unprecedented one hundred million dollars in pension investment capital. In January 1987, Washington signed an executive order that required employers receiving city contracts and economic incentives to use publicly funded employment services as their first source for hiring. (Daley terminated the "first-source" hiring program in 1991.) Equally gratifying, Washington noted, the share of city purchases from locally owned businesses increased from 40 percent to 62 percent. "Every taxpayer benefited from the lessons we learned," he contended, "that when you establish guidelines to specify the details of affirmative action, you simultaneously disrupt the former, costly, cozy arrangements that drove all the prices up."[35]

Washington's wholehearted belief in affirmative action, his commitment to redistribution, and his determination to make government more open and accessible—in short, his headlong pursuit of fairness—established a new tone in city hall that arguably accounted for his greatest achievement and principal legacy as mayor. Such alterations in Chicago's political culture, the mayor and his allies believed, gave hope that fundamental systemic change would follow and that reform could be institutionalized. In the meantime, the openness, inclusiveness, and elevated commitment to equity evinced by the administration were transforming the political culture of the city. For the first time, groups of people sharing certain characteristics or living in particular areas of the metropolis believed that their priorities counted too and that their futures mattered. He rejected spurious distinctions between race and class interests, asserting that indissoluble ligatures bound the two together. By the account of contemporaries observing the mood of the people in the Loop and in remote neighborhoods scattered throughout the city, Chicago crackled with a new sense of purpose and possibility during the Washington era.[36]

What happened to the widespread sense of purpose and possibility after Washington's unexpected death? His administration's emphasis on the neighborhoods produced an immediate backlash, a renewed interest in downtown improvement that surfaced during the Daley regime. The counterattack from the commercial civic elite came quickly. In August 1988, the *Chicago Tribune* published a lengthy series of articles by urban affairs reporter John McCarron on the failure of reform and the economic folly of favoring decentralized development over downtown revitalization. McCarron ridiculed the idea of industrial renewal as hopelessly naive, singling out Rob Mier for special disdain, and argued that excessive concern with social welfare policy had been diverting precious investment capital away from uses more beneficial to the city's economic advancement. After a brief, uncertain transition, Mayor Richard M. Daley's economic agenda solidified in favor of downtown redevelopment, and neighborhood influence correspondingly waned in city hall. The creation and retention of jobs, a momentous matter in the city's forlorn precincts, took a backseat to real estate once again. Especially after a landslide reelection in 1999, by which time Daley's mastery of a subservient city council allowed him to consolidate his hold on local government, the primacy of downtown redevelopment seemed clear. The wariness that characterized relations between city hall and corporate boardrooms during the Washington years gave way during the reign of Daley II to the easy familiarity that prevailed years before under Daley I.[37]

But the enrichment of the central business district—the creation of a beautifully appointed universe where corporate executives completed transactions worth billions of dollars and tourists from around the world consumed fashionable merchandise and high culture—once again raised questions about equity and fairness. While the downtown flourished under Daley and Emanuel and gentrification has revitalized a number of tired neighborhoods, less fortunate portions of the city continue to worsen and become even less habitable to the forlorn populations trapped there. Boosters proudly proclaim Chicago a global city, even as unconscionably high homicide rates turn some areas of the municipality into pitiless killing fields. Residents of tony neighborhoods abutting the Loop and extending into the affluent tracts of the North Side enjoy the best services a flourishing metropolis can offer, while the poor and powerless inhabiting the vast South and West Sides scrape out a hardscrabble existence with little hope of a better life. Chicago in the early twenty-first century too often resembles two cities resting side by side, one basking in prosperity and the other marooned in postindustrial squalor. Washington's plea for balanced growth, fairness, and redistribution—his emphasis on jobs and not real estate—seems to ring hollow in city hall nearly three decades after his death.[38]

To a considerable degree, however, not all transformations from the Washington era have been expunged. Some reforms endure. In part because of the political empowerment sparked in the mid-1980s and in part because of shifting demographics in Chicago, electoral politics in the twenty-first century potentially include more voters and legitimize more issues than in the machine era. The election of an African American mayor ended a decades-old tradition of plantation politics and changed forever the embedded dynamics of racial and ethnic electioneering in Chicago. The Washington victories in 1983 and 1987 provided a template for political change in an increasingly polyglot city. Thus, the younger Daley faced the need to curry favor with expanding voting blocs—Latinos, women, gays, and lesbians, as well as blacks—in ways that had never been necessary for his father. Once the valuable plaything of an elite few, local government has become at least partially accessible to a much greater number of Chicagoans in a healthier, more democratic fashion. Decisions on the appointment of boards, commissions, and task forces by the mayor and other top city officials, once made peremptorily without any regard for diversity, have become in subsequent decades subject to new guidelines designed to include representatives of different backgrounds and interests. Once veiled in secrecy, city hall no longer routinely keeps information from the people or dispenses jobs, contracts, and other perquisites to favored wards or groups of people without explanation. The entrenched customs of exclusion and favoritism have given ground to a more open polity, in considerable degree due to changes in local government rooted in the structural reforms effected under Washington.[39]

Most important, the Washington interlude left Chicagoans in the twenty-first century with compelling memories of an earlier time and a sense of how local government could be retooled to produce a more just society for all of the city's inhabitants. The mayor identified the human building blocks—people of color, the economically disadvantaged, homosexuals, disaffected progressives, and others consigned to the city's margins—that could form a powerful rainbow coalition. With important documents such as *The Washington Papers*, *Chicago Works Together*, and *Chicago Works Together II*, he provided blueprints for effective and efficient municipal governance. In the face of malevolent, unyielding opposition, Washington persevered and demonstrated—at least on a limited scale—what was possible. Nearly thirty years after his death, with the central business district and other flourishing neighborhoods leading the way, Chicago has completed the passage from deteriorating manufacturing center to postindustrial metropolis much more successfully than many other Rust Belt cities. Still, Chicagoans anxiously seek solutions for the problems that pervade much of the forsaken cityscape. The momentous challenges confronting Washington in the 1980s—how to maintain both a vibrant downtown and livable neighborhoods, balance budgets in the face of austerity, retain industry, prioritize jobs rather than real estate development, and make government an agent of fairness—remain just as important thirty years later. The goals and principles articulated by Washington in the 1980s resonate just as strongly in the twenty-first century. His brief tenure in city hall continues in subsequent decades to offer inspiration when gross economic inequality, violence, fear, and distrust threaten to negate Chicago's many glittering achievements.[40]

Washington's legacy likewise stands in stark contrast to the remarkable outcome of the 2016 presidential election. Always quick to comment on national events, the mayor surely would have been shocked that year at the repudiation of the ideals he championed in Chicago, Springfield, and Washington, D.C., during his long political career. He would have felt that many gains in the quest to improve society were suddenly in jeopardy of being lost. In an atmosphere poisoned by incivility and intolerance, the first few months of Donald J. Trump's administration have brought the demonization of immigrants, a failed attempt to roll back health care coverage, proposals for massive spending cuts on domestic programs to fuel an enormous military buildup, relaxation of environmental standards to ensure windfall profits for energy conglomerates, and discussion of a sweeping tax overhaul to benefit the nation's wealthiest citizens. The agenda of the Trump White House seems totally at odds with Washington's call for inclusion, charity, racial and gender equity, openness, and fairness. A rereading of *The Washington Papers* and *Chicago Works Together*, with their emphasis on shared humanity and a benign view of government, could perhaps help to sustain forlorn progressives in a conservative age when very different values prevail.

Notes

Introduction: Race, Reform, and Redistribution

1. *Chicago Tribune*, November 24, 25, 2015; *Chicago Reporter*, February 25, 2015.

2. *New York Times*, November 27, 2015; *Chicago Tribune*, November 28, 2015, September 6, 2016.

3. *Chicago Tribune*, September 6, 2016. See also Larry Bennett, *The Third City: Chicago and American Urbanism* (Chicago: University of Chicago Press, 2010); and Costas Spirou and Dennis R. Judd, *Building the City of Spectacle: Mayor Richard M. Daley and the Remaking of Chicago* (Ithaca, N.Y.: Cornell University Press, 2016).

4. Gary Rivlin, *Fire on the Prairie: Harold Washington, Chicago Politics, and the Roots of the Obama Presidency*, rev. ed. (Philadelphia: Temple University Press, 2013), 1–2; Monroe Anderson, "The Sawyer Saga: A Journalist, Who Just Happened to Be the Mayor's Press Secretary, Speaks," in *Restoration 1989: Chicago Elects a New Daley*, edited by Paul M. Green and Melvin G. Holli (Chicago: Lyceum Books, 1991), 98–99; Harold Washington, *Climbing a Great Mountain: Selected Speeches of Mayor Harold Washington*, commentary by Alton Miller (Chicago: Bonus Books, 1988), 152 (quote).

5. Brian Kelly, "Harold Washington's Balancing Act," *Chicago* 34 (April 1985): 201.

6. Robert Mier, *Social Justice and Local Development Policy* (Newbury Park, Calif.: Sage, 1993), 196.

7. Ibid. See also Robert Mier, "Some Observations on Race in Planning," *Journal of the American Planning Association* 60 (Spring 1994): 235–40.

8. Washington, *Climbing a Great Mountain*, 63. Political scientist William J. Grimshaw notes that Washington's version of reform grew from the black protest tradition, rooted in the African American church, which differed from the traditional brand of white protest. The fullest explication of Grimshaw's ideas can be found in

his *Bitter Fruit: Black Politics and the Chicago Machine, 1931–1991* (Chicago: University of Chicago Press, 1992), especially chap. 8. See also Grimshaw, "Is Chicago Ready for Reform? or, A New Agenda for Harold Washington," in *The Making of the Mayor: Chicago, 1983*, edited by Melvin G. Holli and Paul M. Green (Grand Rapids, Mich.: William B. Eerdmans, 1984), 141–65; and Grimshaw, "Unraveling the Enigma: Mayor Harold Washington and the Black Political Tradition," *Urban Affairs Quarterly* 23 (December 1987): 187–206.

9. *Chicago Tribune*, March 2, 1985; Emily Amine Soloff and Greg Heinz, "Berny Stone and the Boys in the Bloc," *Chicago* 33 (September 1984): 213; Steven P. Erie, *Rainbow's End: Irish-Americans and the Dilemmas of Urban Machine Politics, 1840–1985* (Berkeley: University of California Press, 1988), 260–61; W. Grimshaw, *Bitter Fruit*, 188; Gerald D. Suttles, *The Man-Made City: The Land-Use Confidence Game in Chicago* (Chicago: University of Chicago Press, 1990), 267n6. See also Larry Bennett, "Harold Washington and the Black Urban Regime," *Urban Affairs Quarterly* 28 (March 1993): 427–28.

10. Bill Granger and Lori Granger, *Lords of the Last Machine: The Story of Politics in Chicago* (New York: Random House, 1987), 212, 215; Melvin G. Holli and Paul M. Green, *Bashing Chicago Traditions: Harold Washington's Last Campaign* (Grand Rapids, Mich.: William B. Eerdmans, 1989), 186. Oscar De Priest of Chicago was the first African American elected to the U.S. Congress in the twentieth century; he served three terms, from 1929 to 1935, representing Illinois's First Congressional District.

11. Granger and Granger, *Lords of the Last Machine*, 215.

12. Keith Koeneman, *First Son: The Biography of Richard M. Daley* (Chicago: University of Chicago Press, 2013), 113, 97.

13. Alton Miller, *Harold Washington: The Mayor, the Man* (Chicago: Bonus Books, 1989), 195–97; Rivlin, *Fire on the Prairie*, 175–76.

14. Manning Marable, *Race, Reform, and Rebellion: The Second Reconstruction and Beyond in Black America, 1945–2006*, 3rd ed. (Jackson: University Press of Mississippi, 2007), 214–15.

15. Jacqueline Dowd Hall, "The Long Civil Rights Movement and the Political Uses of the Past," *Journal of American History* 91 (March 2005): 1234. On the long civil rights movement, see Jeanne Theoharis and Komozi Woodard, eds., *Freedom North: Black Freedom Struggles Outside the South, 1940–1980* (New York: Palgrave Macmillan, 2003); and Nikhil Pal Singh, *Black Is a Country: Race and the Unfinished Struggle for Democracy* (Cambridge, Mass.: Harvard University Press, 2004). For a skeptical view of this recent historiographical turn, see Steven F. Lawson, "Long Origins of the Civil Rights Movement, 1954–1968," in *Freedom Rights: New Perspectives on the Civil Rights Movement*, edited by Danielle L. McGuire and John Dittmer (Lexington: University Press of Kentucky, 2011), 9–37; Eric Arnesen, "Reconsidering the 'Long Civil Rights Movement,'" *Historically Speaking* 10 (April 2009): 31–34; and Sundiata Cha-Jua and Clarence Lang, "The 'Long Movement' as Vampire: Temporal and Spatial Fallacies in Recent Black Freedom Studies," *Journal of African American History* 92 (Spring 2007): 265–88.

16. Martha Biondi, *To Stand and Fight: The Struggle for Civil Rights in Postwar New York City* (Cambridge, Mass.: Harvard University Press, 2003); Craig Steven Wilder, *A Covenant with Color: Race and Social Power in Brooklyn* (New York: Columbia University Press, 2000); James Ralph, *Northern Protest: Martin Luther King, Jr., Chicago, and the Civil Rights Movement* (Cambridge, Mass.: Harvard University Press, 1993); Matthew Countryman, *Up South: Civil Rights and Black Power in Philadelphia* (Philadelphia: University of Pennsylvania Press, 2006); Angela Dillard, *Faith in the City: Preaching Radical Social Change in Detroit* (Ann Arbor: University of Michigan Press, 2007); Clarence Lang, *Grassroots at the Gateway: Class Politics and Black Freedom Struggles in St. Louis, 1936–1975* (Ann Arbor: University of Michigan Press, 2009); Patrick D. Jones, *The Selma of the North: Civil Rights Insurgency in Milwaukee* (Cambridge, Mass.: Harvard University Press, 2009); Josh Sides, *LA City Limits: African American Los Angeles from the Great Depression to the Present* (Berkeley: University of California Press, 2003); Robert O. Self, *American Babylon: Race and the Struggle for Postwar Oakland* (Princeton, N.J.: Princeton University Press, 2003); Joan Singler et al., *Seattle in Black and White: The Congress of Racial Equality and the Fight for Equal Opportunity* (Seattle: University of Washington Press, 2011); Thomas J. Sugrue, *Sweet Land of Liberty: The Forgotten Struggle for Civil Rights in the North* (New York: Random House, 2008).

17. Peniel E. Joseph, *The Black Power Movement: Rethinking the Civil Rights–Black Power Era* (New York: Routledge, 2006), 4 (quote); Peniel E. Joseph, *Dark Days, Bright Nights: From Black Power to Barack Obama* (New York: Basic Books, 2010), 196, 207; Wahneema Lubiano, "Black Nationalism and Black Common Sense: Policing Ourselves and Others," in *The House That Race Built: Black Americans, U.S. Terrain*, edited by Wahneema Lubiano (New York: Pantheon, 1997), 232–52; Devin Fergus, *Liberalism, Black Power, and the Making of American Politics, 1965–1980* (Athens: University of Georgia Press, 2009); Jacobi Williams, *From the Bullet to the Ballot: The Illinois Chapter of the Black Panther Party and Racial Coalition Politics in Chicago* (Chapel Hill: University of North Carolina Press, 2013), 10. See also Donna Murch, *Living for the City: Migration, Education, and the Rise of the Black Power Party in Oakland, California* (Chapel Hill: University of North Carolina Press, 2010); and Yohuru Williams, *Black Politics/White Power: Civil Rights, Black Power, and the Black Panthers in New Haven* (Malden, Mass.: Blackwell, 2008). For a different perspective on Black Power, see Adolph Reed Jr., *Stirrings in the Jug: Black Politics in the Post-Segregation Era* (Minneapolis: University of Minnesota Press, 1999).

18. Lawson, "Long Origins of the Civil Rights Movement," 13ff; Jeffrey Helgeson, *Crucibles of Black Empowerment: Chicago's Neighborhood Politics from the New Deal to Harold Washington* (Chicago: University of Chicago Press, 2014), 273. For a description of similar alliances among community-based organizations seeking racial uplift, see Brian Purnell, *Fighting Jim Crow in the County of Kings: The Congress of Racial Equality in Brooklyn* (Lexington: University Press of Kentucky, 2013).

19. Joseph, *Dark Days, Bright Nights*, 196, 207; Lubiano, "Black Nationalism and Black Common Sense"; Erik Gellman, "'The Stone Wall Behind': The Chicago

Coalition for United Community Action and Labor's Overseers, 1968–1973," in *Black Power at Work: Community Control, Affirmative Action, and the Construction Industry*, edited by David Goldberg and Trevor Griffey (Ithaca, N.Y.: Cornell University Press, 2010), 133–34; Helgeson, *Crucibles of Black Empowerment*, 231–34; Mary Pattillo, *Black on the Block: The Politics of Race and Class in the City* (Chicago: University of Chicago Press, 2007), 73–76; J. Williams, *From the Bullet to the Ballot*, 197 (quote). Fred Hampton, chairman of the Black Panther Party's Illinois chapter, died on December 4, 1969, at the hands of Chicago police under highly questionable circumstances.

20. Adam Doster, "How Mayor Harold Washington Shaped the City of Chicago," http://www.chicagomag.com/core/pagetools.php?url=%2FChicago-Magazine%2FThe-31.

21. Pierre Clavel and Robert P. Giloth, "Planning for Manufacturing: Chicago after 1983," *Journal of Planning History* 14 (February 2015): 19–37; Bennett, *Third City*, 6 (quote).

Chapter 1. From Machine Regular to Progressive Democrat

1. On the Great Migration, see James R. Grossman, *Land of Hope: Chicago, Black Southerners, and the Great Migration* (Chicago: University of Chicago Press, 1989); and Christopher Robert Reed, *Knock at the Door of Opportunity: Black Migration to Chicago, 1900–1919* (Carbondale: Southern Illinois University Press, 2014). On segregationist practices in real estate, see Beryl Satter, *Family Properties: Race, Real Estate, and the Exploitation of Black Urban America* (New York: Metropolitan Books, 2009); and N. D. B. Connolly, *A World More Concrete: Real Estate and the Remaking of Jim Crow South Florida* (Chicago: University of Chicago Press, 2014). On restrictive covenants, see Wendy Plotkin, "Deeds of Mistrust: Race, Housing, and Restrictive Covenants in Chicago, 1900–1953" (Ph.D. diss., University of Illinois at Chicago, 1999).

2. St. Clair Drake and Horace R. Cayton, *Black Metropolis: A Study of Negro Life in a Northern City* (Chicago: University of Chicago Press, 1945), remains the best description of African American life in Chicago during the first half of the twentieth century. See also Allan H. Spear, *Black Chicago: The Making of a Negro Ghetto, 1890–1920* (Chicago: University of Chicago Press, 1967); Thomas Lee Philpott, *The Slum and the Ghetto: Neighborhood Deterioration and Middle-Class Reform, Chicago, 1880–1930* (New York: Oxford University Press, 1978); Ethan Michaeli, *The "Defender": How the Legendary Black Newspaper Changed America* (Boston: Houghton Mifflin Harcourt, 2016); and Timuel D. Black Jr., *Bridges of Memory: Chicago's First Wave of Black Migration* (Evanston, Ill.: Northwestern University Press, 2003). Michelle R. Boyd, *Jim Crow Nostalgia: Reconstructing Race in Bronzeville* (Minneapolis: University of Minnesota Press, 2008), cautions against romanticizing African American life in Chicago during the Jim Crow era.

3. Spear, *Black Chicago*, 118–26; Reed, *Knock at the Door of Opportunity*, 184–97.

4. Thaddeus Russell, "Harold Washington," in *African American Lives*, edited by

Henry Louis Gates Jr. and Evelyn Brooks Higginbotham (New York: Oxford University Press, 2004), 853; Florence Hamlish Levinsohn, *Harold Washington: A Political Biography* (Chicago: Chicago Review Press, 1983), 20–23; Gary Rivlin, *Fire on the Prairie: Harold Washington, Chicago, Politics, and the Roots of the Obama Presidency*, rev. ed. (Philadelphia: Temple University Press, 2013), 27–28.

5. Robert McClory, "Up from Obscurity: Harold Washington," in *The Making of the Mayor: Chicago, 1983*, edited by Melvin G. Holli and Paul M. Green (Grand Rapids, Mich.: William B. Eerdmans, 1984), 4; *Chicago Defender*, September 19, 1984.

6. Alfredo S. Lanier, "Congressman Harold Washington," *Chicago* 32 (February 1983): 100 (quote); McClory, "Up from Obscurity," 3.

7. Dempsey J. Travis, *An Autobiography of Black Politics* (Chicago: Urban Research Press, 1987), 468. On the history of black politics in Chicago, see Charles R. Branham, "The Transformation of Black Political Leadership in Chicago, 1864–1942" (Ph.D. diss., University of Chicago, 1981); Charles R. Branham, "Black Chicago: Accommodationist Politics before the Great Migration," in *The Ethnic Frontier: Essays in the History of Group Survival in Chicago and the Midwest*, edited by Melvin G. Holli and Peter d'A. Jones (Grand Rapids, Mich.: William B. Eerdmans, 1977), 211–62; and Christopher Manning, *William L. Dawson and the Limits of Black Electoral Leadership* (DeKalb: Northern Illinois University Press, 2009).

8. William J. Grimshaw, *Bitter Fruit: Black Politics and the Chicago Machine, 1931–1991* (Chicago: University of Chicago Press, 1992), 66–67, 80–81.

9. Dempsey J. Travis, *Harold, the People's Mayor: An Authorized Biography of Mayor Harold Washington* (Chicago: Urban Research Press, 1989), 1–13; Rivlin, *Fire on the Prairie*, 28–29; McClory, "Up from Obscurity," 4; Russell, "Harold Washington," 853.

10. Travis, *Harold, the People's Mayor*, 27–43; Rivlin, *Fire on the Prairie*, 29; Russell, "Harold Washington," 853.

11. Lynn Y. Weiner, "Roosevelt University," in *The Encyclopedia of Chicago*, edited by James R. Grossman, Ann Durkin Keating, and Janice L. Reiff (Chicago: University of Chicago Press, 2004), 722; Jeffrey Helgeson, *Crucibles of Black Empowerment: Chicago's Neighborhood Politics from the New Deal to Harold Washington* (Chicago: University of Chicago Press, 2014), 204; Russell, "Harold Washington," 853–54; Rivlin, *Fire on the Prairie*, 29.

12. Helgeson, *Crucibles of Black Empowerment*, 204–8; Lanier, "Congressman Harold Washington," 100; Levinsohn, *Harold Washington*, 44–58 (quote on 44); Rivlin, *Fire on the Prairie*, 29–30.

13. McClory, "Up from Obscurity," 3–4.

14. Levinsohn, *Harold Washington*, 66–70; Travis, *Harold, the People's Mayor*, 55–57.

15. Rivlin, *Fire on the Prairie*, 30; Travis, *Harold, the People's Mayor*, 59–60.

16. Travis, *Harold, the People's Mayor*, 59–64; Rivlin, *Fire on the Prairie*, 30–31.

17. Travis, *Harold, the People's Mayor*, 64–65.

18. Ibid., 60, 65–66; Levinsohn, *Harold Washington*, 82.

19. Helgeson, *Crucibles of Black Empowerment*, 206–8; Russell, "Harold Washington," 854.

20. Rivlin, *Fire on the Prairie*, 32 (quote); McClory, "Up from Obscurity," 7; Travis, *Harold, the People's Mayor*, 70–71.

21. Levinsohn, *Harold Washington*, 112–15; Lanier, "Congressman Harold Washington," 100.

22. Travis, *Harold, the People's Mayor*, 74 (first quote); McClory, "Up from Obscurity," 6–7; Rivlin, *Fire on the Prairie*, 33; Brian Kelly, "Harold Washington's Balancing Act," *Chicago* 34 (April 1985): 202 (second quote).

23. *Chicago Tribune*, April 3, 1983; Rivlin, *Fire on the Prairie*, 32–34, 37; Travis, *Harold, the People's Mayor*, 76–77. See also the Harold Washington Papers, Illinois State Representative Records, Box 3, Folders 3, 4a, Harold Washington Public Library, Chicago.

24. Rivlin, *Fire on the Prairie*, 34.

25. Kelly, "Harold Washington's Balancing Act," 202; Rivlin, *Fire on the Prairie*, 37 (quote); Roger Biles, *Richard J. Daley: Politics, Race, and the Governing of Chicago* (DeKalb: Northern Illinois University Press, 1995), 177–80.

26. Abdul Alkalimat and Doug Gills, *Harold Washington and the Crisis of Black Power in Chicago* (Chicago: Twenty-First Century Books and Publications, 1989), 51–52; Travis, *Harold, the People's Mayor*, 77, 88 (first quote); Levinsohn, *Harold Washington*, 104 (second quote); *Chicago Defender*, May 17, 1971; McClory, "Up from Obscurity," 11.

27. *Chicago Defender*, May 15, 1965; Travis, *Harold, the People's Mayor*, 81–83; Levinsohn, *Harold Washington*, 110–11. For more documentation of Washington's work on medical malpractice legislation, see the Washington Papers, Illinois State Representative Records, Box 2, Folders 7–15, and Box 3, Folders 1–2.

28. "Equal Job Opportunities under Government Contracts," January 1, 1974, Washington Papers, Illinois State Representative Records, Box 6, Folder 16. On the FEPC, see Washington Papers, Illinois State Representative Records, Box 1, Folders 8–10. See also Washington to Governor Dan Walker, March 15, 1973, Washington Papers, Illinois State Representative Records, Box 6, Folder 2.

29. Washington to Renault Robinson, February 13, 1973, Washington Papers, Illinois State Representative Records, Box 3, Folder 10a; *Daily Illini* (University of Illinois), April 12, 1973 (quotes).

30. "Bonding Barriers Break Black Builder's Back," *Chicago Reporter* 3 (October 1974), 1, 5–7, in Washington Papers, Illinois State Representative Records, Box 3, Folder 7.

31. *Chicago Sun-Times* clipping, December 5, 1976, ibid., Box 2, Folder 3; *Chicago Tribune*, April 12, 1977.

32. Washington to William A. Redmond, November 11, 1976, Washington Papers, Illinois State Representative Records, Box 3, Folder 5a; Travis, *Harold, the People's Mayor*, 83.

33. *Chicago Defender*, July 25, 1973; Travis, *Harold, the People's Mayor*, 81–83. See also the Washington Papers, Illinois State Representative Records, Box 2, Folders 1–5.

34. "Statement to Committee for a Black Mayor by State Representative Harold Washington," September 14, 1974, Washington Papers, Illinois State Representative Records, Box 6, Folder 11b (quote); Travis, *Harold, the People's Mayor*, 82–83.

35. "Statement to Committee for a Black Mayor."

36. *Chicago Tribune*, December 10, 1974, March 21, 1975; W. Grimshaw, *Bitter Fruit*, 136–37; Biles, *Richard J. Daley*, 203–4; William J. Grimshaw, "Unraveling the Enigma: Mayor Harold Washington and the Black Political Tradition," *Urban Affairs Quarterly* 23 (December 1987): 200 (quote).

37. Travis, *Harold, the People's Mayor*, 91 (quote); McClory, "Up from Obscurity," 8–10.

38. Biles, *Richard J. Daley*, 232–33.

39. *Chicago Tribune*, December 29, 1976, January 9, 1977; *Chicago Defender*, January 5, 6, 1977; W. Grimshaw, *Bitter Fruit*, 150–51; Travis, *Harold, the People's Mayor*, 99–101.

40. *Chicago Sun-Times*, January 22, 1977; Rivlin, *Fire on the Prairie*, 35–36; Travis, *Harold, the People's Mayor*, 102–5.

41. W. Grimshaw, *Bitter Fruit*, 151; Travis, *Harold, the People's Mayor*, 107–8; McClory, "Up from Obscurity," 7–8.

42. Jacky Grimshaw, interview by the author, May 8, 2015, Chicago; *Chicago Tribune*, February 19, 20, 1977; *Chicago Defender*, February 22, 1977; Travis, *Harold, the People's Mayor*, 108 (quote). See also *Chicago Sun-Times*, March 18, 1977.

43. Press release, April 7, 1977, Washington Papers, Illinois State Senate Records, Box 11, Folder 3; Paul Kleppner, *Chicago Divided: The Making of a Black Mayor* (DeKalb: Northern Illinois University Press, 1985), 98–99.

44. "Program for a Working City: State Senator Harold Washington," n.d., Washington Papers, Illinois State Senate Records, Box 11, Folder 3.

45. Ibid.; Lanier, "Congressman Harold Washington," 100 (quote).

46. *Chicago Tribune*, February 24, 25, 1977; *Chicago Defender*, March 29, 1977.

47. Daniela Cornescu and Peter d'A. Jones, "Michael Anthony Bilandic," in *Biographical Dictionary of American Mayors, 1820–1980: Big City Mayors,* edited by Melvin G. Holli and Peter d'A. Jones (Westport, CT: Greenwood Press, 1981), 27; W. Grimshaw, *Bitter Fruit*, 151–53; Travis, *Harold, the People's Mayor*, 110–12; Kleppner, *Chicago Divided*, 100–101; Biles, *Richard J. Daley*, 234 (quote). On the 1977 mayoral primary, see Washington Papers, Illinois State Senate Records, Box 11, Folders 1–3.

48. Russell, "Harold Washington," 854 (first quote); W. Grimshaw, *Bitter Fruit*, 153; Travis, *Harold, the People's Mayor*, 114–15; Rivlin, *Fire on the Prairie*, 37; Kleppner, *Chicago Divided*, 103 (second quote). On the 1978 state senate campaign, see Washington Papers, Illinois State Senate Records, Box 11, Folder 4.

49. "Harold Washington to All Black Members of the 81st Illinois General Assembly," January 9, 1979, Washington Papers, Illinois State Senate Records, Box 4a, Folder 1. See also Folders 1–8 for a description of Washington's activities as head of the black caucus.

50. "Senate Bill 745, Statement by State Senator Harold Washington," n.d., ibid., Box 3, Folder 11.

51. "Chicago Legislator Announces State Hearings on Federal Budget Crisis," April 23, 1979, ibid., Box 1, Folder 5.

52. Biles, *Richard J. Daley*, 234–36; Kleppner, *Chicago Divided*, 109–15.

53. Kleppner, *Chicago Divided*, 136 (first quote); Biles, *Richard J. Daley*, 236–37; *Springfield State Journal-Register* clipping, May 9, 1980, Washington Papers, Illinois

State Senate Records, Box 3, Folder 6 (second quote); *Chicago Tribune*, May 22, 1980; *Chicago Defender*, May 12, 1980.

54. *Chicago Tribune*, May 27, 1979; W. Grimshaw, *Bitter Fruit*, 153–54; McClory, "Up from Obscurity," 9–10.

55. McClory, "Up from Obscurity," 9–10.

56. "The Washington Papers," n.d., Washington Papers, Illinois State Senate Records, Box 12, Folder 14. A generous sampling of Washington's 1980 campaign literature can be found in Box 11, Folders 5–21, and Box 12, Folders 1–14.

57. "Sen. Harold Washington: A Leader with a Proud Past," n.d., Washington Papers, Illinois State Senate Records, Box 11, Folder 13.

58. McClory, "Up from Obscurity," 10–14; Travis, *Harold, the People's Mayor*, 117–21; *Chicago Tribune*, March 6, 20, 1980.

59. *Chicago Tribune*, February 4, 1981; *Congressional Quarterly Almanac*, 97th Cong., 2nd Sess., 1982, vol. 38 (Washington, D.C.: Congressional Quarterly, 1983), 21-C; "Civil Liberties Alert," *Legislative Newsletter of the ACLU* (October–November 1982): 11–14; draft of untitled speech, n.d., Washington Papers, U.S. Congressional Records, Box 35, Folder 48 (quote); Rivlin, *Fire on the Prairie*, 38; Washington to James R. Jones, February 25, 1981, Washington Papers, U.S. Congressional Records, Box 11, Folder 32.

60. George W. Crockett Jr. to Washington, December 17, 1981, Washington Papers, U.S. Congressional Records, Box 3, Folder 17; Alkalimat and Gills, *Harold Washington*, 52; Levinsohn, *Harold Washington*, 173 (quote).

61. Walter E. Fauntroy to Congressional Membership, May 3, 1982, Washington Papers, U.S. Congressional Records, Box 11, Folder 6.

62. *Chicago Defender*, March 31, 1982; *Chicago Tribune*, August 27, 1981.

63. Washington to members of the Congressional Black Caucus, April 29, 1981, Washington Papers, U.S. Congressional Records, Box 17, Folder 7; Harold Washington, excerpt from *Congressional Digest*, n.d., ibid., Box 16, Folder 23 (quote); Ronald Reagan to Washington, June 30, 1982, ibid., Box 16, Folder 16; *Chicago Tribune*, June 24, 1982.

64. Lanier, "Congressman Harold Washington," 100.

65. Washington, untitled press release, March 2, 1981, Washington Papers, U.S. Congressional Records, Box 34, Folder 45.

66. *Chicago Defender*, January 22, 1981; Travis, *Harold, the People's Mayor*, chap. 11.

67. W. Grimshaw, *Bitter Fruit*, 169; Levinsohn, *Harold Washington*, 176–79; Travis, *Harold, the People's Mayor*, 135–41.

68. J. Grimshaw, interview.

Chapter 2. The Plan and the Man

1. Roger Biles, "Black Mayors: A Historical Assessment," *Journal of Negro History* 77 (Summer 1992): 109–25; Jeffrey S. Adler, introduction to *African-American Mayors:*

Race, Politics, and the American City, edited by David R. Colburn and Jeffrey S. Adler (Urbana: University of Illinois Press, 2001), 1–4. See also William E. Nelson Jr. and Philip J. Meranto, *Electing Black Mayors: Political Action in the Black Community* (Columbus: Ohio State University Press, 1977); George C. Galster and Edward W. Hill, eds., *The Metropolis in Black and White* (New Brunswick, N.J.: Rutgers University Press, 1992); and several of the essays in Richard M. Bernard, ed., *Snowbelt Cities: Metropolitan Politics in the Northeast and Midwest since World War II* (Bloomington: Indiana University Press, 1990).

2. Paul Kleppner, *Chicago Divided: The Making of a Black Mayor* (DeKalb: Northern Illinois University Press, 1985), 74. On the history of race and politics in Chicago, see the following: Margaret Garb, *Freedom's Ballot: African American Political Struggles in Chicago from Abolition to the Great Migration* (Chicago: University of Chicago Press, 2014); St. Clair Drake and Horace Cayton, *Black Metropolis: A Study of Negro Life in the Northern City*, rev. ed. (Chicago: University of Chicago Press, 1993); Harold F. Gosnell, *Negro Politicians: The Rise of Negro Politics in Chicago* (Chicago: University of Chicago Press, 1967); Allan H. Spear, *Black Chicago: The Making of a Negro Ghetto, 1890–1920* (Chicago: University of Chicago Press, 1967); Charles R. Branham, "A Transformation of Black Political Leadership in Chicago, 1864–1942" (Ph.D. diss., University of Chicago, 1981); John W. Allswang, *A House for All Peoples: Ethnic Politics in Chicago, 1890–1936* (Lexington: University Press of Kentucky, 1971); Alex Gottfried, *Boss Cermak of Chicago: A Study of Political Leadership* (Seattle: University of Washington Press, 1962); Roger Biles, *Big City Boss in Depression and War: Mayor Edward J. Kelly of Chicago* (DeKalb: Northern Illinois University Press, 1984); Christopher Robert Reed, *The Depression Comes to the South Side: Protest and Politics in the Black Metropolis, 1930–1933* (Bloomington: Indiana University Press. 2011); Roger Biles, *Richard J. Daley: Politics, Race, and the Governing of Chicago* (DeKalb: Northern Illinois University Press, 1995); and William J. Grimshaw, *Bitter Fruit: Black Politics and the Chicago Machine, 1931–1991* (Chicago: University of Chicago Press, 1992).

3. Biles, *Big City Boss*, 96–102. See also Christopher Manning, *William L. Dawson and the Limits of Black Electoral Leadership* (DeKalb: Northern Illinois University Press, 2009); and Robert S. Blakely and Marcus Shepard, *Earl B. Dickerson: A Voice for Freedom and Equality* (Evanston, Ill.: Northwestern University Press, 2006).

4. Biles, *Richard J. Daley*, 80–102.

5. Ibid.

6. Kleppner, *Chicago Divided*, 74–78; Biles, *Richard J. Daley*, 178–81; "Clearing the Slate," *Newsweek*, January 3, 1972, 14.

7. Michael Kirkhorn, "Daley Does It," *New Republic*, March 8, 1975, 10–11; W. Grimshaw, *Bitter Fruit*, 126; Kleppner, *Chicago Divided*, 87–89; Biles, *Richard J. Daley*, 204.

8. "How the Daley Machine Rolls," *Time*, March 29, 1976, 14 (quote); Biles, *Richard J. Daley*, 221; W. Grimshaw, *Bitter Fruit*, 136–38.

9. Kleppner, *Chicago Divided*, 97–98; W. Grimshaw, *Bitter Fruit*, 153–56.

10. Ronni Scheier and Laura Washington, "Byrne's Record on Race: Little Fire behind the Rhetoric," *Chicago Reporter* 11 (September 1982): 2; Kleppner, *Chicago Divided*, 110–16; W. Grimshaw, *Bitter Fruit*, 153–56.

11. Scheier and Washington, "Byrne's Record on Race," 2, 4; Gary Rivlin, *Fire on the Prairie: Harold Washington, Chicago Politics, and the Roots of the Obama Presidency*, rev. ed. (Philadelphia: Temple University Press, 2013), 46–49; Kleppner, *Chicago Divided*, 135–43.

12. Kleppner, *Chicago Divided*, 143 (quote); Rivlin, *Fire on the Prairie*, 159–62.

13. Scheier and Washington, "Byrne's Record on Race," 4; Kleppner, *Chicago Divided*, 140–42; *Chicago Tribune*, June 30, 1982 (quote).

14. Jacky Grimshaw, interview by the author, May 8, 2015, Chicago; David Axelrod, *Believer: My Forty Years in Politics* (New York: Penguin Press, 2015), 54.

15. Dempsey J. Travis, *Harold, the People's Mayor: An Authorized Biography of Mayor Harold Washington* (Chicago: Urban Research Press, 1989), 143–45; Axelrod, *Believer*, 55 (quote).

16. *Chicago Defender*, September 1, 1982; Ethan Michaeli, *The "Defender": How the Legendary Black Newspaper Changed America* (Boston: Houghton Mifflin Harcourt, 2016), 481–82; Clarence Page, "Harold Washington's Biggest Challenge," *Chicago* 32 (April 1983): 176; Kleppner, *Chicago Divided*, 147 (quote); Travis, *Harold, the People's Mayor*, 144–45; W. Grimshaw, *Bitter Fruit*, 162–63, 168 .

17. *Chicago Defender*, July 27–31, 1982; *Chicago Tribune*, September 12, 1982; Rivlin, *Fire on the Prairie*, 50; Kleppner, *Chicago Divided*, 145–46; Travis, *Harold, the People's Mayor*, 145–47.

18. *Chicago Tribune*, November 7, 1982; Kleppner, *Chicago Divided*, 150; W. Grimshaw, *Bitter Fruit*, 163–64.

19. *Chicago Tribune*, November 7, 1982.

20. *Chicago Defender*, March 30, October 12, 1982; Kleppner, *Chicago Divided*, 136 (first quote); W. Grimshaw, *Bitter Fruit*, 168 (second and third quotes).

21. *Chicago Tribune*, November 8, 1982; Axelrod, *Believer*, 55 (quote).

22. Travis, *Harold, the People's Mayor*, 157, 158.

23. The emphasis on inclusiveness is evident throughout the publications, correspondence, and memoranda contained in the Mayoral Campaign Records, Harold Washington Papers, Harold Washington Public Library, Chicago. In particular, see the various position papers used in preparation of the Washington Papers.

24. Melvin G. Holli, "Jane M. Byrne: To Think the Unthinkable and Do the Undoable," in *The Mayors: The Chicago Political Tradition*, edited by Paul M. Green and Melvin G. Holli (Carbondale: Southern Illinois University Press, 1987), 174–77; Biles, *Richard J. Daley*, 235–36; *Chicago Tribune*, April 5, 1981; Kleppner, *Chicago Divided*, 126–31; W. Grimshaw, *Bitter Fruit*, 164.

25. Joel Weisman and Ralph Whitehead, "Untangling Black Politics," *Chicagoan* 1 (July 1974): 80 (quote); W. Grimshaw, *Bitter Fruit*, 164.

26. Paul M. Green, "The Primary: Some New Players—Same Old Rules," in *The Making of the Mayor: Chicago, 1983*, edited by Melvin G. Holli and Paul M. Green

(Grand Rapids, Mich.: William B. Eerdmans, 1984), 27; *Chicago Tribune*, February 6, 16, 1983. On public opinion polling, see Richard Day, Jeff Andreasen, and Kurt Becker, "Polling in the 1983 Chicago Mayoral Election," in *Making of the Mayor*, edited by Holli and Green, 85–100.

27. Willie Cole, "Save Our City," *Chicago Reporter* 12 (March 1983): 2; *Chicago Tribune*, February 13, 1984; Kleppner, *Chicago Divided*, 157–60.

28. Cole, "Save Our City," 2–3; *Chicago Defender*, December 25, 1982 (quote); *Chicago Tribune*, January 31, 1983.

29. Keith Koeneman, *First Son: The Biography of Richard M. Daley* (Chicago: University of Chicago Press, 2013), 65 (quote); W. Grimshaw, *Bitter Fruit*, 164; Kleppner, *Chicago Divided*, 126–31; Rivlin, *Fire on the Prairie*, 64–71.

30. Ben Joravsky, "Western Avenue," *Chicago Reporter* 12 (March 1983): 3–5; *Chicago Defender*, November 22, 1982; *Chicago Tribune*, February 21, 1983; Kleppner, *Chicago Divided*, 155–57.

31. Kleppner, *Chicago Divided*, 152–55.

32. Rivlin, *Fire on the Prairie*, 83; Travis, *Harold, the People's Mayor*, 161–70.

33. *Chicago Sun-Times*, March 27, 1983; W. Grimshaw, *Bitter Fruit*, 172–74.

34. J. Grimshaw, interview; Rivlin, *Fire on the Prairie*, 83.

35. Rivlin, *Fire on the Prairie*, 87–88.

36. Ibid., 84–89.

37. Ibid., 94–95.

38. Alfredo S. Lanier, "Congressman Harold Washington," *Chicago* 32 (February 1983): 100 (quote); Kleppner, *Chicago Divided*, 152–55.

39. Alfredo S. Lanier, "Counting the Hispanic Vote," *Chicago* 34 (December 1985): 221; Lanier, "Congressman Harold Washington," 102 (quote).

40. Don Rose, "How the 1983 Mayoral Election Was Won: Reform, Racism, and Rebellion," in *Making of the Mayor*, edited by Holli and Green, 110; Rivlin, *Fire on the Prairie*, 52–63.

41. Harold Baron and Vince Bakeman to Washington, April 26, 1983, Washington Papers, Finance Sub-Cabinet Series, Box 17, Folder 39; Norman Krumholz and Pierre Clavel, eds., *Reinventing Cities: Equity Planners Tell Their Stories* (Philadelphia: Temple University Press, 1994), 99–100; Robert Mier, Kari J. Moe, and Irene Sherr, "Strategic Planning and the Pursuit of Reform, Economic Development, and Equity," *Journal of the American Planning Association* 52 (Summer 1986): 299; Robert Mier and Kari J. Moe, "Decentralized Development: From Theory to Practice," in *Harold Washington and the Neighborhoods: Progressive City Government in Chicago, 1983-1987*, edited by Pierre Clavel and Wim Wiewel (New Brunswick, N.J.: Rutgers University Press, 1991), 71–72. A copy of *The Washington Papers* can be found in Washington Papers, Mayoral Campaign Records, Box 23, Folder 12, Harold Washington Public Library.

42. John Kretzmann, "The Affirmative Information Policy: Opening Up a Closed City," in *Washington and the Neighborhoods*, edited by Clavel and Wiewel, 205–8; Mier and Moe, "Decentralized Development," 75–76.

43. "Neighborhoods: The Washington Papers," n.d., Washington Papers, Mayoral Campaign Records, Box 43, Folder 7.

44. "Harold Washington for Mayor: Economic Development Position Paper," January 1983, ibid., Box 42, Folder 11; Mier and Moe, "Decentralized Development," 67–68; "Mayor Briefs Neighborhood Leaders on Needs Study, City Plan and 10-Year Development Strategy," October 25, 1982, Washington Papers, Development Sub-Cabinet Series, Box 13, Folder 29.

45. "Harold Washington for Mayor."

46. Howard Stanback and Robert Mier, "Economic Development for Whom? The Chicago Model," *Review of Law and Social Change* 15 (1986–87): 13–17.

47. Mier, Moe, and Sherr, "Strategic Planning," 299–300.

48. J. Grimshaw, interview; Rivlin, *Fire on the Prairie*, 89–90; Travis, *Harold, the People's Mayor*, 171.

49. *Chicago Tribune*, January 19, 1983 (quotes); Green, "Primary," 28.

50. *Chicago Tribune*, January 24 (quote), 28, 1983, February 1, 1983; *Chicago Sun-Times*, January 24, 1983.

51. *Chicago Tribune*, February 1, 1983.

52. *Chicago Tribune*, February 3, 1983; Salim Muwakkil, *Harold! Photographs from the Harold Washington Years*, edited by Ron Dorfman (Evanston, Ill.: Northwestern University Press, 2007), 82 (quotes).

53. J. Grimshaw, interview; *Chicago Tribune*, February 2, 3, 1983; Ed McManus, "Chicago's Mayoral Primary," *Illinois Issues* 9 (February 1983): 11 (quote).

54. *Chicago Tribune*, January 23, 1983; *Chicago Sun-Times*, February 3, 1983; Rivlin, *Fire on the Prairie*, 91; Green, "Primary," 28–29; Kleppner, *Chicago Divided*, 174–75.

55. Rivlin, *Fire on the Prairie*, 91–92; W. Grimshaw, *Bitter Fruit*, 169; Kleppner, *Chicago Divided*, 175.

56. *Chicago Defender*, February 7, 1983; *Chicago Tribune*, February 7, 1983; W. Grimshaw, *Bitter Fruit*, 175–76; Kleppner, *Chicago Divided*, 175–76.

57. *Chicago Tribune*, February 7, 1983 (quotes); Kleppner, *Chicago Divided*, 176.

58. *Chicago Tribune*, February 21, 1983; *Chicago Sun-Times*, February 21, 1983; Rivlin, *Fire on the Prairie*, 98–100; W. Grimshaw, *Bitter Fruit*, 176–77.

59. Travis, *Harold, the People's Mayor*, 176–77.

60. *Chicago Tribune*, February 21, 22, 1983.

61. Ibid., February 22, 23, 1983; Rivlin, *Fire on the Prairie*, 102; Page, "Harold Washington's Biggest Challenge," 175 (quote).

62. *Chicago Tribune*, February 26, 1983 (first quote); Kleppner, *Chicago Divided*, 188-89; Rivlin, *Fire on the Prairie*, 105–7; Page, "Harold Washington's Biggest Challenge," 176 (second quote).

63. Muwakkil, *Harold!*, 80; W. Grimshaw, *Bitter Fruit*, 171.

64. Paul M. Green, "Washington's Victory: Divide and Conquer," *Illinois Issues* 9 (April 1983): 15–20; Rivlin, *Fire on the Prairie*, 103 (quote).

65. J. Grimshaw, interview; Rivlin, *Fire on the Prairie*, 104–8; Kleppner, *Chicago Divided*, 189 (first quote); *Chicago Tribune*, February 27, 1983 (second quote).

66. Kleppner, *Chicago Divided*, 191 (first and second quotes); David Orr, interview by the author, May 8, 2014, Chicago (third quote).

67. *Chicago Tribune*, March 6 (Burke quote), 9 (Vrdolyak quote), 1983; Rose, "How the 1983 Mayoral Election Was Won," 104 (Washington quote); W. Grimshaw, *Bitter Fruit*, 178.

68. Travis, *Harold, the People's Mayor*, 182; Kleppner, *Chicago Divided*, 189–90; Adam Doster, "How Mayor Harold Washington Shaped the City of Chicago," http://www.chicagomag.com/core/pagetools.php?url=%2FChicago-Magazine%2fThe-31; Rivlin, *Fire on the Prairie*, 116; Michaeli, *"Defender,"* 490.

69. "Biography," n.d., Bernard J. Epton Papers, Box 1, Folder 1, University of Illinois at Chicago. I consulted three collections of Epton Papers—one box of materials on the 1983 mayoral campaign can be found in Special Collections at the University of Illinois at Chicago, one box at the Chicago History Museum very closely resembles the UIC Collection, and three and a half boxes of materials at the Abraham Lincoln Presidential Library, Springfield, Illinois, mostly deal with Epton's career in the Illinois General Assembly.

70. "Summary of Bernard Epton's Legislative Record, 1977–82," Washington Papers, Mayoral Campaign Records, Box 23, Folder 17; *Chicago Tribune*, April 3, 1983; Travis, *Harold, the People's Mayor*, 189; Rose, "How the 1983 Mayoral Election Was Won," 105–6; Rivlin, *Fire on the Prairie*, 108.

71. *Chicago Defender*, February 24, 1983; *Wall Street Journal*, March 1, 1983; Kleppner, *Chicago Divided*, 202–3; *Chicago Tribune*, February 24–26, 1983.

72. *Wall Street Journal*, March 1, 1983; *Chicago Tribune*, March 6, 1983 (quote); Kleppner, *Chicago Divided*, 200; J. Grimshaw, interview.

73. "The Case against Harold Washington," March 12, 1983, Epton Papers, Box 1, Folder 10, Chicago History Museum; *Chicago Tribune*, March 23, 1983; Travis, *Harold, the People's Mayor*, 190; Kleppner, *Chicago Divided*, 205–6; Rose, "How the 1983 Mayoral Election Was Won," 110 (quote).

74. "Report of Proceedings," *United States of America v. Harold Washington*, U.S. District Court, Northern District of Illinois, Eastern Division, March 27, 1972, Epton Papers, Box 1, Folder 10, University of Illinois at Chicago; "Committee to Elect Harold Washington Mayor of the City of Chicago," n.d., Washington Papers, Mayoral Campaign Records, Box 23, Folder 9; "Case against Harold Washington"; Rivlin, *Fire on the Prairie*, 114–15 (first quote); Lanier, "Congressman Harold Washington," 100 (second quote); Robert McClory, "Up from Obscurity: Harold Washington," in *Making of the Mayor*, edited by Holli and Green, 13 (third quote).

75. "Statement of James R. Thompson, United States Attorney for the Northern District of Illinois," March 27, 1972, Epton Papers, Box 3.5, Folder 3, Abraham Lincoln Presidential Library; "Committee to Elect Harold Washington Mayor of the City of Chicago"; "Text of Special Election-Eve Radio Broadcast by Bernard Epton," April 10, 1983, Epton Papers, Box 3.5, Folder 3, Abraham Lincoln Presidential Library.

76. "Committee to Elect Harold Washington Mayor of the City of Chicago"; "Case against Harold Washington"; McClory, "Up from Obscurity," 13.

77. "Special Election-Eve Radio Broadcast"; Rose, "How the 1983 Mayoral Election Was Won," 116–17.

78. *Chicago Tribune*, March 17, 1983 (first quote); Rivlin, *Fire on the Prairie*, 112; Kleppner, *Chicago Divided*, 194 (second quote).

79. *Chicago Tribune*, March 23, 1983 (quotes); W. Grimshaw, *Bitter Fruit*, 179–80; Kleppner, *Chicago Divided*, 205–6.

80. Paul M. Green, "Chicago Election: The Numbers and the Implications," *Illinois Issues* 9 (August 1983): 14 (first quote); Kleppner, *Chicago Divided*, 207 (second and third quotes); Travis, *Harold, the People's Mayor*, 191 (fourth quote).

81. "Transcript of Statement of Harold Washington," March 22, 1983, Epton Papers, Box 3.5, Folder 3, Abraham Lincoln Presidential Library; Citizens for Epton Press Release, March 23, 1983, Epton Papers, ibid.

82. *Chicago Tribune*, April 3, 1983 (quote); Kleppner, *Chicago Divided*, 227–28; Bill Grimshaw to Al Raby, memorandum, March 2, 1983, Washington Papers, Mayoral Campaign Records, Box 23, Folder 17; "Summary of Bernard Epton's Legislative Record, 1977–82," n.d., ibid.

83. "Candidate Epton Releases Health Statement," n.d., Epton Papers, Box 1, Folder 2, University of Illinois at Chicago; Rivlin, *Fire on the Prairie*, 121–22; Kleppner, *Chicago Divided*, 213–24.

84. *Chicago Tribune*, March 29, 1983; "Chicago's Ugly Election," *Newsweek*, April 11, 1983, 18–21; "Racial Brush Fires," *New Republic*, April 18, 1983, 12–13; Rose, "How the 1983 Mayoral Election Was Won," 119–20.

85. Transcript of John Madigan Editorial, WBBM Newsradio 78, April 7, 1983, Epton Papers, Box 1, Folder 5, University of Illinois at Chicago; Rose, "How the 1983 Mayoral Election Was Won," 117–18; W. Grimshaw, *Bitter Fruit*, 181; *Chicago Tribune*, April 8, 9, 1983.

86. *Chicago Tribune*, April 9, 1983.

87. Rivlin, *Fire on the Prairie*, 124; Kleppner, *Chicago Divided*, 232–33.

88. "Transcript of U.S. Rep. Harold Washington's Response to President Reagan on Behalf of the National Democratic Party," March 12, 1983, Washington Papers, Mayoral Campaign Records, Box 27, Folder 24; *Chicago Tribune*, April 10, 1983; Kleppner, *Chicago Divided*, 229 (quote); W. Grimshaw, *Bitter Fruit*, 182.

89. *Chicago Tribune*, April 13, 1983; Ross Miller, *Here's the Deal: The Buying and Selling of a Great American City* (New York: Alfred A. Knopf, 1996), 181 (first quote); Kleppner, *Chicago Divided*, 235 (second quote); John Schrag, "Washington Mutes Opposition but Gains Few New Supporters," *Chicago Reporter* 16 (May 1987): 8–9; Green, "Chicago Election," 17–18; Gary Rivlin, "The Blacks and the Browns: Is the Coalition Coming Apart?," *Chicago Reader*, November 5, 1987. For background on African American–Latino voting coalitions, see Gordon K. Mantler, *Power to the Poor: Black-Brown Coalition and the Fight for Economic Justice, 1960–1974* (Chapel Hill: University of North Carolina Press, 2013).

90. *Chicago Tribune*, April 14, 1983 (first and second quotes); Kleppner, *Chicago Divided*, 296–97n1 (third and fourth quotes).

91. Kleppner, *Chicago Divided*, 241.

92. Travis, *Harold, the People's Mayor*, 195–96.

93. *Chicago Tribune*, April 14, 1983.

94. Florence Hamlish Levinsohn, *Harold Washington: A Political Biography* (Chicago: Chicago Review Press, 1983), 235 (quote); Rivlin, *Fire on the Prairie*, 125–26; Orr, interview.

Chapter 3. The Devalued Prize

1. *Chicago Tribune*, April 30, 1983; Dempsey J. Travis, *Harold, the People's Mayor: An Authorized Biography of Mayor Harold Washington* (Chicago: Urban Research Press, 1989), 199–203.

2. Travis, *Harold, the People's Mayor*, 205–6. The entire inaugural address is available in Harold Washington, *Climbing a Great Mountain: Selected Speeches of Mayor Harold Washington*, commentary by Alton Miller (Chicago: Basic Books, 1988).

3. Harold Washington to Jane Byrne, April 18, 1983, Harold Washington Papers, Chief of Staff Files, Box 13, Folder 5, Harold Washington Public Library, Chicago; "First Inaugural Address," April 29, 1983, in *Climbing a Great Mountain*, by Washington, 1–7; "1983 Financial Plan," Washington Papers, July 25, 2983, Finance Sub-Cabinet Files, Box 12, Folder 56; *Chicago Tribune*, April 30, 1983; Paul Kleppner, *Chicago Divided: The Making of a Black Mayor* (DeKalb: Northern Illinois University Press, 1985), 242; Travis, *Harold, the People's Mayor*, 203, 206–8.

4. Jon C. Teaford, *The Twentieth-Century American City: Problem, Promise, and Reality* (Baltimore: Johns Hopkins University Press, 1986), 147 (first quote); William Julius Wilson, *The Declining Significance of Race: Blacks and Changing American Institutions* (Chicago: University of Chicago Press, 1978), 139 (second quote); H. Paul Friesema, "Black Control of Central Cities: The Hollow Prize," *Journal of the American Institute of Planners* 35 (March 1969): 77; Roger Biles, "Black Mayors: A Historical Assessment," *Journal of Negro History* 77 (Summer 1992): 115–17; John H. Mollenkopf, "The Post-war Politics of Urban Development," *Politics and Society* 5 (September 1975): 292; Adolph Reed Jr., "The Black Urban Regime: Structural Origins and Constraints," in *Power, Community, and the City*, edited by Michael Peter Smith (New Brunswick, N.J.: Transaction Books, 1988), 161. See also Larry Bennett, "Harold Washington and the Black Urban Regime," *Urban Affairs Quarterly* 28 (March 1993): 423–40. On the shrinking federal commitment to urban America, see Roger Biles, *The Fate of Cities: Urban America and the Federal Government, 1945–2000* (Lawrence: University Press of Kansas, 2011).

5. "The Financial Challenge: 1986 Budget Talking Points," November 4, 1985, Washington Papers, Central Office Files, Box 2, Folder 26; Roger Biles, *Illinois: A History of the Land and Its People* (DeKalb: Northern Illinois University Press, 2005), 289–90.

6. Dominic A. Pacyga, *Chicago: A Biography* (Chicago: University of Chicago Press, 2009), 315, 366; Harold M. Mayer and Richard C. Wade, *Chicago: Growth of a Metropolis* (Chicago: University of Chicago Press, 1969), 426, 428, 430; Robert G. Spinney,

City of Big Shoulders: A History of Chicago (DeKalb: Northern Illinois University Press, 2000), 257–58; Gregory D. Squires et al., *Chicago: Race, Class, and the Response to Urban Decline* (Philadelphia: Temple University Press, 1987), 29.

7. Dominic A. Pacyga, *Slaughterhouse: Chicago's Union Stock Yard and the World It Made* (Chicago: University of Chicago Press, 2015), 166–72; Pacyga, *Chicago: A Biography*, 316–21; Joel Rast, *Remaking Chicago: The Political Origins of Urban Industrial Change* (DeKalb: Northern Illinois University Press, 1999), 22–26, 59–70.

8. Pacyga, *Chicago: A Biography*, 321; David Ranney, *Global Decisions, Local Collisions: Urban Life in the New World Order* (Philadelphia: Temple University Press, 2003), 120. On deindustrialization in the United States and Canada, see Barry Bluestone and Bennett Harrison, *The Deindustrialization of America: Plant Closings, Community Abandonment, and the Dismantling of Basic Industry* (New York: Basic Books, 1982); Saskia Sassen, *The Mobility of Capital and Labor: A Study in International Investment and Labor Flow* (Cambridge: Cambridge University Press, 1988); Jefferson Cowie, *Capital Moves: RCA's Seventy-Year Quest for Cheap Labor* (Ithaca, N.Y.: Cornell University Press, 1999); Steven High, *Industrial Sunset: The Making of North America's Rust Belt, 1969–1984* (Toronto: University of Toronto Press, 2003); and Joseph Persky and Wim Wiewel, *When Corporations Leave Town: The Costs and Benefits of Metropolitan Sprawl* (Detroit: Wayne State University Press, 2000). See also Tracy Neumann, *Remaking the Rust Belt: The Postindustrial Transformation of North America* (Philadelphia: University of Pennsylvania Press, 2016); Allen Dieterich-Ward, *Beyond Rust: Metropolitan Pittsburgh and the Fate of Industrial America* (Philadelphia: University of Pennsylvania Press, 2016); David Koistinen, "Public Policies for Countering Deindustrialization in Postwar Massachusetts," *Journal of Policy History* 18 (2006): 326–61; John T. Cumbler, *A Social History of Economic Decline: Business, Politics, and Work in Trenton* (New Brunswick, N.J.: Rutgers University Press, 1989); and Sean Safford, *Why the Garden Club Couldn't Save Youngstown: The Transformation of the Rust Belt* (Cambridge, Mass.: Harvard University Press, 2009).

9. William J. Grimshaw, *Bitter Fruit: Black Politics and the Chicago Machine, 1931–1991* (Chicago: University of Chicago Press, 1992), 182 (quote); Gary Rivlin, *Fire on the Prairie: Harold Washington, Chicago Politics, and the Roots of the Obama Presidency*, rev. ed. (Philadelphia: Temple University Press, 2013), 152–55.

10. Rivlin, *Fire on the Prairie*, 153–57 (first and second quotes); *Chicago Tribune*, July 30, 1983 (third quote); Arnold R. Hirsch, "Harold and Dutch Revisited: A Comparative Look at the First Black Mayors of Chicago and New Orleans," in *African-American Mayors: Race, Politics, and the American City*, edited by David R. Colburn and Jeffrey S. Adler (Urbana: University of Illinois Press, 2001), 120–27; W. Grimshaw, *Bitter Fruit*, 182–83; Alton Miller, *Harold Washington: The Mayor, the Man* (Chicago: Bonus Books, 1989), 98 (fourth quote).

11. Abdul Alkalimat and Doug Gills, *Harold Washington and the Crisis of Black Power in Chicago* (Chicago: Twenty-First Century Books, 1989), 118; Bennett, "Harold Washington and the Black Urban Regime," 430–31; Rivlin, *Fire on the Prairie*, 153, 158–60.

12. *Chicago Tribune*, August 26, 1984; Rivlin, *Fire on the Prairie*, 179–80.

13. Rivlin, *Fire on the Prairie*, 184 (Oberman quote); David Orr, interview by the author, May 8, 2014, Chicago.

14. David Moberg, "The Man Who Wants to Break the Mold," *Chicago* 6 (October 1983): 180; Larry Bennett, *Fragments of Cities: The New American Downtowns and Neighborhoods* (Columbus: Ohio State University Press, 1990), 113–14; Rivlin, *Fire on the Prairie*, 156 (quote); Larry Bennett, "The Dilemmas of Building a Progressive Urban Coalition: The Linked Development Debate in Chicago," *Journal of Urban Affairs* 9 (October 1987): 267–69.

15. Bennett, "Dilemmas of Building a Progressive Urban Coalition," 274n2 (quote), 268.

16. *Chicago Tribune*, April 27, 30, 1984; *Chicago Reader*, May 4, 1984 (quote); Bennett, "Dilemmas of Building a Progressive Urban Coalition," 268–69.

17. Washington to Byrne, April 18, 1983, Washington Papers, Chief of Staff Files, Box 13, Folder 5; Moberg, "Man Who Wants to Break the Mold," 170; Rivlin, *Fire on the Prairie*, 151.

18. Alton Miller, interview by the author, June 3, 2015, Chicago. See Dick Simpson, *Rogues, Rebels, and Rubber Stamps: The Politics of the Chicago City Council from 1863 to the Present* (Boulder, Colo.: Westview Press, 2001).

19. Orr, interview; Moberg, "Man Who Wants to Break the Mold," 174 (first quote); Hirsch, "Harold and Dutch Revisited," 117 (second quote).

20. *Chicago Tribune*, April 20, May 3, 4, 1983; Moberg, "Man Who Wants to Break the Mold," 173 (quotes); Rivlin, *Fire on the Prairie*, 135–45; Travis, *Harold, the People's Mayor*, 211–15; Christopher Chandler, *Harold Washington and the Civil Rights Legacy* (San Bernardino, Calif.: Woodbury Press, 2014), 95–98.

21. Rivlin, *Fire on the Prairie*, 142 (first quote); Moberg, "Man Who Wants to Break the Mold," 174 (second quote).

22. Kleppner, *Chicago Divided*, 132–33, 244–47; Rivlin, *Fire on the Prairie*, 141–44, 173 (first quote); Moberg, "Man Who Wants to Break the Mold," 173–75; Emily Kamine Soloff and Greg Hinz, "Berny Stone and the Boys in the Bloc," *Chicago* 33 (September 1984): 212 (second quote). See also Roger Simon, "Mayor Vrdolyak?," *Chicago* 33 (December 1984): 176–81, 222–35.

23. Rivlin, *Fire on the Prairie*, 162–63.

24. *New York Times*, May 4, 1983; *Chicago Tribune*, May 3, 1983; Kleppner, *Chicago Divided*, 242–43; Rivlin, *Fire on the Prairie*, 145 (quote).

25. *Chicago Tribune*, May 17, 1983; *New York Times*, June 28, 1983; Moberg, "Man Who Wants to Break the Mold," 174; Travis, *Harold, the People's Mayor*, 213–15.

26. Rivlin, *Fire on the Prairie*, 149; Washington, *Climbing a Great Mountain*, 13 (Washington quote); Travis, *Harold, the People's Mayor*, 215–16.

27. Executive Order 83-1, Washington Papers, Press Office Files, Box 16, Folder 1; Moberg, "Man Who Wants to Break the Mold," 170–72; Judith Walker, "Reforming the Role of Human Services in City Government," in *Harold Washington and the Neighborhoods: Progressive City Government in Chicago, 1983–1987*, edited by Pierre

Clavel and Wim Wiewel (New Brunswick, N.J.: Rutgers University Press, 1991), 157–58.

28. Simpson, *Rogues, Rebels, and Rubber Stamps*, 223–24; Biles, *Fate of Cities*, 190 (first quote); *Chicago Tribune*, May 9, 27, 1983; Barbara Ferman, *Challenging the Growth Machine: Neighborhood Politics in Chicago and Pittsburgh* (Lawrence: University Press of Kansas, 1996), 104 (second quote).

29. *Chicago Tribune*, May 9, 27, 1983; Ferman, *Challenging the Growth Machine*, 104; Simpson, *Rogues, Rebels, and Rubber Stamps*, 223–24.

30. Ester R. Fuchs, *Mayors and Money: Fiscal Policy in New York and Chicago* (Chicago: University of Chicago Press, 1992), 7–8; *Chicago Tribune*, January 20, 28, February 1, 9, 1980; Washington to Byrne, April 18, 1983, Washington Papers, Chief of Staff Files, Box 13, Folder 5; Rivlin, *Fire on the Prairie*, 152; W. Grimshaw, *Bitter Fruit*, 189 (quote); Melvin G. Holli and Paul M. Green, *Bashing Chicago Traditions: Harold Washington's Last Campaign* (Grand Rapids, Mich.: William B. Eerdmans, 1989), 163–64.

31. Holli and Green, *Bashing Chicago Traditions*, 165; R. C. Longworth, "Holding Actions," *Chicago Tribune Magazine*, April 15, 1984, 18 (quote); Elizabeth Hollander, e-mail interview by the author, September 8, 2015; *Crain's Chicago Business*, December 13, 1982.

32. Pierre Clavel and Wim Wievel, introduction to *Washington and the Neighborhoods*, edited by Clavel and Wiewel, 18–24; *Chicago Tribune*, April 15, 1984 (quote).

33. Elizabeth Hollander, "The Department of Planning under Harold Washington," in *Washington and the Neighborhoods*, edited by Clavel and Wiewel, 123; Ross Miller, *Here's the Deal: The Buying and Selling of a Great American City* (New York: Alfred A. Knopf, 1996), 180–86.

34. "Report of Proceedings of Public Hearing before City Council Committee on Economic Development," October 5, 1983, Robert Mier Papers, Box 1, Folder 1, Chicago History Museum; Robert Mier and Kari J. Moe, "Decentralized Development: From Theory to Practice," in *Washington and the Neighborhoods*, edited by Clavel and Wiewel, 65–70; Rast, *Remaking Chicago*, 109–10; *Chicago Tribune*, August 7, 1983 (quote). Mier died at age fifty-two of exposure to the chemical defoliant Agent Orange, to which he had been exposed during his tour of duty in Vietnam. *New York Times*, February 9, 1995.

35. *Chicago Tribune*, April 15, 1984 (quote); Robert Weir, Wim Wiewel, and Lauri Alpern, "Decentralization of Policy Making under Mayor Harold Washington," in *Research in Urban Policy*, edited by Terry Nichols Clark (Greenwich, Conn.: JAI Press, 1992), 4:88; Howard Stanback and Robert Mier, "Economic Development for Whom? The Chicago Model," *Review of Law and Social Change* 15 (1986–87): 11.

36. Stanback and Mier, "Economic Development for Whom?," 13–14; Mier and Moe, "Decentralized Development," 74–76.

37. Rivlin, *Fire on the Prairie*, 158–59.

38. Joan Fitzgerald and Nancey Green Leigh, *Economic Revitalization: Cases and Strategies for City and Suburb* (Thousand Oaks, Calif.: Sage, 2002), 107–9; Rast, *Remak-*

ing Chicago, 111; Mier and Moe, "Decentralized Development," 83–84; Kenneth M. Reardon, "Local Economic Development in Chicago, 1983–1987" (Ph.D. diss., Cornell University, 1990), 165–70; Pierre Clavel, *Activists in City Hall: The Progressive Response to the Reagan Era in Boston and Chicago* (Ithaca, N.Y.: Cornell University Press, 2010), 125–26; Weir, Wiewel, and Alpern, "Decentralization of Policy Making," 89–90.

39. "Protecting Manufacturing Is Essential for Chicago," n.d., Mier Papers, Box 8, Folder 2.

40. Donna Ducharme, "Planned Manufacturing Districts: How a Community Initiative Became City Policy," in *Washington and the Neighborhoods*, edited by Clavel and Wiewel, 227–37; Fitzgerald and Leigh, *Economic Revitalization*, 109–14; Pierre Clavel and Robert Giloth, "Planning for Manufacturing: Chicago after 1983," *Journal of Planning History* 14 (February 2015): 21; Clavel, *Activists in City Hall*, 140–42; Gregory Schrock, "Taking Care of Business? Connecting Workforce and Economic Development in Chicago" (Ph.D. diss., University of Illinois at Chicago, 2010), 114.

41. *Chicago Tribune*, May 10–14, 1981; Mier and Moe, "Decentralized Development," 77–78; Robert Mier, Kari J. Moe, and Irene Sherr, "Strategic Planning and the Pursuit of Reform, Economic Development, and Equity," *Journal of the American Planning Association* 52 (Summer 1986): 299–300; *Chicago Tribune*, August 7, 1983 (quote).

42. Robert Mier, *Social Justice and Local Development Policy* (Newbury Park, Calif.: Sage, 1993), 93.

43. Mier and Moe, "Decentralized Development," 78–81.

44. Robert Mier to Ira Bach, Jerome Butler, Brenda Gaines, Liz Hollander, and Thomas Kapsalis, memorandum, October 12, 1983, Mier Papers, Box 5, Folder 5; "Mayor's Development Subcabinet," May 1986, Washington Papers, Intergovernmental Affairs Files, Box 16, Folder 4; Mier, Moe, and Sherr, "Strategic Planning," 300; Mier and Moe, "Decentralized Development," 81.

45. Roger Biles, *Richard J. Daley: Politics, Race, and the Governing of Chicago* (DeKalb: Northern Illinois University Press, 1995), 226–27; Holli and Green, *Bashing Chicago Traditions*, 139–41.

46. Holli and Green, *Bashing Chicago Traditions*, 139–41; Mier and Moe, "Decentralized Development," 85–86.

47. Anne B. Shlay and Robert P. Giloth, "The Social Organization of a Land-Based Elite: The Case of the Failed Chicago's 1992 World's Fair," *Journal of Urban Affairs* 9 (December 1987): 305–9, 318–20; Squires et al., *Chicago*, 160; William Braden, "Taking a Flier on a World's Fair," *Chicago* 33 (October 1984): 181–82, 248–49.

48. Chicago 1992 Committee, "Employment and the 1992 Chicago World's Fair," September 1984, Washington Papers, Development Sub-Cabinet Files, Box 16, Folder 50; Shlay and Giloth, "Social Organization of a Land-Based Elite," 308.

49. Shlay and Giloth, "Social Organization of a Land-Based Elite," 308–14; Doug Gills, "Chicago Politics and Community Development: A Social Movement Perspective," in *Washington and the Neighborhoods*, edited by Clavel and Wiewel, 48–49; Braden, "Taking a Flier on a World's Fair," 181–83.

50. Gills, "Chicago Politics and Community Development," 48–49; Maria de los Angeles Torres, "The Commission on Latino Affairs: A Case Study of Community Empowerment," in *Washington and the Neighborhoods*, edited by Clavel and Wiewel, 178–79; Chicago 1992 Committee, "Employment and the 1992 Chicago World's Fair"; Braden, "Taking a Flier on a World's Fair," 183.

51. Shlay and Giloth, "Social Organization of a Land-Based Elite," 320–21; Torres, "Commission on Latino Affairs," 178–79; Hollander, "Department of Planning," 132 (quote).

52. *Chicago Tribune*, December 11, 1983; Larry Bennett, "Beyond Urban Renewal: Chicago's North Loop Redevelopment Project," *Urban Affairs Review* 22 (December 1986): 242–60; R. Miller, *Here's the Deal*, 179–91; Squires et al., *Chicago*, 174; Ira J. Bach to Elizabeth Hollander and Rob Mier, March 2, 1984, and Mier and Hollander to Washington, March 5, 1984, Washington Papers, Development Sub-Cabinet Files, Box 6, Folder 19.

53. Douglas Bukowski, "Navy Pier," in *The Encyclopedia of Chicago*, edited by James R. Grossman, Ann Durkin Keating, and Janice L. Reiff (Chicago: University of Chicago Press, 2004), 561; William F. Ware to Ira J. Bach, April 17, 1984, Washington Papers, Chief of Staff Files, Box 9, Folder 8; Mier, Moe, and Sherr, "Strategic Planning," 302–3. On the history of Navy Pier, see Douglas Bukowski, *Navy Pier: A Chicago Landmark* (Chicago: Metropolitan Pier and Exposition Authority, 1996). On James Rouse, see Nicholas Dagen Bloom, *Merchant of Illusion: James Rouse, America's Salesman of the Businessman's Utopia* (Columbus: Ohio State University Press, 2004).

54. Ware to Bach, April 17, 1984, Washington Papers, Chief of Staff Files, Box 9, Folder 8.

55. Norman Krumholz and Pierre Clavel, eds., *Reinventing Cities: Equity Planners Tell Their Stories* (Philadelphia: Temple University Press, 1994), 78.

56. Ware to Bach, April 17, 1984, Washington Papers, Chief of Staff Files, Box 9, Folder 8; "Window on the Future: Final Report Summary of the Mayor's Navy Pier Task Force," 1986, Washington Papers, Office Files, Box 17, Folder 49; Wim Wievel and Pierre Clavel, conclusion to *Washington and the Neighborhoods*, edited by Clavel and Wiewel, 286; "Navy Pier Extension," February 2, 1984, Washington Papers, Press Office Files, Box 15, Folder 80.

57. *Chicago Tribune*, October 21, 23 (first quote), 1983; A. Miller, *Harold Washington*, 163 (second quote); Rivlin, *Fire on the Prairie*, 162–65.

58. Rivlin, *Fire on the Prairie*, 165 (quotes); *Chicago Tribune*, October 23, 1983; A. Miller, *Harold Washington*, 103.

59. Jacky Grimshaw, interview by the author, May 8, 2015, Chicago; Reardon, "Local Economic Development," 234–35; Rivlin, *Fire on the Prairie*, 179–80.

60. Chicago business leaders to Washington, December 15, 1983, Washington Papers, Chief of Staff Files, Box 2, Folder 11; *Chicago Tribune*, November 16, December 9, 11, 1983.

61. *Chicago Tribune*, December 23, 28, 1983, January 1, October 7 (quote), 1984.

62. *Chicago Tribune*, January 1, 1984; Brian Kelly, "Harold Washington's Balancing Act," *Chicago* 34 (April 1985): 206; Rivlin, *Fire on the Prairie*, 180.

63. "Chicago's Bond Rating Reduced," news release, March 13, 1984, Washington Papers, Press Office Files, Box 15, Folder 12; *Chicago Tribune*, May 27, 1984 (quote); Fuchs, *Mayors and Money*, 7–8; Holli and Green, *Bashing Chicago Traditions*, 163–64; "Chicago City Council Committee on Finance Mid-term Report," April 30, 1985, Washington Papers, Chief of Staff Files, Box 26a, Folder 3.

64. "Mayor Washington Calls for Racial Reconciliation," April 12, 1984, Washington Papers, Press Office Files, Box 15, Folder 99; Kelly, "Harold Washington's Balancing Act," 206 (first quote); *Chicago Tribune*, January 1 (second and fifth quotes), April 29, 1984 (third and fourth quotes).

65. A. Miller, *Harold Washington*, 126.

66. Ibid., 128.

67. *Chicago Tribune*, April 15, 1984; Holli and Green, *Bashing Chicago Traditions*, 165; Hollander, "Department of Planning," 131–33.

68. Rivlin, *Fire on the Prairie*, 156 (first quote); *Chicago Tribune*, April 13, 1984 (second, third, and fourth quotes).

69. Holli and Green, *Bashing Chicago Traditions*, 167–69.

Chapter 4. Chicago Works Together

1. *Chicago Tribune*, May 1, 1984; *Chicago: City of the Century*, produced and directed by Austin Hoyt (WGBH Boston, 2003, videocassette); Harold Washington to *Wall Street Journal*, August 23, 1984, Washington Papers, Press Office Files, Box 2, Folder 5, Harold Washington Public Library, Chicago.

2. On inclusiveness, see Harold Washington, *Climbing a Great Mountain: Selected Speeches of Mayor Harold Washington*, commentary by Alton Miller (Chicago: Bonus Books, 1988).

3. Useful discussions of Washington's mayoralty within the larger story of black politics include Manning Marable, *Black American Politics* (New York: Schocken Books, 1985); Michael Preston et al., *The New Black Politics: The Search for Political Power* (New York: Longmans, 1987); Abdul Alkalimat and Douglas Gills, *Harold Washington and the Crisis in Black Power* (Chicago: Twenty-First Century Books, 1988); and William J. Grimshaw, *Bitter Fruit: Black Politics and the Chicago Machine, 1931–1991* (Chicago: University of Chicago Press, 1992).

4. "Mayor Washington Calls for Reconciliation," press release, April 12, 1984, Washington Papers, Press Office Files, Box 15, Folder 99; Alton Miller, *Harold Washington: The Mayor, the Man* (Chicago: Bonus Books, 1989), 20–22.

5. Robert Mier and Kari J. Moe, "Decentralized Development: From Theory to Practice," in *Harold Washington and the Neighborhoods: Progressive City Government in Chicago, 1983–1987*, edited by Pierre Clavel and Wim Wiewel (New Brunswick, N.J.: Rutgers University Press, 1991), 82 (quote); Robert Mier, Kari J. Moe, and Irene Sherr, "Strategic Planning and the Pursuit of Reform, Economic Development, and Equity," *Journal of the American Planning Association* 52 (Summer 1986): 300–301.

6. Elizabeth Hollander, "The Department of Planning under Harold Washington," in *Washington and the Neighborhoods*, edited by Clavel and Wiewel, 125–26. A complete copy of the 1984 Chicago Development Plan can be found in the Washington Papers, Chief of Staff Files, Box 22, Folder 2. On job creation, see Robert Giloth and Kari J. Moe, "Jobs, Equity, and the Mayoral Administration of Harold Washington," *Policy Studies Journal* 27 (February 1999): 129–46.

7. Hollander, "Department of Planning," 125.

8. Commercial Club of Chicago, *Make No Little Plans: Jobs for Metropolitan Chicago* (Chicago: Commercial Club of Chicago, 1984); Barbara Ferman, *Challenging the Growth Machine: Neighborhood Politics in Chicago and Pittsburgh* (Lawrence: University Press of Kansas, 1996), 120–23; Norman Krumholz, Patrick Costigan, and Dennis Keating, review of *Chicago Works Together: 1984 Development Plan*, by City of Chicago, *Journal of the American Planning Association* 51 (Summer 1985): 395–96.

9. Robert Mier, Wim Wiewel, and Lauri Alpern, "Decentralization of Policy Making under Mayor Harold Washington," in *Research in Urban Policy*, edited by Terry Nichols Clark (Greenwich, Conn.: JAI Press, 1992), 4:85–88.

10. *Chicago Tribune*, April 29, 1984; "Statement by Benjamin Reyes, Administrative Assistant to the Mayor," August 30, 1984, Washington Papers, Press Office Files, Box 15, Folder 108.

11. *Chicago Tribune*, May 13, 1984; Ferman, *Challenging the Growth Machine*, 105.

12. *Chicago Tribune*, May 13, 1984.

13. *Chicago Tribune*, June 7, 1984.

14. *Chicago Tribune*, May 24, 1984; A. Miller, *Harold Washington*, 103.

15. *Chicago Tribune*, May 24, 1984.

16. Ibid.

17. Ibid.

18. *Chicago Tribune*, May 31, July 3, 1984.

19. "1984 Capital Budget: 1984 General Obligation Bond Program, July 1984," Washington Papers, Chief of Staff Files, Box 6, Folder 5; Hollander, "Department of Planning," 127–28; Gary Rivlin, *Fire on the Prairie: Harold Washington, Chicago Politics, and the Roots of the Obama Presidency*, rev. ed. (Philadelphia: Temple University Press, 2013), 171; *Chicago Tribune*, July 15, 1984.

20. Gary Rivlin, "City Hall: How Low They Can Go," *Chicago Reader*, July 26, 1985, http://www.chicagoreader.com/chicago/city-hall-how-low-they-can-go/Content?oid=3583.

21. Washington, *Climbing a Great Mountain*, 47 (quote); Rivlin, *Fire on the Prairie*, 188–96; A. Miller, *Harold Washington*, 178.

22. Rivlin, *Fire on the Prairie*, 188–89.

23. *Chicago Tribune*, November 5, 1983, January 4, 1984; Rivlin, *Fire on the Prairie*, 193 (quote).

24. "Labor Backs Mayor Washington's Amendment to Democratic Platform," press release, July 12, 1984, Washington Papers, Press Office Files, Box 15, Folder 41; *Chicago Tribune*, July 16, 18 19, 20, 1984.

25. A. Miller, *Harold Washington*, 103; Rivlin, *Fire on the Prairie*, 194; *Chicago Tribune*, July 19, 20, 1984.

26. *New York Times*, June 29, July 17, 1984; Rivlin, *Fire on the Prairie*, 194–96; A. Miller, *Harold Washington*, 145–46 (quote).

27. A. Miller, *Harold Washington*, 145–46.

28. Ibid., 145–50; Rivlin, *Fire on the Prairie*, 195.

29. Rivlin, *Fire on the Prairie*, 195–96; A. Miller, *Harold Washington*, 143–50.

30. A. Miller, *Harold Washington*, 152.

31. "Mayor Names Kit Duffy as Gay/Lesbian Liaison," press release, February 22, 1984, Washington Papers, Press Office Files, Box 15, Folder 53; A. Miller, *Harold Washington*, 153.

32. Rivlin, *Fire on the Prairie*, 168 (quote).

33. Ibid., 198; *Chicago Tribune*, September 9, 1984.

34. Washington to the Chicago City Council, August 29, 1984, Washington Papers, Press Office Files, Box 2, Folder 3; Washington to Edward M. Burke, September 10, 1984, Washington Papers, Chief of Staff Files, Box 8, Folder 4; *Chicago Tribune*, September 23, 1984.

35. Executive Order 84-7, Washington Papers, Press Office Files, Box 16, Folder 2; Xolela Mangcu, "Harold Washington and the Cultural Transformation of Local Government in Chicago, 1983–1987" (Ph.D. diss., Cornell University, 1977), 146; Ferman, *Challenging the Growth Machine*, 113–18; Howard Stanback and Robert Mier, "Economic Development for Whom? The Chicago Model," *Review of Law and Social Change* 15, no. 1 (1986–87): 16–18; Gregory Schrock, "Taking Care of Business? Connecting Workforce and Economic Development in Chicago" (Ph.D. diss., University of Illinois at Chicago, 2010), 17; A. Miller, *Harold Washington* 174 (quote).

36. "Developing a Minority and Women-Owned Business Enterprise (M/WBE) Procurement Program: Executive Summary," March 1985, Washington Papers, Press Office Files, Box 3, Folder 3; *Chicago Tribune*, March 29, 1985 (quote); Mangcu, "Washington and the Cultural Transformation of Local Government," 150–56; Ferman, *Challenging the Growth Machine*, 113–14; Executive Order 85-2, Washington Papers, Press Office Files, Box 16, Folder 3.

37. Ferman, *Challenging the Growth Machine*, 114–15; Merrill Goozner, "Genesis of a Fraud: Where the City Failed," *Crain's Chicago Business* 8 (March 28, 1985): 1.

38. Goozner, "Genesis of a Fraud," 58; Mangcu, "Washington and the Cultural Transformation of Local Government," 152.

39. *Chicago Tribune*, September 23 (first quote), October 7 (second quote), 1984.

40. "O'Hare Construction to Halt," press release, September 14, 1984, Washington Papers, Press Office Files, Box 15, Folder 83; *Chicago Tribune*, October 7, 1984; Washington to the Chicago City Council, August 29, 1984, Washington Papers, Press Office Files, Box 2, Folder 3.

41. *Chicago Tribune*, September 16 (quote), November 21, 1984.

42. *Chicago Tribune*, November 21, 1984.

43. David Orr press release, December 11, 1984, Washington Papers, Press Office Files, Box 15, Folder 2. On the Summerdale scandal, see Roger Biles, *Richard J. Daley:*

Politics, Race, and the Governing of Chicago (DeKalb: Northern Illinois University Press, 1995); and Richard C. Lindberg, *To Serve and Collect: Chicago Politics and Police Corruption from the Lager Beer Riot to the Summerdale Scandal* (Westport, Conn.: Praeger, 1991).

44. *Chicago Tribune*, December 13, 1984.

45. Ware to Joanna Brown, December 26, 1984, Washington Papers, Press Office Files, Box 2, Folder 69 (quote); *Chicago Tribune*, December 28, 1984; Franklin D. Raines to Washington, December 19, 1984, Washington Papers, Chief of Staff Files, Box 8, Folder 4.

46. Memorandum to Chicago Aldermen, December 31, 1984, Washington Papers, Press Office Files, Box 2, Folder 2; *Chicago Tribune*, January 2, 1985.

47. "Statement by William F. Ware, Chief of Staff," December 10, 1984, Washington Papers, Press Office Files, Box 15, Folder 108; Robert Giloth and Robert Mier, "Democratic Populism in the U.S.: The Case of Playskool and Chicago," *Cities: The International Quarterly on Urban Policy and Planning* 3 (February 1986): 72–74; Rivlin, *Fire on the Prairie*, 180 (quote). The negotiations with Playskool are described in several chapters of Clavel and Wiewel, *Washington and the Neighborhoods*.

48. "Playskool, Inc.," in *The Encyclopedia of Chicago*, edited by James R. Grossman, Ann Durkin Keating, and Janice L. Reiff (Chicago: University of Chicago Press, 2004), 940; Robert Brehm, "The City and the Neighborhoods: Was It Really a Two-Way Street?," in *Washington and the Neighborhoods*, edited by Clavel and Wiewel, 250–51; *Chicago Tribune*, December 5, 1984; Kenneth M. Reardon, "Local Economic Development in Chicago, 1983–1987: The Reform Efforts of Mayor Harold Washington" (Ph.D. diss., Cornell University, 1990), 118.

49. *Chicago Tribune*, November 4, 1984 (quote); *New York Times*, February 2, 1985; Brehm, "City and the Neighborhoods," 251–52.

50. *New York Times*, February 2, 1985 (quote); Robert Giloth, "Making Policy with Communities: Research and Development in the Department of Economic Development," in *Washington and the Neighborhoods*, edited by Clavel and Wiewel, 113–15; Gregory D. Squires et al., *Chicago: Race, Class, and the Response to Urban Decline* (Philadelphia: Temple University Press, 1987), 59.

51. Gene O. Armstrong to Robert Mier, memorandum, January 16, 1987, Washington Papers, Finance Sub-Cabinet Files, Box 15, Folder 25; Giloth, "Making Policy with Communities," 114–15.

52. *Chicago Tribune*, February 20, 1985; Rivlin, *Fire on the Prairie*, 200; A. Miller, *Harold Washington*, 52–53.

53. *Chicago Tribune*, February 20, 21, 1985; Rivlin, *Fire on the Prairie*, 200–201; A. Miller, *Harold Washington*, 53.

54. *Chicago Tribune*, February 20, 1985; Rivlin, *Fire on the Prairie*, 201 (quote); A. Miller, *Harold Washington*, 54–62.

55. A. Miller, *Harold Washington*, 64–67.

56. *Chicago Tribune*, July 26, 1984, May 23, 1985.

57. Alton Miller, interview, June 3, 2015, Chicago; *Chicago Tribune*, March 23, 1985; A. Miller, *Harold Washington*, 154 (quote).

58. Rivlin, *Fire on the Prairie*, 202.

59. Harold Washington, "State of the City," April 11, 1985, Washington Papers, Chief of Staff Files, Box 50, Folder 5; Rivlin, *Fire on the Prairie*, 203–4; Dempsey J. Travis, *Harold, the People's Mayor* (Chicago: Urban Research Press, 1989), 217.

60. *Chicago Tribune*, October 10, 1984.

61. Mayor's Advisory Committee on Latino Affairs, "The Proposed 1992 World's Fair: Consequences for Chicago's Latinos," March 1985, Robert Mier Papers, Box 25, Folder 8, Chicago History Museum; untitled press release, March 29, 1984, Washington Papers, Press Office Files, Box 15, Folder 122; Chicago 1992 Committee, "Employment and the 1992 Chicago World's Fair," September 1984, i–ii, Washington Papers, Development Sub-Cabinet Files, Box 16, Folder 50, ii; Anne B. Shlay and Robert P. Giloth, "The Social Organization of a Land-Based Elite: The Case of the Failed Chicago 1992 World's Fair," *Journal of Urban Affairs* 9 (December 1987): 305–24; Elizabeth Hollander, e-mail interview by the author, September 8, 2015.

62. "Navy Pier Task Force Set," press release, March 1, 1985, Washington Papers, Press Office Files, Box 15, Folder 80; Mier, Moe, and Sherr, "Strategic Planning," 302–5.

63. "Chicago Theater Saved, Mayor Announced," press release, November 2, 1984, Washington Papers, Press Office Files, Box 15, Folder 20; untitled press release, September 10, 1986, Washington Papers, Finance Sub-Cabinet Files, Box 2, Folder 38; Larry Bennett, "Beyond Urban Renewal: Chicago's North Loop Redevelopment Project," *Urban Affairs Review* 22 (December 1986): 249–50; Squires et al., *Chicago*, 174; *Chicago Tribune*, June 1, 1985; Ross Miller, *Here's the Deal: The Buying and Selling of a Great American City* (New York: Alfred A. Knopf, 1996), 182–86; Rachel Weber, *From Boom to Bubble: How Finance Built the New Chicago* (Chicago: University of Chicago Press, 2015), 147.

64. Brenda Gaines, interview, July 20, 2015, Chicago; "Mayor Washington Announces Low-Interest Housing Loans," press release, December 19, 1984, Washington Papers, Press Office Files, Box 15, Folder 58; Brian Kelly, "Harold Washington's Balancing Act," *Chicago* 34 (April 1985): 183. The best history of the CHA is D. Bradford Hunt, *Blueprint for Disaster: The Unraveling of Chicago Public Housing* (Chicago: University of Chicago Press, 2009). See also J. S. Fuerst, *When Public Housing Was Paradise: Building Community in Chicago*, with the assistance of D. Bradford Hunt (Urbana: University of Illinois Press, 2005); and Devereux Bowly Jr., *The Poorhouse: Subsidized Housing in Chicago, 1895–1976* (Carbondale: Southern Illinois University Press, 1978).

65. Rivlin, *Fire on the Prairie*, 244 (first quote); A. Miller, *Harold Washington*, 309 (second quote); Hunt, *Blueprint for Disaster*, 261 (third quote).

66. Rivlin, *Fire on the Prairie*, 245; A. Miller, *Harold Washington*, 307; Hunt, *Blueprint for Disaster*, 261–62.

67. Washington, "State of the City"; Kelly, "Harold Washington's Balancing Act," 183; Edward M. Burke, press release, November 29, 1984, Washington Papers, Development Sub-Cabinet Files, Box 2, Folder 21; Washington, *Climbing a Great Mountain*, 44–45. The city council's Finance Committee attributed the lower bond rating, at least in part, to the mayor's failure to produce a long-term financial plan for the city. "Chicago City Council Committee on Finance, Mid-term Report," April 30, 1985, Washington Papers, Chief of Staff Files, Box 26a, Folder 3.

68. "Chicago Development Plan 1984," Washington Papers, Chief of Staff Files, Box 22, Folder 2; Rivlin, *Fire on the Prairie*, 208–9; Harold Baron, "MPAC's Planning Functions," November 18, 1985, Development Sub-Cabinet Files, Box 5, Folder 24. On the distinction between structural and social reform, see Melvin G. Holli, *Reform in Detroit: Hazen S. Pingree and Urban Politics* (New York: Oxford University Press, 1969).

Chapter 5. Balanced Growth

1. Harold Washington, "State of the City," April 11, 1985, Harold Washington Papers, Chief of Staff Files, Box 50, Folder 5, Harold Washington Public Library, Chicago.

2. Ibid.

3. Ibid.

4. Ibid. (quotes); Alton Miller, *Harold Washington: The Mayor, the Man* (Chicago: Bonus Books, 1989), 168–74.

5. Harold Washington, *Climbing a Great Mountain: Selected Speeches of Mayor Harold Washington*, commentary by Alton Miller (Chicago: Bonus Books, 1988), 90 (quote); A. Miller, *Harold Washington*, 95, 108–9.

6. Melvin G. Holli and Paul M. Green, *Bashing Chicago Traditions: Harold Washington's Last Campaign* (Grand Rapids, Mich.: William B. Eerdmans, 1989), 181–84; Robert McClory, "Up from Obscurity: Harold Washington," in *The Making of the Mayor, 1983*, edited by Melvin G. Holli and Paul M. Green (Grand Rapids, Mich.: William B. Eerdmans, 1984), 3 (quote); Gary Rivlin, *Fire on the Prairie: Harold Washington, Chicago Politics, and the Roots of the Obama Presidency*, rev. ed. (Philadelphia: Temple University Press, 2013), 174–76.

7. Florence Hamlish Levinsohn, *Harold Washington: A Political Biography* (Chicago: Chicago Review Press, 1983), 155.

8. McClory, "Up from Obscurity," 3; Holli and Green, *Bashing Chicago Traditions*, 182–84; Alfredo S. Lanier, "Congressman Harold Washington," *Chicago* 32 (February 1983): 100 (first quote); Rivlin, *Fire on the Prairie*, 174–75; Elizabeth Hollander, e-mail interview by the author, September 8, 2015 (second quote).

9. *Chicago Tribune*, May 25, 1985; Rivlin, *Fire on the Prairie*, 208; A. Miller, *Harold Washington*, 341–42.

10. *Chicago Tribune*, October 8, November 21, 1985; A. Miller, *Harold Washington*, 134 (quote).

11. "O'Hare General Airport Revenue Bond Proceedings," November 5, 1985, Washington Papers, Chief of Staff Files, Box 44, Folder 6 (quotes); *Chicago Tribune*, November 14, 20, 1985; A. Miller, *Harold Washington*, 134–36.

12. "Ten Issues to Clarify in Connection with the CDBG Campaign," June–July 1985, Washington Papers, Chief of Staff Files, Box 27, Folder 3; Barbara Ferman, *Challenging the Growth Machine: Neighborhood Politics in Chicago and Pittsburgh* (Lawrence: University Press of Kansas, 1996), 105–6; Howard Stanback and Robert Mier, "Economic Development for Whom? The Chicago Model," *Review of Law and Social Change* 15, no. 1 (1986–87): 18.

13. Mayor Harold Washington, "The State of the City, 1986," April 10, 1986, Washington Papers, Press Office Files, Box 13, Folder 2; *Chicago Tribune*, July 3, 10, 1985; Ferman, *Challenging the Growth Machine*, 106–7.

14. Executive Order 85-2, Washington Papers, Press Office Files, Box 16, Folder 3; Stanback and Mier, "Economic Development for Whom?," 17; Xolela Mangcu, "Harold Washington and the Cultural Transformation of Local Government in Chicago, 1983–1987" (Ph.D. diss., Cornell University, 1997), 146–48, 158–65; Gregory Schrock, "Taking Care of Business? Connecting Workforce and Economic Development in Chicago" (Ph.D. diss., University of Illinois at Chicago, 2010), 138.

15. David Bensman and Mark R. Wilson, "Iron and Steel," in *The Encyclopedia of Chicago*, edited by James R. Grossman, Ann Durkin Keating, and Janice L. Reiff (Chicago: University of Chicago Press, 2004), 425–27; Robert Lewis, *Chicago Made: Factory Networks in the Industrial Metropolis* (Chicago: University of Chicago Press, 2008), chap. 6. David Bensman and Roberta Lynch, *Rusted Dreams: Hard Times in a Steel Community* (Berkeley: University of California Press, 1988), recounts the story of Wisconsin Steel's closing. On that topic, see also Thomas Geoghegan, *Which Side Are You On? Trying to Be for Labor When It's Flat on Its Back* (New York: New Press, 2004); and Christine J. Walley, *Exit Zero: Family and Class in Postindustrial Chicago* (Chicago: University of Chicago Press, 2013). For a broader view of the steel industry's crisis in the 1970s and 1980s, see Judith Stein, *Running Steel, Running America: Race, Economic Policy, and the Decline of Liberalism* (Chapel Hill: University of North Carolina Press, 1998).

16. "Research Findings on Local Steel Industry and Southeast Chicago Are Presented to Mayor's Task Force," press release, December 2, 1985, Washington Papers, Press Office Files, Box 4, Folder 41; Ann R. Markusen, "Steel and Southeast Chicago: Reasons and Opportunities for Industrial Renewal," a research report to the Mayor's Task Force on Steel and Southeast Chicago, 1985, 19; Bensman and Lynch, *Rusted Dreams*, 71–73; Ann R. Markusen, "Planning for Industrial Decline: Lessons from Steel Communities," *Journal of Planning Education and Research* 7 (April 1988): 180; Stephen Alexander, Robert Giloth, and Joshua Lerner, "Chicago's Industry Task Forces: Joint Problem Solving for Local Economic Development," *Economic Development Quarterly* 1, no. 4 (1987): 352–57; David Ranney, *Global Decisions, Local Collisions: Urban Life in the New World Order* (Philadelphia: Temple University Press, 2003), 109. Obama discussed his time as a community organizer in *Dreams from My*

Father: A Story of Race and Inheritance (New York: Three Rivers Press, 1995), chaps. 7–14.

17. "Building on the Basics: Final Report of the Task Force on Steel and Southeast Chicago," n.d., Washington Papers, Development Sub-Cabinet Files, Box 8, Folder 32; Markusen, "Steel and Southeast Chicago," i (quotes); Pierre Clavel, *Activists in City Hall: The Progressive Response to the Reagan Era in Boston and Chicago* (Ithaca, N.Y.: Cornell University Press, 2010), 134–36; "Research Findings on Local Steel Industry"; Pierre Clavel and Robert Giloth, "Planning for Manufacturing: Chicago after 1983," *Journal of Planning History* 14 (February 2015): 25–26.

18. "Research Findings on Local Steel Industry"; Clavel, *Activists in City Hall*, 134–36; "Building on the Basics"; Markusen, "Planning for Industrial Decline," 180; Alexander, Giloth, and Lerner, "Chicago's Industry Task Forces," 354–55.

19. Clavel, *Activists in City Hall*, 137 (quote); Ranney, *Global Decisions, Local Collisions*, 107–8.

20. Richard G. Hankett to Lake Calumet Airport Task Force members, May 29, 1986, Washington Papers, Development Sub-Cabinet Files, Box 8, Folder 20.

21. Gerald S. Kellman and Maurice Richards to Washington, December 19, 1985; Robert Mier to Washington, memorandum, January 2, 1986; and "LTV Fact Sheet," n.d., all in Washington Papers, Finance Sub-Committee Files, Box 13, Folder 69; "Mayor Washington Issues Statement on Steel Crisis," June 5, 1986, Washington Papers, Press Office Files, Box 13, Folder 5.

22. Kellman and Richards to Washington, December 19, 1985; "Republic Steel Corporation," in *The Encyclopedia of Chicago*, edited by Grossman, Keating, and Reiff, 941; Mier to Washington, memorandum, August 7, 1986; "Mayor's Statement on LTV Plant Layoffs," n.d. (quotes), and "LTV Corporation Fact Sheet," n.d., both in Washington Papers, Development Sub-Cabinet Files, Box 2, Folder 25; Mayor Washington's Statement Regarding LTV's Lobbying Efforts for Increased Trade Protection," June 5, 1986, Washington Papers, Press Office Files, Box 13, Folder 5.

23. Elizabeth L. Hollander to Ad Hoc G. O. Bond Issue Strategy Team, August 1, 1985, Washington Papers, Development Sub-Cabinet Files, Box 3, Folder 24; Elizabeth Hollander, "The Department of Planning under Harold Washington," in *Harold Washington and the Neighborhoods: Progressive City Government in Chicago, 1983–1987*, edited by Pierre Clavel and Wim Wiewel (New Brunswick, N.J.: Rutgers University Press, 1991), 127–28; A. Miller, *Harold Washington*, 136–37; Gary Rivlin, "City Hall: How Low They Can Go," *Chicago Reader*, July 26, 1985, http://www.chicagoreader .com/chicago/city-hall-how-low-they-can-go/Content?oid=3583 (quote).

24. *Chicago Tribune*, July 22, 30, August 2, 6, 1985; Hollander, "Department of Planning," 128; Rivlin, *Fire on the Prairie*, 208–9; "Mayor's Neighborhood Bond Program Approved," press release, August 20, 1985, Washington Papers, Development Sub-Cabinet Files, Box 3, Folder 24 (quote); Rivlin, "City Hall."

25. Rivlin, *Fire on the Prairie*, 239.

26. Development Subcabinet to Washington, memorandum, August 14, 1984, Washington Papers, Development Sub-Cabinet Files, Box 4, Folder 32 (quotes);

Larry Bennett, "The Dilemmas of Building a Progressive Urban Coalition: The Linked Development Debate in Chicago," *Journal of Urban Affairs* 9 (October 1987): 267–69; Robert Brehm, "The City and the Neighborhoods: Was It Really a Two-Way Street?," in *Washington and the Neighborhoods*, edited by Clavel and Wiewel, 253–54.

27. Bennett, "Dilemmas of Building a Progressive Urban Coalition," 269–70; Brehm, "City and the Neighborhoods," 255–59; Larry Bennett, *Fragments of Cities: The New American Downtowns and Neighborhoods* (Columbus: Ohio State University Press, 1990), 117–18.

28. "Draft Proposal for Establishing the Mayor's Advisory Committee on Linked Development," n.d., Washington Papers, Development Sub-Cabinet Files, Box 4, Folder 32; Bennett, *Fragments of Cities*, 117; Barbara Ferman and William J. Grimshaw, "The Politics of Housing Policy," in *Research in Urban Policy*, edited by Terry Nichols Clark (Greenwich, Conn.: JAI Press, 1992), 4:121; Bennett, "Dilemmas of Building a Progressive Urban Coalition," 269–70.

29. Bennett, "Dilemmas of Building a Progressive Urban Coalition," 271–74; Brehm, "City and the Neighborhoods," 258–59.

30. Costas Spirou and Larry Bennett, *It's Hardly Sportin': Stadiums, Neighborhoods, and the New Chicago* (DeKalb: Northern Illinois University Press, 2003), 170; Hollander, "Department of Planning," 141. On professional sports and urban politics, see Michael N. Danielson, *Home Team: Professional Sports and the American Metropolis* (Princeton, N.J.: Princeton University Press, 1997); Neil deMause and Joanna Cagan, *Field of Schemes: How the Great Stadium Swindle Turns Public Money into Private Profit* (Lincoln: University of Nebraska Press, 2008); and Dennis R. Judd and Dick Simpson, "Reconstructing the Local State," *American Behavioral Scientist* 46 (April 2003): 1056–69.

31. Hollander, "Department of Planning," 141; Spirou and Bennett, *It's Hardly Sportin',* 119–20.

32. Ernie Barefield to Robert Mier, memorandum, October 24, 1985, Washington Papers, Chief of Staff Files, Box 60, Folder 6; Spirou and Bennett, *It's Hardly Sportin',* 170; Wim Wiewel and Pierre Clavel, conclusion to *Washington and the Neighborhoods*, edited by Clavel and Wiewel, 286.

33. Robert Mier to Angelo Geocaris, Al Johnson, and Ira Edelson, memorandum, October 9, 1985, Washington Papers, Chief of Staff Files, Box 50, Folder 3; Robert Mier and Kari J. Moe, "Decentralized Development: From Theory to Practice," in *Washington and the Neighborhoods*, edited by Clavel and Wiewel, 86–87; Spirou and Bennett, *It's Hardly Sportin',* 66–67. See also Doug Bukowski, *Baseball Palace of the World: The Last Year of Comiskey Park* (Chicago: Lyceum Books, 1991).

34. Ira J. Edelson, Angelo G. Geocaris, and Albert W. Johnson Jr. to Washington, memorandum, December 16, 1985, Washington Papers, Chief of Staff Files, Box 50, Folder 3.

35. Mier to Washington, memorandum, July 10, 1987, Washington Papers, Central Office Files, Box 34, Folder 55 (quotes); Spirou and Bennett, *It's Hardly Sportin',* 67–75.

36. *Chicago Tribune*, May 3, August 4, 1988; Mier and Moe, "Decentralized Development," 87; Spirou and Bennett, *It's Hardly Sportin,'* 70–82.

37. Robert A. Baade and Allen R. Sanderson, "Bearing Down in Chicago," in *Sports, Jobs, and Taxes: The Economic Impact of Sports Teams and Stadiums*, edited by Roger G. Noll and Andrew Zimbalist (Washington, D.C.: Brookings Institution Press, 1997), 330–31; Spirou and Bennett, *It's Hardly Sportin,'* 145–46.

38. *Chicago Tribune*, January 29, 1987; Mier and Moe, "Decentralized Development," 88.

39. Announcement, February 4, 1987, Washington Papers, Development Sub-Committee Files, Box 8, Folder 30; Michael B. McCaskey to Albert W. Johnson, March 2, 1987, Washington Papers, Central Office Files, Box 43, Folder 24.

40. "Final Report of Mayor Washington's Stadium Review Committee," June 8, 1987, Washington Papers, Chief of Staff Files, Box 50, Folder 4.

41. Amanda Seligman, "North Lawndale," in *The Encyclopedia of Chicago*, edited by Grossman, Keating, and Reiff, 575–76. See also Amanda I. Seligman, *Block by Block: Neighborhoods and Public Policy on Chicago's West Side* (Chicago: University of Chicago Press, 2005); and Beryl Satter, *Family Properties: Race, Real Estate, and the Exploitation of Black Urban America* (New York: Henry Holt, 2009).

42. Mier and Al Johnson to Washington, memorandum, April 14, 1987, Washington Papers, Chief of Staff Files, Box 50, Folder 4; Mier and Moe, "Decentralized Development," 88; *Chicago Tribune*, August 29, 1988; Mayor's West Side Development Committee, "Meeting Minutes," October 2, 1987, Washington Papers, Chief of Staff Files, Box 50, Folder 4.

43. *Chicago Tribune*, September 26, 1986, April 23, 1987, August 29, 1988; Spirou and Bennett, *It's Hardly Sportin,'* 150–53; Mier and Moe, "Decentralized Development," 89 (quote). My reading of the football stadium situation is at odds with the interpretation offered by Keith Koeneman, *First Son: The Biography of Richard M. Daley* (Chicago: University of Chicago Press, 2013), 185–86.

44. Douglas G. Power to Barefield, memorandum, June 28, 1985, Washington Papers, Chief of Staff Files, Box 53, Folder 11; Mier and Moe, "Decentralized Development," 89; Spiro and Bennett, *It's Hardly Sportin,'* 119.

45. Robert Mier to Washington, memorandum, May 5, 1986, Washington Papers, Press Office Files, Box 4, Folder 46; Power to Barefield, memorandum, June 28, 1985; Mier to Washington, memorandum, August 12, 1986, Washington Papers, Central Office Files, Box 12, Folder 4; Hollander, "Department of Planning," 141.

46. Hollander, "Department of Planning," 141 (quotes); Robert Mier to Washington, memorandum, August 12, 1986; Mier and Moe, "Decentralized Development," 89.

47. Hollander, "Department of Planning," 141.

48. Barefield to Mier, memorandum, October 24, 1985, Washington Papers, Chief of Staff Files, Box 60, Folder 6; Hollander, "Department of Planning," 131–33. See also Anne B. Shlay and Robert P. Giloth, "The Social Organization of a Land-Based Elite," *Journal of Urban Affairs* 9 (December 1987): 305–24.

49. Robert Mier to Washington, memorandum, March 23, 1984, Washington Papers, Central Office Files, Box 37, Folder 20; untitled news release, March 29, 1984, Washington Papers, Press Office Files, Box 15, Folder 122 (quote).

50. *Chicago Tribune*, June 21, 23, 27, 1985; Doug Gills, "Chicago Politics and Community Development: A Social Movement Perspective," in *Washington and the Neighborhoods*, edited by Clavel and Wiewel, 48–50 (quote).

51. *Chicago Tribune*, June 21, 1985 (quotes); Hollander, "Department of Planning," 145n5.

52. *Chicago Tribune*, June 27, 1985; *New York Times*, June 25, 1985 (first quote); Hollander, "Department of Planning," 133 (second quote).

53. "North Loop Redevelopment Project Tax Increment Financing Feasibility Study," October 27, 1983, Robert Mier Papers, Box 5, Folder 5, Chicago History Museum; Barefield to Mier, memorandum, October 24, 1985, Washington Papers, Chief of Staff Files, Box 60, Folder 6; Larry Bennett, "Beyond Urban Renewal: Chicago's North Loop Redevelopment Project," *Urban Affairs Review* 22 (December 1986): 249–50; "Projects under Negotiation and Construction: North Loop Redevelopment and Conservation," July 1985, Washington Papers, Chief of Staff Files, Box 44, Folder 5; Rachel Weber, *From Boom to Bubble: How Finance Built the New Chicago* (Chicago: University of Chicago Press, 2015), 147; Ross Miller, *Here's the Deal: The Buying and Selling of a Great American City* (New York: Alfred A. Knopf, 1996), 186 (quote).

54. Barefield to Mier, memorandum, October 24, 1985, Washington Papers, Chief of Staff Files, Box 60, Folder 6; Robert Mier, Kari J. Moe, and Irene Sherr, "Strategic Planning and the Pursuit of Reform, Economic Development, and Equity," *Journal of the American Planning Association* 52 (Summer 1986): 305; "Navy Pier Task Force Set," March 1, 1985, Washington Papers, Press Office Files, Box 15, Folder 80; Robert Mier to Washington, memorandum, September 13, 1985, Washington Papers, Chief of Staff Files, Box 44, Folder 1.

55. "Mayor Washington Receives Navy Pier Recommendation," January 17, 1986, Washington Papers, Central Office Files, Box 17, Folder 57; Mier, Moe, and Sherr, "Strategic Planning," 305; Washington to Citizens of Chicago, undated news release, Washington Papers, Central Office Files, Box 50, Folder 7 (quotes); "Navy Pier Fact Sheet," n.d., Washington Papers, Development Sub-Cabinet Files, Box 6, Folder 12.

56. Robert Mier to Washington, March 9, 1987, Washington Papers, Development Sub-Cabinet Files, Box 6, Folder 11; *Chicago Tribune*, January 4, 1987; Koeneman, *First Son*, 131; http://navypier.com (quote).

57. Heywood T. Sanders, *Convention Center Follies: Politics, Power, and Public Investment in American Cities* (Philadelphia: University of Pennsylvania Press, 2014), 3–8, 23, 68–71, 234–35; http://www.mccormickplace.com; *Chicago Tribune*, September 2, 22, 1986; Hollander, "Department of Planning," 125.

58. Barefield to Mier, memorandum, October 24, 1985, Washington Papers, Chief of Staff Files, Box 60, Folder 6; Robert Mier, *Social Justice and Local Development Policy* (Newbury Park, Calif.: Sage, 1993), 107.

59. *Chicago Tribune*, November 1, 1987.

60. *Chicago Tribune*, March 14, 1986 (quote); Hollander, "Department of Planning," 141–43.

61. *Chicago Tribune*, December 4, 24, 25, 29, 31, 1985; Hollander, "Department of Planning," 133–34; Washington, *Climbing a Great Mountain*, 123 (quote); A. Miller, *Harold Washington*, 199–200; Barefield to Philip G. Schreiner, May 28, 1986, Washington Papers, Finance Sub-Committee Files, Box 5, Folder 25.

62. "Working Together: Chicago Federal Agenda, Legislative and Budgetary Issues," 1985, Washington Papers, Chief of Staff Files, Box 22, Folder 3; Rivlin, *Fire on the Prairie*, 248 (quote). On the Reagan administration's treatment of U.S. cities, see Roger Biles, *The Fate of Cities: Urban America and the Federal Government, 1945–2000* (Lawrence: University Press of Kansas, 2011), chap. 8.

63. Washington, press release, March 4, 1985, Washington Papers, Intergovernmental Affairs Files, Box 1, Folder 15 (quotes); "Working Together"; Kenneth M. Reardon, "Local Economic Development in Chicago, 1983–1987: The Reform Efforts of Mayor Harold Washington" (Ph.D. diss., Cornell University, 1990), 272.

64. "Mayor Initiates 'Fair Return' Campaign, Will Travel around the State to Lobby for Federal Funds," May 22, 1986, Washington Papers, Intergovernmental Affairs Files, Box 17, Folder 10; *Champaign-Urbana News-Gazette*, June 3, 1986 (quote); *Chicago Tribune*, May 24, 1986; "Statement by Mayor Harold Washington, Fair Return Campaign, Champaign-Urbana, Illinois," June 2, 1986, Washington Papers, Intergovernmental Affairs Files, Box 13, Folder 3.

65. Biles, *Fate of Cities*, 188–89, 284; *Champaign-Urbana News-Gazette*, June 3, 1986 (quote); "Organizers of the Scientists' Boycott of Star Wars to the Mayors of Illinois Cities and Towns," June 12, 1985, Washington Papers, Intergovernmental Affairs Files, Box 21, Folder 8.

66. "Statement by Mayor Harold Washington, Fair Return Campaign."

67. "Mayor Washington Presents 'Chicago Federal Agenda' to Illinois Legislators and Businesspeople," May 8, 1986, Washington Papers, Intergovernmental Affairs Files, Box 1, Folder 16; *Chicago Tribune*, June 19, 1986; "Mayor Sells National Fair Return Petition Campaign to U.S. Conference of Mayors," June 19, 1986, Washington Papers, Press Office Files, Box 13, Folder 12.

68. Biles, *Fate of Cities*, 284; Alice O'Connor, "Swimming against the Tide: A Brief History of Federal Policy in Poor Communities," in *Urban Problems and Community Development*, edited by Ronald F. Ferguson and William T. Dickens (Washington, D.C.: Brookings Institution Press, 1999), 113–15; Peter Dreier, John Mollenkopf, and Todd Swanstrom, *Place Matters: Metropolitics for the Twenty-First Century*, 2nd ed. (Lawrence: University Press of Kansas, 2004), 138–40.

69. *Chicago Tribune*, June 4, December 31, 1985, January 1, 1986; Dick Simpson, *Rogues, Rebels, and Rubber Stamps: The Politics of the Chicago City Council from 1863 to the Present* (Boulder, Colo.: Westview Press, 2001), 190–91.

70. *Chicago Tribune*, December 26, 30, 1985; Dempsey J. Travis, *Harold, the People's Mayor: An Authorized Biography of Mayor Harold Washington* (Chicago: Urban Research Press, 1989), 232–33.

71. A. Miller, *Harold Washington*, 166–67; Travis, *Harold, the People's Mayor*, 233; Rivlin, *Fire on the Prairie*, 210–11.

72. A. Miller, *Harold Washington*, 208 (quotes); *Chicago Tribune*, December 31, 1985, January 8, 1986; Travis, *Harold, the People's Mayor*, 233–41; Executive Order 86-1, Washington Papers, Press Office Files, Box 16, Folder 4.

73. *Chicago Tribune*, March 20, 1986.

74. *Chicago Tribune*, March 22, 23, April 20, 1986; Luis Gutierrez, *Still Dreaming: My Journey from the Barrio to Capitol Hill* (New York: W. W. Norton, 2013), 198–209.

75. A. Miller, *Harold Washington*, 273–75; Rivlin, *Fire on the Prairie*, 226; Travis, *Harold, the People's Mayor*, 245 (quote); Gutierrez, *Still Dreaming*, 210–27.

76. *New York Times*, May 1, 1986; *Chicago Tribune*, April 30, 1986; A. Miller, *Harold Washington*, 273; Travis, *Harold, the People's Mayor*, 248 (quote).

77. Washington, "State of the City, 1986," April 10, 1986, Washington Papers, Press Office Files, Box 13, Folder 2 (quote); A. Miller, *Harold Washington*, 283–84; Rivlin, *Fire on the Prairie*, 226.

Chapter 6. In Search of a Mandate

1. *Chicago Tribune*, May 1, 4, 9, 1986. See also Louis H. Masotti and Paul M. Green, "Battle for the Hall," *Chicago* 36 (February 1987): 105–7, 134.

2. Gary Rivlin, *Fire on the Prairie: Harold Washington, Chicago Politics, and the Roots of the Obama Presidency*, rev. ed. (Philadelphia: Temple University Press, 2013), 226 (quote); *Chicago Tribune*, June 7, 1986; Alton Miller, *Harold Washington: The Mayor, the Man* (Chicago: Bonus Books, 1989), 274.

3. *Chicago Tribune*, May 10, 31, June 3, 4; Dempsey J. Travis, *Harold, the People's Mayor: An Authorized Biography of Mayor Harold Washington* (Chicago: Urban Research Press, 1989), 249–51.

4. *Chicago Defender*, June 9, 1986; Rivlin, *Fire on the Prairie*, 227; Travis, *Harold, the People's Mayor*, 251–52.

5. Basil Talbott Jr., "Jesse Madison's Big Bout," *Chicago* 36 (November 1987): 145, 184; A. Miller, *Harold Washington*, 258–60; Melvin G. Holli and Paul M. Green, *Bashing Chicago Traditions: Harold Washington's Last Campaign* (Grand Rapids, Mich.: William B. Eerdmans, 1989), 35.

6. *Chicago Tribune*, July 15, 1986; Timothy Wright, "Throwing Rocks on the Inside: Keeping a Progressive Administration Progressive," in *Harold Washington and the Neighborhoods: Progressive City Government in Chicago, 1983–1987*, edited by Pierre Clavel and Wim Wiewel (New Brunswick, N.J.: Rutgers University Press, 1991), 192–93; Jesse D. Madison to Michael J. Hennessy, June 17, 1986, Harold Washington Papers, Press Office Files, Box 2, Folder 74, Harold Washington Public Library, Chicago; A. Miller, *Harold Washington*, 274; Holli and Green, *Bashing Chicago Traditions*, 35–36; Talbott, "Jesse Madison's Big Bout," 187–91. The battle to reform harbor management in the Park District is discussed in R. J. Nelson, *Dirty Waters: Confessions of Chicago's Last Harbor Boss* (Chicago: University of Chicago Press, 2016).

7. *Chicago Tribune*, August 12, 1986; A. Miller, *Harold Washington*, 275–81. The administration's planned budget for the next year can be found in Harold Washington,

"The 1987 Budget Message," Washington Papers, Development Sub-Cabinet Files, Box 10, Folder 10.

8. *Chicago Tribune*, August 27, September 24, 1986.

9. Ibid., September 24, 25, 28, 1986; Ronald D. Picur to Ira Herenstein, October 10, 1986, Washington Papers, Finance and Administration Files, Box 31a, Folder 4 (quote); A. Miller, *Harold Washington*, 277–81.

10. *Chicago Tribune*, September 25, 1986 (quotes); A. Miller, *Harold Washington*, 279–81. The *Chicago Tribune* reported that Natarus spoke with someone in the city hall business office during the recess; Alton Miller wrote that the alderman conversed with his ward committeeman George Dunne.

11. "President Reagan's Proposed 1987 Budget Impact on Chicago," February 18, 1986, Washington Papers, Chief of Staff Files, Box 54, Folder 14; Kenneth M. Reardon, "Local Economic Development in Chicago, 1983–1987: The Reform Efforts of Mayor Harold Washington" (Ph.D. diss., Cornell University, 1990), 272; "President Reagan's Proposed 1988 Budget Impact on Chicago," February 1987, Washington Papers, Central Office Files, Box 48, Folder 8 (quote).

12. *New York Times*, February 23, 1986; *Chicago Tribune*, January 23, 1986 (quote); "North River Commission: Impact of Federal Cuts," n.d., Washington Papers, Intergovernmental Affairs Files, Box 13, Folder 4.

13. Ben Joravsky, "Hispanics: Chicago's Unregistered, Undecided Voters," *Chicago Reporter* 14 (August 1985): 1–6; Maria de los Angeles Torres, "The Commission on Latino Affairs: A Case Study of Community Empowerment," in *Washington and the Neighborhoods*, edited by Clavel and Wiewel, 172–73; Rivlin, *Fire on the Prairie*, 124–25; Wilfredo Cruz, *City of Dreams: Latino Immigration to Chicago* (Lanham, Md.: University Press of America, 2007), 58–59.

14. Maria Torres, Ben Reyes, and Gini Sorrentini to Ernest Barefield, December 11, 1986, Washington Papers, Development Sub-Cabinet Files, Box 11, Folder 8; Alfredo S. Lanier, "Counting the Hispanic Vote," *Chicago* 34 (December 1985): 224; Rivlin, *Fire on the Prairie*, 223 (quote).

15. Executive Order 83-3, Washington Papers, Press Secretary Files, Box 16, Folder 1; Torres, "Commission on Latino Affairs," 174–75; Gary Rivlin, "The Blacks and the Browns: Is the Coalition Coming Apart?," *Chicago Reader*, November 5, 1987, http://www.chicagoreader.com/chicago/the-blacks-and-the-browns/Content?oid=871364.

16. Cruz, *City of Dreams*, 177–79 (quote on 178).

17. Torres, Reyes, and Sorrentini to Barefield, December 11, 1986; Executive Order 85-4, Washington Papers, Press Office Files, Box 16, Folder 3.

18. Rivlin, "Blacks and Browns."

19. John Schrag, "Competing Demands for 'Our Fair Share' Strain Ties That Bind Tenuous Alliance," *Chicago Reporter* 16 (July 1987): 1 (first quote); Rivlin, "Blacks and Browns" (second quote).

20. Rivlin, "Blacks and Browns"; Torres, "Commission on Latino Affairs," 176.

21. Rivlin, "Blacks and Browns"; Torres, "Commission on Latino Affairs," 176; Schrag, "Competing Demands."

22. Lanier, "Counting the Hispanic Vote," 224; Alton Miller, oral history interview, June 3, 2015, Chicago (quote).

23. Lanier, "Counting the Hispanic Vote," 224 (first quote); Larry Bennett, "Harold Washington and the Black Urban Regime," *Urban Affairs Quarterly* 28 (March 1993): 434; Rivlin, *Fire on the Prairie*, 233 (second quote); A. Miller, *Harold Washington*, 172–73; Schrag, "Competing Demands," 7.

24. Lisa Goff, "Despite Woes, Mayor Firm on Minority Jobs," *Crain's Chicago Business* 10 (March 23, 1987): 1; A. Miller, *Harold Washington*, 172 (quote); Washington to Dr. Armando Triana, November 6, 1986, Washington Papers, Development Sub-Cabinet Files, Box 11, Folder 8; Bennett, "Washington and the Black Urban Regime," 435. On the shrinking federal aid to cities, see Roger Biles, *The Fate of Cities: Urban America and the Federal Government, 1945–2000* (Lawrence: University Press of Kansas, 2011).

25. Holli and Green, *Bashing Chicago Traditions*, 36–37.

26. Rivlin, *Fire on the Prairie*, 227–28; Holli and Green, *Bashing Chicago Traditions*, 37–38; A. Miller, *Harold Washington*, 286–87.

27. *Chicago Tribune*, August 28, 1986; A. Miller, *Harold Washington*, 287 (quote).

28. *Chicago Tribune*, August 21, 1986; A. Miller, *Harold Washington*, 288–89.

29. *Chicago Tribune*, July 30, 1986 (quote); Holli and Green, *Bashing Chicago Traditions*, 38–39; Rivlin, *Fire on the Prairie*, 228.

30. *Chicago Tribune*, August 26, October 2, 1986; Holli and Green, *Bashing Chicago Traditions*, 41 (quote).

31. Dominic A. Pacyga, *Chicago: A Biography* (Chicago: University of Chicago Press, 2009), 376–77.

32. *Chicago Tribune*, July 17, 1985; Lanier, "Counting the Hispanic Vote," 221; Pacyga, *Chicago: A Biography*, 377. See the briefing papers that outline Byrne's attacks on the administration in the Washington Papers, Chief of Staff Files, Box 17, Folder 12.

33. Holli and Green, *Bashing Chicago Traditions*, 50 (quote); Rivlin, *Fire on the Prairie*, 231–32.

34. Holli and Green, *Bashing Chicago Traditions*, 55–65; Travis, *Harold, the People's Mayor*, 256 (quote).

35. *Chicago Tribune*, August 14, 1986; Holli and Green, *Bashing Chicago Traditions*, 52; A. Miller, *Harold Washington*, 290.

36. Rivlin, *Fire on the Prairie*, 233.

37. A. Miller, *Harold Washington*, 297–98; Rivlin, *Fire on the Prairie*, 233 (quote).

38. *Chicago Tribune*, February 1, 1987 (quote); Travis, *Harold, the People's Mayor*, 262–63; Pacyga, *Chicago: A Biography*, 378.

39. *Chicago Tribune*, February 12, 1987; Rivlin, *Fire on the Prairie*, 235–36.

40. "Issue Summary and Background: Neighborhood Infrastructure," Washington Papers, Chief of Staff Files, Box 17, Folder 12; Rivlin, *Fire on the Prairie*, 236 (quote); *Chicago Tribune*, January 23, 1987.

41. *Chicago Tribune*, February 1, 9, 1987; Holli and Green, *Bashing Chicago Traditions*, 69–71, 76–78.

42. *Chicago Tribune*, February 9, 10, 1987; Holli and Green, *Bashing Chicago Traditions*, 78 (quote).

43. *Chicago Tribune*, February 16, 1987; Holli and Green, *Bashing Chicago Traditions*, 79–83; *Chicago Tribune*, February 8, 1987 (quote).

44. *Chicago Defender*, February 25, 1987; *Chicago Tribune*, February 25, 26, 1987; Rivlin, *Fire on the Prairie*, 238–39; Holli and Green, *Bashing Chicago Traditions*, 84–89.

45. *Chicago Tribune*, February 25, 1987; Holli and Green, *Bashing Chicago Traditions*, 72–73, 88.

46. Pacyga, *Chicago: A Biography*, 378; Rivlin, *Fire on the Prairie*, 240–41; Holli and Green, *Bashing Chicago Traditions*, 88–92.

47. *Chicago Tribune*, March 9 (quote), April 1, 2, 1987; Holli and Green, *Bashing Chicago Traditions*, 106–9.

48. *Chicago Tribune*, April 1, 2, 1987; A. Miller, *Harold Washington*, 303 (quote).

49. *Chicago Tribune*, March 24, 1987; Pacyga, *Chicago: A Biography*, 378.

50. Holli and Green, *Bashing Chicago Traditions*, 94–97; Rivlin, *Fire on the Prairie*, 241 (quote).

51. *Chicago Tribune*, January 8, 14, February 1, March 20, 1987; A. Miller, *Harold Washington*, 306–7.

52. *Chicago Tribune*, February 17, 1987 (quote); A. Miller, *Harold Washington*, 310–11; D. Bradford Hunt, *Blueprint for Disaster: The Unraveling of Chicago Public Housing* (Chicago: University of Chicago Press, 2009), 264–66.

53. *Chicago Tribune*, January 14, 1987; Hunt, *Blueprint for Disaster*, 266–67; A. Miller, *Harold Washington*, 306–9.

54. *Chicago Tribune*, March 11, 1987 (first quote); Pacyga, *Chicago: A Biography*, 378; Travis, *Harold, the People's Mayor*, 269 (second quote).

55. Holli and Green, *Bashing Chicago Traditions*, 109 (first quote); Rivlin, *Fire on the Prairie*, 241 (second quote).

56. *Chicago Tribune*, February 13, 1987; Rivlin, *Fire on the Prairie*, 241 (quotes); Judith Walker, "Reforming the Role of Human Services in City Government," in *Washington and the Neighborhoods*, edited by Clavel and Wiewel, 160–62; Mike Holewinski to Washington, May 28, 1986, Washington Papers, Public Safety Files, Box 8, Folder 5. See also "Department of Human Services, Chicago Intervention Network," June 11, 1986, Washington Papers, Public Safety Files, Box 8, Folder 5.

57. *Chicago Tribune*, March 19, 1987 (quote); Holli and Green, *Bashing Chicago Traditions*, 99–101.

58. *Chicago Tribune*, March 19, 1987; Holli and Green, *Bashing Chicago Traditions*, 99–100.

59. "Statement of Mayor Washington on Campaign Finances," March 23, 1987, Washington Papers, Press Office Files, Box 100, Folder 42; *Chicago Tribune*, February 18, 22, 24, March 30, 31, 1987; Holli and Green, *Bashing Chicago Traditions*, 101–2.

60. Barefield to Department Heads, memorandum, September 17, 1986, and Executive Order 86-2, both in Washington Papers, Chief of Staff Files, Box 72, Folder 5; Jacky Grimshaw, interview, May 8, 2015, Chicago; A. Miller, *Harold Washington*, 296–302.

61. Travis, *Harold, the People's Mayor*, 267–70.

62. Goff, "Mayor Firm on Minority Jobs," 1; Holli and Green, *Bashing Chicago Traditions*, 98.

63. "Mayor Washington Announces $2 Billion Neighborhood Program," February 1, 1987, Washington Papers, Press Office Files, Box 14, Folder 6.

64. Elizabeth Hollander to Benjamin Reyes, May 6, 1987, Washington Papers, Development Sub-Cabinet Files, Box 7, Folder 15; *Chicago Tribune*, March 29, 1987; Hollander to Washington, January 29, 1987, Washington Papers, Finance Sub-Cabinet Files, Box 16, Folder 31; "City Closes on North Loop Financing: Over $18 Million in Bonds Sold," Washington Papers, Press Office Files, Box 13, Folder 39.

65. "Appendix I: Trend Analysis from April 7, 1987, General Election," Washington Papers, Finance Sub-Cabinet Files, Box 9, Folder 59; *New York Times*, April 8, 9, 1987; *Chicago Tribune*, April 8, 1987. See also Gordon K. Mantler, *Power to the Poor: Black-Brown Coalition and the Fight for Economic Justice, 1960–1974* (Chapel Hill: University of North Carolina Press, 2013), 246.

66. *Chicago Tribune*, April 8, 1987; Holli and Green, *Bashing Chicago Traditions*, 112 (quote).

67. *Chicago Tribune*, April 8, 1987; Alton Miller, interview, June 3, 2015, Chicago; *Chicago Tribune*, April 8, 1987 (quote).

68. John Schrag, "Washington Mutes Opposition but Gains Few New Supporters," *Chicago Reporter* 16 (May 1987): 8; Rivlin, *Fire on the Prairie*, 242; A. Miller, *Harold Washington*, 305 (quote).

69. "Appendix I: Trend Analysis"; *New York Times*, April 8, 1987; Rivlin, *Fire on the Prairie*, 240 (first quote); Holli and Green, *Bashing Chicago Traditions*, 113–15; Adam Doster, "How Harold Washington Shaped the City of Chicago," *Chicago Magazine*, http://www.chicagomagazine.com/core/pagetools.php?url=%2FChicago -Magazine%2FThe-31 (second quote).

70. *Chicago Tribune*, April 8, 9, 1987; *New York Times*, April 9, 1987 (quote).

Chapter 7. The Final Months

1. "Mayor Washington Calls for Tough Manifesto on the Needs of America's Cities," April 28, 1987, Harold Washington Papers, Press Office Files, Box 14, Folder 16, Harold Washington Public Library, Chicago; Jacquelyne D. Grimshaw to Ernest G. Barefield, September 23, 1987, Washington Papers, Chief of Staff Files, Box 36, Folder 1.

2. Harold Washington, "Toward an Urban Manifesto," April 28, 1987, Washington Papers, Press Office Files, Box 14, Folder 16.

3. "Second Inaugural Address of Mayor Harold Washington, Grant Park, Chicago," May 4, 1987, Washington Papers, Press Office Files, Box 14, Folder 17 (quotes); *Chicago Tribune*, May 5, 1987.

4. *Chicago Tribune*, April 15, 19, 1987; Gary Rivlin, *Fire on the Prairie: Harold Washington, Chicago Politics, and the Roots of the Obama Presidency*, rev. ed. (Philadelphia: Temple University Press, 2013), 246–47.

5. "Mayor Washington Leads Media on Downtown Redevelopment Tour," July 16, 1987, Washington Papers, Press Office Files, Box 14, Folder 27.

6. Ibid. (quote); "Mayor Harold Washington's Press Statement on Chicago's Economic Climate," July 16, 1987, Washington Papers, Press Office Files, Box 14, Folder 27; "Moody's Municipal Credit Report: Chicago, Illinois," October 6, 1987, Washington Papers, Finance Sub-Cabinet Files, Box 31, Folder 12.

7. "Downtown Real Estate Development Overview," July 16, 1987, Washington Papers, Press Office Files, Box 14, Folder 27; "Downtown Hotel Market Fact Sheet," July 16, 1987, ibid.; "Downtown Retail Market Fact Sheet," July 16, 1987, ibid. See also Elizabeth Hollander to Ben Reyes, May 6, 1987, Washington Papers, Development Sub-Cabinet Files, Box 7, Folder 15.

8. "Downtown Residential Market Fact Sheet," July 16, 1987, Washington Papers, Press Office Files, Box 14, Folder 27.

9. Timothy Wright, interview, June 16, 2015, Chicago; Robert Mier to Reyes, memorandum, May 6, 1987, Washington Papers, Development Sub-Cabinet Files, Box 3, Folder 3; Timothy Wright, "Throwing Rocks on the Inside: Keeping a Progressive Administration Progressive," in *Harold Washington and the Neighborhoods: Progressive City Government in Chicago, 1983–1987*, edited by Pierre Clavel and Wim Wiewel (New Brunswick, N.J.: Rutgers University Press, 1991), 197–98.

10. James Andrews to Mayor Harold Washington, "Personal & Very Confidential," memorandum, July 26, 1987, Washington Papers, Finance Sub-Cabinet Files, Box 9, Folder 58; "Four Year Workplan for the Political Organization of Mayor Harold Washington," n.d., ibid.

11. Chicago Works Together Planning Task Force, "Chicago Works Together II: Recommended Changes to the 1984 Chicago Development Plan," August 1987, Washington Papers, Chief of Staff Files, Box 26, Folder 9.

12. D. Bradford Hunt, *Blueprint for Disaster: The Unraveling of Chicago Public Housing* (Chicago: University of Chicago Press, 2009), 262–66; William Peterman, *Neighborhood Planning and Community-Based Development* (Thousand Oaks, Calif.: Sage, 2000), 120–28.

13. *Chicago Tribune*, May 21, July 21, 1987; Alton Miller, *Harold Washington: The Mayor, the Man* (Chicago: Bonus Books, 1989), 306–7. On Reagan and public housing, see Roger Biles, *The Fate of Cities: Urban America and the Federal Government, 1945–2000* (Lawrence: University Press of Kansas, 2011), especially chap. 8.

14. Harold Washington, *Climbing a Great Mountain: Selected Speeches of Mayor Harold Washington*, commentary by Alton Miller (Chicago: Bonus Books, 1988), 185.

15. Carl Covitz to Alan J. Dixon, June 24, 1987, Washington Papers, Chief of Staff Files, Box 22, Folder 5 (quote); Hunt, *Blueprint for Disaster*, 264–66.

16. Brenda J. Gaines, "Interim Executive Director's Report," April 23, 1987, Washington Papers, Chief of Staff Files, Box 24, Folder 12; Rivlin, *Fire on the Prairie*, 245–46; *Chicago Tribune*, September 26, 1987; Carl Covitz to Alan J. Dixon, June 24, 1987.

17. Miller, *Harold Washington*, 309.

18. *Chicago Tribune*, May 29, August 6, 1987; Miller, *Harold Washington*, 310–11.

19. Brenda Gaines, interview, July 20, 2015, Chicago; *Chicago Tribune*, May 29, 1987 (quotes); Miller, *Harold Washington*, 308–15.

20. Ernest G. Barefield to Dr. James E. Baugh, June 5, July 21, 24, 1987, Washington Papers, Chief of Staff Files, Box 22, Folder 6; Paul Simon et al. to Samuel R. Pierce Jr., June 26, 1987, Washington Papers, Chief of Staff Files, Box 22, Folder 5; Miller, *Harold Washington*, 312–14; Hunt, *Blueprint for Disaster*, 267; Neil F. Hartigan to Samuel R. Pierce Jr., August 1, 1987, Washington Papers, Chief of Staff Files, Box 22, Folder 7.

21. "Notes on CHA-HUD Issues from July 21 Discussions," July 22, 1987, Washington Papers, Chief of Staff Files, Box 22, Folder 6; Barefield to Baugh, July 24, 1987, ibid.

22. Wayne A. McCoy to Reverend B. Herbert Martin, September 28, 1987, Washington Papers, Chief of Staff Files, Box 35, Folder 3; *Chicago Tribune*, September 24, 26, 1987; Gaines, interview; Hunt, *Blueprint for Disaster*, 267.

23. *Chicago Tribune*, September 24, 1987 (first and second quotes); Hunt, *Blueprint for Disaster*, 267; Rivlin, *Fire on the Prairie*, 246 (third quote); Gaines, interview.

24. *Chicago Tribune*, October 30, 1987; Rivlin, *Fire on the Prairie*, 247.

25. *Chicago Tribune*, October 30 (quote), November 1, 1987.

26. *Chicago Tribune*, August 29, October 30, November 1, 1987.

27. *Chicago Tribune*, October 30, November 1, 1987.

28. *Chicago Tribune*, October 5, 1987 (quotes); Rivlin, *Fire on the Prairie*, 249–50. For a concise statement of the administration's approach to labor negotiations, see Ronald Litke (assistant corporation counsel) to Barefield, November 18, 1987, Washington Papers, Chief of Staff Files, Box 36, Folder 6.

29. *Chicago Tribune*, September 14, 29, October 4, 1987.

30. Jacquelyne D. Grimshaw to Barefield, September 29, 1987, Washington Papers, Chief of Staff Files, Box 36, Folder 1; *New York Times*, October 4, 1987; *Chicago Tribune*, September 14, 1987 (quotes); Rivlin, *Fire on the Prairie*, 249–50.

31. *New York Times*, October 4, 1987; *Chicago Tribune*, September 10, October 4, 5, 1987.

32. *Chicago Tribune*, September 20, October 5 (quote), 1987.

33. James Carlton to Toni Preckwinkle, memorandum, July 24, 1987, Robert Mier Papers, Box 2, Folder 3, Chicago History Museum; *Chicago Tribune*, September 20, 1987; David Orr, "The Harold Washington Legacy," undated press release in possession of the author.

34. Alton Miller to Washington, November 23, 1987, Washington Papers, Finance Sub-Committee Files, Box 15, Folder 32; *Chicago Tribune*, October 12, 1987; Carlton to Preckwinkle, memorandum, July 24, 1987.

35. *New York Times*, November 8, 1987; *Chicago Tribune*, November 7, 1987 (quotes).

36. Grimshaw to Barefield, September 29, 1987, Washington Papers, Chief of Staff Files, Box 36, Folder 1; *Chicago Tribune*, November 8, 1987 (quotes); Miller to

Washington, November 23, 1987,Washington Papers, Finance Sub-Cabinet Files, Box 15, Folder 32.

37. Wright, interview; Washington, *Climbing a Great Mountain*, 167; Miller, *Harold Washington*, 305; "Notes on CHA-HUD Issues from July 21 Discussions"; Rivlin, *Fire on the Prairie*, 249; *Chicago Tribune*, May 2, 21, 1987.

38. *Chicago Tribune*, March 25, May 23, 1987; Roger Biles, *Richard J. Daley: Politics, Race, and the Governing of Chicago* (DeKalb: Northern Illinois University Press, 1995), 52–53.

39. *Chicago Tribune*, March 25, 1987 (quote); Wright, interview; Wright, "Throwing Rocks on the Inside," 193.

40. *Chicago Tribune*, July 7, September 21, 1987; Heywood T. Sanders, *Convention Center Follies: Politics, Power, and Public Investment in American Cities* (Philadelphia: University of Pennsylvania Press, 2014), 68–69.

41. *Chicago Tribune*, August 30 (quotes), November 3, 1987.

42. Wright, interview (first quote); Melvin G. Holli and Paul M. Green, *Bashing Chicago Traditions: Harold Washington's Last Campaign* (Grand Rapids, Mich.: William B. Eerdmans, 1989), 187–88; Dominic A. Pacyga, *Chicago: A Biography* (Chicago: University of Chicago Press, 2009), 379 (second and third quotes).

43. *Chicago Tribune*, September 8, 9, 1987; Miller, *Harold Washington*, 316–17.

44. *Chicago Tribune*, September 9, 1987.

45. Miller, *Harold Washington*, 316–18.

46. Ibid., 317–19.

47. Miller to Washington, November 23, 1987, Washington Papers, Finance Sub-Committee Files, Box 15, Folder 32; "Mayor Delivers Fifth Annual Budget Briefing to 1,200 Community Leaders," October 24, 1987, Washington Papers, Chief of Staff Files, Box 69, Folder 3.

48. "Design/Build Architectural Competition for New Central Library Begins Today: Requests for Qualifications Sent Out," October 16, 1987, Washington Papers, Chief of Staff Files, Box 69, Folder 3; Elizabeth Hollander, "The Department of Planning under Harold Washington," in *Washington and the Neighborhoods*, edited by Clavel and Wiewel, 141–42; *Chicago Tribune*, November 1, 15, 1987.

49. Hollander, "Department of Planning," 142–43; "Design/Build Architectural Competition."

50. Miller, *Harold Washington*, 9–17.

51. Rivlin, *Fire on the Prairie*, 255 (quote); Jacky Grimshaw, interview, May 8, 2015, Chicago; Miller, *Harold Washington*, 17.

52. Barack Obama, *Dreams from My Father: A Story of Race and Inheritance* (New York: Three Rivers Press, 1995), 147; Salim Muwakki, *Harold! Photographs from the Harold Washington Years*, edited by Ron Dorfman (Evanston, Ill.: Northwestern University Press, 2007), 191.

53. Muwakki, *Harold!*, 191; *New York Times*, December 1, 1987 (first and second quotes); *Chicago Tribune*, December 1, 1987 (third quote); Holli and Green, *Bashing Chicago Traditions*, 188–91.

54. Monroe Anderson, "The Sawyer Saga: A Journalist, Who Just Happened to Be the Mayor's Press Secretary, Speaks," in *The Mayors: The Chicago Political Tradition*, edited by Paul M. Green and Melvin G. Holli (Carbondale: Southern Illinois University Press, 2005), 206; Rivlin, *Fire on the Prairie*, 251–59; William J. Grimshaw, *Bitter Fruit: Black Politics and the Chicago Machine, 1931–1991* (Chicago: University of Chicago Press, 1992), 198.

55. W. Grimshaw, *Bitter Fruit*, 199.

56. *New York Times*, December 2, 1987; W. Grimshaw, *Bitter Fruit*, 197; Anderson, "Sawyer Saga," 200; Rivlin, *Fire on the Prairie*, 256.

57. *Chicago Tribune*, December 1, 1987 (Jarrett and Gutierrez quotes); *New York Times*, December 2, 1987 (Rush quote); *Chicago Tribune*, December 1, 1987; Luis Gutierrez, *Still Dreaming: My Journey from the Barrio to Capitol Hill* (New York: W. W. Norton, 2013), 250 (Jackson quote).

58. David Orr, interview, May 8, 2014, Chicago; Rivlin, *Fire on the Prairie*, 252.

59. *Chicago Tribune*, December 2, 1987; Holli and Green, *Bashing Chicago Traditions*, 194; Rivlin, *Fire on the Prairie*, 259–60.

60. *New York Times*, December 2, 1987; *Chicago Tribune*, December 2, 1987; Rivlin, *Fire on the Prairie*, 259–60; Holli and Green, *Bashing Chicago Traditions*, 194.

61. Alton Miller, interview, June 3, 2015, Chicago; *Chicago Tribune*, December 7, 1987 (quote); Rivlin, *Fire on the Prairie*, 260.

62. *New York Times*, December 3, 1987; Anderson, "Sawyer Saga," 207; Rivlin, *Fire on the Prairie*, 261.

63. Rivlin, *Fire on the Prairie*, 261–62.

64. Ibid., 262; W. Grimshaw, *Bitter Fruit*, 200 (quote).

65. *New York Times*, December 3, 1987.

66. *Chicago Tribune*, December 3, 1987.

67. *New York Times*, December 3, 1987.

68. J. Grimshaw, interview; Pierre Clavel, *Activists in City Hall: The Progressive Response to the Reagan Era in Boston and Chicago* (Ithaca, N.Y.: Cornell University Press, 2010), 153; Gaines, interview; Miller, *Harold Washington*, 349–50 .

Chapter 8. Harold Washington and Chicago

1. Monroe Anderson, "The Sawyer Saga: A Journalist, Who Just Happened to Be the Mayor's Press Secretary, Speaks," in *Restoration 1989: Chicago Elects a New Daley*, edited by Paul M. Green and Melvin G. Holli (Chicago: Lyceum Books, 1991), 94 (first quote); Alton Miller, *Harold Washington: The Mayor, the Man* (Chicago: Bonus Books, 1989), 351; William J. Grimshaw, *Bitter Fruit: Black Politics and the Chicago Machine, 1931–1991* (Chicago: University of Chicago Press, 1992), 201 (second quote).

2. *Chicago Tribune*, July 14, 1988 (quote); Paul M. Green, "The 1989 Mayoral Primary Election," in *Restoration 1989*, edited by Green and Holli, 6.

3. *Chicago Tribune*, September 19, 1988; Green, "1989 Mayoral Primary Election," 5–15.

4. *Chicago Tribune*, December 30, 1988; Green, "1989 Mayoral Primary Election," 9 (quotes).

5. Anderson, "Sawyer Saga," 107; Green, "1989 Mayoral Primary Election," 7–8.

6. *Chicago Tribune*, May 2–5, 1988.

7. Keith Koeneman, *First Son: The Biography of Richard M. Daley* (Chicago: University of Chicago Press, 2013), 111–16; Green, "1989 Mayoral Primary Election," 12 (quote).

8. *Chicago Tribune*, January 2, 1989; Green, "1989 Mayoral Primary Election," 22–23.

9. *Chicago Tribune*, February 24, 25, 1989.

10. *Chicago Tribune*, March 1, 1989.

11. *Chicago Tribune*, March 5, 14, 1989;

12. Paul M. Green, "The 1989 General Election," in *Restoration 1989*, edited by Green and Holli, 37–46; *Chicago Tribune*, April 4, 1989.

13. *Chicago Sun-Times*, March 26, 1989; *Chicago Tribune*, March 10, 19, 21, 31, 1989.

14. *Chicago Tribune*, March 28, April 4, 1989; Green, "The 1989 General Election," 42–45.

15. Green, "The 1989 General Election," 53n33; *New York Times*, April 5, 1989; *Chicago Tribune*, April 5, 1989.

16. *New York Times*, April 5, 1989. See also David Moberg, "The Fuel of a New Machine," *Chicago Reader*, March 30, 1989, http://www.chicagoreader.com/chicago/the-fuel-of-a-new-machine/Content?oid=873612. On the "new Daley machine," see Dick Simpson, *Rogues, Rebels, and Rubber Stamps: The Politics of the Chicago City Council from 1863 to the Present* (Boulder, Colo.: Westview Press, 2011), 287–90.

17. Melvin G. Holli, "The Daley Era: Richard J. to Richard M.," in *The Mayors: The Chicago Political Tradition*, edited by Paul M. Green and Melvin G. Holli, 3rd ed. (Carbondale: Southern Illinois University Press, 2005), 229–34; John J. Betancur and Douglas Gills, "Community Development in Chicago: From Harold Washington to Richard M. Daley," *Annals of the American Academy of Political and Social Sciences* 594 (July 2004): 101; Koeneman, *First Son*, 317–23; Dominic A. Pacyga, *Chicago: A Biography* (Chicago: University of Chicago Press, 2009), 398–400. On the Daley mayoralty, see Costas Spirou and Dennis R. Judd, *Building the City of Spectacle: Mayor Richard M. Daley and the Remaking of Chicago* (Ithaca, N.Y.: Cornell University Press, 20116). The contrast between the Washington and Daley mayoralties is presented emphatically in Paul L. Street, *Racial Oppression in the Global Metropolis: A Living Black Chicago History* (Lanham, Md.: Rowman and Littlefield, 2007).

18. Timothy Wright, interview, June 16, 2015, Chicago; Pierre Clavel and Robert Giloth, "Planning for Manufacturing: Chicago after 1983," *Journal of Planning History* 14 (February 2015), 24–25; Koeneman, *First Son*, 127–28; Laura Washington, "Putting Harold to Rest," in *Mayors*, edited by Green and Holli, 283; Robert Giloth, "Making Policy with Communities: Research and Development in the Department of Economic Development," in *Harold Washington and the Neighborhoods: Progres-*

sive City Government in Chicago, 1983–1987, edited by Pierre Clavel and Wim Wiewel (New Brunswick, N.J.: Rutgers University Press, 1991), 110.

19. Wright, interview; Elizabeth Hollander, e-mail interview by the author, September 8, 2015; John J. Betancur and Douglas Gills, "Community Development in Chicago," in *The Collaborative City: Opportunities and Struggles for Blacks and Latinos in U.S. Cities*, edited by John J. Betancur and Douglas C. Gills (New York: Garland, 2000), 102 (quote); Spirou and Judd, *Building the City of Spectacle*, xii; Rachel Weber, "Selling City Futures: The Financialization of Urban Redevelopment Policy," *Economic Geography* 86 (July 2010): 251–74; Joel Rast, "The Politics of Alternative Economic Development: Revisiting the Stone-Imbroscio Debate," *Journal of Urban Affairs* 27, no. 1 (2005): 62–64; Dan Immergluck, "Building Power, Losing Power: The Rise and Fall of a Prominent Community Economic Development Coalition," *Economic Development Quarterly* 19 (August 2005): 215–19; Stephen Alexander, "Black and Latino Coalitions: Means to Greater Budget Resources for Their Communities?," in *The Collaborative City*, 203–4; Larry Bennett, *The Third City: Chicago and American Urbanism* (Chicago: University of Chicago Press, 2010), 92–93; Pacyga, *Chicago: A Biography*, 384–89.

20. Koeneman, *First Son*, chap. 20; Spirou and Judd, *Building the City of Spectacle*, 136–40.

21. *New York Times*, December 31, 2015.

22. L. Washington, "Putting Harold to Rest," 286–87.

23. Xolela Mangcu, "Harold Washington and the Cultural Transformation of Local Government in Chicago, 1983–1987" (Ph.D. diss., Cornell University, 1997), 174.

24. Barbara Ferman and William J. Grimshaw, "The Politics of Housing Policy," in *Research in Urban Policy*, edited by Terry Nichols Clark (Greenwich, Conn.: JAI Press, 1992), 4:118; Roger Biles, *The Fate of Cities: Urban America and the Federal Government, 1945–2000* (Lawrence: University Press of Kansas, 2011), 284–85; Howard Stanback and Robert Mier, "Economic Development for Whom? The Chicago Model," *Review of Law and Social Change* 15 (1986–87): 11, 21–22; "Mayor Harold Washington on Affirmative Action," July 17, 1987, Harold Washington Papers, Press Office Files, Box 100, Folder 39, Harold Washington Public Library, Chicago (quote).

25. David Orr, interview, May 8, 2014, Chicago; Miller, *Harold Washington*, 94, 335–36; Wim Wiewel and Pierre Clavel, conclusion to *Washington and the Neighborhoods*, edited by Clavel and Wiewel, 274; David Moberg, "The Man Who Wants to Break the Mold," *Chicago* 32 (October 1983): 182 (quote).

26. Wright, interview; Robert Mier and Kari J. Moe, "Decentralized Development: From Theory to Practice," in *Washington and the Neighborhoods*, edited by Clavel and Wiewel, 97n21; Jacky Grimshaw, interview, May 8, 2015, Chicago; Wim Wiewel and Pierre Clavel, conclusion to *Washington and the Neighborhoods*, edited by Clavel and Wiewel, 289; Brenda Gaines, interview, July 20, 2015, Chicago (quote).

27. Miller, *Harold Washington*, 99 (first quote); L. Washington, "Putting Harold to Rest," 286 (second quote).

28. Harold Washington, *Climbing a Great Mountain: Selected Speeches of Mayor*

Harold Washington, commentary by Alton Miller (Chicago: Bonus Books, 1988), 157; Wright, interview; Mier and Moe, "Decentralized Development," 85–95.

29. Washington, *Climbing a Great Mountain*, 157; Mier and Moe, "Decentralized Development," 85–95; J. Grimshaw, interview; Rachel Weber, *From Boom to Bubble: How Finance Built the New Chicago* (Chicago: University of Chicago Press, 2015), 147; "Protecting Manufacturing Is Essential for Chicago," n.d., Robert Mier Papers, Box 8, Folder 2, Chicago History Museum (quote).

30. Wright, interview (quote); Giloth, "Making Policy with Communities," 103–7, 110–11; J. Grimshaw, interview; Mier and Moe, "Decentralized Development," 91–95.

31. Doug Gills, "Chicago Politics and Community Development: A Social Movement Perspective," in *Washington and the Neighborhoods*, edited by Clavel and Wiewel, 56; Simpson, *Rogues, Rebels, and Rubber Stamps*, 222; David Orr, "The Harold Washington Legacy," undated press release, copy in possession of the author (quote).

32. Executive Order 83-1, Washington Papers, Press Office Files, Box 16, Folder 1; Washington, *Climbing a Great Mountain*, 49; Stephen Alexander, Robert Giloth, and Joshua Lerner, "Chicago's Industry Task Forces: Joint Problem Solving for Local Economic Development," *Economic Development Quarterly* 1, no. 4 (1987): 352–57; J. Grimshaw, interview; Barbara Ferman, *Challenging the Growth Machine: Neighborhood Politics in Chicago and Pittsburgh* (Lawrence: University Press of Kansas, 1996), 119–20. A copy of *Chicago Works Together II* can be found in the Washington Papers, Chief of Staff Files, Box 26, Folder 9.

33. Executive Orders 84-1 and 84-2, Washington Papers, Press Office Files, Box 16, Folder 2; Executive Order 85-4, Washington Papers, Press Office Files, Box 16, Folder 3; Gary Rivlin, *Fire on the Prairie: Harold Washington, Chicago Politics, and the Roots of the Obama Presidency*, rev. ed. (Philadelphia: Temple University Press, 2013), 186; Miller, *Harold Washington*, 154 (quote).

34. *Chicago Tribune*, July 8, 1987 (quotes); Washington, *Climbing a Great Mountain*, 196–98.

35. Executive Order 85-2, Washington Papers, Press Office Files, Box 16, Folder 3; Gregory Schrock, "Taking Care of Business? Connecting Workforce and Economic Development in Chicago" (Ph.D. diss., University of Illinois at Chicago, 2010), 17–18, 138–45; Washington, *Climbing a Great Mountain*, 200 (quote).

36. "Mayor Harold Washington's 'Chicago's War against Crime Week, August 9 thru 15, 1987,'" n.d., Washington Papers, Public Safety Files, Box 18, Folder 3; Alton Miller, interview, June 3, 2015, Chicago; Christopher Chandler, *Harold Washington and the Civil Rights Legacy* (San Bernardino, Calif.: Woodbury Press, 2014), 153–57.

37. *Chicago Tribune*, August 28, 31, 1988; Pierre Clavel, *Activists in City Hall: The Progressive Response to the Reagan Era in Boston and Chicago* (Ithaca, N.Y.: Cornell University Press, 2010), 153–56, 163–67; Robert Weir, Wim Wiewel, and Lauri Alpern, "Decentralization of Policy Making under Mayor Harold Washington," in *Research in Urban Policy*, edited by Clark, 95; Pacyga, *Chicago: A Biography*, 384.

38. *New York Times*, December 31, 2015.

39. Clavel, *Activists in City Hall*, 162–67; Miller, *Harold Washington*, 352–53; Timothy Wright, "Throwing Rocks on the Inside: Keeping a Progressive Administration Progressive," in *Washington and the Neighborhoods*, edited by Clavel and Wiewel, 198–99; Hollander, e-mail interview; Chandler, *Washington and the Civil Rights Legacy*, 153–57.

40. For a reform alderman's assessment of the Washington mayoralty, see Simpson, *Rogues, Rebels, and Rubber Stamps*, 221–24.

Index

ROGER BILES is Professor Emeritus of History at Illinois State University. His books include *Richard J. Daley: Politics, Race, and the Governing of Chicago* and *The Fate of Cities: Urban America and the Federal Government, 1945–2000.*

The University of Illinois Press
is a founding member of the
Association of American University Presses.

————————————————————————

Composed in 10.25/14 Chaparral Pro
with Bureau Eagle display
by Lisa Connery
at the University of Illinois Press
Manufactured by Sheridan Books, Inc.

University of Illinois Press
1325 South Oak Street
Champaign, IL 61820-6903
www.press.uillinois.edu